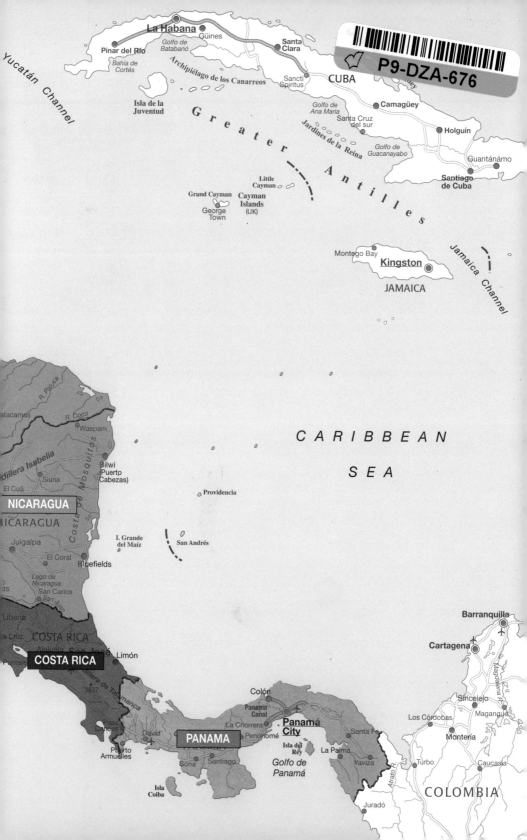

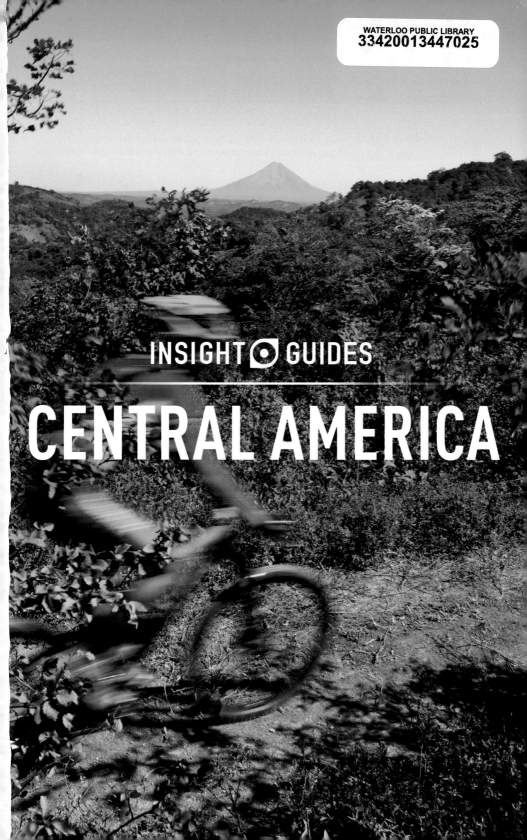

INSIGHT ◉ GUIDES

CENTRAL AMERICA

⊙ Walking Eye App

YOUR FREE DESTINATION CONTENT AND EBOOK AVAILABLE THROUGH THE WALKING EYE APP

Your guide now includes a free eBook and destination content for your chosen destination, all for the same great price as before. Simply download the Walking Eye App from the App Store or Google Play to access your free eBook and destination content.

HOW THE WALKING EYE APP WORKS

Through the Walking Eye App, you can purchase a range of eBooks and destination content. However, when you buy this book, you can download the corresponding eBook and destination content for free. Just see below in the grey panels where to find your free content and then scan the QR code at the bottom of this page.

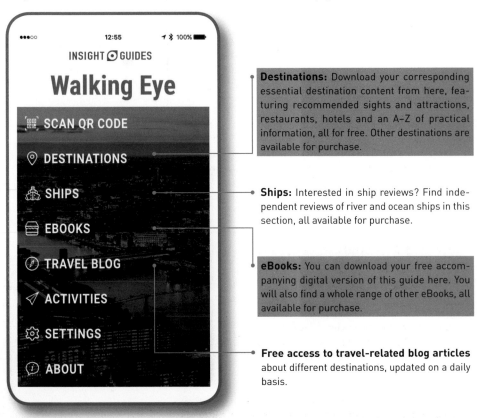

Destinations: Download your corresponding essential destination content from here, featuring recommended sights and attractions, restaurants, hotels and an A–Z of practical information, all for free. Other destinations are available for purchase.

Ships: Interested in ship reviews? Find independent reviews of river and ocean ships in this section, all available for purchase.

eBooks: You can download your free accompanying digital version of this guide here. You will also find a whole range of other eBooks, all available for purchase.

Free access to travel-related blog articles about different destinations, updated on a daily basis.

HOW THE DESTINATION CONTENT WORKS

Each destination includes a short introduction, an A–Z of practical information and recommended points of interest, split into 4 different categories:

- Highlights
- Accommodation
- Eating out
- What to do

You can view the location of every point of interest and save it by adding it to your Favourites. In the 'Around Me' section you can view all the points of interest within 5km.

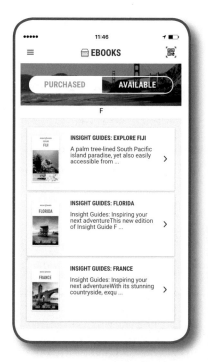

HOW THE EBOOKS WORK

The eBooks are provided in EPUB file format. Please note that you will need an eBook reader installed on your device to open the file. Many devices come with this as standard, but you may still need to install one manually from Google Play.

The eBook content is identical to the content in the printed guide.

HOW TO DOWNLOAD THE WALKING EYE APP

1. Download the Walking Eye App from the App Store or Google Play.
2. Open the app and select the scanning function from the main menu.
3. Scan the QR code on this page – you will then be asked a security question to verify ownership of the book.
4. Once this has been verified, you will see your eBook and destination content in the purchased ebook and destination sections, where you will be able to download them.

Other destination apps and eBooks are available for purchase separately or are free with the purchase of the Insight Guide book.

CONTENTS

LEGEND
○ Insight on
○ Photo Story

THE BEST OF CENTRAL AMERICA: TOP ATTRACTIONS

△ **The Riviera Maya**. From Cancun's resort lined hotel strip to Tulum's eco-chic vibe, some of the world's finest, softest white-sand beaches are found here, providing the setting for Mexico's biggest tourist region. See page 116.

▽ **Chichén Itzá**. Declared one of the 'New Seven Wonders of the World,' this great Maya city is intensely dramatic in both style and scale. See page 113.

△ **Osa Peninsula**. Wilderness, wildlife, and adventure: everything the eco-minded traveler comes to Costa Rica to find is here, located in the remotest part of the southern Pacific region with its legendary biodiversity. See page 301.

△ **Diving in Belize**. Part of the Mesa American reef, the world's second largest stretch of coral provides countless opportunities for diving and snorkeling, such as the famous Blue Hole and the Hol Chan Marine Reserve. See page 91.

△ **Arenal Volcano**. Picture-perfect, cone-shaped Arenal stands out as the quintessential volcano. Although it is temporarily dormant on the outside, it still supplies the geo-thermal power on the inside to heat the ever-popular hot springs. See page 292.

◁ **Panama Canal**. Cutting between the Atlantic and the Pacific, this recently expanded canal is one of the world's most strategic waterways and a marvel of modern engineering. See page 315.

▷ **Tikal**. Soaring above jungle canopy, the colossal temple-pyramids of this once powerful Maya city, which dates to the 4th century BC, seem built to an unearthly scale. See page 160.

△ **Lake Atitlán**. This exquisite highland lake in a giant *caldera* (collapsed volcano) in Guatemala's Sierra Madre is lined by laid-back towns and Maya villages with distinctive customs and shrines. See page 140.

△ **Ometepe Island**. Two volcanoes, Concepción and Maderas, connected by a low isthmus, form Lake Nicaragua's largest island, which is marked with wide beaches, petroglyphs, and rich farmland. See page 258.

▽ **Joya de Cerén**. Covered in volcanic ash and not discovered until 1976, this village in El Salvador – still being unearthed – is a Mayan Pompeii, revealing what life was like in the 6th century. See page 208.

THE BEST OF CENTRAL AMERICA: EDITOR'S CHOICE

Plumed basilisk lizard, Tortuguero National Park.

BEST WILDLIFE WATCHING

Tortuguero National Park. With a sharp-eyed guide, you'll see myriad birds, mammals, and reptiles in this labyrinth of natural jungle canals. See page 208.

Cockscomb Basin Wildlife Sanctuary. One of the best-preserved, most pristine expanses of rainforest in the Americas, Belize's most important reserve is a refuge for jaguars, ocelots, and many species of birds. See page 193.

Pico Bonito National Park. Taking in both low lying tropical rainforest and mountainous cloud forest, Honduras' most impressive national park offers sublime birding, hiking, and whitewater rafting. See page 234.

Manuel Antonio National Park. Small but exquisite, this park packs a wealth of monkeys and birds into a compact jungle edged by three long arcs of white-sand beach. No wonder it's the most popular national park in Costa Rica. See page 300.

Golfo de Chiriquí. This marine reserve on Panama's Pacific Coast is the meeting point for humpback whales migrating from both Alaska and South America. See page 321.

BEST BEACHES

Nosara. Two Costa Rican beaches side by side, Playas Pelada and Guiones offer surfing, swimming, spectacular Pacific sunsets, and yoga on the beach. See page 299.

Playa El Tunco. A quick jaunt from San Salvador, this black sand beach is basecamp for famed nearby surf spots like El Sunzal and Punta Roca. See page 216.

West Bay. Though it gets busy when cruise ships come to Roatán, the calm, clear waters make West Bay the most perfect beach in the Bay Islands. See page 236.

Tulum. It may have gone jet set, but this former hippie outpost still has the white powdery sands backed by thick jungle that continues to enchant. See page 123.

San Juan del Sur. A crescent-shaped bay on Nicaragua's Pacific is home to this mellow expat town with surf shacks, thatched-roof bars, and sail boats. See page 261.

Playa Venao. This remote beach on Panama's Azuero peninsula has seen a surge of new hotels, restaurants, and yoga retreats, making staying here as cushy as Panama City. See page 320.

Puerto Viejo de Talamanca. There are rastas peddling bicycles and sloths in trees in this laid back surf town near the Salsa Brava, on Costa Rica's Caribbean coast. See page 290.

Kuna Yala (San Blas) Islands, Panama. Nearly 400 postcard perfect isles in the Caribbean form the Comarca Kuna Yala, the home of the Kuna people, who have preserved their own laws, norms, and values. See page 327.

A San Blas islet.

BEST MUSEUMS

Museo de Oro, Costa Rica.

BioMuseo. Designed by starchitect Frank Gehry, this museum dedicated to biodiversity on the Amador Causeway took 15 years to build. See page 312.

Museo del Oro Precolombino. Central America's largest collection of pre-Columbian gold artifacts is held here, arranged to show how gold was woven into indigenous cultures. See page 282.

Museo Ixchel del Traje Indigena. Indigenous textile traditions and jewelry are explored in this massive collection that considers many of Guatemala's different cultures. See page 139.

Museo de Arte. At El Salvador's largest art museum, pay particular attention to the collection made during El Salvador's civil war. See page 211.

Museum of the Revolution. Nicaragua's Sandinista uprising of the 1970s is explored at this Leon museum though photos, documents and other artifacts. See page 253.

BEST COLONIAL CITIES AND TOWNS

Antigua. Guatemala's former colonial capital is a gracious city of ornate Baroque churches and rich and colorful traditions. See page 140.

Granada. Established in 1524, Granada is the oldest colonial city in the Americas and shares some of the Moorish architecture of its Spanish namesake. See page 255.

Comayagua. Most of the cobblestone plazas, churches, and colonial houses in this small Honduran town, once the country's capital, have been immaculately maintained. See page 228.

Suchitoto. This colonial town in the Salvadoran highlands is known for its indigo, migrating birds, and hikes to waterfalls and caves. See page 211.

Mérida. The cultural capital of the Yucatán retains its original cobblestone streets, leafy plazas, and houses with white stucco walls and courtyards. See page 110.

Vendors at Mercado de Chichicastenango.

BEST MARKETS

Mercado de Chichicastenango. Twice a week, this mountain town holds the region's biggest market. This astonishing bazaar is one of the most vivid, colorful expressions of the Highland Maya way of life. See page 148.

Mercado Central. San Salvador's crowded, chaotic market isn't just a place for exotic juices and pupusas; there are car stereos and hi-top sneakers too. See page 206.

Mercado de Mariscos. An artisanal fishing fleet from every part of Panama's Pacific Coast descends upon this market near Casco Viejo. Don't miss the ceviche vendors! See page 310.

Mercado Lucas de Galvéz. Mérida's main marketplace features a dizzying array of local foods and ingredients like *panuchos*, *queso de bola*, and *recados*. See page 110.

Mercado Municipal de Granada. A few blocks from the plaza lies this labyrinth of produce and traditional foods aimed at locals, housed in a century-old neoclassical building. See page 255.

Santa Catalina arch in Antigua.

Fried tilapia and crab soup in Guatemala.

BEST CUISINE

Afro-Panamanian. Mix fresh fish, shellfish, and coconut milk with the culinary traditions of Jamaica, China, and numerous indigenous groups, and you have some idea of what this is.

Garifuna. The descendants of ship-wrecked African slaves have created a cuisine of their own that utilizes the fresh seafood, plantains, and cassava found along the Caribbean from Belize to Nicaragua.

Yucatecan. Achiote-rubbed pork roasted in a banana leaf and lime-infused chicken soup are just a couple of the sumptuous dishes of this southern Mexican region.

Guatamalan. Corn, chillies, and beans are the primary staples of this diverse cuisine with Spanish and Mayan influences. Be on the lookout for the hundreds of varieties of tamales.

Modern Panamanian. Panama City's fine dining scene is the region's best, with indigenous ingredients like *boda* and *pixbae* finding their way on to elegant tasting menus.

Atop Pacaya Volcano.

BEST OUTDOOR ADVENTURES

Whitewater rafting the Pacuare River. Steep canyon walls and lush green rainforest define the Class III-IV rapids of this warm Costa Rican river in the Talamanca mountain range. See page 287.

Hiking Celaque National Park. With luck, pumas, ocelots, quetzals, and endangered salamanders can be seen at this rich cloud forest reserve surrounding Honduras' highest peak. See page 231.

Fishing Panama's Pacific. Whether it's Azuero, the Gulf of Chiriquí, or the Pearl Islands, there's easy access to reeling in monster marlin, wahoo, and yellowfin tuna. See page 321.

Climb Guatemala's Pacaya Volcano. Get up close to molten lava on a half-day hike up one of Central America's most active volcanoes. See page 140.

Río Plátano Biosphere Reserve. A combination of rafting and hiking are required to cross the rugged jungles and rivers of La Mosquitia's gorgeous, yet rarely experienced terrain. See page 239.

BEST FOR FAMILIES

Cancún. Self-contained resorts with many of the features of home, plus kid-friendly activities all over town. Maybe skip Spring Break time though. See page 116.
Monteverde Cloud Forest. A misty cloud-forest preserve protects an astonishing range of butterfly, mammal, and bird species. See page 291.
The Canal Zone. Aside from seeing ships traverse the Miraflores Locks on Panama's famed canal, there's a railroad through the jungle, boat trips to Emberá villages, and phenomenal birdwatching to enjoy. See page 315.
Belize coast. Dozens of eco-resorts offer snorkeling, river kayaking, and wildlife-spotting walks along jungle trails, followed by stays in a tree house. See page 178.
Lake Arenal. What kid wouldn't like spotting howler monkeys, waterfall rappelling, zip lining, hot springs, and seeing a smoking volcano? See page 293.

Capuchin monkey, Monteverde Cloud Forest.

BEST RUINS

Tulum. Overlooking the sea, this walled city served as a major port for Cobá deeper in the jungle and was one of the last cities built by the Maya. See page 123.
Palenque. In the lush jungles of Chiapas, this archeological site is anchored by the largest Mesoamerican step pyramid, the Temple of Inscriptions, whose hieroglyphics have been an important tool for understanding Mayan civilization. See page 129.
Copán. One of the greatest Maya cities during the Classic Period, this Honduran site was home to major cultural achievements, most visibly the Hieroglyphic Stairway, with more than 1,800 individual glyphs. See page 229.
Xunantunich. Reached by ferry, the most famous of Belize's Mayan ruins is home to El Castillo, a 40-metre-high pyramid with an impressive stucco frieze. See page 190.
Panamá Viejo. Surrounded by the suburbs of modern Panama City, the first European settlement on the Pacific was destroyed by fires and pirate attacks before being moved to the west. See page 311.

Palenque's temples.

TOP TIPS FOR TRAVELERS

Learn to bargain. Never accept the first price when haggling at markets for handicrafts and clothing. Lowballing an offer isn't considered rude even from a Westerner, it's the nature of the game.
Cheap diving. That two-tank dive or certification course on the Rivera Maya is going to cost half as much in places like the Bay Islands, Belize, or Panama, some of the cheapest dive destinations on earth.

Skip the Nescafé. Panama's Geisha is the most expensive coffee in the world, though buy a bag of beans from a local farmer in Costa Rica, Nicaragua, El Salvador, or Honduras and you'll rarely be disappointed.
Sand flies. Mosquitoes aren't the biggest annoyance in Central American travel. That honor goes to sand flies, the size of gnats, which leave little red bumps and are hard to swat away.

Drink the local hooch. Guatemala and Nicaragua produce fine rums, but don't miss out on the region's lesser known spirits like Costa Rican Guaro or Salvadoran Tíc Táck.
Corn Masa. In El Salvador it's the pupusa. In Honduras the baleada. In Mexico the taco. In Guatemala the tamale. Everywhere you go there's a cheap eat made of corn stuffed with some succulent filling to satisfy your noshing.

Thatched houses and palm tree forest in the Kuna Yala archipelago, Panama.

Grabbing a lift in Suchitoto,
El Salvador.

Altun Ha, Belize.

A REGION OF FIRE AND FOREST

From lush rainforests to coffee plantations, smoking volcanoes and tropical beaches, Central America is a place you won't forget in a hurry.

Vibrant flower, Costa Rica.

When American explorer John Lloyd Stephens was traveling through Central America in 1840, he couldn't believe his eyes when he stumbled upon Copán in Honduras. He thought that it couldn't have been built by the Maya, but perhaps some long-forgotten civilization – and he was able to buy the ruins outright for $50. It was that easy back then.

For decades, Central America was seen as a series of unstable, backwater banana republics that had never quite recovered from colonial rule. Only the most adventurous travelers made their way here. Today, those days are long gone. While security concerns occasionally bubble up around the region, the region's era of civil wars and uprisings has mostly faded away. Few tourists are scared away these days, and they're hiking their way to the top of active volcanoes and doing yoga in eco-lodges in the middle of the thickest jungle. In parts of Belize, Costa Rica, and Panama, expats seem to outnumber those born there.

The region's rich cultural legacy permeates the landscape. The ancestors of the Maya still carry on their traditions in the northern half of the region, while their once-grand stone cities – many of which are still being carved out of the jungle – have only begun to reveal themselves. The Spanish left colonial plazas and churches, while the African diaspora has left a lasting impression on music, dance, and cuisine along

Cenote at Xel-Ha, Cancún.

the Caribbean coast. There are modern, maze-like metropolises with millions of inhabitants who order the wine pairing with their tasting menu and shop at the same designer stores frequented in North American cities, as well as isolated indigenous groups like the Lenca or Guna Yala, who maintain their ways despite the rapidly developing world around them.

All-inclusive beach resorts and package bus tours may lure many travelers to the region, but a 10-minute bicycle ride out of town often leads to a world where ancestral farming practices and howler monkeys still reign supreme. As compact as it may be, there are still vast pieces of terrain that remain unexplored, such as Panama's roadless Darien and the rich forests of La Mosquitia. While buying ancient cities is no longer realistic, the feeling of stepping out into the great unknown is still there.

Nicaragua's Masaya volcano.

LAND AND ENVIRONMENT

With more than 100 volcanoes, two coastlines, and forests with some of the highest biodiversity on earth, Central America is a natural marvel.

Less than 50km (31 miles) between the Pacific and the Caribbean Sea at its narrowest point, the thin strip of land that connects North and South America is home to an astounding 7 percent of the world's biodiversity. Central America is one of the rare places on earth where in a single day you can walk on a beach beside one ocean, climb an active volcano, hike through cloud forest, and watch the stars come out over an entirely other ocean before going to sleep. Despite the region's compact size, there is a lot going on.

Once covered in water, Central America began to rise out of the ocean some 15 million years ago when, beneath the Earth's crust, the Cocos Plate began to slide under the Caribbean Plate. Underwater volcanoes developed from the pressure, grew large enough to form islands, and over millions of years sediment filled in the gaps until an isthmus was formed, connecting the two continents. This happened around 4.5 million years ago and the world has never been the same. Animals migrated north and south over the land bridge, leading to the immense biodiversity that we find there today.

A Kuna Yala islet, Panama.

EARTHQUAKES AND HURRICANES

Natural disasters are nothing new to Central America. The path of destruction left in the wake of Tropical Storm Agatha in May 2010 was the latest in a long series of major natural disasters that have left their mark on the history of this region. One of the earliest recorded hurricanes was the Great Hurricane of 1780, which struck the eastern Caribbean, killing approximately 20,000 people.

Devastating tropical storms build in the Gulf of Mexico before winging their way through the Central American isthmus. Possibly because of climate change, these storms seem to have been increasing in frequency and severity in recent years. Positioned to the west of the hurricanes' usual path, Belize has managed to avoid a good many of the Caribbean storms of the past 40 years, but those that have scored a direct hit have been disastrous, like 1961's Hurricane Hattie, which leveled Belize City, prompting the building of the modern, planned capital of Belmopan and the relocation of all government offices. While Honduras and Nicaragua bore the brunt of the havoc wreaked by Hurricane Mitch in 1998, Guatemala suffered from heavy rains brought by the storm, which caused landslides and flooding, resulting in 260 deaths and the homelessness of tens of thousands. The Yucatán is also periodically blasted by extreme winds – the damage inflicted by 320kph (200mph) Hurricane Dean in 2007 destroyed the resort of Mahahual, though it has since been rebuilt. Few tropical storms find their way to the southern portion of the region, though they are not unheard of. In 2016, Hurricane Otto followed the Nicaragua and Costa Rica border and caused significant damage in Panama, where landslides and unusually strong winds surprised a population unused to them.

Beneath the earth's crust, minute movements of continental tectonic plates cause seismic convulsions and volcanic eruptions in a region

tremendous reach of this disaster exposed and exacerbated governmental corruption alongside the progressive suffering of the poor. San Salvador has been hit by earthquakes again and again, several of them measuring greater than 7 on the Richter Scale. In 2001, a 7.7 quake left more than 900 dead and 200,000 homeless.

VOLCANOES

With more than 100 large volcanoes, Central America is one of the most active volcanic zones in the western hemisphere. The Sierra Madre in

Serenity and solitude at Lake Atitlan in the Western Highlands of Guatemala.

plagued by the most powerful natural forces that planet Earth can muster. Historically, Guatemala and El Salvador have been on the receiving end of much of the region's seismic activity, located as they are between the Pacific and Caribbean coasts, and with a chain of volcanoes spanning the countries. The Mesoamerican Pacific coast of the two countries belongs to the continent's active tectonic field, where the small Cocos Plate is pushed and shoved by the forces of the larger Caribbean Plate to the east. Guatemala City was virtually flattened by quakes in 1917 and 1918, and again most recently in 1976, when at least 25,000 people were killed and a million left homeless. With its epicenter in Chimaltenango and measuring 7.5 on the Richter Scale, the

Between the peaks of the spine-like ranges that traverse Central America are cool highland valleys with gently rolling, wooded pasture land that reminds visitors more of Switzerland than of a tropical country.

the southern Mexican state of Chiapas marks the beginning of a long volcanic chain that stretches down along the Pacific coast. Forming the backbone of the Central American isthmus, this rugged range of mountains and volcanic peaks cuts a swathe through the land of the Maya, dividing it into highlands and tropical lowlands with just two major interoceanic passes at the mouth of the San Juan River to Lake Nicaragua and along what is now the Panama Canal. The rich volcanic soils, fed by ash spewed out millions of years ago, also proved perfect for growing crops like coffee, which have helped shape Central American history and society since the late 19th century.

Many of the region's volcanoes are concentrated in the Guatemalan highlands, where there are 33 volcanoes, which are mostly inactive or dormant. Several do remain active, however, such as Volcán Pacaya, which has been in

the two coasts help contribute to Central America's vast array of microclimates, which are the primary factor in the immense biodiversity found here. As you travel around Central Amer-

In Costa Rica's Central Valley, Poás Volcano, at 2,700 meters (8,900ft), has one of the world's largest craters, measuring nearly 2km (1.5 miles) in diameter.

an almost constant state of eruption since 1965. This activity ranges from minor gaseous emissions and gentle steam eruptions to explosions so powerful as to hurl 'bombs' up to 12km (7.5 miles) into the air. Although such serious outbursts are rare, Pacaya – which looms over the south of Guatemala City – does emit regular lava flows, and an ashy pall often hangs over the immediate area. Occasionally local villages need to be evacuated, and in 2010 a large eruption closed Guatemala City's airport for a week and blanketed the capital in volcanic ash.

BIODIVERSITY

This central mountain range that runs down the funnel shaped land mass and the proximity of

ica, you'll notice how drastically the landscape changes, even within a short distance. Each region has its own ecological characteristics.

Across much of the region's lowlands, the climate is wet and warm enough for trees to keep growing for much of the year. The result of this nonstop growth is generally called rainforest. Strictly speaking, though, botanists restrict use of this term to the wettest forests of all. Unlike the trees in tropical dry forests, rainforest trees are evergreen, and their dense crowns form a continuous canopy that casts a deep and almost unbroken shade. These rainforests – both on low ground and at higher altitudes – harbor an immense variety of life. While they only cover 2 percent or so of the total surface area of the

Earth, rainforests harbor roughly 50 percent of all flora and fauna on the planet.

In the drier parts of Central America, where little rain falls for four or five months of the year, the natural vegetation is dry tropical forest, with most trees shedding their leaves soon after the dry season begins. The trees are rarely more than 30 meters (98ft) high, and there is usually a tangled understory of spiny and thorny shrubs. Although the trees are leafless during the dry season, few of them are fully dormant, and many burst into flower soon after their leaves have been shed. Patches of dry forest can be found in southeastern Mexico, Guatemala, El Salvador, Nicaragua, and Costa Rica.

On the low-lying coasts of Central America, mangroves are the natural vegetation, and they form extensive forests on both the Caribbean and Pacific shores. These ecoregions are important nesting sites for many bird species and also provide a habitat for fauna like monkeys, caimans, and pumas.

The region's coastlines are home to extensive beaches – often of dark volcanic sand – punc-

Giant buttress roots on a rainforest tree at Hacienda Baru, Costa Rica.

☉ GREAT BALLS OF FIRE

The highest peaks in the cordillera are Guatemala's Volcán Tajumulco and Volcán Tacaná, which rise above 4,000 metres (13,123ft). Additionally, there are 35 other peaks that stand at 2,000m (6,562ft) high, scattered about the region in every country except Belize. On the highest peaks of the cordillera, the forest gives way to a treeless landscape known as *páramo*. Cold and frequently swathed in cloud, *páramo* seems a world away from the warmth and lushness of lower altitudes. This ecosystem is dominated by tough, low-growing shrubs that can withstand strong winds. *Páramo* is found in patches in Guatemala, Costa Rica and Panama.

tuated by low-lying rocks and a small number of offshore islands. The Mesoamerican Barrier Reef System stretches over 1,000km (621 miles) from Isla Contoy off the top of the Yucatán Peninsula down to the Bay Islands. Smaller reefs can be found along both coasts. Reef-building corals need sunlight to grow, and they can only survive in clear water. This limits them to areas well away from the mouths of silt-laden rivers, but it also makes them vulnerable to any increase in silt run-off. The longest rivers of Central America flow to the Caribbean, though some smaller ones drain into the Pacific. Additionally, there are three large lakes: Lake Nicaragua and Lake Managua in Nicaragua and Gatún Lake in Panama, which forms part of the Panama Canal.

ENVIRONMENTAL PROTECTION

Despite accounting for only 0.1 percent of the Earth's surface, Central America boasts 7 percent of the world's biodiversity. While the region's enormous collection of flora and fauna is impressive, much of it is threatened. More than 100 species are classified as critically endangered, plus another 200 or so that are threatened. In recent history, money has taken precedence over conservation and forests have been chopped down to make room for cattle. The soil has been depleted and a wide range of

of all land territory in Belize has some form of protected status, which is more than anywhere else in the Americas. Additionally, countries such as Panama, Costa Rica, and Honduras have maintained at least 40 percent of their forest cover. While the threats are not going away anytime soon, the path they can take gets narrower every year.

Marine territory is also under threat around the Central America. The region's network of coastal wetlands, lagoons and mangroves supports nearly 60 types of coral like brain and

Tropical beach at Laughingbird Caye National Park, Belize.

rare habitats has been destroyed. Deforestation and rainforest fragmentation is a major concern and an estimated 80 percent of the vegetation in Central America has already been converted to agriculture. While economically important, tourism, mining, and farming have taken a toll on the environment. There is some hope, however.

National parks, biological preserves, wildlife refuges and other categories of protected areas, both private and public, now cover significant portions of many Central American nations. More than 25 percent of several nations in the region has been set aside in some form or another by human beings to protect it from the potential exploitation and ravages of other human beings. Over 36 percent

elkhorn, 350 mollusk, and 500 fish species. The Mesoamerican Barrier Reef System, extending from Mexico to Honduras, is one of the most diverse ecosystems on earth and only around 10 percent of all species here have been discovered. While healthy marine ecosystems support the region's multi-billion-dollar tourism industry, overfishing, pollution from agriculture, invasive species like lionfish, and changing coastlines endanger much of it, not to mention the effects of climate change that are pushing the limits of natural systems. NGOs are working with local governments to help establish no-take zones for fish stocking and re-population, fishery management systems, and zoning laws to combat unsustainable development.

An engraving of washerwomen on the river Chagres at Matachin, Panama, from 1879.

DECISIVE DATES

THE PRE-HISPANIC ERA

c.10,000 BC
Earliest animal remains: mammoth bones found at Loltún in Yucatán.

c.6000–2000 BC
Early settlers farm maize and beans, make pottery, and probably speak a Proto-Maya language.

c.2000 BC
First evidence of fixed Maya settlements at Nakbé, Cuello, Loltún, Mani, and along the Pacific coast at Ocos.

500 BC
Period of first monumental buildings at sites such as Tikal. Influence of the Olmec culture.

100 BC
El Mirador established as the first Maya 'superpower'; 70-meter (230ft) temples are completed and fabulous murals of San Bartolo painted.

c.AD 1
Emergence of Teotihuacán in Mexico.

AD 150
Collapse of Preclassic cities, including El Mirador, probably due to environmental breakdown.

250–450
Maya region and much of Mexico influenced, or even dominated, by Teotihuacán.

300
Start of Classic period. First stelae found with exact date in

Pre-Columbian artifacts, San José.

central region: Stela 29 at Tikal, dated AD 292.

426
Yax K'uk Mo' (probably from Teotihuacán) founds dynasty at Copán.

550–695
Rival 'superpowers' Tikal and Calakmul fight for dominance in the central region. In AD 695 Tikal avenges a bitter earlier defeat by overrunning Calakmul, and the city never recovers its former glory.

700–800
Peak of Maya Classic period, all through the region: sites such as Uxmal, Kabah, and Chichén Itzá at their height in Yucatán, Palenque in Chiapas. Population in central region reaches an estimated 10 million by 750.

800–900
Decline of Classic Maya sites, possibly due to overpopulation

and drought, leading to environmental collapse. The last recorded inscription at Palenque is from AD 799; at Tikal it is AD 869.

1000
Postclassic period, with the emergence of fortified sites in Yucatán region and several competing groups in Guatemala.

1250
The fall of Chichén Itzá and emergence of Mayapán as center of influence in Yucatán. In Guatemala the K'iche', Kaqchikel, and Mam tribes dominate region. Tulum emerges as important trading center.

1440
Decline of Mayapán, and breakup of Maya groups in Yucatán into small areas of influence.

THE SPANISH CONQUEST

1519
Hernán Cortés arrives on island of Cozumel off Yucatán at the start of the discovery and conquest of Mexico; the first Mass on the American continent is held.

1523
Spanish exploration and conquest of Guatemala under Pedro de Alvarado, who defeats the K'iche'.

THE COLONIAL ERA

1527
First Spanish capital of Guatemala founded. Francisco de Montejo begins his conquest of Yucatán.

1541
Capital of Guatemala is moved to Antigua.

1542
Foundation of Mérida, which becomes the Spanish capital of Yucatán.

1540s
Franciscan friars set out to bring Christianity to Maya.

1600s
First 'Baymen' begin to settle near mouth of Belize River, and exploit forests of the region and trade in logwood for dyes.

1638–40
Maya rebellion drives Spanish out of Belize.

1671
Pirate Henry Morgan captures Panama.

1697
Last Maya stronghold in Guatemala falls with conquest of the Itzá on a Lake Petén Itzá island.

1739
First of the Maya manuscripts rediscovered in Vienna and taken to the German city of Dresden, to become known as the Dresden Codex.

1746
Father Antonio de Solis is first European to discover the site of Palenque in Chiapas, Mexico.

1765
A set of regulations, 'Burnaby's Code,' drawn up as first constitution for what becomes British Honduras (Belize).

1786
Spanish captain Antonio del Río explores Palenque for Spanish king.

INDEPENDENCE MOVEMENTS

1798
The Battle of St George's Caye between British and Spanish naval forces. Defeat of Spanish fleet firmly establishes British rule of Belize region.

1821
Mexico and Central America win independence from Spain. Guatemala, Honduras, Nicaragua, and El Salvador form Central American Federation. Yucatán and Chiapas also join federation, but then join Mexico in 1823. The Garífuna establish first settlement in Dangriga, Belize.

1823
San José replaces Cartago as the capital in Costa Rica.

1838
Central American Federation splits. Guatemala, El Salvador, Honduras, Nicaragua, and Costa Rica become independent.

1841
Incidents of Travel in Central America, Chiapas and Yucatán by the explorer John Lloyd Stephens, illustrated by Frederick Catherwood, begins the era of scientific investigation of the great Maya sites. Maya of Yucatán declare independence from Mexico. A republic is declared, which lasts until 1848.

1847
Guatemala becomes an independent republic. War of the Castes erupts in Yucatán, a Maya revolt that simmers for more than 50 years.

1848
Declaration of the Republic of Costa Rica.

1854
Earthquake destroys San Salvador, El Salvador.

1856
American adventurer William Walker becomes president of Nicaragua.

Illustration from 'Incidents of Travel in Central America, Chiapas, and Yucatán.'

1857

The *Popol Vuh*, the sacred book of the K'iche' Maya, is published in a French translation.

1858

Costa Rica defeats William Walker, who sought to turn Central America into a colony of the southern American states.

1859

Convention between the UK and Guatemala recognizes the boundaries of British Honduras, but these are subsequently disputed by Guatemala.

1862

British Honduras becomes an official British colony.

THE MODERN ERA

1893

Mexico renounces its longstanding claim to territory of British Honduras and signs a peace treaty. Guatemala still claims sovereignty.

1903

The United States is granted exclusive control of a 16km (10-mile) corridor across Panama.

Aftermath of the 1976 earthquake in Guatemala.

1910

Mexican revolution led by Francisco Madero against Porfirio Díaz. An earthquake destroys Cartago, Costa Rica, killing 700.

1914

The Panama Canal is completed.

1923

Yucatán governed by revolutionary socialists.

1924

Yucatán's Socialist leader, Governor Felipe Carrillo Puerto, assassinated during a failed military revolt.

1931

Dictator Jorge Ubico president in Guatemala: banana boom led by United Fruit Company. Belize City destroyed by hurricane.

1932

30,000 killed during peasant uprising in El Salvador.

1939

As coffee exports stagnate, Costa Rica declares war on Germany, Japan, and Italy.

1944–54

Progressive nationalist governments in Guatemala under presidents Arévalo and Jácobo Arbenz. Land reform and attempts to curb power of US-owned banana companies.

1948

Civil War erupts in Costa Rica, and a junta led by José Figueres takes over. Under the new con-stitution, the army is disbanded.

1954

Che Guevara arrives in Guatemala City. A CIA-backed coup in Guatemala leads to the overthrow of Arbenz, start of military rule, and civil war.

1970s

Oil is discovered off the Campeche coast and Cancún is developed for mass tourism.

1973

British Honduras is renamed Belize.

1976

Earthquake in Guatemala leaves 23,000 dead.

1979

The Sandinistas in Nicaragua topple the Somoza dictatorship; civil war ensues. Over 30,000 killed in El Salvador by government-sponsored death squads.

1981

Belize gains independence from the UK.

1982

Guatemalan guerrillas form Guatemalan National Revolutionary Unity (URNG). US funded attacks by Contra rebels based in Honduras begin in Nicaragua.

A meeting of Central American presidents, 1986.

1986
Guatemala returns to civilian government. Costa Rican president Oscar Arias Sánchez helps restore peace to the region and is later awarded the Nobel Peace Prize.

1988
US charges Panamanian president Manuel Noriega with drug smuggling; following year US invades Panama and ousts Noriega.

1991
Guatemala recognizes self-determination of the people of Belize in return for Caribbean coastal waters.

1992
Rigoberta Menchú is awarded the Nobel Prize for Peace.

1994
On January 1, Mexico joins the North American Free Trade Agreement with the US and Canada. The same day, Lacandón Maya Indians and the Zapatista National Liberation Army rebel in Chiapas.

1996
Final peace accords signed in Guatemala end more than 30 years of civil war in which about 200,000, mostly Maya, were killed or disappeared.

1998
Hurricane Mitch sweeps Central America.

1999
US transfers control of the Panama Canal to Panama.

2004
Military numbers and budget cut in Guatemala; CAFTA trade agreement approved; Panama Canal earns a record $1 billion in revenue.

2005
Hurricane Wilma wreaks havoc in Mexico's Yucatán Peninsula; several people are killed.

2009
Honduran President Jose Manuel Zelaya is overthrown by the military.

2010
Laura Chinchilla (PLN) becomes the first female president of Costa Rica.

2012
Festivities planned across the Maya world to mark the end of a Great Cycle in the Maya calendar on December 21.

2013
Chinese billionaire Wang Jing is granted a 50-year concession to build and operate a canal across Nicaragua.

2015
Chinese stock market crash puts plans for Nicaragua's Grand Interoceanic Canal on hold. Costa Rica's Turrialba volcano erupts, spewing a column of ash 2,500 meters (8,202ft) high.

2016
The Panama Canal finishes a nine-year, $5.4 billion expansion that more than doubles its capacity. The Nicaraguan government frees 8,000 prisoners in an effort to ease overcrowding in Nicaragua's jails.

2017
Costa Rica sues Nicaragua over the military camp at Isla Portillos on Costa Rican territory.

Ash rising from Turrialba volcano.

Mayan ceramic figurine of a
Lord, circa 600–900 AD, Mexico.

EARLY HISTORY

More than 12,000 years of history has riddled the Central American isthmus with mysteries that are only just beginning to be solved.

Human settlement of Central America dates back thousands of years. Hunter-gatherers are first thought to have arrived in the region around 10,000 BC, and spears and tools dating from 9000 BC have been unearthed in the Guatemalan highlands. By 2000 BC villages were beginning to be established along the Pacific coast. These Pacific coast people seem to have subsisted primarily on shellfish, fish, and iguanas. Meanwhile, evidence has emerged that villages up in the Petén were in place by around 1700 BC, and by 1100 BC the first rudimentary ceremonial structures were being built at Nakbé; the first temples were added by 750 BC. Gradually more and more Preclassic settlements began to flourish in the northern Petén, above all the giant city of El Mirador. The hub of the first empire in the Americas, El Mirador grew to obtain superpower status by the time of Christ, when its population approached 100,000 – its center crowned by

Mayan mosaic disk, circa AD 900–1200,Chichen Itza.

In the courtyards in front of the palaces, the Maya placed stelae or free-standing stone columns on which the figure of the ruler who put up the building is shown, with elaborate dating and details of his dynastic position inscribed in hieroglyphic writing.

a triadic temple complex that reached over 70 meters (230ft). Outside the northern Petén, most Maya still lived as farmers, cultivating maize and other vegetables, living in small family units.

These ordinary Maya were governed by an elite who enjoyed religious and military power, and who passed the power on in dynasties. They increasingly celebrated that power in vast ceremonial buildings, and in inscriptions and stelae (carved stone monuments) that recalled their deeds as well as depicting their gods. By AD 250–300, what is known as the Classic period of Maya civilization had begun. This lasted until approximately AD 900 and is the period when most of the great Maya centers were built.

One of the most important early centers was at Kaminaljuyú, close to modern Guatemala City. Here, local obsidian was worked into tools and traded all over Maya territory. More than 400 ceremonial mounds have been located at Kaminaljuyú, though these have mostly been lost to urban sprawl.

ARCHEOLOGICAL REMAINS

Tikal (see page 160), the second great city to emerge in Petén, is one of the few Maya centers to have been fully excavated, giving a good idea of how a settlement might have looked some 1,200 years ago. Archeologists estimate it was home to a population of perhaps 80,000 at the peak of the Classic period. The city was grouped around an imposing ceremonial core of palaces, courtyards, and pyramids, with broad causeways connecting the center to other parts of the city. The temple-pyramids were built on a

Detail of a fresco depicting a warrior, Cacaxtla.

base of earth and rubble and covered with limestone blocks. At the summit of these pyramids were narrow rooms decorated with plaster and vividly painted with murals, probably reserved for sacred rituals. The whole construction was topped off with a further extension – a roof comb of stone that adds height and solemnity, and was usually covered in brightly painted stucco reliefs.

The other main ceremonial centers, such as Palenque, Calakmul, Piedras Negras, Yaxchilán, Copán, Yaxhá, Uxmal, and part of Chichén Itzá were also built during the Classic period. These sites show not only the complexity of the religious beliefs of their inhabitants, but also their fascination with astronomy and time, the strong hierarchy in their society, and their sense

of history as reflected in the written inscriptions on the many stelae erected.

The Classic Maya held deep religious beliefs. They thought that the gods found their purpose in the creation of mankind, who repaid them for their existence by showing fidelity to them and the rituals the gods demanded. They conceived of the world as flat and square (some paintings and codices suggest it was seen as the back of a huge crocodile floating in a pond full of waterlilies), and among their most important gods were the four Bacab who occupied each corner of the square. Each god was identified with a color (white for north, yellow for south, red for east, and black for west), and between them they held up the heavens, where the other gods lived.

The Maya not only engraved monuments with hieroglyphs depicting their gods and their history; they also wrote and drew about their beliefs on long strips of tree bark or animal hides. These were then folded like a screen to form books, or codices. When the Spaniards arrived in the 16th century, hundreds of these sacred books were in existence. Bishop Diego de Landa in Yucatán had an important collection of them, but in 1562 he decided they were all heretical, and so organized a huge burning of his collection of manuscripts.

Because of this and other accidents or deliberate acts of destruction, only four of the ancient Maya codices have survived to our day. Three of them are known after the cities where they can be found: Dresden, Madrid, and Paris. The fourth, which came to light in the 1970s, is named the Grolier Codex after the association of bibliophiles who helped identify it; this is the only one still in Mexico.

WAR AND SACRIFICE

Although for many years the idea prevailed that the Maya were a peaceful people, interested only in science and art, we now know they were just as warlike as any of the other civilizations of Mesoamerica. In the ever-changing power politics of the time, the elite cities formed a network of alliances with minor settlements, contested trade routes, and fought for hegemony in outright warfare, such as Tikal's famous defeat at the hands of Calakmul and Caracol in the battle of 562. Warfare was essential for the capture of prisoners, as the Maya used human sacrifice as a guarantee of cosmic order, to help ensure that nature did not destroy mankind. These sacrifices were used to mark important dates in the Maya calendar and to glorify victories in battle, with prisoners ritually killed (by decapitation or by the removal of their hearts) to appease the Maya gods and mark the accession of a new ruler.

RELIGION AND CLASS

Maya rulers were also religious leaders, governing the masses along with shamans and priests, who were experts on calendrics and ritual. In the tomb of one of these leaders, Pakal, at Palenque, he is carrying a jade sphere in one hand and a dart in the other, representing the powers of heaven and earth. On the lid of his sarcophagus is a sculpture of a dragon in the form of a cross. This is the dragon Itzamna, the most powerful god in the Maya pantheon; dozens of other gods were associated with everything from planting corn to sex. Religious ritual was primarily concerned with honoring the correct god on the correct day of the calendar. Preceding an important event, the Maya priests and rulers would fast and remain abstinent. Then a ceremony would take place, involving

Image of an Amerindian sacrifice.

⊙ THE MAYAN CALENDAR

The observation of the heavens, and the calculation of time based on the movement of the stars, the sun, and the moon, was of the utmost importance to the Maya. Many great Maya sites, such as Chichén Itzá, had observatories from where the experts could calculate the calendar, and they proved to be extremely accurate.

Over the centuries, the Maya developed three different calendar systems. The first consisted of 20 named days, which interlocked like a cogwheel with the numbers one to 13, giving a total cycle of 260 days. Alongside this system was one more closely based on the sun's movement. In this calendar, there were 18 months of 20 days. At the end of the year came five days to complete the solar cycle.

These two calendars, one based on 260 days, the other on 365, came back to their starting point every 18,980 days, or 52 years.

In addition to their two intermeshing calendars, the Maya also developed a system for calculating longer dates. Confusingly, this seems to have been based on a year made up of 360 rather than 365 days, known as a *tun*. The system, called the Long Count, came into use during the Classic Maya period, and is based on the great cycle of 13 *baktuns* – a period of 1,872,000 days, or 5,125 years. The present cycle was said to end on December 21, 2012, which doomsayers thought would be the end of the world, but for the Maya it meant the start of another great cycle.

bloodletting (by pricking the tongue, ears, and genitals), the participants under the influence of alcohol and hallucinogenic mushrooms.

Maya society was highly structured, with strict divisions between the classes. Most numerous were the *peones*, at the bottom of the scale, whose primary role was to work the land intensively to provide food for the community. In addition, they performed regular military service duties. But their most lasting contribution was to provide the labor needed to construct the temples found in the center of every Maya city. These great structures

corn, *pejibaye* (the bright orange fruit of the peach palm), and numerous other plants. They supplemented their diets with wild fruits and game from the forests, fish and shrimp from the rivers, and crustacea and small oysters from the ocean. Some groups even had small stone cities, such as Guayabo near present day Turrialba in the Costa Rican highlands, which was built with wide, cobblestone walkways, freshwater springs bubbling out of stone-lined pools, and a stone aqueduct system carrying fresh water to some of the stone mounds on which houses were built.

Restored roadway and wall at the Guayabo National Monument and Park.

were achieved by human power alone, without the use of wagons or wheelbarrows – the Maya did not have the wheel – and without the aid of any draft animals such as horses, mules, or oxen.

DOWN SOUTH

Beyond El Salvador and down through Panama, the pre-Columbian cultures were predominantly speakers of the Chibchan languages at the time of European contact. These were mostly small agrarian and trading societies that were influenced by their Mesoamerican neighbors, learning to fashion goods from stone, jade, and gold.

These groups with diverse languages and cultures lived throughout the southern region in small chiefdoms, cultivating crops like yuca,

The Maya had no metal tools – they were ignorant of iron and bronze – yet they produced a mass of finely worked gold objects, jade carvings, and pottery.

The Spanish colonists gave the Amerindians the names by which we know them today (which was often the name of the chief at the time of the Conquest). We do not know what the people called themselves. Since some groups were completely wiped out before the Spanish arrived, we do not have names for them or know what languages they spoke. Because of this, archeologists usually refer to Amerindian groups by the areas in which they lived.

A CULTURE IN DECLINE

By the 9th century AD, there were signs that Maya culture was in decline. Most experts now concur that a long drought was the primary factor, perhaps brought on by forest clearance and overpopulation.

Whatever the reason for this decline, the large centers in Guatemala and Chiapas were abandoned. Other archeologists argue that there was no sudden collapse, but that the hub of Maya culture moved to the northern lowlands of the Yucatán, to the Puuc region, and above all, to the great center of Chichén Itzá. Over a lengthy period of time, an immense and elaborate ceremonial center was built on this site in the north of the Yucatán Peninsula. At its heart was the sacred *cenote* or pool, which was a place of pilgrimage for people throughout the region. Thousands of votive offerings, as well as the remains of human sacrifice, have been discovered in the mud at the bottom of this pool.

Chichén Itzá itself is a hybrid of styles and influences, which suggests that the Maya came into contact with, or had been conquered by, groups from farther north in Mexico. The Toltecs brought in the worship of Kukulcán, a feathered serpent worshiped in other Mexican cultures as Quetzalcoatl. The most important building at Chichén Itzá, the so-called Castillo, is a temple built in his honor, which is clearly in the style of the Toltec Maya. At some point in the 13th century, however, Chichén Itzá was also abandoned, as power shifted at the start of the Postclassic era.

DEFENSIVE STRONGHOLDS

The center of Postclassic Yucatán was Mayapán, a walled city in the west of the Yucatán Peninsula. As many as 12,000 people are thought to have lived in this important trading city, which covered more than 5 sq km (2 sq miles) of land and where up to 2,000 dwellings have been discovered. Although the Itzá did build temples and various other ceremonial buildings, they had lost many of the skills of the Classic Maya. Mayapán appears to have been the defensive redoubt of a warlike group of people who exacted tribute from neighboring tribes.

Another center built during this last phase of the Classic Maya culture was the breathtaking site of

Tulum, on the Caribbean coast of the Yucatán Peninsula (see page 123). This too was a defensive stronghold, surrounded by walls on three sides and the ocean on the fourth. Its buildings, paintings, and inscriptions show it to have been a mixture of styles and influences. Its isolated position means that it may have survived into the Spanish era.

In 1441, Mayapán was overrun by its enemies. Mayapán was the last of the major Maya centers; when the Spaniards arrived 150 years later they found the sites deserted, and the Maya of Mexico living in small, dispersed groups.

The ruins of Mayapán.

WARRING LOCAL FACTIONS

The Maya in the Guatemalan highlands underwent a similar fate. Toltecs arrived in the region from farther north in the 13th century. They appear to have overcome the local indigenous Maya, and formed several local empires. The most powerful of these were the K'iche', whose capital was K'umarkaaj. Other groups included the Kaqchikel and the Mam, but these last two were conquered by the K'iche' in the 15th century. But when Quicab, the powerful leader of the K'iche', died in 1475, the other Guatemalan Maya tribes broke away from their rule. As in Mexico, when the Spanish arrived they found the local tribes at war with each other, and were quick to exploit this enmity to their own advantage.

TIKAL

Possibly the most visually impressive of all the Maya cities, Tikal stands majestically in the Petén jungle, occupied now only by monkeys, toucans, and other exotica.

As the first sunlight filtered through the early morning mist, the high priest, Iahca Na, emerged from the inner sanctum of Temple I. Yik'in Chan K'awiil, waiting to be crowned the 27th ruler of the great city, was clad in jaguar pelt and jade jewels, awaiting approval from the shaman who had consulted the gods for their blessing. A discreet nod from the priest confirmed Yik'in Chan's accession and the expectant multitude gathered in the plaza below erupted in celebration, heralding a new era for Tikal.

COSMOPOLITAN CITY

As you walk through the ruins today, it is easy to forget that Tikal was previously a thriving metropolis with a population of around 100,000. The Maya city was home to a multi-layered society: as well as the nobility there was a large middle class, comprising merchants, craftsmen, and bureaucrats, and a workers' class, which included farmers, builders, and servants.

Tikal represents over 1,200 years of continuous construction. Wherever you stand, beneath your feet lie many layers of previous eras; more than 100 structures lie beneath the North Acropolis as we see it today.

Temple I: being closer to heaven, the small room at the top of the temples was used for sacred rituals and ceremonies.

Carved stelae depicted major events in Tikal's history and tales from Maya mythology.

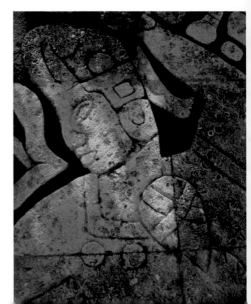

A Mayan Classic-period censer of a deity holding a human head, displayed at Museo Tikal.

Birdlife, such as this colorful montezuma oropendola, is abundant around the temples of Tikal.

Tikal's natural wonders

In addition to its awesome archeological heritage, the Tikal National Park offers visitors one of the richest rainforest environments in Central America. The protected territory saves trees, hundreds of years old, from logging, and rare animals from both the black market and the dining table.

Tikal has an incredible variety of animal life, and as you wander around the site, you can tell that they have made it their home. Racoon-like coatimundis scurry around the undergrowth, and troupes of spider monkeys playfully pelt you with berries from the treetops. The park is also home to over 250 species of birds, such as the keel-billed toucan, the ocellated turkey, parrots, and eagles. Most thrilling of all are five of the world's rarest wildcats that live in the area; you might be lucky enough to catch sight of a jaguar, puma, ocelot, jaguarundi, or margay. As you enter the site, pause by the Tikal reservoir, which is a good place to spot a turtle or even a small alligator.

As seen from the top of Temple IV, the tallest of all the Tikal structures, the massive temple roof combs rise out of the dense tree canopy.

The ceiba is a symbol of national pride in modern Guatemala. In ancient times, the sacred tree was seen as a link to heaven.

Look up as you stroll along the jungle paths between the temples and you are likely to spot all kinds of wildlife, including spider and howler monkeys.

A depiction of Hernan Cortes being honored by the conquered Amerindians.

EUROPEAN CONQUEST

As the Spanish subdued the Maya, they quickly overtook the continent, except for a stretch of Caribbean coast that was claimed by the British.

When Christopher Columbus set sail from Spain in 1492 on his first voyage to the New World, he was hoping to find a group of islands near Japan, which he conceived to be about 2,400 nautical miles (4,445km) to the west of Spain. There, he determined, he would build a great city and trade gold, gems, and spices from the Indies with the cities of Europe. He imagined himself as a rich governor, lord of it all.

His ambitions coincided with the interests of the Spanish Crown. The wars to oust the Moors from Spain had depleted the royal treasury and the promise of the wealth of the Indies was very attractive indeed. On returning from his first journey to the New World, Columbus was given a grand reception. He was named Admiral of the Ocean Sea and was ordered to organize a second voyage to further explore Hispaniola.

His second and third voyages had mixed results, ranging from exploring the Atlantic

Baymen in the swamps, Belize.

The Amerindians of Costa Rica, wearing gold necklaces, guided the Spaniards around the area, and spoke of great mines of gold – pointing south.

coast of South America to being sent back to Spain in chains after a rebellion by settlers on Hispaniola. Somehow, he persuaded the Spanish sovereigns, Ferdinand and Isabella, to agree to finance his fourth and final voyage to the Americas in search of gold and a passage to the West. He landed on the Bay Island of Guanaja on July 30, 1502. For the rest of the year, he charted

the coastal area from Honduras to Panamá and named it Veragua. He was so enamored by the golden mirrors that the Amerindians of Costa Rica wore about their necks, and by their many stories of gold and gold mines along the coast to the south, that he named the area the Rich Coast of Veragua.

Rich though it seemed to Columbus at the time, the newly discovered area was not to be a great, rich jewel in Spain's crown. In fact, the 'Rich Coast' turned out to be one of the poorest of Spain's American colonies. Impassable mountains, impenetrable forests, raging rivers, unbearable heat, floods, disease, swamps, shortages of food and of labor, internal rivalries, lack of natural resources, or a way to generate wealth all oppressed the settlers. They were often reduced to living like the 'savages' they had come to conquer: wearing goat-hair garments or clothing made of bark; using cacao (chocolate) beans for currency; eking out a bare subsistence in the fields, using native methods to cultivate native crops. This bleak reality was yet to come. Columbus naively returned to Spain brimming with dreams of great riches and grandeur, to the point of asking the king to confer on him the title of Duke of Veragua, which was eventually granted to his descendants.

Central America. They were capturing Amerindian slaves and sending them to work in the mines of Hispaniola, stealing their gold and desperately searching for a passage across the continent to the other ocean. Finally, in 1513, Vasco Nuñez de Balboa, a young stowaway escaping debts on Hispaniola, led an expedition across the isthmus and discovered the Pacific Ocean. It wasn't long before rudimentary shipyards appeared on the Pacific coast to accommodate would-be explorers who had sailed into Atlantic ports and then walked across the isthmus,

Hernan Cortes (1485–1547) arriving in Mexico, from 'The Codex Azcatitlan.'

MORE EXPEDITIONS

In 1506, two years after Columbus returned to Spain, King Ferdinand sent Governor Diego de Nicuesa and a group of settlers to establish a colony at Veragua. It was the first of many ill-fated attempts to establish settlements. Nicuesa's ship ran aground in Panamá and he and his group set about walking up the coast to their destination. Food shortages and tropical diseases were acute; the terrain was devastating. Indigenous peoples along the way burned their own crops rather than yield their food. By the time the settlers finally arrived, their numbers had been halved.

Around this time, expeditions from Spain were landing throughout the Atlantic coast of

ready to set sail on the Pacific and continue their explorations. The unexplored Pacific had better anchorages, and was thought to have more gold.

The first Spanish expedition to land in the Maya world was led by Francisco Hernández de Córdoba in 1517. Hernán Cortés followed two years later. He landed on the island of Cozumel, where the first Christian Mass was said on the American continent.

One of Cortés's lieutenants, Francisco de Montejo, returned to the Yucatán in 1527 to extend Spanish rule to the Maya living there. At first he was unsuccessful, both on the Caribbean coast near Campeche and on the Atlantic side. It was Montejo's son and nephew who began a second conquest of the Yucatán in 1540, and this time the Spaniards succeeded in establishing their rule. In 1542 they founded the city of Mérida, and as in Mexico City, built their new cathedral directly on top of the ruins of a Maya temple.

LEGENDARY FEROCITY

The Spanish conquest of the Maya in Guatemala was entrusted to Pedro de Alvarado. He achieved it with a ferocity that became legendary. In 1523, he and some 800 men defeated the main army of the K'iche' and slew their leader, Tecún Umán. Alvarado then advanced on the

and a half later, in 1697, that the last descendants of the independent Maya kingdoms, who lived in Tayasal, an island on Lake Petén Itzá in northern Guatemala, were finally subdued.

PESTILENCE AND SLAVERY

The Spanish expeditions to Central America had brought smallpox, influenza, and plague to the area, and tens of thousands of Amerindians died. Survivors of the epidemics faced another danger: enslavement. Indigenous peoples that lived in large population centers, and were vul-

Pedro de Alvarado.

K'iche' capital, K'umarkaaj, and burned it down. He was equally ruthless with the Kaqchikel, and set about conquering the many mountain tribes. In 1527, Alvarado founded the first Spanish capital of Guatemala at Santiago de los Caballeros, close to the modern-day city of Antigua.

Resistance to Alvarado's rule continued through the 1530s, especially in the highlands of Verapaz, where in the end it was Christian missionaries led by Fray Bartolomé de las Casas who managed to get the Maya to accept Christianity and Spanish rule. By the time of Alvarado's death in 1541, almost the entire Maya population of Guatemala was under Spanish control. As in Mexico, however, this did not mean a complete end to resistance, and it was more than a century

nerable to such attacks, were captured, branded with hot irons, and shipped off to Panamá and Peru to be sold as slaves.

During this period, the *conquistadores* who arrived in Central America were free to exploit the indigenous population in virtually any way they wished. The Spanish policy of *requerimiento*, which went into effect in 1510, permitted settlers to wage war on those who refused to be baptized, a convenient justification for killing Amerindians and plundering their gold.

Later, *encomienda*, a royal grant from the Crown, gave settlers in Central America the right to force indigenous peoples to labor without compensation – or to demand goods as tribute. It was, in effect, slavery. The Amerindians were relocated to live on the land where they worked, and were considered the property of the grant holder. Without the system of *encomienda*, the *conquistadores* could not realize their aspira-

> *Bartolomé de las Casas was to chronicle the methods of Spanish colonization in Latin America in his History of the Indies. He later became bishop of Chiapas, in Mexico.*

City. The Yucatán and Guatemala (from where Honduras and Chiapas were governed) were far from these centers, and this distance on the one hand led to greater abuses, but on the other protected the Maya way of life, as it was never entirely dominated by the newcomers.

Among the first measures taken by the Spanish administration was the concentration of the native population in villages and towns, known as *reducciones*. Each of these was laid out in the Spanish style, with a central square where the Catholic church and the town hall or *ayuntamiento* were

Cruelty of the Spanish encomienda system on a plantation.

tions of becoming landed aristocracy. All of the rights and assumed privileges of title had no real value without Amerindians to work the land.

Many Amerindians did not adapt well to slavery and fiercely resisted its imposition. Many fought and died avoiding enslavement, and many others fled to the mountains where they could not be followed. Finally, the practice of *encomienda* was abolished well before large numbers of Spanish settlers started arrived in the region.

LIFE UNDER SPANISH RULE

By the mid-16th century, the original Spanish conquistadors had died, and Spanish rule was directed more impersonally from Spain and from the capital of the viceroyalty in Mexico

located. The local population was brought into these new villages for several reasons. It was easier for the Spaniards to control them, and to make sure they paid their taxes. They were on hand for the communal work demanded of them, while at the same time it facilitated the missionaries' work of evangelization. In this way, the Maya were forced to become part of Spanish colonial society – which, in a very racist way, always regarded them as the lowest element in that society.

As the Spaniards developed agriculture and their estates or *haciendas* extended throughout the region, they also forced the Maya to work there – and in Guatemala, for example, began the wholesale transfer of laborers from the highlands down to the plantations on the Pacific coast. Spain's Central American colonies gradually developed, with administrative centers springing up in Panama, Nicaragua, and Guatemala, while the name 'Costa Rica' was used for the first time in 1539, to distinguish the territory between Panama and Nicaragua.

SKILLFUL ADAPTATION

Although some Maya were given posts of minor authority in the new Spanish villages, there was little chance of them wielding any real power. Instead, they continued their traditional practices and communal organization in parallel with the Spanish system. Authority in the more remote villages continued to be held by *principales,* or elders. Communal efforts were organized among Maya *cofradías* or brotherhoods, who used their role as keepers of the local saints to run self-help schemes, joint work on the *milpas* (maize fields), or even land transfers among villagers. Together with this, the colonial Maya were skillful at adapting the Christian religion to their own beliefs, continuing to worship the old gods in the guise of the Christian pantheon.

The cathedral and city of León, Nicaragua.

⊘ REPARTIMIENTO

When slavery was abolished, the Crown still had to support the need for labor. The unethical system of *encomienda* was replaced by a system called *repartimiento* (meaning to divide up) which required all Amerindian men between the ages of 16 and 60 to labor for one week of each month for private individuals, religious institutions, municipalities, and/or government offices. Indeed, this was one form of slavery replacing another. On paper, the system was supposed to provide indigenous peoples with compensation for their labor and leave them free to work their own fields for the remaining three or so weeks of the month. But, in practice, things were very different; abuses became commonplace and slavery-like conditions arose.

Local people were required to devote considerably more than a week's labor to the Spaniards, since they had to walk very long distances, sometimes for days on end, from their villages to their places of work. And they were charged for the food and any other goods they consumed – thus using up their miserably small amount of pay. Many Amerindians were forced to escape the *repartimiento* system by leaving their communities, although the practice eventually faded away in the 17th century as the number of native people declined and many laborers became directly employed by hacienda owners.

BOURBON INFLUENCE

For more than two centuries after the Spanish Conquest, these efforts and the isolation of much of the Maya world from the centers of Spanish interest helped to protect the Maya from the worst ravages of the empire. The Maya's position worsened during the second half of the 18th century, however, when the Bourbon monarchy in Spain sought to regain effective control of its rebellious colonies. The provinces were reorganized into *intendencias* and *partidos,* and indigenous officials were removed from office.

Captain Edward Teach, or Blackbeard.

> No pirates are as enduringly remembered as Blackbeard – Bristol-born Edward Teach, who allegedly spent much time hiding out in the Belizean cayes off the Gulf of Honduras.

At the same time, an effort was made to redistribute land and to make the *haciendas* more productive. The profitable new crops of sisal, tobacco, sugar cane, and cotton demanded more land, which was seized from communal Maya holdings. Increasingly, the Maya were employed as laborers on these estates, often in conditions of near-slavery.

When the struggle for independence began in Spanish America during the first decades of the 19th century, the Maya were still regarded as the lowest sector of society. Their customs and beliefs were largely ignored, if not despised. By this time they had little idea of their ancestors' glorious achievements, and yet many elements of their distinctive culture – language, dress, social habits – had managed to survive against the odds.

BRITISH COLONIZATION

While Spain had claimed Belize, the Bay Islands, and the Mosquito Coast, the Spanish had not been able to settle there, partially because they were unable to fight off the native inhabitants, while the challenging terrain – coral reefs, murky swamps, and mosquito-filled forests – proved a deterrent. However, English and Scottish adventurers began arriving in search of logwood trade – with no interest in taxing or converting the locals, they got on much better with them. Gradually, the sparsely-inhabited coastline of Belize began to attract another kind of British entrepeneur: the buccaneer, or pirate. Plundering Spanish cargo ships and selling on the loot, the buccaneers used the Belizean reef, with its mud flats and treacherous coral heads, to their advantage by utilizing fast, shallow draft ships. By 1670, the death-knell for Caribbean freebooting was sounded when a treaty between Britain and Spain pledged to suppress high seas piracy.

Many British settlers, known as the Baymen, had been forming settlements and logging since the 1630s, and despite regular attacks by the Spanish until the end of the 18th century, when the Battle of St George's Caye was won decisively by the Baymen, they prevailed in establishing a colony around the logwood and later, mahogany trade. They brought in boatloads of African slaves from Jamaica to help cut down the trees, who soon outnumbered the white settlers roughly ten to one. Slave laws were more liberal than in, for instance, the southern United States, and it was possible for slaves to buy their freedom, while female slaves taken as mistresses by settlers were also freed. Conditions for slaves, however, could be as brutal as anywhere else.

Even after the emancipation of Central America from the Spanish, the British continued to administer the region and formally declared Belize a Crown Colony in 1862, calling it British Honduras.

Baymen working in the rainforest of British Honduras.

INDEPENDENCE

A power vacuum brought on by the end of Spanish rule left the region in disarray and vulnerable to outside forces.

Under the supervision of the Spanish viceroy in Mexico City, much of Central America was loosely united as the Captaincy General of Guatemala until the early 19th century. This included part of the state of Chiapas, Guatemala, El Salvador, Honduras, Nicaragua, and Costa Rica. As Napoleonic forces and Spain, Portugal, and Britain battled for control of the Iberian Peninsula in the Peninsular War between 1807 and 1814, the Central American union began to fray.

Independence movements first broke out in El Salvador in 1811, and again in 1814, but the rebellions didn't amount to much. However, in Guatemala City on September 15, 1821, a group of Central American Criollos declared the region's independence from Spain. It didn't last long. A year later, despite the objections of liberal factions, conservative leaders allowed the annexation of Central America by Mexico, which had been the center of the Spanish viceroyalty and was now ruled by an emperor, Agustín de Iturbide. The following year Mexico became a republic and on July 1, 1823, the congress of Central America broke away and declared its independence.

Modeled after the United States of America, this new nation became known as, according to the Constitution of 1824, 'The Federal Republic of Central America.' It consisted of the states of Guatemala, El Salvador, Honduras, Nicaragua, and Costa Rica, as well as – for a short time – Los Altos, which included parts of Mexico and Western Guatemala. The Guatemalan Manuel José Arce became the federation's first president. Liberals hoped that Central America would develop into a democratic nation that could build on trade from goods crossing from the Atlantic to the Pacific and vice versa, though it only lasted six years before rebel troops, calling

Coin of the Federal Republic of Central America.

themselves 'the allied army for the protection of the law' under General Francisco Morazán from Honduras, took Guatemala City in 1829. The final nail in the coffin was when Nicaragua separated from the federation in 1838 and the union soon dissolved.

COFFEE POWER

The provinces became their own republican states, though tensions grew more aggressive throughout the rest of the 19th century. There were many attempts at uniting Central America as a single nation, though results never panned out.

In 1843 William Le Lacheur, an Englishman on his way back home with a cargo of pelts, put in to Puntarenas, a Costa Rican port on the Pacific coast, in search of ballast for his ship, which had been battered by storms off the Mexican coast. He loaded some 230,000kg (500,000lbs) of coffee into his hold and the Costa Rica–Liverpool connection was established. Thus were the British Isles and, ultimately, the European continent, opened up as an important new market for Costa Rican coffee.

Members of the budding coffee oligarchy called on General Francisco Morazán, a hero of the Central American Federal Republic, to free them from what they perceived as President Braulio

William Walker praying before his execution in 1860.

Carrillo's despotism. Morazán was welcomed as a liberator when he arrived in Costa Rica in April of 1842, with an army of 500 mostly Salvadoran volunteers. The head of Carrillo's army, Vicente Villaseñor, met up with Morazán just as the general and his men neared Alajuela on their march from the Pacific port of Caldera, and offered to join forces with him. The *Pacto de Jocote* sealed, Carrillo fell and was forced into exile in El Salvador. A special assembly named Morazán provisional head of the state of Costa Rica.

Morazán wore out his welcome when he attempted to use Costa Rica as a base to revive his moribund confederation. The general sent missives to the other Central American countries calling for a National Constituent Assembly to revive his dream of a unified Central American nation. He threatened to impose compliance by force of arms. When Morazán tried to conscript Costa Ricans to enforce his ultimatum, the people of San José revolted. After three days of fierce fighting, Morazán was captured and, on September 15, 1842, he was executed in San José's Central Park. Less than three years later, Braulio Carrillo, too, was to meet a violent end, assassinated in El Salvador.

WILLIAM WALKER

A decade after Morazán's attempt at unification, El Salvador, Honduras, and Nicaragua created the Federation of Central America, but it too fell apart. In the 1880s, Guatemalan President Justo Rufino Barrios tried to take over the region by force and was killed in the process. Other attempts were made in 1896 and 1921 and didn't last more than a year or two. While the different nations of Central America were never able to unite politically, they were able to form a military coalition in 1856–7 to fight off an invasion by US adventurer William Walker.

In 1855, the Tennessee-born Walker took control of Nicaragua after conducting a farcical election. One of his aims was to institutionalize slavery there and in neighboring countries so that he could sell slaves to the United States. Certain US industrialists liked the plan and gave support to Walker. The following year, with an army of 300 mercenaries, called *filibusteros*, he invaded Costa Rica, advancing as far as the site of the present Santa Rosa National Park. Walker and his men entrenched themselves in the fortified

⊘ FLYING THE FLAG

Central America's strategic location between the Atlantic and the Pacific was emblematic for the formation of the short-lived Federal Republic of Central America. The federation's flag displayed a white band between two blue stripes, epitomizing the land between two oceans, while the coat of arms showed five mountains, each signifying a different state, between two oceans. Even after the federation fell apart, the idea remained symbolic. Even today, Guatemala, El Salvador, Honduras, Nicaragua, and Costa Rica still fly flags that retain the old federal motif of two outer blue bands bounding an inner white stripe.

Santa Rosa mansion. Costa Rican President Juan Rafael Mora, a member of the coffee oligarchy, had been monitoring the threat and had already mustered a force of *campesinos* (farm workers) to repel Walker. The Costa Ricans were numerically superior, though many were poorly armed with little more than farming implements and rusty rifles. On May 20, 1856, they engaged Walker in a 14-minute-long battle and forced him to retreat toward the Nicaraguan border.

The Costa Rican army pursued them and, at Rivas in Nicaragua, trapped Walker in a wooden

Two waves of immigration changed Belize considerably: 2,000 people from the Mosquito Coast, a British settlement, came in the late 1700s; then, after 1800, the Garífuna, of mixed Amerindian and African blood, arrived from St Vincent.

fort. A young drummer boy named Juan Santamaría volunteered to torch the fort, but was shot dead in the process. With the fort in flames, Walker's men were routed. Three years later, he met his end in front of a firing squad in Honduras.

BELIZE

It took Belize many years to win its independence. Even then, it was a good few years before the country achieved true political freedom. Relations with the Spanish rulers of neighboring Guatemala were frequently tense throughout the 17th and 18th centuries, as British pirate ships used Belize's sheltered waters as harbors from which to attack Spanish ships. As a result of the American War of Independence, Spain declared war on Britain and in 1779 a sizeable Spanish force attacked St George's Caye, burning it and Belize Town to the ground. The settlement was rebuilt, but in 1798 the Spanish attacked again. Despite the fact that the Spanish force had far superior firepower, a decisive sea battle was fought at St George's Caye, and the Spanish were soundly defeated.

Following this victory, the local inhabitants considered themselves part of the British Empire, although officially the colony still did not exist. In 1802, Spain was obliged to acknowledge British sovereignty over the area

in the Treaty of Amiens. When Guatemala and Mexico won their independence from Spain in 1821, both laid claim to the territory of Belize. It was formally declared a British Crown Colony in 1862 and stayed that way all the way up until 1973, while the Bay Islands and Mosquito Coast were ceded to Honduras and Nicaragua in 1859 and 1860.

GRAN COLOMBIA

Panama shares a political history closer to neighboring Colombia than with the rest of

The British Honduras Volunteer Guard on parade, 1972.

Central America. After its independence from Spain on November 28, 1821, Panama became part of the Republic of Gran Colombia, which included Colombia, Venezuela, and Ecuador. The Isthmus fought for its independence with little success until 1903. After a failed French attempt at building a canal linking the Atlantic and Pacific Oceans, the Roosevelt administration proposed to Colombia that the US should build and control such a canal, offering to pay off the stockholders of the company still in control, though the Colombian government refused. A rebellion ensued and in 1903 the Hay–Bunau-Varilla Treaty was signed, giving the US permission to build a canal and then administer, fortify and defend it 'in perpetuity.'

A man runs from a huge ash cloud as Costa Rica's Mount Irabu volcano erupts, 1963.

MODERN HISTORY

Natural disasters, civil wars, and foreign intervention have dominated headlines in recent decades, but stability in the region finally seems to be within reach.

The 20th and 21st centuries have seen many ups and downs in Central America. There has been no shortage of drama to say the least. Civil Wars, uprisings, revolutions, outside interference, and major natural disasters have all played a part, giving a sense of mass disorder. However, recent years have seen economic growth and development, as well as the stabilization of the political situation in many countries.

DOMINATION OF US FRUIT COMPANIES

Throughout the 20th century, countries like Costa Rica, Guatemala, and Honduras were effectively controlled by American fruit corporations, which consolidated large landholdings throughout the region.

In 1899, New Orleans-based Vaccaro Brothers and Company, which would later become Standard Fruit, arrived in Roatán, in the Bay Islands of

An El Salvadoran rebel child soldier, 1983.

> *The United Fruit Company grew so big in the 1950s, taking over the railroad, radio, telegraph, and electricity companies, it was nicknamed 'El Pulpo' – the Octopus.*

Honduras, to buy fruits like coconuts, oranges, and bananas. Two years later they set up on the mainland in La Ceiba and soon controlled the entire banana industry along the coast from Boca Cerrada to Balfate, a stretch of about 80km (50 miles).

Around the same time, another American fruit corporation, United Fruit, came to Honduras to take over banana plantations. With enormous wealth, they were able to gain extraordinary access to the Honduran government. They were granted concessions to build railroads from Tela to Progreso and from Trujillo to Juticalpa. With the two railroads, the Tela Railroad Company and Trujillo Railroad Company, United Fruit was able to dominate the banana trade in the country.

By taking over large concessions of land mostly to grow bananas, peasant farmers who were growing and exporting their crops were forced out of business. Additionally, as these corporations favored workers from the West Indies and Belize, who were usually better-educated and spoke English, resentment grew.

Over time, the fruit companies began to look more and more like foreign occupations. Conflicts over land ownership and workers' rights led to armed conflicts and multiple invasions by US armed forces, who were lobbied by the US-aligned elites to protect their investments. In the first decades of the 20th century, US military incursions took place in Honduras in 1903, 1907, 1911, 1912, 1919, 1924, and 1925.

The strife within the banana industry helped bring about the region's first organized labor movements. The first major strike occurred in 1917 against the Cuyamel Fruit Company, which was quickly suppressed by the Honduran military. Protests against the Standard Fruit Company's holding in La Ceiba in 1920 elicited the response of a US warship being dispatched to the Caribbean coast. The strike only ended when Standard Fruit offered a new wage, equivalent to $1.75 per day.

CONSTRUCTION OF THE PANAMA CANAL

There has been no more significant imitative in the history of Central America than a trade route between the Atlantic and Pacific Oceans. The construction of a shipping route across the isthmus was first proposed in Nicaragua – using the San Juan River and Lake Nicaragua, as well as a series

Steam shovel trains excavating the Panama Canal channel in 1913.

⊘ BANANA REPUBLICS

While companies such as United Fruit and Standard Fruit – which would grow up to become Dole and Chiquita – profited wildly from the banana, the people in the places that grew bananas rarely shared their success. In fact, the power and influence that these American corporations held in Central America resulted in the mass destabilization of several countries. In exchange for land, these companies built sorely-needed infrastructure. However, they used government ties to control railroads and ports, and when they didn't get their way they even supplied weapons to opposition groups in return for favorable conditions.

Under the system, workers were often exploited and overall economic development was uneven. Despite so much money coming to the country, the local people remained poor and the government corrupt.

While in Honduras in 1904 escaping an embezzlement charge, American writer O. Henry wrote the short story *The Admiral*, later published in his book *Cabbages and Kings*. The story describes life in a fictional, dysfunctional country called Anchuria, where the entire economy revolved around the banana. He described it as a 'small, maritime banana republic,' and that's how the phrase was coined.

of locks and tunnels from the lake to the Pacific Ocean – during the early colonial era. There were studies done as early as 1551 by the Viceroyalty, and the short-lived Federal Republic of Central America commissioned a study in 1825 and asked the US for financing and engineering technology to explore the idea. It never came to fruition and the idea would be explored again and again by a variety of parties until the end of the 19th century.

In Panama, the idea of transisthmian has been around since the time of conquest. Work was done as early as 1519 when the Spanish crown began dredging the Chagres River , which allowed for traffic for two-thirds of the way across the isthmus. When the French attempt at building a sea-level canal in the late 1800s was in disarray because of disease and faulty engineering, the US took over. From 1904 to 1913 the 83-km (50-mile) lock canal, considered one of the world's great engineering triumphs, was built by the US Army Corps of Engineers. On October 10, 1913, President Woodrow Wilson detonated the dike at Gamboa, which isolated the Culebra Cut from Gatún Lake, via telegraph from Washington. The canal opened to traffic the following August, just as World War I had broken out.

The canal became an important strategic and economic asset to the US and changed world shipping patterns by saving the extra 12,600km (7,800 miles) of travel around Cape Horn at the foot of South America. In total, the canal cost the US about $375 million, including $10 million paid to Panama and $40 million paid to the French operators. A total of roughly 75,000 people worked on the project and 5,609 lives were lost by workers who died from disease and accidents during the construction.

The canal brought mostly positive changes to Panama. Infrastructure was developed to treat water, sewage, and garbage within the Canal Zone and the cities of Panama and Colón. The area was even rid of yellow fever using techniques pioneered by Cuban physician Carlos Finley by 1905. Although the US originally signed a contract to operate the canal in perpetuity, its operation and all US military bases were turned over to Panama on December 31, 1999.

GUATEMALA IN THE 20TH CENTURY

A series of weak presidents and military coups characterized the first decades of the 20th century in Guatemala. Then, in 1931, General Jorge Ubico was elected as president; he was to rule until 1944. During his 13 years in power, Ubico managed to improve Guatemala's economic situation and bring about political stability. But individual freedoms were restricted and he manipulated constitution, legislative, and legal powers for his own ends. Ubico imposed military discipline throughout Guatemala, so that even the national symphony orchestra played in military uniforms.

Ubico was finally overthrown in 1944 and the reformist Juan José Arévalo was elected presi-

United Fruit Company plantation in Guatemala, 1961.

dent under a new constitution in 1945. Arévalo set in motion important changes in education, land ownership, and labor laws. These measures brought resistance from the more conservative sectors of Guatemalan society and there were several attempts to depose him. Despite these plots, Arévalo succeeded in completing his six years in office, and in 1950 handed over to another reform-minded president, Jácobo Árbenz Guzmán. His attempts to break up the huge rural estates through land reform programs and to control the power of the United Fruit Company soon led to protests.

The United States branded Árbenz a communist, and in 1954 they backed a coup by Colonel Carlos Castillo Armas and the National

Liberation Movement. Faced with an invasion from Honduras led by Castillo Armas, Árbenz was forced to resign on June 27, 1954, paving the way for Castillo Armas to take over. The civil war that rocked Guatemala for more than three decades is widely regarded to have started with the 1954 coup that overthrew Árbenz.

For the next 30 years, Guatemala was governed by a succession of military rulers. The US-supported Castillo Armas was assassinated in the National Palace in 1957; from then on the country was subject to increasing violence, as

of military victories, but the army hit back using scorched-earth tactics and a murderously successful terror campaign in the highlands. Several thousand people were killed each year during this period; the vast majority were indigenous Maya peasants who had nothing to do with the struggle.

THE LONG ROAD TO PEACE

In 1982 a military junta toppled the government of Lucas García and, in 1983, General Ríos Montt took control. It was during his period in power that the repression in the countryside reached

Supporters of Colonel Castillo Armas' anti-Communist government marching in Guatemala City in 1954.

trade unions, left-wing guerrillas, and other groups fought against the brutal military rule.

The Castillo government had built up a 'blacklist' of more than 40,000 politicians, trade unionists, grass-roots leaders, and intellectuals whom it regarded as a threat. Many were imprisoned, or forced into exile. The Church, too, was subjected to violence by the armed forces, who resented the clergy for their support of Maya villagers. Between 1978 and 1983, 13 Catholic priests were killed and more than 100 fled the country.

Left-wing groups responded by forming a variety of organizations including, by the beginning of the 1960s, guerrilla armies. During the late 1970s and early 1980s the civil war reached its climax. The guerrillas initially scored a number

> "In Guatemala there are two presidents, and one of them has a machine gun with which he is always threatening the other." Juan José Arévalo (President 1945–50)

a peak. Counter-insurgency techniques ruthlessly implemented by the Guatemalan army led to the murder, torture, and displacement of many thousands of peasants in these years, among Guatemala's darkest. In 1984, the military ruler General Óscar Mejía Víctores ordered the establishment of a new constitution, which led to the election of Guatemala's first civilian president in more than 30 years, Vinicio Cerezo Arévalo, a Christian Democrat.

With the return of civilian government in 1986, the attempts to achieve peace began in earnest. The guerrilla organizations realized that they could not overthrow the Guatemalan state by violence. One of the chief problems for these negotiations was the fact that the army considered it had eliminated what it called 'subversion,' and therefore there was nothing to negotiate. Cerezo moved only cautiously during his four years in office to try to curb the power

powers in 1993, though he was quickly ousted. Elections were organized for the end of 1995, which gave victory to Álvaro Arzú, a center-right candidate. In March 1996, the guerrilla organization URNG agreed to a ceasefire. This was followed by rapid progress in other areas of the peace negotiations, and on December 29, 1996, an agreement for a firm and lasting peace was signed by the government and the rebels in Guatemala City. The principal parts of the agreement were to carry out an investigation of the human-rights abuses committed during the civil

Guatemalan Labor Party (PGT, associated with Communist Party) guerrillas with their weapons, Guatemala City, 1981.

of the armed forces and to bring the continuing civil war to an end.

Cerezo's successor as president from 1990 was Jorge Serrano, who fared even worse. Although talks between the armed forces and the Guatemalan National Revolutionary Unity (URNG) guerrillas began in Mexico City in 1991, very little progress was actually made toward peace. The guerrillas wanted peace accords that would guarantee substantial change in Guatemala. The armed forces were anxious not to be held responsible for the 200,000 deaths that had occurred during the violence. They also wished to avoid any sweeping reforms to the army or the police.

The deteriorating situation within Guatemala led Serrano to attempt to assume dictatorial

war, a commitment to demilitarize society, and to introduce constitutional changes to safeguard indigenous rights in Guatemala.

Initially, the outlook was positive as the guerrillas handed in their weapons and formed a political party, while MINUGUA (the United Nations Mission to Guatemala) arrived to oversee the implementation of the accords. Some reforms of the armed forces were carried out and a new constitution was framed (which promised an inclusive role for indigenous people). A commission was also established to investigate human rights crimes committed during the civil war. Progress proved very slow, however, as the Guatemalan military stalled on key commitments and proved reluctant to relinquish its power base.

Army personnel were later implicated in the assassination of Bishop Juan Geradi in 1998, two days after his offices had published a report that blamed the military and civil-defense patrols for 93 percent of civil war deaths. Meanwhile, a referendum rejected a constitutional amendment to legitimize Maya rights.

THE NICARAGUA REVOLUTION

With the backing of the US, the Somoza family political dynasty came to power in Nicaragua in 1912 and would rule for the next seven dec-

kidnappings, which earned them national recognition as the opposition force. The Somoza's regime retaliated hard, using their US-trained military and police forces to torture, intimidate, and censor the Nicaraguan public. A destructive 1972 earthquake added to the unease.

In 1978 the administration of Jimmy Carter cut off aid to the Somozas because of human rights violations. Riots broke out in Managua after the editor of the leftist Managua newspaper *La Prensa* was murdered and a general strike followed in Nicaragua's large cities calling

General Anastasio Somoza, the President of Nicaragua, 1975.

ades. With wealth from US-based multinational corporations and the backing of the US military, their rule was characterized by rising inequality and widespread political corruption.

The Sandinista National Liberation Front (FSLN) arose in response to the Somoza family. In 1961, Carlos Fonseca Amador, Silvio Mayorga, and Tomás Borge Martínez formed the rebel group along with students, peasants, and other anti-Somoza elements, such as the Communist Cuban government, the Panamanian government of Omar Torrijos, and the Venezuelan government of Carlos Andrés Pérez. By the 1970s they were strong enough to begin plotting against the regime of long-time dictator Anastasio Somoza Debayle. They began a campaign of

for the end of the Somoza regime. The violence continued to worsen. In 1978, the FSLN took around 2,000 people hostage at the National Palace in Managua and the government agreed to pay $500,000 and release certain prisoners. A year later, negotiations took place, managed by the Organization of American States, but they broke down. Within months, the FSLN took over the country and President Somoza resigned.

When the Sandinistas took over, the country was in ruins. Of the total population of 2.8 million, around 600,000 Nicaraguans were homeless and 150,000 had become refugees or were in exile. All wealth was concentrated in Managua, while the rest of the country had little. The revolution brought about a restructuring of all sectors of the economy. Agrarian reforms gave away much of the land to farmers. Ceremonies were held around the country where President Daniel Ortega gave peasants titles to land and a rifle with which to defend it.

While the Carter administration tried to work with the FSLN, the subsequent Ronald Reagan administration was bent on a strict anti-communist strategy that would isolate the Sandinista regime. An anti-Sandinista movement was begun by former members of the Somoza regime's National Guard unit along the border

> Ríos Montt was ousted in 1982 by his defense minister, Mejía Víctores, who observed that "Guatemala doesn't need more prayers, it needs more executions."

with Nicaragua, which was known as the *Contrarrevolución* (Counter-revolution), aka Contras. Other minority groups along the Mosquito Coast also began demanding more autonomy. Reagan cancelled economic aid to Nicaragua and covertly began supporting anti-Sandinista forces.

Central America was already destabilized by ongoing civil wars in El Salvador and Guatemala, so Nicaragua was a powder keg waiting to explode. The CIA-backed Contras secretly opened a 'second front' on Nicaragua's Atlantic coast and Costa Rican border. So instead of reform and development, more than 50 percent of the FSLN's budget was dedicated to the military. By 1982, Contra forces launched a series of assassinations of government officials and the following year began planting mines in Nicaragua's harbors to stop shipments of weapons from reaching Managua. The US Congress enacted legislation to suspend further aid to the Contras later that year, although Reagan attempted to illegally supply them out of the proceeds of arms sales to Iran, an act known as the Iran-Contra Affair. With the help of mediation by other Central American nations, the Sapoa ceasefire between the Sandinistas and the Contras was signed on March 23, 1988, which called for a democratic election to be held in 1990. The FSLN lost the election to the National Opposition Union, though they still controlled the army and courts. For the next seven

years, Violeta Chamorro's presidency would be dedicated to consolidating democratic institutions and stabilizing the economy.

SALVADORAN CIVIL WAR

At the start of the 20th century, the Salvadoran economy revolved around coffee, sugar cane, and cotton, which were controlled by just a few families. Rural resistance began to bubble up, most notably in 1932 when peasants around the country began to protest. The government retaliated in what has become known as La Matanza,

House after a Salvadoran army and guerrilla battle, 1983.

or the slaughter. Roughly 40,000 indigenous farmers and political opponents were murdered, imprisoned or exiled during the act.

From the 1930s to the 1970s there was widespread instability and El Salvador's authoritarian governments quashed any form of rebellion. Attempts at democratic reform were extinguished and government opposition turned to armed resistance. In 1979 the reformist Revolutionary Government Junta took power, angering both the left and the right. Civil war broke out. The army became involved in indiscriminate killings, most notoriously the El Mozote massacre in December 1981, when 800 civilians were brutally murdered.

As the US backed the government and Cuba and other communist states supported the growing insurgency, a proxy war ensued. The Chapultepec Peace Accords marked the end of the war in 1992, and the Farabundo Martí National Liberation Front (FMLN), initially formed from guerilla groups, became one of the major political parties. Many military functions were transferred to civilian control and the size of the armed forces were dramatically reduced; it has since become one of the most respected institutions in the country. Many guerrillas and soldiers who fought in the war received land under the peace accord-mandated land transfer program, which ended in January 1997.

COSTA RICA'S WAR OF NATIONAL LIBERATION

Costa Rica's War of National Liberation began on March 11, 1948. It consisted of a well-planned offensive carried out by men with no formal military background, trained by guerrilla fighters from the Dominican Republic and Honduras, and armed with guns flown in from Guatemala. Forty-four days later, 2,000 men, one in every 300 Costa Ricans, had been killed during the violent, sad war of liberation. José Figueres' forces were victorious, despite the efforts of the former Nicaraguan

Costa Rican government troops, 1948.

⊘ MIGRANT WORKERS

The US is home to millions of immigrants from the Northern Triangle countries of El Salvador, Guatemala, and Honduras, many of whom are undocumented. Upticks of instability throughout the region increase the drive to move north. The surge of Central American migrants hit new heights in 2014 after the US increased its deportation of undocumented gang members back to places like El Salvador and Honduras, where murder rates then soared. El Salvador's homicide rate, for example, increased in 2015 to 104 murders per 100,000 population, the highest rate worldwide. Honduras was not far behind. Fleeing the violence at home, more undocumented people are then driven to seek sanctuary in the US.

Severe drought and food insecurity in these Central American countries only adds to the problem, as does shifting US policy. Past US administrations have allowed for unaccompanied children and families apprehended at the border to be released and remain in the country, in some cases, while they await the outcomes of immigration court hearings. With the 2016 election of Donald Trump as president, that policy seems to be in flux, while tension has been raised again with talks of a border wall with Mexico, which could lead to more desperate means of entering the US. Smuggling networks continue to adapt and are already finding new ways to circumvent Mexico's increased southern border enforcement.

dictator Anastasio Somoza García, and his invasion of the north of Costa Rica. President Teodoro Picado, who had never really believed an armed insurrection would occur, and who had no heart for conflict, saw that a swiftly negotiated peace was essential; he announced his surrender.

Don Pepe Figueres, as both the acknowledged winner of the battle and head of the victorious junta, entered San José five days after the ceasefire and led a triumphant parade. Figueres addressed the people, outlining his goals and fundamental concepts, of what he called his

Manuel Noriega.

Second Republic: the re-establishment of civic ethics, elimination of the spoils system in public administration, social republic progress without Communism, and a greater sense of solidarity with other nations.

One of Figueres' first acts was to place a 10 percent tax on wealth, a law that was resented, badly administered, and in most cases, evaded by the affluent. He expanded the social security system; enacted full voting rights for all women; created a minimum wage; established low-cost national health care services for all; passed legislation on child support; and proposed nationalizing the banks. The firing of large numbers of bureaucrats and schoolteachers, in an attempt to reorganize government agencies, exacerbated

his declining popularity. And then the assets of individuals connected with the Calderón-Picado governments were frozen. Figueres' extreme – and to some, arbitrary – politics alienated many. Even the press became hostile to him.

The constitution of 1949 did reflect many of the goals of the Second Republic. It included political and individual freedoms, and added new social guarantees. It established the principle of public regulation of private property and enterprise, and empowered the state to take actions assuring the widest distribution of wealth possible. But arguably its finest social guarantee was to extend citizenship to everyone born in Costa Rica. This was an important issue for Afro-Caribbean residents, who until that time had been treated as second-class people.

The new constitution also abolished the military. This was perhaps Figueres' most celebrated and memorable achievement, one that he would point to over and over again. In a public ceremony, he delivered the keys of the Bella Vista military fortress to the minister of public education and told him to convert it into a national museum. Don Pepe knew how to exploit the moment: with photographers standing by, he raised a sledgehammer and symbolically smashed at the wall of the fortress. His supporters considered it a final blow to militarism. His enemies regarded the abolition of the military as a clever move: lacking the full backing of the military, he simply decided to get rid of it.

THE US INVASION OF PANAMA

Although Panama collaborated with the Reagan Administration by delivering drugs and arms by airplane to the Contras in Nicaragua, relations between the two countries worsened in the 1980s. The US froze economic and military aid to Panama in the summer of 1987 after an attack on the US embassy. The following year, President Manuel Noriega was indicted in US courts for drug-trafficking and the Panamanian Government had their assets frozen in US banks, withholding fees for using the canal. An election in May 1989 was marred by accusations of fraud, though Noriega's regime promptly annulled the election and refused to leave.

The US began sending thousands of troops to American bases in the canal zone. Tensions quickly flared up. US troops left their bases and started stopping and searching vehicles; then an American Marine was killed by Panamanian police in Panama City. On December 20, 1989, US troops began an invasion of Panama that would last for one week. Hundreds of Panamanians would die during the conflict and Guillermo Endara was sworn in as president at a US military base on the day of the invasion. Afterward, US President George H. W. Bush announced a billion dollars in aid to Panama, though much of it was incentives for US business. Noriega is now serving a 40-year sentence for drug trafficking.

Protesting gun violence on a march in Guatemala.

HURRICANE MITCH

In 1998, the third major hurricane of the season, named Mitch, formed in the western Caribbean Sea on October 22, 1998, and quickly strengthened to peak at Category 5 status. In preparation, Honduras evacuated roughly 45,000 citizens on the Bay Islands. Belize alerted citizens on offshore islands to head for the mainland, while much of Belize City was also evacuated for fears of a repeat of Hurricane Hattie 37 years earlier. In Guatemala, 10,000 were evacuated along the coasts and rivers.

At peak intensity, Mitch sustained winds of 285 km/h and had one of the lowest barometric pressures for any Atlantic hurricane. The hurricane weakened as it reached the shores of Honduras, yet moved so slowly across Guatemala and Nicaragua that it dropped historic amounts of rainfall. Deaths due to catastrophic flooding made it one of the deadliest hurricanes in history after the Great Hurricane of 1780.

Nearly the entire country of Honduras saw significant damage. On the Bay Islands, water facilities were damaged and nearly all the mangroves and trees of every sort on Guanaja were uprooted. The high rainfall caused rivers in the country to overflow and widespread mudslides on the mainland. An estimated 70–80 percent of roads and bridges were destroyed, as were power lines and access to fresh water. The overall impact represented about 70 percent of the country's GDP. In Nicaragua, as much as 630mm (25 inches) of rain fell on coastal areas, 368,300 people were displaced and roughly 2,700km (1,678 miles) of roads were destroyed. The rains left a trail of damage from flooding and mudslides through Belize, Guatemala, El Salvador, Costa Rica, and Panama, as well as elsewhere in the Caribbean region. In the aftermath, nearly 11,000 people were killed, more than 11,000 were missing, and 2.7 million were left homeless. The region, already recovering from civil wars, was left with more than $6 billion in damages.

THE CURRENT SITUATION

Dictatorships and bloodshed have plagued the region since the birth of the independent states, but peace and stability finally seem to be taking hold. Still, natural disasters, corruption, security, and uneven economic development occasionally give way to general instability, which could become worse with the unpredictability of the Trump administration's hawkish immigration policy and potential border wall. Rising crime rates and the influence of criminal cartels are two of the most pressing issues facing countries like Guatemala, Honduras, El Salvador, and Mexico. Mafia-style networks, many with ties to the military and corruption-riddled police forces, have established the region as key in the drug trade. Gang membership in urban areas also threatens social stability, as has the return of deported gang members that were previously living illegally in the US. Still, security and development throughout the region is far better than it once was, with steady growth economically.

GUATEMALA'S NOBEL PEACE PRIZE WINNER

Rigoberta Menchú, an activist for the rights of the world's indigenous peoples, is a controversial figure in Guatemala today.

Globally, the best-known Guatemalan is not the president, a pop star, or even a sporting figure, but the K'iche' Maya peasant turned human rights activist Rigoberta Menchú, who won the 1992 Nobel Peace Prize for her work on behalf of Guatemala's and the world's indigenous peoples. Menchú is a controversial figure in Guatemala, feted by the political left, but also provoking vitriolic polemic from her ideological opponents, who consider her a subversive ex-guerrilla.

Rigoberta Menchú was born in 1959 in Quiché. In the first volume of her autobiography, *I, Rigoberta Menchú*, published in 1983, she describes how the horrific brutality of the Guatemalan civil war affected her family, how her mother, father and brothers were branded guerrilla-sympathizers and killed by the military in their fight to protect the family's farmland. In powerful, unambiguous language, Menchú castigates the inequalities of that ruptured Guatemalan society: the cultural chasm between *ladino* and Maya, the gross disparity of wealth, health education, and opportunity between the country's rich and poor. She also details that she had no formal schooling, how her family had to work in the plantations of the Pacific coast to survive, and her flight to exile in Mexico in 1980.

I, Rigoberta Menchú sold strongly all over the world, catapulting the author into the international limelight. Menchú became a familiar face at the United Nations in Geneva, tirelessly campaigning for the rights of the Guatemalan Maya and forging connections with other oppressed minorities. This period of her life is recounted in *Crossing Borders* (1998), the second volume of her autobiography. It tackles the controversy over her Nobel Peace Prize award, which split the country along familiar lines as ecstatic supporters celebrated in San Marcos, while the president failed to turn up to a rally in the capital, citing an earache.

A CONTROVERSIAL FIGURE

The Nobel laureate returned to Guatemala in 1994 as an iconic if contentious figure, but internationally she remained beyond reproach until the publication of David Stoll's biography *Rigoberta Menchú and the Story of All Poor Guatemalans*, in 1998. Stoll's book shook this enshrined reputation, contending that important parts of *I, Rigoberta Menchú* were false: that Menchú had been educated at a convent school and that her family's land dispute was an internecine family quarrel rather than a racially charged indigenous–*ladino* clash. He also alleged a guerrilla past.

Menchú has since admitted that she received some education at the convent, but remained silent about other allegations. Despite doubts over certain details

Rigoberta Menchu.

of Menchú's story, her reputation remains largely intact and the Nobel Committee dismissed calls to revoke her prize. It is not in dispute that her mother, father, and brothers died at the hands of the military.

Menchú's success bringing global attention to the suffering of the Guatemalan Maya is unquestionable. Her work on behalf of the world's indigenous peoples for the UN has been tireless, and she continues to campaign in Guatemala for political and social justice and on healthcare issues. She has also fought to prosecute armed forces leaders for civil war atrocities. Menchú formally entered politics in 2005, serving as a goodwill ambassador for the peace accords, and went on to contest the 2007 and 2011 presidencies, but only polled 3 percent of the vote in both elections.

A mother and daughter cook traditional Guatemalan food at their outdoor food stall in Quetzaltenango.

Traditionally dressed Mayan man from Panajachel, Guatemala.

PEOPLE

The people of Central America are as diverse as the natural landscape in which they live, but collectively they share a distinct Latin American heritage.

Latino (*ladino* or *mestizo*) culture dominates Central America and competes with the US for cultural hegemony. The influence of the rest of the Latin world is very evident throughout the isthmus, especially in its music. You will be lambasted with rhythms from all over the Americas in the buses, bars, and clubs: merengue tunes from the Dominican Republic; salsa from Colombia; reggaetón from Puerto Rico; and Hispanic hip-hop from California add lyrical joy, sorrow, and social comment to everyday life.

A *ladino* is, strictly speaking, someone who is identifiably 'Western' in outlook, someone who speaks Spanish, who sees themselves as Latin American rather than Native American. There are also *ladinos* who are pure-blood Maya or from other indigenous groups but no longer speak a Mayan language or dress in indigenous style. Many have more Maya than Spanish blood in their veins, though there are a few *ladinos* who are of pure European ancestry.

The region's elite is largely of white, European origin and concentrated within a select group of families. Sometimes called *criollos*, this oligarchy retains ties with Spain, but also increasingly with Miami and the US's Latino diaspora.

OF AFRICAN DESCENT

The Garífuna, a people with an extremely rich history that they trace back to Africa, arrived to the region on two shipwrecked slave boats, via the Caribbean islands of St Vincent and Roatán. The Garífuna are sometimes called Black Caribs – ethnically quite accurate as the Garífuna are also descendants of Africans and the indigenous Caribs – though the people themselves now prefer the name Garífuna. There are some 22,000 Belizean Garífuna, mainly around Dangriga and

Local man in Tortuguero, Costa Rica.

in the southern Toledo district, though many more live in Honduras (and the United States). There are also Garífuna villages in Nicaragua and Guatemala.

Some Garífuna, well liked by the Amerindians, intermarried and, over the years, developed an identity and language of their own, called Miskito. British pirates joined forces with the Miskitos, and together they wreaked havoc along the Atlantic coast of Costa Rica and in the cacao plantations. For the Miskitos, the undefended plantations offered little resistance. They sailed in for their biannual raids, took the cacao, captured the black slaves, and set off again. Traces of Miskito influence remain in the Atlantic coast area, where many of the place names come from their language, including Talamanca (Talamalka), Sixaola, and Cahuita.

There are many other groups of Central Americans of African descent, especially along the Caribbean coast. In Belize, English-speaking Creoles (black and mixed black-white) form around a third of the country's tiny 330,000-strong population, living mainly in Belize City and the towns. Culturally, most Creoles feel much closer to Jamaica and the islands of the British West Indies than the rest of Latin America, and listen to reggae, soca, punta, and

oppressive management. Some were ultimately given land along the railroad right of way, and others, thanks to their command of English, rose from the ranks of laborers to become managers in the banana business and on the railroads. Most originally planned to earn whatever they could and then return to their islands. The maltreatment of workers in the banana fields of the Caribbean United Fruit Company is well documented. However, these Afro-Caribbeans were certainly not invulnerable and they, too, died in their thousands while working in the region.

Slum-dweller in Bonacca Cays, Honduras.

other Caribbean rhythms. The African-American influence has also grown noticeably: musically, hip-hop and R&B are becoming much more prevalent, and on the sports fields, basketball is now more widely played than cricket.

From Honduras to Panamá, many Afro-Caribbean islanders found work in the region in the 19th and 20th centuries. In Panama they came to help build the canal, while in Guatemala, Honduras, Nicaragua, and Costa Rica they found employment on banana and sugar-cane plantations. Others harvested cacao or worked on barges and railroads, proving willing to tolerate hazardous working conditions, which included exposure to yellow fever, malaria, and venomous snakes, as well as severe physical labor and

THE MAYA

There are around 9 million Maya spread across Guatemala, Mexico, Belize, El Salvador, and Honduras today – about half of the region's total population. These are the survivors of the region's great civilization: the descendants of the temple builders, astronomers, mathematicians, architects, artists, artisans, farmers, and soldiers.

They are a far from homogeneous race – speaking some 30 different languages, they worship at Catholic, Protestant, and Evangelical churches. Yet many still also continue to honor Maya religious practices forged over thousands of years, and blend pagan and Western faiths: prayer keepers use the Tzolkin 260-day calendar while celebrating Christianity's holy days. After centuries of cultural attack, ridicule, and humiliation at the hands of the state, this unique fusion of Western and indigenous faiths prevails in most indigenous communities and permeates many more mixed-race minds.

Most of Mexico's 2 million or so Maya live in the southeastern state of Chiapas and in the Yucatán Peninsula. The Chiapaneco and Yucateco Maya form two distinct communities, each with their own languages and traditions. The vast majority of Chiapas Maya are highlanders, with

strongest and continue to defy mainstream Latin American and North American cultural influence. The K'iche' Maya are the most numerous (more than 1 million), the descendants of the warrior Tecún Umán, who was defeated in 1535 by Pedro de Alvarado the conquistador, close to the modern-day town of Quezaltenango. The K'iche' have adapted relatively well to life in modern Guatemala and have a reputation as skillful entrepreneurs and traders. Rigoberta Menchú, the 1992 Nobel Peace Prize winner, is from a K'iche' family (see page 63).

Indigenous Mayan women in Chiapas, Mexico.

customs that are very similar to those in Guatemala just over the border (indeed, the state was part of Guatemala until the early 19th century). Their rugged, mountainous homeland, with peaks reaching over 3,200 meters (10,500ft), has always been isolated from the rest of Mexico, allowing traditions to survive, particularly around the town of San Cristóbal de las Casas. This is also the poorest corner of Mexico, with the highest illiteracy, birth, and child mortality rates in the region.

In Guatemala, the Maya mainly live in the western highlands, between the Mexican border and the capital. In these highlands they form some 80 percent of the population, and it is here that Maya customs and traditions remain

⊘ END OF A CIVILIZATION

There's still no definitive explanation for the breakdown of the Classic Maya civilization, roughly between AD 800 and 900. It now seems that it was not caused by cataclysmic natural forces. The latest evidence now suggests that a prolonged drought caused harvest failures, almost certainly due to man-made environmental over-exploitation. In turn, widespread hunger may have brought about a class-based uprising against the ruling elite. Some academics even hypothesize that the failure of calendar-based prophesies could have triggered revolt. Whatever the reasons, all the cities in the heartland of the Maya world were all but deserted by AD 909.

OTHER INDIGENOUS PEOPLE

While the Maya are the predominant indigenous group in the region, they are by no means the only indigenous group. Like the Maya, however, they have suffered much the same fate. The Europeans brought diseases to which the native populations had no immunity and entire tribes were obliterated. Many lived in patrimonial groups, grew corn, and were culturally similar to groups from southern Mexico. These peoples were devastated during the Spanish Conquest by disease and by slave traders who shipped

today, mostly living in dispersed mountain villages, despite historically being based along the coasts. In Costa Rica, clans such as the Terraba, Boruca, and – in the Talamanca mountains – the Bribri and Cabecar fled to the almost inaccessible jungle regions of the southern mountains on the arrival of Europeans. Much of their culture has been preserved by their descendants, who still speak their original languages and live in the remote regions of the Talamanca Mountains. Despite the influence of Christian missionaries, many native people have not forsaken their ani-

San Pedro locals, Belize.

them off to Panama and Peru. Their surviving descendants are today mostly integrated into contemporary Central American life.

In southwestern Honduras and eastern El Salvador, the Lenca are believed to have migrated to the region from South America some 3,000 years ago. In Honduras, they number around 100,000, while El Salvador's Lenca population is about half of that. The Guaymí, now called the Ngäbe (pronounced 'Nobe'), reside on both sides of the Panama–Costa Rica border. Most live within the Ngäbe-Buglé comarca in the Western Panamanian provinces of Veraguas, Chiriquí, and Bocas del Toro, as well as five territories in southwest Costa Rica. There are approximately 200,000–250,000 speakers of Ngäbere

mistic religious traditions. The Bribri call their deity Sibu and trust in shamans, with their vast knowledge of the rainforest's medicinal herbs, to cure a range of illnesses.

On the Caribbean coast of Panama, the Chibchan-speaking Kuna, also known as the Guna or Cuna, live in three autonomous comarcas, as well as several small villages in Colombia. Most of the population lives on a group of small islands off the coast, known as Kuna Yala, or the San Blas Islands, as well as in communities in Panama City and Colón.

In the late 1700s, the Emberá began migrating from the Choco region of Colombia to the Darién province of Panama, pushing the Kuna farther toward the coast. There are an estimated

PEOPLE | 71

In Costa Rica, the most dramatic influx of people today is the result of the flourishing tourism industry. People of all ages come to carry out ecological work, stimulating major changes in the environmental awareness of the country.

33,000 Emberá people living in Panama, most in the Darién, as well as Lake Gatún and throughout the Canal Zone.

IMMIGRANT GROUPS

Throughout the region, some immigrant communities may seem completely out of place on the beaches and rainforests of Central America. For example, Chinese immigrants arrived in large numbers to work on the railroads in the 19th century. As their fortunes improved, Chinese immigrants set up small eateries, groceries, and liquor stores. The steady trickle of Chinese immigrant laborers that followed the first railroad workers benefitted from those who were already established. Through work contracts and credit assistance from other Chinese, they set up commercial ventures along the railroad, in the port cities, and in growing rural communities throughout the country. Their small-scale businesses required little capital investment, only a minimal acquaintance with the language, and allowed all members of the growing family network to become involved in tending the business. Chinese family traditions upheld the authority of elders and reinforced an already strong generational hierarchy. Well-defined divisions of labor, plus a strong work ethic, ensured that their businesses flourished.

In an attempt to find an alternative working force, railroad managers imported thousands of Italians, though the disagreeable working conditions soon led them to leave the rail projects. Many remained throughout the region and settled in government-sponsored colonies, like San Vito, in the southern Pacific region of Costa Rica.

THE GRINGO

They are unmistakable in places like San José and Panama City, their heads sticking out above the throng of people crowding the chaotic city sidewalks. *Gringos*, fairer and usually taller than local people, easily catch the eye. A pejorative word in much of Latin America, *gringo* is a much milder term here, applied not only to US citizens but also to Canadians and Europeans. Early in the 19th century, attracted by the promise of wealth from coffee, French, German, and British entrepreneurs, along with teachers, scientists, and professionals, emigrated to Central America. Many married local women and most became thoroughly assimilated. Today, many powerful families in the arts and politics bear British or German surnames.

Farmer with ox-cart, Central Valley, Costa Rica.

Since the 1960s, laws favoring North American and European retirees have led to the establishment of a large number of comparatively wealthy *gringos* throughout the region, particularly in Costa Rica's Central Valley, the Chiriquí highlands, the Pacific coast of Panama, and coastal areas of Belize and Honduras. These retirees come for the warm climate and for the higher standard of living their dollars afford them. With the growing disparity in the country between haves and have-nots, foreigners are sometimes viewed less favorably these days, especially those who come to Costa Rica in order to make a quick buck in what are sometimes shady or environmentally insensitive property developments.

RACIAL HIERARCHY

In many places in Central America the melting pot has been so thoroughly blended that locals are unexpectedly homogeneous. Wealth tends to be concentrated in the hands of the lighter skin, more European-looking residents, alongside those of newcomers from North America and Europe that are quickly establishing themselves among the elite.

In many Central American countries, skin color and racial origins have a distinct bearing on status. The fairest people are frequently

Mennonite children playing, Spanish Lookout, Belize.

> *Belize is home to the Mennonite community (see page 185), a religious sect who are descended from members of the Anabaptist Movement in Europe. Conservative Mennonites farm the land and life a lifestyle akin to the Amish in the US.*

concentrated in the professional establishments or in front of television cameras. One can often detect a striking color difference between the faces that appear on the television screen and those watching it, with the few dark or black on-screen faces relegated to servile roles. But this situation is now changing, and has even been spoofed in more recent television dramas and comedies.

Many indigenous people, while clinging to their customs and traditions in the face of overwhelming odds, have historically been marginalized by other segments of society. The conquistadors and the church pushed indigenous cultures to convert to Catholicism and give up their traditional dress and customs, resulting in a hybrid system of beliefs and practises in many communities. While in past decades the ways of indigenous groups have been looked down upon, recent years have seen an appreciation of their culture by wider Central American society, such as Panamanian chefs working with the Ngäbe to develop their native ingredients, or the art community recognizing the value in Lenca pottery and Emberá tribal masks.

GROWING PAINS

Much of Central America continues to be some of the most unequal part of the world. The lingering effects of civil wars and corruption have caused an uneven development of society. While the middle and upper classes, which tend to be concentrated in a few neighborhoods in the largest urban areas, have access to the same education and consumer goods as their Western counterparts, many others have been left behind. Modernization begs the question of what kind of society and political model these countries should aspire to.

More often than not, aspirations have transformed into aggressive consumerism. Consumer debt is on the rise even as wages remain low amid poor productivity. Social cohesion and respect for the environment remain rare as many of the wealthy lock themselves into gated communities and new immigrants from the countryside fight for turf in the poor barrios barely reached by government services.

Other challenges include widespread corruption and the spread of violent crime. As the international prohibition of drugs continues, maintaining the value of black market smuggling as a lucrative practice, drug cartels have increased their presence in the countries south of Mexico and the resulting violence is an ongoing problem to which these societies have yet to find a solution.

WOMEN IN CENTRAL AMERICA

Despite significant gains, women throughout Central America are still held back by unequal pay, violence, and antiquated attitudes.

In recent years, Central American women have been playing an ever more prominent role in political and professional life. In 1990, Nicaragua elected its first woman president, Violeta Chamorro, who would hold office until 1997. She was followed by Panama's first female president, Mireya Moscoso, in 2009, and Laura Chinchilla in Costa Rica a year later. As doctors, lawyers, and in civil society pressure groups, women are to the fore. Young women are often the best and most enthusiastic students in many academic disciplines, while Latin America and the Caribbean has seen the largest gains in female labor force participation in the world during the last two decades, with women becoming increasingly active in paid work, closing the gap with men, and catching up to their counterparts in more advanced economies.

Yet in this mainly Catholic region, there is still a general assumption that a woman's purpose should above all be to be a good wife and mother, and they are often expected to combine motherhood with a full day's work, although they are rarely paid as much as their menfolk. On the streets, catcalling and overt harassment of women is common. The word machismo was, after all, coined to describe the Latin male. Women's rights are not always guaranteed and there is ongoing criminalization of abortion in all Central American countries, with El Salvador and Nicaragua not permitting it under any circumstances; the former has perhaps the most draconian laws in the world, which can criminalize mothers for miscarriages or complex premature births under charges for 'aggravated murder.'

EARNING POWER

Poor working conditions and low wages can prevent many women and their families from climbing up from the lowest rungs of the economic ladder. Social protection programs in the region concentrate on social assistance and less on promoting life skills and job training, which limits a woman's ability to attain the necessary tools and qualifications to enter the labor force on more favorable terms. While many Central American countries have enacted laws to protect and encourage gender equality, other challenges such as endemic violence and the outbreaks of infec-

Women going to church in Campeche, Mexico.

tious diseases often take priority over gender issues. Still, across Central America, women are increasingly playing a crucial role in maintaining social stability and meeting the basic needs of their families.

THE CHALLENGE OF VIOLENCE

Soberingly, rates of violence toward women are especially high in the countries with substantial gang problems. El Salvador has the highest female homicide rate in the world, while Guatemala is rated third and Honduras seventh on this grim list. With many women fleeing violence in these countries, the issue is rapidly becoming a major refugee crisis. More than eight out of 10 women from the region who reach the US come from areas controlled by criminal armed groups, called *maras*, or drug cartels, where rapes, kidnappings, and various threats have become common. The increasing reach of such groups has surpassed the capacity of governments in the region to respond.

Procession during Semana Santa (Holy Week), Antigua, Guatemala.

RELIGION

From indigenous beliefs and the Spanish push for Catholicism to the recent rise of Evangelicals, religion has helped shape Central America.

'The first aim of your expedition is to serve God and spread the Christian faith,' were the orders that the Spanish crown gave to conquistador Hernán Cortés on his expedition into Mexico to conquer the Aztecs. As Latin America came under Spanish control, wave after wave of Franciscan, Dominican, Augustinian, and Jesuit missionaries soon followed. Some reports claim that the Franciscans alone baptized as many as five million people in the first years of European settlement in the New World.

CONVERSION BY THE CONQUISTADORS

During the Age of Discovery, Spanish governors encouraged the spread of Catholicism among the native populations, which was supported by the Vatican and allowed them to control the region with only a small military. Missions and other colonies were established, and spreading Christianity to the newly discovered continent became a top priority, although just one piece of the wider Spanish colonization system.

Throughout the region, massive stone churches were built, as grand as any in Europe, and they anchored the towns and villages where the converts lived. Schools, trades, civil government, and hospitals were established there too. The church became the center of life in every village and city. Priests controlled books and education. Life revolved around the church bells, letting villagers know when it was time to wake up or eat. The indigenous people were legally defined as children in some cases, leading the clergy to take on an almost paternalistic role, sometimes enforced with corporal punishment.

While there was fierce resistance among local populations, priests began fusing elements of

Salvadoran woman at Mass.

native beliefs into Catholicism. 'Folk Catholicism,' as it is sometimes called, incorporated elements of local spirituality, legend, and shamanism into orthodox Catholic dogma, resulting in a fusion of indigenous and Catholic beliefs that could resonate in local communities. In Guatemala, the Maya population adapted Catholicism to their traditional cosmovision, while in other places indigenous gods were simply swapped with Catholic saints and virgins. Costa Rica, the most European of the Central American nations, created the Virgin de los Angeles or La Negrita – a small, black, stone image – which became Costa Rica's patron saint in 1824. Early attempts were made to prepare indigenous clergy, but many in the church were suspicious, seeing them as not entirely dependable. Some monastic orders specifically forbade the ordination of non-Spanish priests.

THE INFLUENCE OF CATHOLICISM

The influence of Catholicism allowed Spain's other objectives to be reached, such as the extension of Spanish language, culture, and political control in the New World. However, this proved to be a double-edged sword. Central America became so fervently Catholic that when Spain tried to assert control of the church, the clergy became politically active and helped

Shrine of El Maximon in Santiago de Atitlan, Guatemala.

initiate calls for independence. In the 1960s, growing social awareness and politicization of the Church gave birth to liberation theology that openly supported anti-imperialist movements.

Still, in the near-five centuries after the Conquest, the Church hierarchy made little effort to reach out to the indigenous groups in Central America – there were few attempts to translate the Bible into the indigenous languages, and the liturgy was remote and often inexplicable to the local population. During the turbulent years from the 1950s onward, the Catholic Church hierarchy largely sided with the armed forces and with repression, and consequently was viewed with increasing suspicion as violence in many Central American countries increased.

In spite of this growing tension in places like Guatemala, many rural Catholic priests had made efforts to win over Maya communities, supporting development projects and campesinos' unions. Unfortunately these activities provoked the suspicions of the military authorities, who labeled the priests as communists and troublemakers. Paramilitary death squads hunted down and brutally murdered many of these campaigning Catholic priests, to such an extent that by the early 1980s the Catholic Church had withdrawn altogether from some of

> *In Panama City, one of the world's eight Baha'i Houses of Worship can be found. This monotheistic religion, which emphasizes the spiritual unity of all humankind, was founded in Persia in the 19th century and arrived in Panama in the 1940s. It currently has about 60,000 members in the country, including around 10 percent of all Ngäbe people.*

the guerrilla-based areas of the highlands, by way of protest and for its own self-preservation. The vacuum thus created by the Catholic Church left many highland Maya wary and fearful of being associated with the guerrilla movement.

EVANGELISTS

Evangelical missionaries from the United States adopted a very different approach in Central America to their Catholic counterparts. They lived in the indigenous communities, and from the start learned and translated the Bible into the local tongues. They also taught converts a way of life that was strict but appealing, forbidding alcohol and openly condemning social behavior they saw as sinful, whereas the Catholic Church had remained aloof on these matters. Significantly, some Evangelists openly voiced their support for the army over the guerrillas, a policy which gained acceptance from those keen to survive further military oppression.

They also attracted many converts because of their promise that by leading a 'proper' Christian life, the faithful would advance in their lives on this earth as well as in the next world. This Evangelical message was extremely seductive for many indigenous peoples who felt they had been excluded from all levels of society. As a result, by the start of World War II, Central American Evangelical churches had become a powerful force around the region, something that was accelerated by mass migrations to cities; their influence continues to grow today.

OTHER CHRISTIAN SECTS

While the region remains overwhelmingly Catholic – Latin America has more than 425 million faithful, accounting for about 40 percent of the world's total Catholic population – the movement and toward Protestantism has gained significant momentum in the span of a single lifetime. The numbers are quickly changing. In 1938 Protestants totaled about 600,000 in Latin America, but a decade later there were close to 3 million. Over the last two decades the numbers have exploded and there are now an estimated 40 million Protestants in the region. In Guatemala, for example, Evangelists currently make up around 53 percent of the population, and in El Salvador, it's 45 percent. Dozens of sects of Christianity have made in-roads in the region, including Seventh-day Adventists, Jehovah's Witnesses, and Episcopalians, although they still only make up small segments of the population.

In Belize, La Mosquitia, and the Bay Islands – places settled by or aligned with the British – the Anglican Church once battled with the Roman Catholic church for converts, but today there are just an estimated 35,000 members in the entire region. Additionally, there are small communities of Mennonites in Belize, whose fascinating culture originated in the Netherlands in the 16th century (see page 185) For the past 50 years they have made a tremendous contribution to the agricultural sector. In the 1950s, Quakers from the US came to Costa Rica looking for peace. They found it in the cloud forest of Monteverde, where they formed a community dedicated to a life of harmony with the land. They have created a successful dairy and cheese industry, which today supplies much of Costa Rica's specialty cheese market.

ANIMISTIC TRADITIONS

Despite the influence of Christianity, many of the more remote indigenous groups still cling to their animistic religious traditions. The Bribri in Costa Rica, for example, call their deity Sibu

and put their trust in shamans, with their vast knowledge of the rainforest's medicinal herbs, to cure a range of illnesses. The Garífuna believe that the departed ancestors mediate between the individual the external world, though their religion combines elements of Catholicism as well. In Panama, the Kuna religion is called the 'Father's Way,' and has a creation myth that references *Pab Dummat* (Big Father) and *Nan Dummat* (Big Mother). They hold regular church-like services where *caciques* (chiefs) chant religious and historical songs full of symbolism.

Wood statues used by Kuna shaman in Panama.

⊘ BORN AGAIN

The strength of Evangelical churches was reinforced when General Efraín Ríos Montt came to power in Guatemala. Montt, who had become a born-again Christian in the 1970s, was the first Protestant president of Guatemala. Although condemned for the vicious counter-insurgency war that he fought in the countryside, his uncompromising message of bringing law and order to a godless society won him a substantial following. This support continued in the 1990s as his Republican Front of Guatemala (FRG) won the 1999 elections. However, the disastrous term of office that followed ended the Montt myth. In 2012 he was charged with genocide and crimes against humanity.

Water carriers, Chichicastenango, Guatemala.

ARTS, MUSIC, AND DANCE

Whether its reggaetón or calypso, salsa or cumbia, Modernismo or Vanguardia, the vivid culture of Central America is a part of everyday life.

As in the rest of Latin America, art, literature, and music are fundamental parts of everyday life. Popular Latin music dominates the airwaves here, not to mention the inside of buses and taxis. Few Central Americans are shy about blasting reggaetón or cumbia into the street at decibel levels that humans in other parts of the world deem offensive. In each country, mainstream forms of salsa, mariachi, reggae, and calypso take on a new life. And in the other cultural forms, while few of the art and stories from the days before European arrival remain, post-conquest artistic expression has proved integral to making sense of the often-tumultuous political system.

All around the region, distinct forms of art have been created by and adapted to Central America's diverse cultures and landscapes. In Panama, salsa and reggae have taken on new life, while on the rural coasts of Belize and Honduras, traditional Garífuna music has been modernized and exported to a mainstream audience. In Guatemala, the Maya have their own Bible and the literary movement of Modernismo found its origins. In the world of visual arts, the landscape – displayed in all its glory – has made its way to the fore, idealizing a simple life amidst the stunning natural surroundings of the countryside, even as civil wars and corruption raged in the cities.

EARLY WRITINGS

As Pre-Columbian cultures were primarily oral, few of their stories have survived post conquest. While the Aztecs and Mayans produced elaborate codices, most mythological and religious beliefs were recorded by Europeans, such as with the historical narratives of the Post Classic K'iche' kingdom, known as *Popol Vuh*, sometimes called the Mayan Bible. Considered one of the most

Garifuna Punta rock drummers in Dangriga, Belize.

significant works of Guatemalan literature, *Popol Vuh* is a collection of Mayan stories and legends, aimed at preserving Mayan traditions. The first known text dates to the 16th century, though it wasn't translated into Spanish until the beginning of the 18th century by the Dominican priest, Francisco Ximénez. There's no other work as integral to the understanding of the culture of Pre-Columbian America as the *Popol Vuh*.

During the colonial period, Central American countries were centers of European culture and literary activity flourished. There were poetic contests, theater, public recitations, and literary gatherings like those that would be found in European villages and cities. This era saw the first Central American authors writing in Spanish. Important writers included the region's first playwright, Sor Juana de Maldonado, and the Guatemalan poet and Jesuit, Rafael Landívar. In Nicaragua, the satirical drama *El Güegüense*, written by an anonymous author, is a folkloric masterpiece combining music, dance, and theater.

MODERN LITERATURE

In the late 19th century, a poetic movement called Modernismo materialized. It blended three European forms: Romanticism, Symbolism, and Parnassianism. Félix Rubén García

Miguel Angel Asturias Rosales.

Sarmiento, better known as Rubén Darío, was a Nicaraguan poet born in 1862. He's considered the father of the Spanish-American literary movement of Modernism, and his works had a great influence in the Spanish literature of the 20th century.

In the 20th century, Central American literature was strongly influenced by the political situations in each country, and many works were written by authors and poets who were in exile from their respective countries. In the late 1920s, the Vanguardia literary movement emerged in Granada, Nicaragua, led by the poet José Coronel Urtecho. Modeled after European movements like Surrealism, Vanguardia's aim was to attract the public's

attention through artistic expression, scandal, and aggressive criticism via confrontational themes. One of the most important writers in this period was the Guatemalan novelist Miguel Ángel Asturias, author of *El Señor Presidente* and *Hombres de Maíz*. He won the Nobel Prize for Literature in 1967.

DANCE

To understand the evolution of musical and dance forms on the subcontinent is to attempt to fathom the tremendous demographic upheaval

> *Despite his given name, Felix Ruben Garcia Sarmiento, Darío started using his pen name at the age of 14. The name was adopted from a great grandfather.*

that took place over 500 years. The richness and diversity of Latin music reflects the many colonizing and colonized forces present over the centuries. Along with native elements, Africa, Europe and the United States all had a hand in the shaping of this magical music. Music grew from a brutal and loveless relationship, out of enslaved indigenous people and Africans, European settlers, and colonial power brokers. Often oceans away from their homelands, these early inhabitants all had their music and dances. These were a way of remembering home and identity in an uncertain landscape. Thrown together in an ethnic melting pot, many traditions were either discarded or bonded together. Out of this struggle was born regional and national musical traditions that represent different colonial experiences and development.

SONGS OF STRUGGLE

Used by dictatorial powers as a propaganda tool, traditional music has, nevertheless, also been a useful source of social revolution and protest. The *Nueva Canción* (New Song) movement that emerged in Chile in the 1960s and 1970s put music at the forefront of the struggle all over Latin America. *Nueva Canción* was designed to voice the struggle and suffering of those with no lyrical accompaniment – but this has changed recently. The music is now accompanied by ballads sung most often in indigenous languages or in Spanish. These plaintive yet raucous songs record the daily lives, romances, and ribald interludes of rural indigenous communities. In Nicaragua, *Nueva Canción* musicians were credited with transmitting social and political messages, which helped aid the populace during the Sandinista revolution.

A SPICY MIX

Arguably the most international of all Latin American rhythms is what we now call salsa.

really a jazzed-up version of *son*, whose origins date back to eastern Cuba in the 1880s.

Son intermingled African rhythms with Spanish verse forms, and its early means of expression were drums, maracas, Cuban *tres* guitar, and claves or sticks tapping out the beat. The beat is syncopated and loaded with polyrhythms of regular pulses provided by the clave (two sticks that beat at a 2–3 or 3–2 tempo), the *campana* (cowbell), and accents that are offbeat (piano, bass, and brass). This is all useful to know if you want to blame

A dance troupe in the Joy of Life carnival, Managua, Nicaragua.

The term itself is really nothing more than a marketing ploy adopted by the US music industry in the late 1960s, which assumed that people could not cope with the many different types of music Latin America had to offer. *Son*, *mambo*, *guaracha*, and many other styles were lumped together so that they could be easily packaged for consumption. Salsa means 'sauce' and the name was inspired by many musicians who would scream 'Salsa!' at a pulsating audience to excite them even further. This artificial grouping of many different styles means that most discussions about the origin of salsa become as hot and spicy as the dancing the music inspires. Most unbiased opinion, however, takes the view that today's salsa is

⊙ THE MARIMBA

Developed by African slaves in Central America, the marimba has become the most important folk instrument in the region since being introduced in the 16th or 17th century. The instrument was descended from an ancestral balafon, which consisted of a set of wooden bars, arranged like keys on a piano, struck with mallets. The marimba is like a xylophone, but with a more resonant and lower-pitched tessitura. During the 18th and 19th centuries the instrument became more prevalent and its sound is now widespread in musical genres throughout the region, from woodwind and brass ensembles to marching bands and contemporary orchestras.

your partner for messing up when he or she is clearly the better dancer. If salsa means sauce, then the musical ingredients in these complex arrangements need a master chef to work with them. As music is food for the soul

> In Panama, salsa musician Rubén Blades has achieved international stardom and is a national icon.

Casco Viejo. Minor jazz scenes can be found in large metropolitan areas throughout the region, such as San José and Guatemala City.

AFRO-CARIBBEAN MUSIC

Along Central America's Caribbean coast the music is influenced by Jamaica and other West Indian islands that have had a long history of migration. Originating in Trinidad and Tobago in the early to mid-20th century, calypso found its way to Costa Rica and Panama, particularly the stretch of coast from Puerto Limón to Bocas del

A jazz drummer applique design by a Kuna Indian artist, Panama.

to Latin Americans, culinary references in the lyrics are compulsory.

LATIN JAZZ

Central America has a strong jazz legacy, particularly Panama. The country has a long history in the musical genre. In the 1940s, the port city of Colón boasted at least ten local jazz orchestras, with local legends that included pianist and composer Victor Boa, bassist Clarence Martin, singer Barbara Wilson, and French horn player John 'Rubberlegs' McKindo. This jazz legacy was recently reinvigorated when the US-based Panamanian pianist Danilo Perez organized the first jazz Festival in January 2004, then opened a jazz club in 2015 inside the American Trade Hotel in

Toro. In Cahuita, Panama-born musician Walter Ferguson had some minor success in the 1970s and 1980s, but his fame was resurrected in 2002 with the release of the album *Dr. Bombodee*, from Costa Rican label Papaya Music.

Reggae en Español, or Spanish reggae, originated in Panama, and is similar to Jamaican dancehall music. Some songs are simply Jamaican songs translated into Spanish, something often criticized as plagiarism, though many original reggae artists can be found from Belize to Bocas del Toro. Spanish reggae is a predecessor in the region to reggaetón, a mix of hip hop, bachata, salsa, and electronic music born in Puerto Rico in the 1990s. Central American reggaetón artists have found considerable success on the larger Latin American scene, such as Panamanian rapper Lorna's 2003 hit *Papi Chulo (Te Traigo el Mmm)*.

Punta, a style developed by the Garífuna, is a contemporary adaptation of traditional Garífuna songs and dance. In its original form, punta consisted of a man and woman competing against each other by shaking their hips and moving their feet to the beat of a drum, though the sexual undertones have now been toned down somewhat. Modern punta mixes Garífuna rhythms with a little bit of reggae, R&B, and rock.

> *The Congo dance, passed on from generation to generation, tells a story of characters in a fight with the devil, who is loose during Carnival.*

In Colón and Portobleo on Panama's Caribbean coast, Congo is a form of music and dance with colorful costumes that originated with escaped slaves that lived in the rainforest, known as Cimarrones. Performed mostly during festival times, Congo is distinguished by the use of upright drums and wild, lascivious movements and lyrics. The primary performances take place on the Tuesday and Wednesday before Lent, allowing practitioners to celebrate and share their oral history and traditions.

VISUAL ARTS

In Central America, the visual arts have mostly been a response to indigenous traditions and Western European movements. The rich history of art in the Maya region predates the arrival of Europeans, with murals and carved stone stelae by the Mayans. During the colonial period, the church not only exerted enormous power over the lives of the European and indigenous peoples, but also the nature of the visual arts. Indigenous traditions merged with the Christian teachings of Franciscan, Augustinian and Dominican teachings, resulting in unique mestizo works from mostly anonymous artists.

In the late 1920s in Escazú southwest of San José, a group of artists developed the 'Landscape' movement in Costa Rica. Calling themselves the Group of New Sensibility, they portrayed rural Costa Rica in bright vibrant colors. Throughout the 20th century, however, rather than portray natural settings, most art produced in the region has embodied critiques of social, political, and economic conditions, often in the hopes of bringing international awareness to the poor conditions in which many live. For example, the Indigenismo movement advocated for a dominant social and political role for indigenous peoples in countries where they constitute a majority, such as Mexico and Guatemala. This often romanticized view of native culture can be a in the murals and paint-

Alfredo Galvez Suarez's Mayan mural, Guatemala.

ings of Alfredo Gálvez Suárez (1899–1946) and Carlos Mérida (1891–1984).

Originating in the 1970s on the islands of Solentiname in Lake Nicaragua, the Primitivista painting movement was influenced by the Haitian painting renaissance of the late 1940's and 50's, and idealized scenes of everyday life in natural environments in bright colors and intricate detail. The idea embodied hope and possibility, something at odds with the Somoza regime, which eventually bombed the artist community on the islands and forced the remaining artists into hiding. After the Sandinista revolution, the painting workshops reemerged; subsequently, many members of the group have won national prizes and exhibited in North America, Europe, and Japan.

📷 CRAFTS

Despite the efforts of the conquistadors, the Maya and other indigenous groups of Central America carry on many craft traditions from their ancestors.

Unique styles of textiles, ceramics, carving and jewelry have developed across Central America, many dating from the days of ancient civilizations. Many cultures have their own form of ceramics, such as the Guatil in Guanacaste, who create pottery decorated with beasts that are half-bird, half-man, and people with exaggerated genitals, suggesting a fertility-rite culture. In western Honduras, the Lenca are known for their ceramics decorated with black and white geometric designs.

Textiles are important as well. In the Kuna culture on Panama's Caribbean coast, *molas* (traditional clothing) originated with the tradition of body painting geometrical designs, but are now a hand-sewn appliqué method on pieces of cloth. In the Guatemalan highlands, intricate weavings are made on simple hip-strap looms identical to those used by the ancient Maya, which consist of nothing more than a series of sticks. They're decorated with a wide range of bird, animal, and plant motifs as well as geometric forms, many of which figure in Maya mythology. Some are recalled from memory, without the use of patterns. Momostenango, near Quetzaltenango, is Guatemala's best place for traditional woolen blankets.

Masks, carved from balsawood or woven from plant fibers, are a common form of folk art in dozens of indigenous cultures in the region, such as the Boruca in Costa Rica, the Emberá in Panama, and Maya in Guatemala. Often used for ceremonial purposes, many designs merge human, spiritual, and natural elements. Basketry, made of palm, wicker, or bamboo, is another age-old process that has changed little in centuries.

A pottery artisan in Guatil, Guatamala.

A Mayan man displays his traditional wares at the Textile Market in Tecpan.

Guanacaste Devils walk through the streets with elaborately painted masks during the Juegos de los Diablitos, an indigenous ceremony in Boruca, Costa Rica

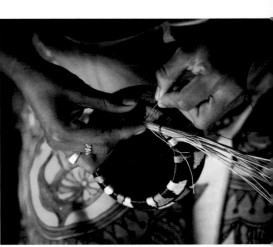

A Wounaan woman weaves an intricate shallow basket in Puerta Lara, Panama.

Fair trade products

While many handicrafts produced in Central America are of extremely high quality, much of what is found in markets and souvenir stores are cheap, mass-produced designs that sell for a fraction of the costs of an original handmade item, which was constructed using a centuries-old tradition. Many tourists are fine with paying less and having more ponchos and straw baskets, though they should be aware that little of that money goes toward the community from which they bought it.

Authentic indigenous handicrafts might cost just a little bit more than the items produced by a machine, though the benefits they give back to those who produce them are tenfold. The creation of handicrafts is fundamental for many indigenous groups all over the world, mostly because they can be produced with relatively limited resources. For women and families, it is one of the most accessible forms of income available to them – even though they are often subjected to exploitation, such as getting unfair prices for the work they do. The term fair trade gets thrown around a lot in the region, often in relation to coffee, but it's important for craftsmen and women too. To prevent unfair trading practices, many NGOs help to inform producers about their rights and the worth of their skills and help them organize into cooperatives to enable producer empowerment.

...ola, or traditional clothing, crafted by Kuna Indians from ...e San Blas Archipelago, Panama.

...ayan wooden masks for sale at Mercato de ...hichicastenango in Guatemala.

A Mayan girl weaving in Chiapas, Mexico.

Tourists white water rafting at Pozo Azul near Virgen de Sarapiqui in Costa Rica.

ADVENTURE SPORTS AND ACTIVITIES

Adventurers: behold a compact world with abundant opportunities to surf world-class waves, dive primeval coral reefs, raft raging rivers, and hike jungle trails.

Central America is one of the world's great destinations for outdoor enthusiasts. With two oceans to choose from, not to mention mountains, active volcanoes, and vast expanses of undisturbed forests, there's no shortage of opportunities for adventure. This diverse landscape boasts rainforest trails for hiking, beaches for horseback riding, remote trails for mountain biking through isolated villages, and world-class kayaking and whitewater rafting. Along the Caribbean coast, you'll find the world's second-longest barrier reef where you can scuba dive, snorkel, or swim with whale sharks, while in the Pacific there's superb surfing and sport fishing. Adrenaline sports such as ziplining, paragliding, and bungee jumping are on the rise – but note that there is little regulation of the adventure travel business, so choose your operator with care.

Zip lining in Dominical, Costa Rica.

For a wet and wild adventure, try waterfall rappelling. Instead of zipping along a cable, you step off the top of a waterfall and rappel your way down, attached to ropes secured by guides at both the top and bottom of the waterfall.

CANOPY TOURS

The most popular and readily accessible adventure sport is ziplining, also known as a canopy tour. Modern canopy tours were invented in the 1970s, when botanists and ecologists began looking to the mostly unstudied rain and cloud forest canopies and strapping on climbing gear to get close to them. Over time, this transitioned into a tourist activity and ziplines are now found all over the region, from the Rivera Maya and the Bay Islands to the jungles of Panama.

The region's original canopy tour was established in Costa Rica and involved donning a waist harness, climbing inside a huge, hollowed-out *matapalo* (strangler fig) tree up to a wooden platform, hooking your harness onto a wire cable, then stepping off the platform into thin air, perhaps 30 meters (100ft) off the ground, and whizzing along, suspended from the cable, to the next platform in the tree tops. The idea is a refinement of the method used by biologists to get up into the canopy to perform research. Some tours retain that focus on natural history and the chance to get close-up looks at life in the canopy. But most zipline tours today are focused on fun. Taking that first step into thin air is quite a thrill. Cables, harnesses, and safety equipment have to meet high government standards, but you are still at the mercy of human error, so choose a canopy tour operator who talks a lot about safety measures and gives careful, complete instructions to neophytes.

WHITEWATER RAFTING AND KAYAKING

Whitewater rafting (also known as river running) and kayaking offer anyone of moderately good fitness an exhilarating way to observe the scen-

The Talamanca range and the Cordillera Central have many steep, wide, perennial rivers that are regularly supplied with bounteous rainfall.

The variety of these rivers provides an enormous range of wilderness experiences. Some offer idyllic float trips through luscious landscapes with abundant wildlife, while others contain explosive whitewater and raging rapids that challenge the most experienced rafter. Primary rafting rivers include the Sarapiquí River, flowing through the lowlands of Heredia; the Reventazón River, with continuous rapids of moderate

Kayaking through Cacao Lagoon, Honduras.

ery and wildlife of the country. Dozens of professional outfitters around the region will provide all of the necessities: life preservers, helmets, and rafts or kayaks. You can be assured that you are in good hands: guides have been through training in the classroom and on the rivers. Many head guides have been trained at whitewater schools in the US and have worked with the world's best.

Costa Rica has more accessible whitewater rivers and rapids than any other place in the world. It is, of course, the unique geography of the country that makes it one of the world's great destinations for rafting. To have the right kind of rapids, you need a river that descends in a fairly steep gradient. The four mountain chains that wind down the axis of Costa Rica provide the perfect conditions.

to high difficulty; the Pacuare, passing through a deep gorge in dense jungle that contains rich flora and wildlife; and the Corobicí, ideal for rafters who are also keen birdwatchers.

In Honduras, the Cangrejal River, on the border of Pico Bonito National Park, has Class III-IV rapids in turquoise water, dodging giant boulders as toucans fly overhead. The region's longest rafting experience is in La Mosquitia, however, where 13-day expeditions run through the remote Río Plátano Biosphere Reserve, giving spectacular views of rare wildlife, glimpses into little-known indigenous cultures, and looks at mysterious petroglyphs. In Guatemala, the Cahabon River offers one to five-day expeditions through jungle canyons and caves, stopping at the remote Mayan ruins of Quiriguá. From Guatemala City and Antigua, there are easy one-day trips to the Esclavos, Motagua, and Naranjo rivers. There's also rafting in the highlands of Panama near Boquete, on the Mopan River in Belize, and on the Paz and Lempa rivers in El Salvador.

WINDSURFING

Since Costa Rica held its first windsurfing contest on Lake Arenal in the early 1990s, the country has been recognized as an outstanding destination for international windsurfers. With strong trade

the right conditions to practice acrobatic speed runs, jumps, and loops. The water is a comfortable 18 to 21°C (64 to 70°F) all year round.

Elsewhere in the region there are a handful of excellent wind surfing spots, such as Punta Chame in Central Panama, Bahía Salinas in northwestern Costa Rica, Llopango Lake in El Salvador, and on Roatán in the Bay Islands of Honduras.

SURFING

Central America's unending beaches are a fixture on the international surfing circuit and

A surfer enjoying perfect waves and clear water in Playa Santana, Nicaragua.

winds whipping the picturesque lake into a sea of whitewater and waves, it compares favorably with the world's best windsurfing locations, such as the Columbia River Gorge in Oregon and Maui in the Hawaiian Islands (with the only caveat that the waves are sometimes rather choppy).

Almost every other day between January and April, consistent winds of around 20 knots whip the waves to a meter-high (3ft) swell along the length of Arenal, creating excellent short-board sailing conditions. For the rest of the season, lighter winds predominate and are ideal for longboard sailing. Lake Arenal is not a suitable place for beginners. Sideshore winds are consistent and blow across the full width of the lake. During high winds, steep swells provide

⊘ WHITEWATER SAFETY

Sadly, every year whitewater accidents happen. Even the most experienced rafters, caught in a powerful river eddy, can drown. So choose your trip according to your level of expertise and find an outfitter that sticks to safety precautions: life vest, helmets, and accompanying safety/rescue kayaks. Before you enter the water in the raft you should have a practice drill to ensure everyone understands the instructions (often shouted over the thundering water). Also, check your travel insurance policy to ensure that you are covered for rafting. River water is unsafe to drink, so if you do tumble in, keep your mouth closed!

attract hordes of surfers from North America, Australia, and Europe. The region is blessed with masses of beaches: there are thousands of kilometers of Caribbean coast and Pacific shores, sculpted with sandy beaches, rocky headlands, offshore reefs, and river mouths close to coastal jungles. There are also a large number of open beaches that are exposed to ocean swells coming from many directions. However, much of the coastline is removed from civilization, so there may be no amenities, food, or emergency services of any kind within many kilometers. A four-

of the Barranca River produces what is reputed to be one of the world's longest left-breaking waves. Far to the north, the beaches of Guanacaste province have some of the best surf anywhere, particularly during the dry season when steady offshore winds help to create the waves. The break near Roca de la Bruja at Playa Naranjo is one of the most spectacular waves; the number of surfers is officially limited because it is in Santa Rosa National Park. Surfers need to make advance reservations with one of the many local surf shops and travel by boat to this surfing spot.

Scuba diving group swimming from a dive boat, Half Moon Caye, Belize.

wheel-drive vehicle is often essential, especially during the rainy season.

Costa Rica, in particular, gets high marks. Aficionados generally concur that the quality of Costa Rica's surf is firmly in the top four – along with California, Hawaii, and Australia. Moreover, they find that the surf here is plentiful and relatively uncrowded, the water temperature is a comfortable 27°C (80°F) throughout the year, and there is still the chance of experiencing the rare thrill of having a wave all to yourself, just offshore from a pristine and empty beach.

On the Pacific Coast, many gravitate toward Jacó, for its easy access from San José; Playa Hermosa, site of many a surfing competition; and near Puntarenas, where the sandspit at the mouth

Near Limón, two and a half hours east of San José, Playa Bonita is a good, popular surfing beach. About one hour south of Limón, Puerto Viejo de Talamanca, a tranquil Caribbean village, is the site of the sometimes awesome Salsa Brava, a surf break that has acquired an international reputation. From December through March, consistent, large north swells hit the coral reef with tremendous force.

While Nicaragua does not get the same amount of attention as Costa Rica, the country's Pacific coast is not lacking in surf spots. Locals have only begun surfing in the country in the last 15 years, but surf shops and hotels catering to the sport have been steadily increasing. This is a year-round surfing destination, although the best

From December to April, large swells caused by winds originating in the Caribbean arrive at Costa Rica's east coast beaches. The steep, fast-moving waves break over shallow coral reefs, often in shapes and sizes that rival those of the north shore of Oahu in Hawaii.

swells occur from April to November. Most facilities center in the area around San Juan del Sur.

With warm water and right-breaking waves, El Salvador is quickly finding its way on the region's surf circuit. Many of the best waves can be found in the West, such as at La Libertad, Playa El Tunco, Playa El Sunza, and Playa El Zonte. The season here runs from about March to October, the rainy season. In Panama, some of the best waves are to be found on the Azuero peninsula, as well as at other points along the Pacific coast.

DIVING AND SNORKELING

With the Pacific Ocean on one side and the Caribbean Sea on the other, Central America is paradise for scuba diving. Some of the most inexpensive certification courses can be found in the region, plus there's a wide range of dive sites, from easy offshore locations in the Bay Islands to Belize's Blue Hole.

Tracking the entire Caribbean coast of the Maya region – from Puerto Morelos in Mexico and south through Belizean waters to the Bay Islands of Honduras – is the world's second-longest barrier reef, the Mesoamerican Barrier Reef System, an aquatic paradise for scuba divers. Like the Australian Great Barrier Reef, it is not just one continuous barrier or coral wall, though in many places the reef crest stretches for miles just below the surface. Additionally, there are hundreds of large and small coral-fringed islands or cayes, underwater seamounts and ridges, and four coral atolls.

Starting in the north, there's some good diving around Isla Mujeres and Cancún, and there are several well-established dive schools on both islands. If you are in the area between May and September, you have the chance to snorkel with whale sharks, which gather off the coast and near Isla Holbox. Cozumel is the next important location, with some world-class diving on rich

coral reefs, with deep trenches, coral patches, and steep drop-offs. Palancar Reef, which was first popularized by the French underwater explorer and marine biologist Jacques Cousteau, is justly famous throughout the diving world for its incredible coral wall. Other spectacular sites include Columbia Shallows, a dazzling coral garden, and Punta Sur, which offers wonderful coral formations (and also strong currents). There are plenty of dive schools in Cozumel.

Belize offers arguably the best diving in the western hemisphere. The sheer number and

Snorkeling from Isla de Perro, Panama.

variety of dive sites is astonishing, the marine environment is well protected, and there are some excellent dive schools. Lighthouse Reef, one of the atolls, is where you'll find the much-touted Blue Hole, which looks as if it was created by a bomb blast but is actually the result of a collapsed cavern. There are several shipwrecks in the area that have formed artificial reefs, which you can explore, and there's the Half Moon Caye Natural Monument, which in 1982 became the first marine location in Belize to be made into a preserve. In southern Belizean waters there is good diving around most of the cayes – Tobacco Reef, Columbus Reef, and South Water Caye particularly – but Glover's Reef, farther offshore, is the place that people rave about. Designated as a marine preserve, it is a large atoll with some epic wall diving and beautiful snorkeling gardens.

The Bay Islands of Honduras – Roatán, Utila, and Guanaja – are each a world class diving destination. Aside from the benefit of being inexpensive, the diversity of the species here is impressive. Dolphins, sea turtles, nurse sharks, manta rays, and whale sharks are all frequently seen.

CAVING

To the ancient Maya, caves were entrances to the underworld – *Xibalba* – the 'Place of Fright.' Recent

Cave Branch Jungle Lodge, on the bank of the Caves Branch River, midway between the huge St Herman's Cave and the Blue Hole National Park, has a range of accommodations, from dorm rooms to secluded cabaña suites.

In Guatemala, the huge Candelaria cave systems, extending for around 80km (50 miles) in length, contain some vast caverns. Confusingly, there are at least four separate access points, but the Complejo Cultural de Candelaria near the town of Raxrujá contains the most impressive chambers. There are more remarkable caves

A cenote in Chichen Itza.

research indicates that every major Maya settlement was built near a cave, usually a natural one, though in some cases an artificial chamber was hollowed out of the rock. Caves were essential elements in the Maya belief system and, although the ancient Maya never made permanent settlements in caves, every cave so far explored in the region exhibits evidence of a Maya presence long ago. From cave entrances to deep underground, records of ceremonial visits remain in the form of pottery, petroglyphs, carvings, and fire-hearths.

In Belize, visitors can take an amazing journey into the realm of *Xibalba*. Caves Branch Jungle Lodge, on the Hummingbird Highway, 21km (13 miles) south of Belmopan, has the best guided caving trips in the Maya world. Ian Anderson's

> *The Belize Barrier Reef reserves were given Unesco World Heritage Site status in 1996, confirming the global importance of the Caribbean reefs and their marine life.*

near Semuc Champey, including the Lanquín cave, which is best visited at dusk to view the thousands of bats that emerge from the main cavern.

Yucatán is riddled with cave networks. Some of the most impressive are the Río Secreto, a wet and dry cave system which you explore in a wetsuit and by torchlight, clamboring over rocks and swimming part of the way; it is near Xcaret, south of Playa del Carmen. The caves of Loltún, which are well organized for visitors, include the chance to see rock art and carving dating back to ancient Maya times. Other possibilities for a caving trip include the multiple cave systems around Oxkintok, Balankanché, and Dzitnup.

HIKING

With dozens of national parks scattered in some of the world's most biodiverse terrain, Central America offers some of the finest walking – jungle, mountain, and coastal hikes – in the world.

Pedro La Laguna is especially picturesque, as it passes through some of the least populated parts of the lakeshore, the path clinging to the edge of the caldera at times.

Honduras' national park system contains several impressive trail networks, such as in Montaña de Celaque, Pico Bonito and La Tigra. Funding for the country's parks fluctuates and they can be sorely understaffed, so it's important to get updated travel information before visiting. Costa Rica has dozens of great hikes on well trodden trails, such as those in Manuel Antonio, the Are-

Hiking in Bocawina National Park, Belize.

The spellbindingly dramatic landscape of lofty peaks, verdant river valleys, empty beaches, thick rainforests, and traditional indigenous villages are linked by a web of trails, paths, and dirt tracks in various states of repair.

Lake Atitlán, a mandatory destination for every visitor to Guatemala, is world-class trekking country. An idyllic network of trails snakes around the steep banks and volcanic slopes of the lake, connecting all of the 13 shoreside settlements, past patchwork cornfields and vegetable gardens. Sadly, as there have been incidents of walkers being robbed in recent years, it is best to take a local guide with you. If you only want to walk one section of the lake, then the five-hour trail between Santa Cruz La Laguna and San

nal Volcano, and Monteverde. The country's top hike is through the rich biodiversity of Corcovado National Park. In El Salvador, the cloud forest trail to El Trifinio in Montecristo National Park is the most celebrated trek.

SPORT FISHING

One of the premier destinations on earth for big game sport fishermen is Central America's Pacific coast. Marlin, sailfish, yellowfin tuna, and dorado are all attracted to the calm, warm waters and the numbers here are staggering. Billfish and dorado can be caught year round, while sailfish boats can often release dozens in a day. On jungle rivers and freshwater lakes, peacock bass, tarpon, and rainbow bass are commonly caught.

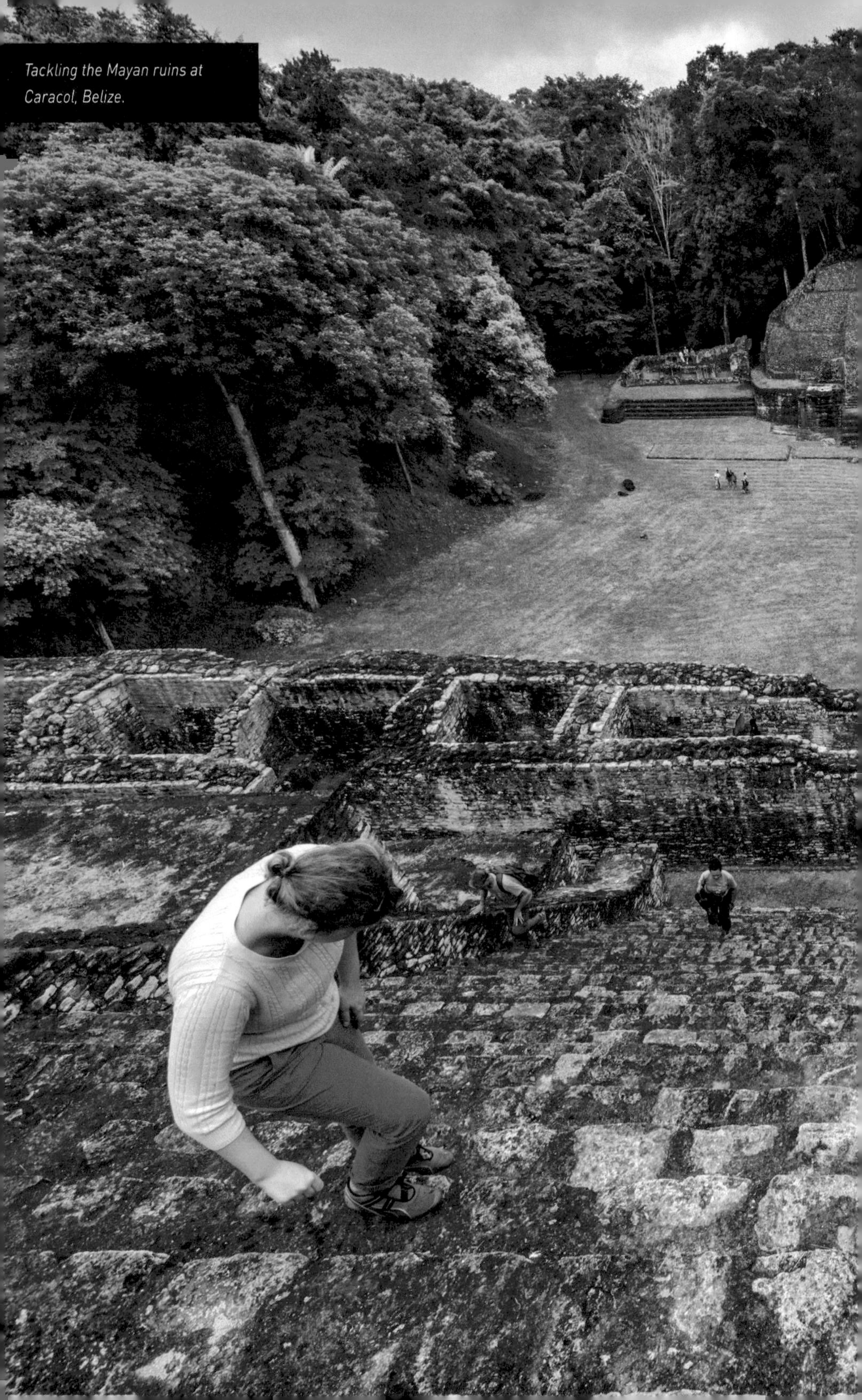

Tackling the Mayan ruins at Caracol, Belize.

Descending Nicaragua's Cerro Negro volcano in the Cordillera de los Maribios, the youngest volcano in Central America.

Swimming in Cénote dos Ojos,
Yucatán.

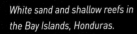
White sand and shallow reefs in the Bay Islands, Honduras.

INTRODUCTION

A detailed guide to the whole of Central America, including southern Mexico, with principal sites clearly cross-referenced by number to the maps.

Hummingbirds, Central Valley, Costa Rica.

Despite Central America's small size, the array of sights and adventure activities is substantial. Exploring Mayan ruins lost within the jungle, seeking out resplendent quetzals in the cloud forest, and kicking back on unspoiled beaches are all on offer here. On a short visit, it's best to confine yourself to a limited geographical area, although flights within countries can save you a significant amount of travel time.

The Maya region, encompassing Southern Mexico, Belize, and Guatemala, is rife with history and diverse landscapes. Aside from the pleasures of some of the world's top beaches at Cancún and along the Rivera Maya, Mexico's Yucatán Peninsula is covered with thick jungle that contains Mayan cities like Chichén Itzá and dreamy *cenotes*. Guatemala, home to the ruins of Tikal and the colonial city of Antigua, is more mountainous, with the tallest peaks in the region, which include active volcanoes. English-speaking Belize, with a Caribbean vibe and some of the world's best diving on the Mesoamerican Barrier Reef, is also filled with archeological sites and adventure activities.

To the south, El Salvador, Honduras, and Nicaragua are still being discovered by modern travelers, yet have no less to offer. The natural diversity here is astounding: mangroves, cloud forests, mountains, volcanoes, and lakes. Surfing on El Salvador's Pacific coast and diving in the Bay Islands is as good and as inexpensive as anywhere in the world. Upscale beach resorts and eco-lodges have established themselves in biodiversity hotspots like Pico Bonito National Park and Lake Nicaragua.

At Volcan Masaya.

Then there's Costa Rica and Panama, which have the region's most developed tourist infrastructure. Within minutes of bustling capitals like San José and Panama City, good highways and a network of short range aircraft can drop travelers on remote tropical islands and in dozens of well-maintained national parks. While the Panama Canal, recently expanded, crosses the Panamanian isthmus in dramatic fashion, both countries have delightful Atlantic and Pacific coastlines dotted with quaint beach towns.

Note: While the region of Central America covers the seven nations south of Mexico's border, we have included the southern Mexican states here as they often form part of a journey to the region, and for Mayan cultural continuity.

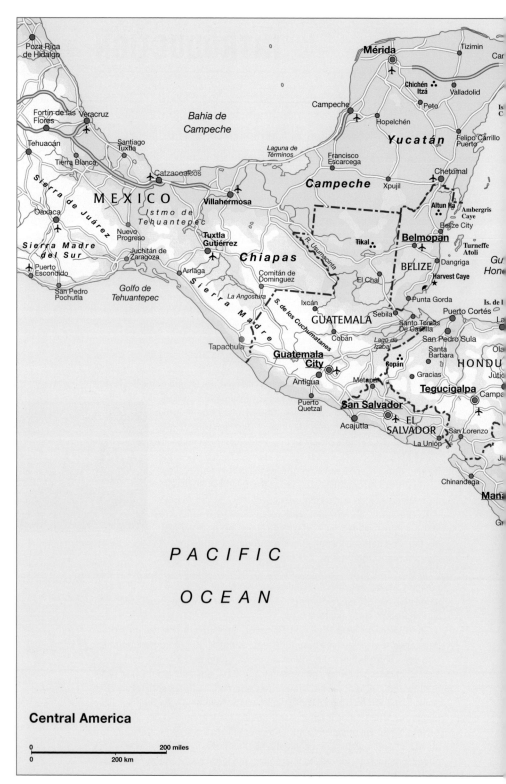

Poza Rica de Hidalgo

Mérida

Tizimin

Car

Chichén Itzá

Valladolid

Campeche

Peto

Is C

Fortín de las Flores

Veracruz

Hopelchén

Bahia de Campeche

Tehuacán

Santiago Tuxtla

Laguna de Términos

Yucatán

Felipo Carrillo Puerto

Tierra Blanca

Catzacoalcos

Francisco Escarcega

Chetumal

MEXICO

Villahermosa

Campeche

Xpujil

Oaxaca

Istmo de Tehuantepec

Altun Ha

Ambergris Caye

Sierra de Juárez

Belize City

Sierra Madre del Sur

Nuevo Progreso

Tuxtla Gutiérrez

Tikal

Belmopan

Turneffe Atoli

Juchitán de Zaragoza

Puerto Escondido

Arriaga

Chiapas

R. Usumacinta

BELIZE

Dangriga

Gu Hon

Comitán de Dominguez

El Chal

Harvest Caye

San Pedro Pochutla

Golfo de Tehuantepec

La Angostura

S. de los Cuchumatanes

Ixcán

Punta Gorda

Is. de l

Sierra Madre

GUATEMALA

Sebila

Puerto Cortés

La

Cobán

Santo Tomas De Castilla

Tapachula

Lago de Izabal

San Pedro Sula

Santa Barbara

Ola

Guatemala City

Copán

HONDU

Jútic

Antigua

Metapan

Gracias

Tegucigalpa

Campa

Puerto Quetzal

San Salvador

Acajutla

EL SALVADOR

San Lorenzo

La Unión

Ji

Chinandega

Man

Gr

PACIFIC

OCEAN

Central America

0   200 miles

0   200 km

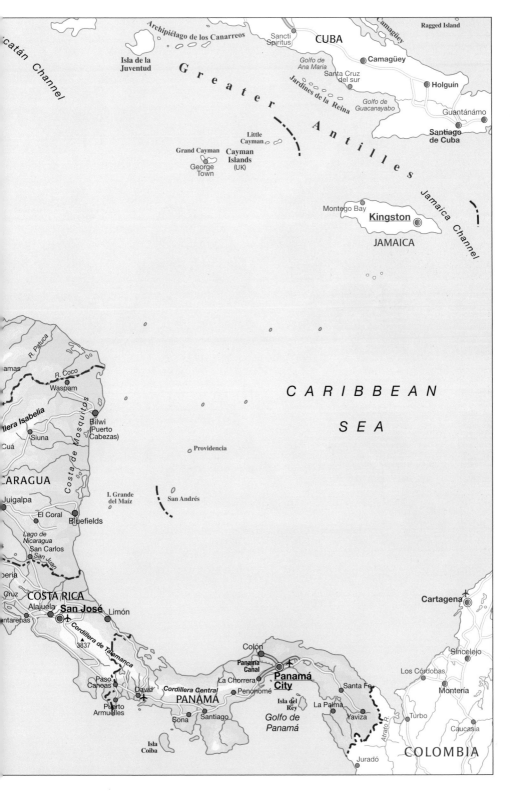

Yucatán Channel

Archipiélago de los Canarreos

Sancti
Spiritus

CUBA

Camagüey

Ragged Island

Isla de la
Juventud

Golfo de
Ana Maria

Santa Cruz
del sur

Camagüey

Holguín

G r e a t e r

Jardines de la Reina

Golfo de
Guacanayabo

Guantánamo

A n t i l l e s

Santiago
de Cuba

Little
Cayman

Grand Cayman

**Cayman
Islands**
(UK)

George
Town

Montego Bay

Jamaica Channel

Kingston

JAMAICA

C A R I B B E A N

S E A

R. Patuca

amas

R. Coco

Waspam

llera Isabelia

Bilwi
(Puerto
Cabezas)

Cuá

Siuna

Providencia

C o s t a   d e   M o s q u i t o s

:ARAGUA

Juigalpa

I. Grande
del Maíz

San Andrés

El Coral

Bluefields

Lago de
Nicaragua

San Carlos

San Juan

:eria

Cruz

COSTA RICA

Cartagena

Alajuela

San José

Limón

antarenas

Cordillera de Talamanca

3837

Colón

Sincelejo

Panama
Canal

Los Córdobas

Paso
Canoas

David

Cordillera Central

La Chorrera

**Panamá
City**

Santa Fe

Montería

Penonomé

Puerto
Armuelles

PANAMÁ

Isla del
Rey

La Palma

Tùrbo

Sona

Santiago

*Golfo de
Panamá*

Yaviza

Caucasia

Isla
Coiba

Juradó

COLOMBIA

Atrato R.

Temple V towers out of the jungle in Tikal, Guatemala.

THE MAYAN REGION

The magnificent architecture of the ancient Maya, legendary beaches, and renowned diving are attracting a growing tide of visitors.

Performer at Xcaret.

With thousands of years of history and a glittering coastline, the Maya region of Central America is now a global travel destination, attracting visitors from every part of the world. This is where the rich Mayan culture had its center and where its remnants are still part of the landscape today. Away from the resorts, the interior has changed at a much slower pace, and many Maya continue to farm *milpas* (cornfields), planting the maize and beans that have been harvested here for perhaps five millennia under the relentless sun.

While the Maya influence cannot be denied, mainstream Latino *(ladino)* culture dominates the region, pushing farther and farther into the interior from the beaches of the Riviera Maya and sprawl of Guatemala City. In coastal Belize, the Caribbean influence is very evident, with thunderous reggae bass lines direct from Jamaica shaking the dancehall, while the inimitably reflective wit and harmonies of Trinidadian calypso fill the airwaves. In southern Belize and on the Caribbean coast of Guatemala, there are several Garífuna communities.

The beaches around Cancún and along the Riviera Maya, lined with all-inclusive resorts and eco-cool boutique hotels, are the biggest attraction in the entire region, luring cruise ships to Cozumel and hipsters to Tulum. Yet, just off the beach, thick jungle extends across the Yucatán, where the rich culture of Mayan villages and colonial cities like Mérida can be found. Extending across the border into Guatemala and Belize, one-time Mayan settlements form a loosely

Ambergris Caye, Belize.

connected network of city-states centered around groups of awesome temple-pyramids, decorated with fine murals and carved stelae. The ruins at Chichén Itzá, Uxmal, Palenque, Copán, Tikal, Calakmul, and El Mirador are some of the most impressive archeological remains in the Americas. There's no shortage of adventure here, from diving the world's second largest barrier reef to discovering the vast cave network that includes underground rivers and cenotes; climbing to the summit of active volcanoes; or paddling dugout canoes through mangrove forests.

Cenote Choo-Ha near Coba, Yucatán.

SOUTHERN MEXICO

The Yucatán Peninsula contains a wealth of cultural and ecological treasures, not least the Mayan archeological wonders and cave systems – and, of course, miles of beautiful beaches.

With seemingly endless sunshine enhancing fascinating ancient cultural sites and resorts of every type, the southern states of Mexico are well known as a major tourist destination. Visitors to the Yucatán Peninsula spend their time clambering over awe-inspiring ruins; sunning themselves on golden beaches; discovering the natural splendors of the environment; and exploring old colonial towns, all supported by a cohesive and well-established tourism infrastructure.

Everything began to change in the region in the 1970s and development has been accelerating ever since. The Mexican government decided on tourism as a foreign currency earner, and chose the beaches of the eastern Yucatán, especially the near-deserted island of Cancún, as ideal sites for development. Since then, Cancún has become a major world resort, and the once-remote beaches to the south have been dubbed the *Riviera Maya*.

For those seeking an insight into the Maya, ruins can be found all over the peninsula, many only partially excavated, or even buried in the forest. No visit is complete without a look at Chichén Itzá, perhaps the most famous ruin in the Maya world. Despite the crowds, its Castillo temple, sacred *cenote* sacrificial pool, and group of a Thousand Columns are still inspirational,

unforgettable sights. Edzná has a remarkable five-story temple. Tulum, a minor site in every sense, has an incomparable location, framed with white-sand Caribbean beaches and turquoise waters. In the far south are the remains of Calakmul, one of the two superpowers of the Classic Maya era (along with Tikal). Aside from Mayan ruins, there's the colonial charm in the majestic core of Mérida and the pastel-painted buildings of Campeche. Few of the henequen plantations that once brought great wealth to Yucatán landowners are still

⊙ **Main Attractions**

Mérida
Chichén Itzá
Cancún
Cozumel
Playa del Carmen
Tulum
Sian Ka'an
Palenque
San Cristóbal de las Casas

Maps on pages 108, 114, 117, 128

The ruins of Becán.

The Yucatán

0   50 km

0   50 miles

N

G U L F   O F

Reserva Ecológica Es
Bocas de Da

Telchac   Boca de Dzilam
Puerto   Dzilam
Progreso   Chicxulub   Chábihau de Bra
Chuburna   Puerto   **Xcambo**   Dzidzantún
Sisal   Chicxulub
Punta Baz   Baca   Cansahcab
261   Temax

Reserva de la Biosfera
Ría Celestún   Dzibilchaltún   Motul   Tepakán
Punta Boxcohuo   Hunucmá   **Mérida** ❶
Kinchil   Umán   Aké   **Izamal**
Celestún   Seyé   Hóctun
281   Acancéh   Kantunil
Bella Flor   1800 Libre
Chocholá   261   Yaxcopoil   Tecoh   Union
180   Y   u   Telchaquillo   Chichén I
Maxcanú   **Mayapán**   Sotuta
Muna   Mama   Tekit
Tankuché   **Oxkintoc**   Lázaro   Mayapán
Halachó   Becal   Cárdenas   Ticul   Teabo
Reserva de la   Calkini   Maní
Biosfera Petenes   **Uxmal** ❷   Oxkutzcab
Jaina   Pochoc   **Kabáh**   Grutas de Loltún
(Zac-Pol)   Tekax de A.O.
Punta Nitún   Pomuch   Hecelchakán   **Sayil**   **Labná**   Peto
Xcalumkin   Xlapak   Ticum   Tzucacab
Tenabó   261   184

B a h í a   d e   C a m p e c h e

24   Boxol   Dzuiché
Campeche ❶⑦
Lerma   Chencoyi   **Santa Rosa**   José María
Xtampak   Hunto Chac   Morelos
180D   Cayal   **Hopelchén**
Seybaplaya   Tixmucuy   Nohyaxché   Iturbide   **Dzibilnocac**   Q   u
Balneario Acapulco   261   **Edzná**   Chunh
Haltunchén   Pich   Chenko   **Dzibalchén**
Champotón   Moquel   Ruíz   **Hochob**
180   Cortines
San Enrique   **M**   **E**   **X**   **I**
Chencán
Huayahaca   Pustunich   212 ▲
Reserva de la
180   Pixoyal   **M e s e t a**
261   250 ▲   **Biosfera de**
Isla del   Puerto   Chicbul   **C**   a   m   p   e   c   h   e   **de Zoh**   **a g u n a**
Carmen   Real   Dieciocho   Ponte   Francisco   Lechugal   **Balamkú**   **Calakmul**   Dzibanché-
Ciudad del   de Marzo   Díaz Ordaz   Escárcega   Kinichná
Carmen   Zacatal   Laguna   186   Lago   Dzinapara   Conhuas   **Becán**   **Xpuhil**   Francisco
de Términos   Coyoc   Francisco   Sivituc   **Chicanná**   Xpuhil   Villa
Villa   **Chicanná**   186
Buenavista   **Río Bec**   **Kohunlich**
Candelária   **Tortuga**   **Reserva de la**
365 ▲   Tomás
El Tigre   **B i o s f e r a   d e**   Garrido
Chiapas   **Calakmul** ⑯   Or
Chablé   Nueva   **C a l a k m u l**   Neustadt
Coahuila
⑱   ⑲ **Bonampak** ⑳ **Yaxchilán**   G U A T E M A L A

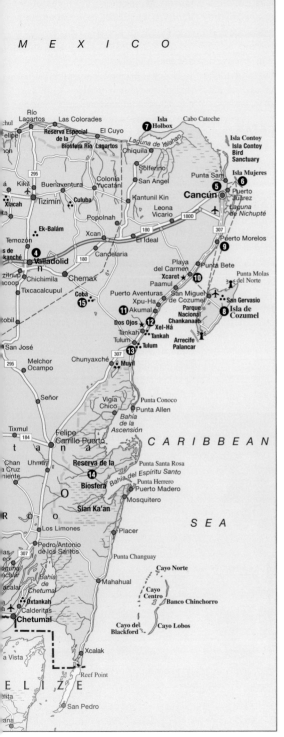

operating today, though some have been resurrected as luxury rural hotels.

Famously, the Yucatán's Caribbean coastline is stunning. The white beaches and azure waters between Cancún and Tulum attract the most visitors, and there are many delightful beaches and lagoons down this way, such as Akumal and Tankah. Offshore is the island of Cozumel, its coral walls the talk of dive magazines the world over, and the more intimate beaches of tiny Isla Mujeres. National parks and preserves are extensive and varied. Most impressive is the Calakmul Biosphere Reserve with its pristine jungle and wildlife. The Sian Ka'an Biosphere Reserve is another vast protected territory, whose boundaries also include the offshore reef. The Río Lagartos and Celestún wetlands are superb for birders, especially for the flocks of flamingos. Finally, there are hundreds of atmospheric *cenotes* across the Yucatán to swim in: a must-do experience for any visitor.

THE YUCATÁN MAYA

Yet, not far from the tourist resorts, many Yucatán Maya live in much the same way as they have for centuries. There are almost half a million Maya in the region, most of whom speak Yucatec Maya. In more remote areas, many still own and farm the land communally. They cultivate maize, chili peppers, and beans as they have always done, and most families have beehives for the Yucatán's celebrated honey. Nevertheless, the Maya still struggle to survive. Traditional farming gives only a meager income. The tourism boom has, naturally, provided new kinds of work; newer tourist towns like Playa del Carmen are full of Yucatecan migrants, and many Maya spend a few months each year on the coast, working in construction or hotels, before returning home with their savings.

The more fluid political situation in Mexico since the ending of the one-party rule of the PRI in 2000 has made it a little easier for village people to be heard, but the Maya's right to own and farm land is still constantly threatened by development. Maya cultural traditions are often seen only as a picturesque part of the tourist industry. Although they are the most Mexican of Mexico's inhabitants, they are still often excluded socially and treated as outcasts in their own land. In Chiapas, conflicts have been more intense, and led to the revolt by the Zapatista National Liberation Army (EZLN) in 1994, when, as so often in the past, the Maya emerged from remote jungle areas and took over towns to press their claims for more land and other social demands.

THE NORTHERN YUCATÁN

The northern section of the Yucatán Peninsula is occupied largely by the wedge-shaped state of Yucatán. The landscape up here is flat, dry, and covered in scrub bush. The sacred *cenotes* of the Maya (deep natural wells in the limestone crust) provided the only access to fresh water. Second to the peninsula's Caribbean beach resorts, this is the region that draws the most visitors for its sheer quantity of superb archeological sites, crowned by the magnificent Chichén Itzá and Uxmal, and for the special charm of the Yucatecan way of life.

MÉRIDA

Around Plaza Mayor in Mérida.

The ideal base for exploring the Yucatán is its elegant colonial capital,

Mérida **❶**. Formerly the home of millionaires who made their riches during the henequen heyday, today this thriving city is visited by more than 2 million people annually.

In spite of this year-round human traffic, Mérida remains a pleasant city. Once enclosed by walls, Mérida's downtown area is compact, its narrow streets and closely packed buildings originally laid out in the era of the horse and buggy, and now filled by motor traffic. It operates on a grid plan with numbered streets: even numbers run north–south, odd numbers east–west.

AROUND THE PLAZA MAYOR

At the heart of the city center, the wonderfully shady **Plaza Mayor** is bound by calles 61 and 63, and 60 and 62. On its northern side, the Pasaje Picheta leads to an internal plaza with café tables under a glass roof. Across on the south side of the laurel-shaded plaza is the **Casa de Montejo,** built in 1549 for the first Spanish governor of the Yucatán, Francisco de Montejo. It has been partially rebuilt as a bank, but still retains

its extraordinary Renaissance portico, with carvings of armed warriors standing on screaming heads.

The Maya name for the city on the site, Tihó, means 'the Place of the Five Temples.' Many of their stones were used to erect the **Catedral de San Ildefonso**, diagonally opposite the Montejo mansion on the northeast corner. Built from 1562 to 1598, this was only the second cathedral built anywhere in the Americas, after Santo Domingo in the Dominican Republic. Next to the cathedral, housed in the former archbishop's palace, is the **Museo de Arte Contemporáneo de Yucatán** or **MACAY** (tel: 999 928 3258; www.macay.org; Wed–Mon 10am–6pm; free), Mérida's major modern art museum, containing an important collection of works from local and national artists.

On the plaza's northern side is the **Palacio del Gobierno** (Governor's Palace), built in 1892, on whose murals Fernando Castro Pacheco worked for 25 years. The restored **Teatro Mérida**, in an Art Deco building around the corner on Calle 62, has a bar and a movie theater. The west side of the square is dominated by the **Ayuntamiento** or city hall, with an elegant 18th-century colonnaded facade. Next to it, the corner of Calle 61 is now occupied by the **Centro Cultural de Olimpo** (shows Tue–Sat 7pm), an attractive modern cultural center, with a planetarium.

CALLE 60 AND AROUND

Running across the east side of the Plaza Mayor in front of the cathedral, Calle 60 is Mérida's traditional main street, and you will find many sights on and just off this thoroughfare. East of Calle 60 is the the giant **Mercado** on Calle 65, where shops and stalls sell products ranging from traditional hammocks, panama hats, and embroidery to electronics and giant cooking pots. At the corner of calles 65 and 56, the former post office is now the **Museo de la Ciudad** (tel: 999 924 4264; Tue–Fri 9am–8pm, Sat–Sun 9am–2pm; free).

One block north of the cathedral, the **Parque Hidalgo** is dominated by the Jesuit-built church of **La Tercera Orden**, completed in 1618 and containing a

⊘ THE YUCATÁN'S GILDED AGE

The late 19th century was a boom time for the Yucatán, with a prosperity based on 'green gold,' henequen from the agave plant, used to make the rope known as sisal. Such was the demand from Europe's and the United States' farms, ships, and factories for sisal rope that the Yucatán became the wealthiest state in Mexico, and by around 1900, Mérida could boast more millionaires per capita than any other city in the world. Railroads were built for exporting the rope, and politicians hailed the sisal boom as the triumph of progress. A broad new avenue was created, Paseo Montejo, flanked by mansions in ornate European styles. Henequen plantation owners lived like kings, their children educated at the best schools in Europe, their wives dressed in the latest Parisian finery – all attained, however, at the expense of their Maya laborers, who were practically slaves. Henequen was exported and the French bricks and tiles that came back as ballast were used to build mansions for the tycoons in Mérida.

At the same time, the Maya peasants employed on henequen plantations were cruelly abused with near-slave status, and often paid in tokens that could be exchanged only in stores owned by the landowners. The situation in rural Mexico, under the regime of dictator Porfirio Díaz, was exposed by American journalist John Kenneth Turner in his 1910 book *Barbarous Mexico*. This led even the London *Daily Mail* to protest: 'If Mexico is half as bad as she is painted by Mr Turner, she is covered with the leprosy of a slavery worse than that of San Thome or Peru, and should be regarded as unclean by all the free peoples of the world.'

Today, many of the plantation *haciendas* lie abandoned and crumbling, but some are open to visitors, such as the one at Yaxcopoil (www.yaxcopoil.com), which offers tours, a restaurant, and accommodations. A giant Moorish-style double arch on the highway leads to the main house, a series of large, airy rooms full of period furniture; next to the private chapel with its shiny marble floor, an ancient kitchen opens onto a garden of citrus trees and banana plants. Other *haciendas*, such as Temozón between Mérida and Uxmal, or San José Cholul toward Izamal, have now been turned into the Yucatán's most distinctive luxury hotels.

painting that depicts the meeting in 1542 of Montejo and Tutul Xiú, the first Maya ruler to convert to Christianity. The sparsely equipped **tourist office** (daily 8am–8pm) is in the domed **Teatro Peón Contreras** (built in 1900), with an ornate marble staircase designed by the Italian architect Enrico Deserti, who was also responsible for the city's Anthropology Museum. Opposite the theater stands the **University of Yucatán**.

UXMAL

About 80km (50 miles) south of Mérida you come to **Uxmal ❷** (daily 8am–5pm), one of the most impressive ruins in the Maya world and a Unesco World Heritage Site. Uxmal was the most important Puuc center, reaching its peak between 800 and 1000, and its architecture is stunning. In 1840, the US explorer John Lloyd Stephens compared the **Palacio del Gobernador** (Governor's Palace) favorably with Grecian, Roman, and Egyptian art. 'The designs are strange and incomprehensible, very elaborate, sometimes grotesque, but often simple, tasteful, beautiful,' he wrote. The palace,

The Nunnery Quadrangle at Uxmal.

100 meters (330ft) wide with an impressive facade, sits atop a hill. In the Puuc style of building, rubble-filled walls were faced with cement and the whole edifice was covered with limestone mosaic panels, 20,000 of them in this case.

To the north of the palace is the 39-meter (128ft) high **Pyramid of the Magician**, legendarily built in one night by an *alux*, a spirit that was the son of a witch, but actually the product of several generations of builders (Uxmal means 'three times built'). Immediately west is the 74-room quadrangle referred to as the **Cuadrángulo de las Monjas** (Nunnery Quadrangle), because its form reminded the Spanish priest Father Diego López de Cogolludo, who named Uxmal's main buildings, of a convent. Though made up of four separate buildings, it forms an elegant ensemble; the entire complex is built on an elevated man-made platform and typifies the Puuc architectural style, which is based on the Maya hut, the *na*, with its wooden walls and high-peaked thatch roof. To the south of the Nunnery is a ball court, beyond which, sharing the Governor's Palace platform, is **Casa de las Tortugas** (House of the Turtles), which gets its name from the turtle carvings on the cornice, an animal associated with rain in Maya legend.

West of the pyramid is **El Palomar** (House of the Pigeons), while southeast of the Governor's Palace, is the pyramid called the **Casa de la Vieja** (House of the Old Woman), which Maya legend avers was the house of the sorcerer-mother of the dwarf magician who built Uxmal.

The **Visitors' Center** at the entrance includes a shop, museum, and restaurant. The 45-minute sound and light show is at 8pm (Nov–Mar 7pm); an English translation is provided through headphones. Regular buses connect the site with Mérida, and a daily tour bus also leaves Mérida's second-class bus station at 8.30am for Uxmal and the other main Puuc sites.

CHICHÉN ITZÁ

Just off Highway 180 about 116km (72 miles) east of Mérida is **Chichén Itzá** ❸ (named from the Yucatec Maya *chi* = mouths; *chen* = wells; *Itza* = the people believed to have settled here), the best known of all Maya sites. It is a Unesco World Heritage Site and was also voted one of the 'New Seven Wonders of the World' from a selection of 200 monuments in 2007.

Curiously, Chichén Itzá is a very atypical Maya site. Its largest buildings – the Pyramid of Kukulcán, the Temple of the Warriors – are very 'un-Maya' in style, and much more similar to buildings in central Mexico. It used to be thought that Chichén Itzá had initially been a purely Maya city, which around the year 1000 was taken over by warlike invaders from central Mexico called the Toltecs, who were later replaced by another non-Maya people, the Itzaes. However, as more and more of the blanks in Maya history have been partially filled in, this theory has been largely discredited, as the successive invasions do not seem to match with any established dates.

Instead, Chichén Itzá seems from its beginnings to have been a mixed community, combining Maya traditions with those of migrants from central Mexico. It grew up late in the Classic Maya era, around 700, but from around 800 dominated the north-central Yucatán for several centuries. The city declined more slowly than other Maya centers, and only finally disintegrated as a political entity around 1200.

EXPLORING THE SITE

On entering Chichén, the view is dominated by the 24-meter (80ft) high **Pyramid of Kukulcán (El Castillo)** ❹. It represents the Maya calendar, with four 91-step staircases plus a single step at the top, adding up to 365. Eighteen terraces divide the nine levels that represent the 18 months, each 20 days long. The nine terraces symbolize the nine underground worlds. Each side has 52 panels, representing the 52-year cosmic cycle, the point at which the Mayas' two calendars coincided and they considered that a cycle ended, only to begin anew.

⊙ **Fact**

One of the most influential early explorers of Maya sites was the Frenchman Désiré Charnay. It was he who first photographed Palenque, Uxmal, and Chichén Itzá, and these superb photographs and lithographs led the way for the first scientific archeological expeditions.

El Castillo at Chichén Itzá.

The giant carved serpents beside the great stairway are picked out by sunlight at sunset during the spring equinox, interpreted as a time to sow the crops, just as the snake's apparent ascension of the pyramid at the fall equinox signified harvest time. Thousands of visitors come to see this phenomenon – known as the 'Descent (or Ascent) of Kukulcán,' from the Maya name for the plumed serpent god Quetzalcoatl – on March 21 and September 21 every year. The illusion, which lasts more than three hours, is imitated more briefly every night during the *Luz y Sonido* (Light and Sound) show (Nov–Mar 7pm, Apr–Oct 8pm).

Centers of sacrifice at Chichén were the three small platforms in the great plaza to the north of the main pyramid, the **Plataforma de Venus B** (with stairways at each side guarded by feathered serpents), the **Plataforma de Águilas y Jaguares** (with relief carvings of eagles and jaguars holding human hearts), and the **Tzompantli**, from which human heads were hung. Around it are carved grinning stone skulls in horizontal rows, on all four sides.

The east side of the plaza is filled by the **Temple of the Warriors C**, another of the most imposing buildings at Chichén. This is another structure that you are no longer allowed to climb, to see the most famous of all the Chac-Mool sculptures at Chichén Itzá. The temple takes its name from the rows of columns at its front, carved with over 200 separate images of warriors, priests, and other figures of Chichén, each one different, almost like a 'picture gallery' of the city. The Warriors' columns form a corner with the plainer pillars of the huge quadrangle called the **Court of the Thousand Columns**, which probably served as a market and center for public business in Chichén Itzá. A sacbé-style path to the left of the Warriors temple leads through woods to the **Sacred Cenote D**, 60 meters (197ft) in diameter and 35 meters (115ft) deep.

The enormous **Juego de Pelota E** (96 meters/315ft long, 30 meters/98ft wide) or ball court of Chichén Itzá, completed in the year 864, is the largest ancient ball court in Mesoamerica, and on a vastly different scale from the

Chichén Itzá's El Osuario.

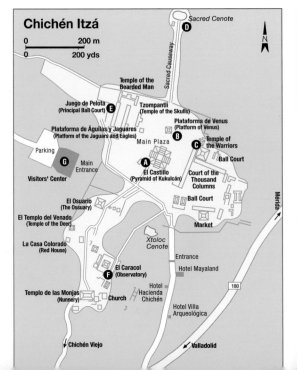

Chichén Itzá

| 0 | 200 m |
| 0 | 200 yds |

N

Sacred Cenote D

Sacred Causeway

Temple of the Bearded Man

Juego de Pelota E
(Principal Ball Court)

Tzompantli
(Temple of the Skulls)

Plataforma de Águilas y Jaguares
(Platform of the Jaguars and Eagles)

Plataforma de Venus
(Platform of Venus) B

Main Plaza

Temple of the Warriors C

Parking

Main Entrance A

Visitors' Center G

El Castillo
(Pyramid of Kukulcán)

Ball Court

Court of the Thousand Columns

El Osuario
(The Ossuary)

Ball Court

Mérida

El Templo del Venado
(Temple of the Deer)

Market

La Casa Colorado
(Red House)

Xtoloc Cenote

Entrance

El Caracol F
(Observatory)

Hotel Mayaland

Templo de las Monjas
(Nunnery)

Church

Hotel Hacienda Chichén

180

Hotel Villa Arqueológica

Chichén Viejo

Valladolid

courts usually found in Maya cities. On either side it has stone rings high on the walls, and it seems likely players had to get the solid latex ball through them to score.

There are several other structures around the site, particularly to the south of the great plaza. **El Osuario**, a 10-meter (33ft) tall pyramid that seems almost a 'model' for the later Castillo, contains an opulent tomb, the origin of its alternative name 'The High Priest's Grave'; **La Casa Colorada**, the Red House, was named for the red paint on its doorway mural. **El Caracol** , the fascinating observatory of Chichén Itzá, is a domed, circular tower shaped like a snail (hence its name), with roof slits through which astronomical observations could be made with remarkable precision. Farther south again, the complex the Spaniards called **Las Monjas** (the Nunnery) is purely Maya in style, with fantastically elaborate carved friezes, made-up stone Chac masks and mythological *bacabs*.

At the entrance to the ruins (daily 8am–5pm) is a large **Visitors' Center** ,

with stores, restaurants, and a museum. Chichén Itzá is inundated with tourist buses every day of the year, but regular buses from Mérida and Valladolid also pass the site or stop in the nearby village of **Piste**, on the highway 1.5km (2 miles) before the site, about US$3 by taxi.

VALLADOLID

Valladolid  (population 56,000), some 40km (25 miles) east of Chichén Itzá, was once a Maya center called Zaci, but was taken over by the Spanish in 1545. Its attractively calm feel today belies its dramatic history, as Valladolid was the scene of a historic massacre of most of its white citizens during the War of the Castes, the great Maya uprising that began nearby in 1847.

The city's colonial atmosphere is maintained by its well-preserved churches and mansions. The convent-church of **San Bernardino Sisal** is one of the oldest churches in the Yucatán (1552), and sits at the end of a row of colonial houses leading from the center, Calle 41-A or the *Calzada de los Frailes* (Street of the Friars). The **Museo**

Painted ceramic on display at Museo de San Roque in Valladolid.

Developments line the coast in the hotel strip, Cancún.

San Roque (daily 9am–6pm), just east of the plaza on Calle 41, has an engaging display of local relics. Valladolid still has its town *cenote*, **Cenote Zaci** (daily 8am–6pm) at the intersection of calles 36 and 39, which is fine for a refreshing dip, though its waters are a little murky. Nearby, however, there is one of the great must-sees of the Yucatán, **Cenote Dzitnup**, 7km (4.5 miles) west and well signposted off the highway.

CARIBBEAN COAST

Mexico's Caribbean coast is best known for **Cancún ❺**, the country's purpose-built global resort with its enormous hotels lining dazzling beaches, and the 130km (80-mile) strip of coast to the south now known as the *Riviera Maya*, with more fabulous beaches and resorts of different sizes running all the way down to the spectacular Maya ruins of Tulum. Tourists flood to Cancún and the Riviera year-round, drawn by their turquoise waters and white sands, the range of outdoor leisure activities, and glitzy nightlife. The sun-soaked coastline offers numerous attractions: tranquil

islands such as Isla Mujeres, fascinating archeological sites such as Tulum and Cobá, and pristine wildlife preserves such as Sian Ka'an in the south.

Modern Cancún was born in 1969, after the government agency Fonatur was set up to identify potential new tourist sites, draw master plans, and solicit investment. At first there was only jungle here, and a narrow sand strip enclosing the brackish Laguna de Nichupté. A tiny village at the northwestern end of the number 7-shaped island was transformed into a modern town to house all the workers needed to service the big hotels – the first of which opened in 1971 – and bridges connected the island to the mainland at both ends. Building has continued ever since, with ever-bigger hotels replacing the first ones of the 1970s. The permanent population is now around 700,000, and around 6 million visitors arrive every year.

CANCÚN'S HOTEL STRIP

For those in search of a lazily luxurious vacation, sunbathing on a soft

white beach and swimming in glorious turquoise waters (or your own pool), Cancún is tailor-made. Honeymooners are not the only people who check into a world-class hotel and rarely leave it. All the hotels are huge and, although next to each other, getting between them can be such a trek it hardly seems worthwhile to go visiting. Most hotels are self-contained, with restaurants, pools, beachfront, discos, lobby bars with soaring atriums, and shopping malls, and often operate on an all-inclusive plan. The hotel strip has just one long street, Boulevard Kukulcán, with no street numbers but kilometer indicators to help locate addresses.

These monumental resort hotels have been built in every conceivable architectural style, from the verdant lobby of the **Paradisus Cancún ⓐ** at Km 16.5, whose leafy plant tendrils drift over the balconies to create a lush tropical atmosphere, to the modernist Dreams Sands Cancún Resort & Spa at Km 9.5.

Just before the halfway point where the boulevard turns sharp right is the **Centro de Convenciones ⓑ** (Km 9),

the scene of concerts and other cultural events. Across the boulevard from the Convention Center is another very important part of Cancún, its main nightlife hub (at Km 9.5), around the **Forum by the Sea Mall ⓒ**, with huge franchises of chains like the Hard Rock Café. Outside, crowds stand in line every night outside the giant multi-space nightclubs – some of the world's biggest – like The City Nightclub and Coco Bongo, all offering a choice of music, light shows and live acts, non-stop energy, and fantastically efficient air conditioning.

Against all odds, some Mayan sites have survived: the major one, **El Rey ⓓ**, now stands beside the Hilton Hotel golf course. Most of El Rey dates from the Post-classic era of Maya civilization just before the Spanish Conquest.

DOWNTOWN CANCÚN

Travelers less addicted to glitz, or maybe on a budget, stay in Ciudad Cancún (downtown), in one of the inexpensive hotels near reliable Sanborns and the bus station where Avenida Uxmal

⊙ **Fact**

The bright lights of big box retailers and advertising hoardings can make parts of the Riviera Maya seem quite urban. Their fast growth has caught many creatures unawares: jaguars are still spotted wandering through the woods behind Playa del Carmen and pumas are occasionally seen in residential areas south of Cancun.

Party time at Coco Bongo.

🔍 TOURIST TRAP

The turnover of the region to tourism may have brought much-needed wealth – but at what cost?

Bathed with water so turquoise it seems to define the Caribbean dream, blessed with mile after mile of ravishing sandy beaches and boasting a climate that's utterly tropical, it is easy to understand the meteoric rise of Cancún from desert island to über-resort. Present-day visitors will probably have trouble imagining how pristine the area was back in the 1960s.

The statistics relating to Cancún and the *Riviera Maya* – a tag only dreamed up in 1998, but which has become an inescapable part of the scenery – defy the imagination. The growth of Cancún in 30 years from a few first hotels to a city of 700,000 is widely recognized; it is less well known that neighboring Playa del Carmen, which in 1995 could still be talked about as a sleepy off-Cancún retreat, has grown in population by more than 500 percent in little over 10 years.

Much is made of the idea that Cancún's creation came about through a rational, planned process, after Mexican officials concluded that the northern Quintana Roo coast was one of the most beautiful places on earth, and ideally located for easy access

Crowds on Playa del Carmen.

from North America and Europe. The explosive expansion of the Riviera has created new urban realities, in downtown Cancún – conceived as just a 'dormitory' for hotel workers, but now very much a real city – or the sprawl of Playa del Carmen. Tourism is now inseparable from the Yucatán, its economic motor. Few have not benefited in some way from it, from middle-class car-rental agents to Maya farmers who spend a few months each year working on construction sites – although the wealth from tourism is distributed extremely unequally.

The big potential problems of the Riviera – beyond the open sore of inequality – stem from its sheer, unceasing momentum. Many developers seem to work on the assumption that there are no limits to tourist growth. Many sneer at Cancún on taste grounds, but as a source of environmental damage it is less significant than the self-contained, all-inclusive resorts spreading down the coast that are blocking the flow of nutrients between the mangroves and the reefs, which is essential for their survival. And the Riviera's people – tourists and residents – produce vast amounts of garbage. There are now more than a dozen golf courses around the Riviera, although this is one of the worst places in the world to build one as they're fed a cocktail of chemicals that later sinks through the thin limestone subsoil and into the sea.

Many are trying to develop alternatives. For tourists, there are of course other ways of enjoying the region than going straight from the airport to an enclosed resort, such as diving or taking wildlife tours with small-scale operators. Many such operations are based around preserves and work closely with Maya communities, aiming to ensure a more equitable distribution of the tourist dollar.

Non-utopian environmentalists suggest there are three essential measures needed on the *Riviera Maya*: a solution to the garbage problem; a complete ban on new building within half a kilometer of the coast; and strict enforcement of proper, filtered drainage standards.

Many developers may only think in terms of their first five-year results, but the future of this coast is tied to its ability to supply its visitors with a beautiful natural environment, and allow its inhabitants, ultimately, to share in the benefits.

meets the main drag, tree-shaded Avenida Tulum. Explore the side streets for authentic restaurants. Between the **Monumento a la Historia de México** (Mexican History Monument) at the bus station end and the **Monumento Diálogo Norte–Sur** (dedicated to North–South dialogue) is everything a visitor might need: markets, shops, money-changers, hotels, bars, and tourist offices. Buses on the R-1 route, conveniently marked Hotel Zone or Downtown, run continually from downtown all the way along the wide boulevard, turning back at the southern end. Taxis are everywhere, and because of the distances in Cancún, they are often indispensable. Tariffs are worked out on a zonal system, with rates around downtown about US$5, while downtown to Km 9.5 (for nightlife) is around US$15.

ISLA MUJERES

A very different atmosphere can still be found on **Isla Mujeres ⑥**, about 8km (5 miles) long, with only two main roads and nowhere more than 1km (0.6 miles) wide. Some have suggested the name 'Island of Women' derives from 17th-century pirates who kept their women sequestered here, but it was actually given by some of the first Spaniards who arrived on the island because of the many female idols they saw honoring Ixchel, the Maya goddess of fertility. At the island's southern tip are the tiny ruins of the Temple of Ixchel.

Passenger ferries to Isla Mujeres run from Puerto Juárez just north of Cancún, operated by the Magana and Ultramar companies; both have boats every half-hour, usually 6am–12.30am (from Isla, 5am–midnight). The trip takes 20 minutes. Car ferries run from Punta Sam, about 8km (5 miles) north of Cancún, with five boats a day 8am–8.15pm (from Isla, 6.30am–7.15pm).

Many of today's Isla visitors spend their time on the compact town beach, **Playa Norte**, where the water is very shallow, or snorkeling a couple of miles south in **El Garrafón Reef Park** (winter daily 10am–5pm, summer until 6pm), a natural rock pool. Taxis run all around the island, but the most popular way to get around Isla is by renting a golf cart.

Playa Norte on Isla Mujeres.

Isla Mujeres is the best scuba-diving and snorkeling center close to Cancún. At **Los Manchones**, a reef off the southern tip, crystal-clear waters flow around a 3-meter (10ft) bronze crucifix, placed there in 1994 to mark the 140th anniversary of the island becoming a township. The **Cave of the Sleeping Sharks**, in deep waters off the southeast coast, is so called because sharks lie there immobile for hours at a time, a rare phenomenon explained by the fact that an underground river emerges into the sea there.

ISLA HOLBOX

Just around Cabo Catoche, the meeting point of the Caribbean and the Gulf of Mexico, is **Isla Holbox** ❼. A narrow strip of mangrove and beach, Holbox has just one village, with sand streets and very few motor vehicles – golf carts and bicycles are the main traffic. Along the beach there are several laidback, palm-roofed hotels, from simple to luxurious. Idyllically relaxing, Holbox is also a wonderful place for fly-fishing, birdwatching, or snorkeling,

Island style at Hotel Las Palapas on Isla Holbox.

especially around **Isla de Pájaros** in Laguna de Yalaháo, between Holbox and the mainland. Holbox also has a special attraction: the gathering off Cabo Catoche, every year from May to September, of large numbers of whale sharks, the world's largest fish, which mass to feed on a rich soup of tunny fish spawn and plankton that the sea serves up at that time of year.

To get to Holbox you must first get to the little port of Chiquilá, 160km (110 miles) or a 2.5-hour drive from Cancún, from where passenger ferries leave about every two hours.

COZUMEL

South of Isla Mujeres is the much larger island of **Cozumel** ❽, 47km (30 miles) long with a lighthouse at each end, and 16km (10 miles) wide. Cozumel was another island that was a place of pilgrimage for Maya Yucatán in the Postclassic era, with several shrines dedicated to Ixchel. The principal relic of Maya Cozumel is the site of **San Gervasio** (daily Sept–May 8am–4pm, June–Aug until 5pm), in the middle of

the island. Similar in style to Tulum and other Post-Classic Maya sites, it is quite widely spread out, so exploring involves an enjoyable walk through the woods, often full of flowers and birds. Among the principal structures is the **Chichan Nah** complex, probably the residence of the chief lord of Cozumel.

Cozumel was actually discovered for tourism before Cancún even existed, particularly by divers and fishermen drawn by the riches of its reefs. Things remained fairly low-key, however, until Cancún took off: today Cozumel welcomes about 400,000 visitors a year, especially from cruise ships. Frequent passenger ferries run back and forth between the island and **Playa del Carmen**, and there is a less frequent car ferry service from **Puerto Calica**, just to the south.

There are over 20 reefs along Cozumel's west coast, providing dives of every degree of difficulty. In many places you can also see a great deal just with a snorkel, or you can observe the underwater wonderland from the comfort of glass-bottomed boats. Nearby are some of Cozumel's best beaches, such as popular **Playa San Francisco**, which stretches for 3km (2 miles). Scuba-divers favor reefs a little farther offshore, such as the famous **Palancar Reef**, often filmed by Cousteau, **San Francisco**, or **Santa Rosa**, known for its spectacular wall dives.

The island's only town, **San Miguel de Cozumel** on the west coast, is spread alongside the 14-block waterfront Avenida Rafael Melgar. Local musicians perform on Sunday evenings in the central Plaza del Sol, surrounded by restaurant terraces. The **Museo de la Isla de Cozumel** (daily 9am–5pm), on the waterfront in a former hotel, is a charming little museum with exhibits on Maya Cozumel, pirates, hurricanes, the local flora and fauna with information in Spanish and English.

The east side of the island is deserted aside from beaches and, at the southern tip, the **Faro Celarain** lighthouse, surrounded by a nature preserve. The northeast side of Cozumel is virtually empty, with only a dirt road to the Molas lighthouse at the island's tip.

ALONG THE RIVIERA MAYA

On the mainland, Highway 307, the 'spine' of the Riviera, runs south from Cancún behind the coast, usually about 2–3km (1–2 miles) inland. At many points, elaborate gateways announce the entrances to all-inclusive resort complexes, while at others side roads turn off to more open communities. **Puerto Morelos ❾**, 36km (22 miles) from Cancún, was the only village on this coast before tourism started up, and is a remarkable survivor with a small-town plaza right on the beach, with playing kids and fishermen.

Back on the highway, more side roads turn off to white-sand beaches, nearly all of which now have some building on them. The exquisite **Playa del Secreto** is backed by opulent beach houses. The beaches around the 'bend' in the coast at **Punta Bete**

A Gonzalo Guerrero painting at Museo de la Isla de Cozumel.

Tourists join a snorkeling tour off Cozumel.

A beach hotel in Playa del Carmen.

Souvenir shopping in tourist mecca, Playa del Carmen.

were until a few years ago only reachable by very bad dirt tracks, but most have now been paved and occupied by upscale hotels. A little to the south are perhaps the two most luxurious resort complexes on the Riviera, the giant **Mayakoba**, with five hotels and a PGA-standard golf course within the same carefully landscaped area, and the **Hacienda Tres Ríos**.

PLAYA DEL CARMEN

About 68km (42 miles) south of Cancún, **Playa del Carmen** ⓾ is an even more astonishing phenomenon than the capital of the Riviera itself. In 1980 it had about 1,000 residents; now it has more than 150,000. Then it had only one sand street, parallel to the beach; this is now the Avenida Quinta (5th Avenue), the pedestrianized main thoroughfare that links up the many new areas of Playa and provides tourists with a day and night promenade, lined with restaurants, bars, shops, and hotels.

The second hub of the Riviera, Playa del Carmen still has a different style from Cancún. Since it began as a real

town by a beach, most of its attractions and services are within walking distance of each other rather than strung out over kilometers like the Cancún Hotel Zone. Its streets are conducive to strolling, whether you enjoy the crowds on the Quinta or wandering along the more tranquil avenues elsewhere, picking out a restaurant that looks attractive.

Playa's hotels cover a complete range, from backpacker favorites through charming small lodges to chic boutique hotels and resorts. There are also several excellent dive and snorkel operators based in the town. Cozumel ferries run frequently from a dock right on the town plaza.

The biggest resort hotels are in the Playacar development on the south side of the town, which also has an 18-hole golf course, condos, and even some Maya ruins, relics of what was once a departure point for pilgrimages to Cozumel. Just down the coast is **Xcaret** (tel: 998 879 3077; www.xcaret.com; 8.30am–9.30pm), one of the Riviera's most popular attractions, where a natural lagoon – once a Maya harbor – has

been made into a 'snorkel park' with an artificial underground river, and surrounded by an ecological preserve with a zoo of local wildlife, an orchid farm, butterfly garden, aquarium, an open-air theater, and several restaurants. Buses are also provided direct from Cancún (call for times, tel: 998 883 3143), and most visitors stay until night.

PUERTO AVENTURAS TO XEL-HÁ

Puerto Aventuras, 20km (12 miles) from Playa del Carmen, is a purpose-built, Mediterranean-style resort village of hotels and villas created around a lavish marina and another beautiful beach. Just beyond is the series of seven bays known as **Xpu-Ha**, which are among the Riviera coast's greatest beauties.

On the inland side of the highway near Xpu-Ha there are several *cenotes* (natural sinkholes) that are open to visitors for snorkeling and swimming. **Cenote Kantun-Chi** (daily 9am–5pm) is a low-key 'ecopark' with four gorgeous *cenotes*, a forest walk, and a little zoo.

The clear waters of the Yal-Ku lagoon (where the Spanish ship *Matancero* sank in 1741) flow into the sea at the northern end of the resort town of **Akumal ⓫**, set around some of the most beautiful bays on the coast, above all the arching **Media Luna** ('Half Moon') bay on the north side. While mostly as new as Puerto Aventuras, Akumal also has a real village at its center, and has a more relaxed feel, with hotels, villas, and condos spread along the long beaches. Akumal is Maya for 'place of the turtles,' and the beaches here and at Xcacel just to the south are among the region's most important turtle-breeding beaches, where from around May to August, green, hawksbill, and loggerhead turtles crawl up onto the sands to lay their eggs. The **Centro Ecológico Akumal** (tel: 984 875 9095; www.ceakumal.org), a conservation and research center that organizes 'turtle watch' trips at night in the summer season, and is a good source of information.

Easy snorkeling is the biggest attraction at **Xel-Há ⓬** (tel: 998 884 7165; www.xelha.com; daily 8.30am–6pm), just beyond Akumal, where freshwater underground rivers mingle with the ocean in a natural lagoon at the center of an ecological park run by the same organization as Xcaret. An expensive daily admission ticket includes snorkel rental, and swimming with dolphins and bicycle rides through the surrounding forest.

The southern Riviera is the most important area in the world for cave diving, with the *cenote* entrances to several spectacular cavern systems such as the celebrated **Dos Ojos**, 2km (1.5 miles) south of Xel-Há, which stretches for at least 61km (38 miles) under the ground – though it may well be longer.

TULUM

Some 27km (17 miles) south of Akumal is the clifftop site of **Tulum ⓭**. Originally called Zama, which means 'dawn,' due to its location facing the sunrise, Tulum was the largest of the communities that grew up along the coastal trade route

Snorkelers enjoy the tropical weather and waters at Xcaret.

in the Post-Classic era, between about 1300 and the Spanish Conquest.

Tulum is estimated to have had a population of only about 600 at the time of conquest. The priestly and noble classes perhaps resided within the stone walls that still flank the 6.5-hectare (16-acre) core of the site on three sides, with the rest of the population outside. A supreme lord or *Halach Uinich* headed a council of the leading families, which collected taxes, raised armies, and negotiated alliances with neighboring communities.

Tulum's fortress, if this is what it was, sits on dramatic limestone cliffs above powdery white beaches, giving it the most spectacular location of any Maya ruin. The perimeter wall has five entrances and the remains of what may have been watchtowers. The **Temple of the Frescos**, a two-story structure with columns on the bottom level and a much smaller room on top, has a fresco of human figures in a style that suggests central Mexican influence, and masks of the rain god Chac around the corners of the facade.

To the left of the platform in front of El Castillo is the **Temple of the Diving God**, which has a relief of this strange personage – thought, logically, to be related to fishing – in a relatively good state of preservation over the door. The carvings above doorways are protected with *palapa* (thatched) canopies.

Tulum's most imposing building is naturally **El Castillo** (The Castle), fronted by serpent columns, which was built on top of two earlier pyramids, and probably served as a watchtower and lighthouse as well as a temple. When Grijalva's Spanish expedition first saw it in 1518, they recorded that a flame was kept burning here day and night. Sadly – as is now the case with most structures at Tulum – you can no longer climb up the Castillo to enjoy the view, but must admire it from behind wire cordons.

TULUM BEACH AND SIAN KA'AN

Tulum is also one of the finest of all the Riviera's beaches, stretching 11km (7 miles) from the ruins down to the entrance gate to the Sian Ka'an preserve. Tulum beach was once the

Ruins overlooking the beach at Tulum.

⊘ CENOTES

The elusiveness of water has always marked life in the Yucatán. There are no surface rivers anywhere north of Champotón, on the west coast, and the Belize border on the east. Rainwater sinks straight through the rock, and the Yucatán is honeycombed with caves and sinkholes (*cenotes*), including the longest underwater cave systems in the world. These majestic water-filled caverns and deep, open are pools formed when the limestone surface collapses, exposing water beneath. *Cenotes* and the Yucatán's caverns are magical places, and have always had great significance for the Maya, particularly associated with the rain god Chac. At his first sight of a *cenote*, early explorer John L. Stephens raved about 'a spectacle of extraordinary beauty...a bathing place for Diana and her nymphs.'

laid-back, bohemian destination on the Riviera, the foremost home of the palm-roofed beach *cabaña* or hut. However, since its beauty has been recognized by a much broader range of people, the area has gone jetset, with bikini boot camps, yoga studios, and eco-chic hotels that are pushing the backpackers out. Nevertheless, it is still possible to find wonderfully mellow spots along the beach for some thorough relaxation. Some local 'traditions' are maintained, such as that Tulum beach has no permanent electricity, but most hotels now have solar power or their own generators functioning for at least part of the day.

Tulum village, just inland, was one of the most traditional Maya communities in northern Quintana Roo until the 1990s, but is now an untidy little town developing fast to service the burgeoning tourist trade.

South of Tulum, the beach road continues south to enter the 500,000-hectare (1.25 million-acre) **Reserva de la Biosfera de Sian Ka'an ⑭**, a vast, scarcely inhabited expanse of tropical forest, mangrove swamps, reef, and wetland lagoons, which nurtures 300 species of bird and an abundance of such animals as jaguars, pumas, white tail deer, crocodiles, tapirs, and monkeys. Day tours, including boat trips through the lagoons, are run from Tulum by the **Centro Ecológico Sian Ka'an** (tel: 984 871 2499). The access road is unpaved from partway down Tulum beach and in the preserve, and often has basin-sized potholes, particularly after rain.

COBÁ

From the main crossroads in Tulum, an almost straight, monotonous road leads to Cobá, 45km (28 miles) to the northwest, toward Valladolid. There are a few villages and several *cenotes* on the way. Many examples of Maya homes can still be seen, constructed in the traditional way on a base of stone with upright poles (Y-shaped at the top) supporting branches covered with palm leaves. These roofs shift and shake during hurricanes but, unlike some more solid structures, usually stay in place. Maya houses stay cool, too, aided by

Cobá's ruins.

always-open front and back doorways and a breeze blowing between the poles.

The pyramids and temples at **Cobá** ⑮ (daily 8am–6pm) are widely dispersed around the forest, so exploring the site involves a fairly long walk, surrounded by greenery and the sounds of tropical birds (bicycles and tricycle-taxis can be rented at the entrance to make things a little easier). En route you might be able to admire the delicate flights of butterflies and orioles. Toucans and snakes are rarely encountered here, but crocodiles are quite easy to spot in the lakes – so resist the urge for a dip.

CAMPECHE AND CHIAPAS

Filling the southwestern corner of the Yucatán, the state of Campeche is the least-known part of the peninsula, and still devotes as much energy to its fishing and oil industries as to tourism. The main draws here are the magnificent Maya sites – some still only partly uncovered – and the highly atmospheric walled city of Campeche. Champotón marks the site of the Spaniards' first landing on Mexican soil (after their

Climbing the Nohoch Mul pyramid at Cobá.

brief landing on Isla Mujeres), under Francisco Hernández de Córdoba, on March 20, 1517.

The adjacent state of Chiapas to the south has a huge allure thanks to its superb Maya sites: Bonampak, Yaxchilán and, above all, Palenque, with graceful temple pyramids in a jungle setting. In contrast to the pancake-flat Yucatán, much of Chiapas is covered in forested mountains, with crystalline rivers and sparkling waterfalls gushing down steep gorges. It is home to over a million Maya, from eight different main groups, each retaining its own culture and language.

ON THE HIGHWAY INTO CAMPECHE

Heading west into Campeche from Chetumal, Highway 186 traverses the base of the Yucatán Peninsula. This hot, humid region has been partly repopulated around the Highway, which is now an important link between central Mexico and the *Riviera Maya*; around 1,500 years ago, this area was one of the heartlands of ancient Maya civilization. Some of the sites, such as **Xpuhil** and **Becán**, are just off the road, while

⊘ A CLASSIC TRAVELOGUE

John L. Stephens, North American explorer and travel writer, and his colleague, the English artist and architect Frederick Catherwood, came to Central America in 1839, inspired by an edition they had found of Captain del Río's expedition to Palenque in 1786. This, in Stephens's blunt prose, had 'roused our curiosity.'

Over the next three years, the two men traveled throughout the region, overcoming illnesses and the threats posed by ongoing civil wars. They visited dozens of Maya cities, including Chichén Itzá, Palenque, Quiriguá, and Copán, and described many places never seen before by outsiders, such as Kabah, Sayil, and Tulum. Stephens and Catherwood were captivated by these fabulous sites, and were among the first to recognize that their creators had to have been the region's indigenous Maya inhabitants, and not some Egyptians or Greeks who had somehow wandered across the Atlantic. In 1841, Stephens published *Incidents of Travel in Central America, Chiapas and Yucatán*, beautifully illustrated with Catherwood's finely detailed lithographs, and after a second trip the pair produced *Incidents of Travel in Yucatán* in 1843. Both are still in print today, as true travel 'classics.' They never did manage to decipher the glyphs, but they did bring the culture to the attention of the outside world, attracting further study that continues unabated today.

the giant city of **Calakmul** lies hidden in the forest far to the south.

Roads have been built to the most important sites, and much of southern Campeche state is within the **Reserva de la Biosfera de Calakmul**, extending north and south of the Highway, and the largest rainforest preserve in Mexico. This forest is home to monkeys, armadillos, tapirs, jaguars, and many other kinds of wild cat, so as you visit the ruins – especially Calakmul itself – you are likely to see plenty of animals as well. The preserve's jungles merge with Guatemala's Maya Biosphere Reserve and Belize's Río Bravo Conservation Area to form a huge, vitally important, subtropical forest.

The most important site in the region is **Calakmul** ⑯ (daily 8am–5pm), in the southern portion of the Calakmul Biosphere Reserve, 60km (37 miles) down a winding road that turns south off Highway 186 52km (32 miles) west of Xpuhil. At the turn-off you must pay an admission fee to the Biosphere Reserve, and there is a separate entry charge to the ruins. The way there is a lonely drive – keep a look out for flocks of wild turkeys and toucans in the treetops – and bring drinking water and insect repellent. The immense site of Calakmul is the largest known city in the Maya world, comprising over 6,000 structures, including Structures 1 and 2, vast Maya pyramids, both around 50 meters (165ft) high. The city dates back to the 5th century BC, but its prosperity really took off in the early Classic era, from AD 350.

CAMPECHE

Traveling north 150km (93 miles) from Escárcega brings you to Campeche's state capital. Founded in 1540 by Francisco de Montejo on the site of a Maya chiefdom called Ah Kin Pech, **Campeche** ⑰ suffered for 200 years from attacks from pirates attracted by the wealthy galleons that set sail from here for Spain. This led the Spanish crown to encircle the city with massive fortifications, built between 1685 and 1704. Nearly 3.5 meters (8ft) thick in places, the walls were originally 2,536 meters (8,320ft) long and stretched along today's Avenida Circuito de los Baluartes, making

Colorful streets in Campeche city.

Campeche one of the few fortress cities in the Americas, a hexagonal stronghold guarded by eight towers. Faced with the now impregnable port, the pirates redirected their energies elsewhere.

The **Puerta del Mar** (Sea Gate) is a natural beginning to an exploration of the Old City. Calle 59 runs right through the Old City, a Unesco World Heritage Site from there to the **Puerta de Tierra** (Land Gate), which now contains an entertaining museum dedicated to pirates, the **Museo de la Piratería** (Mon–Fri 9am–5pm, Sat–Sun 9am–5pm).

THE PLAZA PRINCIPAL

The hub of Old Campeche is its **Plaza Principal** Ⓐ. **Baluarte de la Soledad** Ⓑ, on the coast near the Puerta del Mar, hosts the **Museo de Arquitectura Maya** (daily 9.30am–5.30pm), with fine carved stelae and other relics from Maya sites around Campeche state. On the west side of the square, **Casa Seis** Ⓒ (daily 9am–9pm; free) is a 19th-century merchant's house with lovely shaded patios that has been beautifully restored and now houses the main tourist office.

The Fuerte de San Miguel Museum in Campeche is home to many important Mayan artifacts.

On the opposite side of the plaza, the **Catedral de la Concepción** Ⓓ is topped with twin towers, flying buttresses, and a dome. Campeche's other interesting architecture includes the 1540 church of **San Francisco**, some 20 minutes' walk from the center northeast along the seafront; and the **Mansión Carvajal** Ⓔ, on calles 10 and 53, once the home of a wealthy *hacienda* owner, which has undulating Moorish arches, checkered floors, and a sweeping staircase.

The lively market at calles 18 and 51, where Avenida Gobernadores begins, is near the **Baluarte de San Pedro** Ⓕ, which houses a small **crafts museum** (Tue–Sat 9am–8pm, Sun 9am–1pm; free). Not far away, the rebuilt **Baluarte de Santiago** Ⓖ encircles the **Jardín Botánico X'much Haltún** (daily 9am–9pm), filled with tropical plants.

THE FORTRESS MUSEUMS

Campeche's two biggest museums occupy two dramatic Spanish forts on hills north and south of the city, built from 1779 to 1801. The **Museo de Cultura Maya** (Tue–Sat 9.30am–7pm,

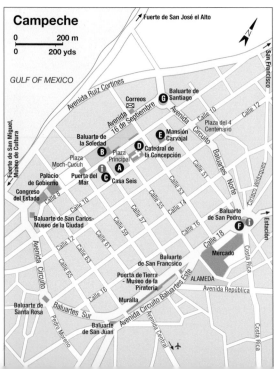

Sun 9am–2pm) in the **Fuerte de San Miguel**, above the coastal avenue south of the city, holds one of the most important collections of Maya artifacts in Mexico, its greatest treasures the jade funeral masks discovered at Calakmul in the 1990s (although these are often on loan to other museums).The best way to get to the museum is by taxi, but a special tourist bus called 'El Guapo' runs from the Plaza Principal.

One of Campeche's main attractions, the **Fuerte de San José el Alto**, north of the city, is equally imposing on its massive hill, but the museum it contains, the **Museo de Barcos y Armas** (Tue–Sun 9.30am–5.30pm) is less exciting, with exhibits on colonial and maritime history. A tourist bus runs there a few times each day.

CHIAPAS

Leaving the Yucatán Peninsula proper, the state of Chiapas to the south provides an adventurous extension to many visitors' itineraries, to explore some fascinating Maya settlements and ancient ruins deep in the forest.

PALENQUE

Looming out of the dense tropical undergrowth of Chiapas, 355km (220 miles) from Campeche, the Maya ruins at **Palenque** ⓲ (daily 8am–5pm) are for many visitors the highlight of their trip to Mexico. The complex site inspires awe, and yet what one sees today represents just a fraction of the incredible complex of chambers, terraces, staircases, temples, palaces, and other structures that graced Palenque at its peak in the 7th century AD.

The name Palenque simply means palisade in Spanish; its original name was perhaps Lakam-ha or 'Big Water,' although it was also known just as Bak or 'the Bone Kingdom.' It was the largest and most powerful Maya city in the Río Usumacinta region from around AD 400, but went into a precipitate decline around 800, when its ruling dynasty soon collapsed. It was the first Maya site to be investigated in the modern era, when Spanish priests began to explore it in the 1770s.

A battlement over the Gulf of Mexico shoreline at Fuerte de San Miguel.

THE RUINS

Concealing its treasures almost until you stumble into them, the wall of jungle divides beyond the entrance to reveal the two most important and magnificent structures of the site: the pagoda-like tower complex of the palace and, to its right, the **Temple of Inscriptions**, a superb example of Classic Maya architecture, crowned with the characteristic roof comb.

The temple is in fact a pyramid with a temple on top, which, at 26 meters (85ft) high, dominates the whole site. The hieroglyphic inscriptions on the walls – giving a detailed list of the kings of Palenque with their dates – give the temple its name. In 1952, Mexican archeologist Alberto Ruz Lhuillier discovered a sealed stone passageway that led to a burial chamber 25 meters (82ft) down, at the center of the pyramid. It contained the tomb of King Pakal (ruled AD 615–83), greatest of all Palenque's rulers, wearing a mosaic jade death mask with shell and obsidian eye insets, and his body richly adorned with jade jewelry.

Pakal's tomb and the rest of the Temple of Inscriptions are no longer open to visitors. However, in the site museum (by the entry road to the site, and included in the ticket) there is a full-size reconstruction of the tomb, the **Sala Tumba de Pakal**. Nearby, in the smaller **Temple XIII**, one can now visit the **Tomb of the Red Queen**, a three-chamber tomb where a sarcophogus of a woman was discovered in 1994, stained with unusually large amounts of the red cinnabar pigment that was used by the Maya to symbolize rebirth. She is believed to have been Pakal's queen, Lady Tzakbu Ajaw.

Almost directly opposite the pyramid is the **Palace**, a complex of buildings with courtyards, passages, and tunnels, arranged around a unique, four-story, square-sided tower. The walls are embellished with finely detailed stucco panels, and its grassy courtyards have low walls decorated with hieroglyphics and impressive sculptures of giant human figures.

There is a **ball court** and another group of lesser temples in a grassy clearing to the north of the Palace,

The Temple of Inscriptions at Palenque.

called the **North Group**. To the east are three important temples known as the **Cross Group**. All were built during the rule of Pakal's son Kan B'alam II (684–702), in order to glorify himself, his father, and their dynasty. The imposing Temple of the Cross is the largest of the three, with a frieze inside its main temple showing Kan B'alam II receiving the attributes of kingship from his father. Many spectacular discoveries have been made within the last 25 years in the group of buildings just south of the Cross Plaza, known as the **South Group**.

The site itself lies about 8km (5 miles) from the town of Palenque, from where there are regular *combi* minibuses to the ruins. The museum is about 1km (0.6 miles) back from the site on the entry road, but you can also walk there from the main site, down a beautiful jungle path. The forest around Palenque is a national park, so visitors must pay a small park entry fee as well as the ruins admission charge.

BONAMPAK AND YAXCHILÁN

The other two most important Maya sites in Chiapas, Bonampak and Yaxchilán, are located deep in the jungle near the Río Usumacinta, which marks the international border with Guatemala.

Bonampak ⓲, 140km (87 miles) to the southwest, is reached from Palenque via a good paved road parallel to the Usumacinta valley. Take the turning at San Javier for Bonampak (13km/8 miles), stopping at the Lacandón village of Lacanjá after 9km (5.5 miles). Bonampak is in a Lacandón-run preserve, and only their vehicles are allowed to take you to the site. Lacanjá is also the best place to stay in the area, with several small *campamentos* of cabañas near the sparkling Lacanjá River. Bonampak was only 'discovered' by outsiders in 1946, and its vividly colored murals are the only large Maya paintings that have survived.

An essential part of the same trip is the journey to the larger Maya site of **Yaxchilán ⓴**, spectacularly located on lofty slopes above the Usumacinta. To get there you must continue 20km (12.5 miles) past San Javier and then turn down a 19km (12-mile) road to the river village of Frontera Corozal, where local *lanchero* (boatmen's) co-operatives offer boat trips to the ruins, which take about an hour each way. Agencies in Palenque offer tours to both sites.

One of Mexico's most enjoyable and picturesque colonial towns, **San Cristóbal de las Casas** is located at an altitude of over 2,100 meters (6,900ft) and enjoys a beautifully temperate climate. It is highly popular with visitors, and has a cosmopolitan array of restaurants, cafes, and boutiques, as well as some wonderful historic hotels. San Cristóbal is especially atmospheric around the central plaza, which is framed by elegant buildings, including a stately Baroque cathedral. **Na Bolom** (daily 10am–5pm, tours in English at 4.30pm), a beautiful 19th-century house with surrounding gardens, is another prime attraction. Tour operators organize trips to the region's indigenous villages and natural places of interest.

A mural at Bonampak.

Semuc Champey, Guatemala.

Lago de Atitlán at Panajachel, with Volcan Toliman in the background.

GUATEMALA

From ancient Maya pyramids and beautifully preserved colonial architecture to mighty mountains and sparkling lakes, Guatemala is rich in culture and offers everything for a memorable adventure.

Guatemala is both the ancient and modern heart of the Maya world. More than 6 million Maya live in Guatemala, forming around 50 percent of the country's population, and it is their dynamic, unique cultural tradition that is the nation's most distinctive feature. Guatemala is one of the least Latin of all Latin American countries – a land where sophisticated pre-Conquest traditions, language, religion, culture, and dress still endure over 500 years after the Spanish first arrived on the continent.

For such a small country, Guatemala combines a multiplicity of landscapes. Vast tropical forests cover the Petén, a sparsely populated northern region rich in wildlife and studded with the ruins of dozens of ancient Maya cities. The east of the country has an extreme juxtaposition of geophysical systems: cloud forests, gorge systems, and a humid Caribbean coastline. The southern swathe of the nation is mountainous and crowned by volcanoes. In the beautiful highlands, the rural population is mostly indigenous, and life revolves around traditions that have evolved since the Conquest. Though most Maya are nominally either Catholic or belong to Evangelical churches, ancient Maya spiritual beliefs are integrated into highland worship and fiesta celebrations. Maize remains a key crop – it also retains a sacred status, since in Maya

mythology man was created from corn.

Guatemala has been the center of power in Central America since Preclassic Maya times, when the great trading cities of the region, El Mirador and Kaminaljuyú, first emerged. Tikal later dominated the Classic period. When the Spanish conquistadors arrived from Mexico in 1523 they established their first capital in Guatemala before moving down through the rest of the isthmus. The colonial capital of Antigua was one of the glorious cities of the Americas, ranking alongside Mexico City and Lima

◉ Main Attractions

Guatemala City
Antigua
Lago de Atitlán
Panajachel
Chichicastenango
Santa Cruz del Quiché
Quetzaltenango
Cobán
The Petén and Tikal

Maps on pages 136, 141, 144, 162

Traditionally dressed Guatemalans.

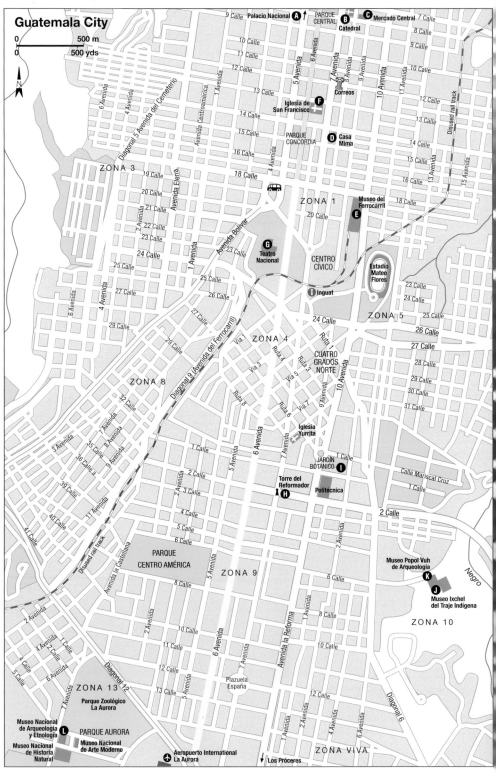

Guatemala City

0   500 m
0   500 yds

N

ZONA 3

ZONA 1

ZONA 5

ZONA 4

ZONA 8

CUATRO GRADOS NORTE

ZONA 9

ZONA 13

ZONA 10

ZONA VIVA

9 Calle   Palacio Nacional **A**
PARQUE CENTRAL **B**
Catedral
Mercado Central **C**   7 Calle
8 Calle
10 Calle
9 Calle
11 Calle
10 Calle
12 Calle
Correos
13 Calle   12 Calle
Iglesia de San Francisco **F**
14 Calle   13 Calle
15 Calle   Casa Mima **D**
PARQUE CONCORDIA   14 Calle
16 Calle   15 Calle
18 Calle   16 Calle
19 Calle
Museo del Ferrocarril   18 Calle
20 Calle
21 Calle   20 Calle
22 Calle   **E**
23 Calle
24 Calle
Teatro Nacional **G**
25 Calle
CENTRO CÍVICO
Estadio Mateo Flores
26 Calle
27 Calle
i Inguat
23 Calle
24 Calle
29 Calle   24 Calle   25 Calle
26 Calle
27 Calle
28 Calle
29 Calle
30 Calle
31 Calle
Iglesia Yurrita
JARDÍN BOTÁNICO **I**
Calle Mariscal Cruz
Torre del Reformador **H**
Politécnica   1 Calle
2 Calle
1 Calle
2 Calle
3 Calle
4 Calle
5 Calle
6 Calle
Museo Popol Vuh de Arqueología **K**
PARQUE CENTRO AMÉRICA
8 Calle
Museo Ixchel del Traje Indígena **J**
10 Calle
11 Calle
12 Calle
T3 Calle
Plazuela España
12 Calle
Parque Zoológico La Aurora
Museo Nacional de Arqueología y Etnología **L**
PARQUE AURORA
Museo Nacional de Historia Natural
Museo Nacional de Arte Moderno
Aeropuerto International La Aurora
Los Próceres

Diagonal 5 Avenida del Cementerio
Avenida Centroamérica
Avenida Elena
Avenida Bolívar
Diagonal 9 (Avenida del Ferrocarril)
Disused rail track
Avenida la Castellana
Diagonal 12
Avenida la Reforma
Diagonal 6
Negro
CUATRO GRADOS NORTE

as one of the greatest in the continent. Today, Guatemala is the most populous of the seven Central American nations, with a population of around 15 million.

GUATEMALA CITY

A vortex of humanity and belching traffic, **Guatemala City** ❶, colloquially known as 'Guate,' is in many ways everything that the rest of the country is not. The streets of the central zone are crumbling, but increasingly, parts of the historic center are being revitalized. In the more upscale suburbs in the south of the city the atmosphere is very different, but even here the bougainvillea flowers draped over residential homes are intertwined with razor wire, put up to deter intruders. Nevertheless, if you want to get a real flavor of the complexities (and inequalities) of the country, then a day or two in 'Guate' is essential. In fact, for many travelers, Guate's grit and noise has a special appeal, particularly as a uniquely urban counterpoint to the country's natural and cultural riches.

Stroll the Parque Central – the emotional and geographic heart of the city – and the store-lined La Sexta (6a avenida, or 6th Avenue) in the historic center, and then mingle with the Guatemalan elite in the Zona Viva, a cosmopolitan mix of restaurants, bars, and clubs. Guatemala City also has a variety of top-notch museums. And the climate, as the city is at 1,500 meters (4,900ft), is also benign, and never gets oppressively hot.

Getting around is fairly straightforward because almost everything of interest is in five zones: Zona 1 in the north of the city, Zona 4 in the center, and Zonas 9, 10, and 13 in the south. In common with most Latin American capitals, Guatemala City is organized according to the Spanish grid system: all calles run east to west and all avenidas north to south.

ZONA 1 AND PARQUE CENTRAL

The Parque Central is considered both the heart of the city and the nation; indeed, all distances are measured from here. It is surrounded by some of the most historic and prestigious edifices in the country. Presiding over the northern side is the monumental bulk of the **Palacio Nacional** Ⓐ (tel: 2253 0748; daily

Looking out over Zona 10, or 'Zona Viva,' in Guatemala City.

⊘ SAFETY IN THE CITY

Guatemala City can present security concerns for travelers, and you should always take basic precautions to minimize the risk of being robbed: keep your valuables (including smartphones) out of sight. Though Zona 1 looks run down, it is considered safe to explore during daylight hours and in the early evening. The Zona Viva (in Zona 10) is a spirited upscale area, and the great number of cafés and restaurants here make it fine to explore on foot, except perhaps very late at night. The Transmetro bus network is a safe, fast way to get around the city, but after 8pm or so stick to taxis – Amarillo (tel: 2470 1515) is a reliable company with metered cabs.

10am–4pm), designed by the architect Rafael Pérez de León during the Ubico dictatorship between 1939 and 1943. The Palacio contained the presidential offices until 1998; if you visit you can take a guided tour (in English and Spanish). The sober grey-green stone exterior belies an eclectically decorative interior of Moorish and neoclassical influences. Giant stairwell murals by Alfredo Gálvez Suárez depict an idealized history of Guatemala. Don't miss the two attractive Mudéjar (Moorish) inner courtyards planted with palm trees.

Dominating the east side of the Parque Central is the city **Catedral** Ⓑ (daily 7am–noon, 3–7pm; free), constructed in a mixture of Baroque and neoclassical styles between 1782 and 1809, though its blue-tiled dome and towers were added later, in 1868. Around the corner from the Catedral is the **Mercado Central** Ⓒ (daily 6am–7pm), with a huge variety of textiles, leather goods, basketry, and other handicrafts, as well as food stands on the middle floor serving up a range of *caldos* (stews), fresh produce, seafood, meat, and snacks. The salmon-pink Correos

Discover Guatemala's rail history at the Museo del Ferrocarril.

(post office), on 12 Calle and 7 Avenida, looms just south of the Mercado, with a great arch that spans 12 Calle. A block south of is **Casa Mima** Ⓓ (8 Avenida; tel: 2253 4020, www.casamima.org; Mon–Sat 10am–5pm), a beautifully preserved 19th century townhouse with fine period furniture and furnishings. Guatemala City's former train station has been converted into the excellent **Museo del Ferrocarril** Ⓔ (18 Calle and 9 Avenida; tel: 2232 9270; Tue–Fri 9am–4pm, Sat–Sun 10am–4pm), devoted to the history of Guatemalan railroads. There are several superb old steam locomotives, plus a small collection of classic cars and train paraphernalia.

If you head west from here you can return to the Parque Central via traffic-free La Sexta Avenida (6th Avenue), a delight to stroll as it takes you past fine 19th-century and Art Nouveau buildings and cafés. The **Iglesia de San Francisco** Ⓕ (tel: 7882 4438; daily 9am–5.30pm) was built in 1780 in an Italianate neoclassical style, and the mortar used to construct it consisted of milk, cane syrup, and egg white. There is a terrific collection of paintings of martyrs, and the relics include the sacred heart of Trujillo. A small but worthwhile museum inside the church houses the belongings of Fray Francisco Vásquez, a Franciscan friar (daily 9am–noon, 3–6pm).

THE CENTRO CÍVICO – ZONA 4

Bridging the divide between the old quarter of Zona 1 and the richer, leafy environs of Zonas 9 and 10 is the cluster of concrete buildings known as the Centro Cívico. The Centro Cultural Miguel Ángel Asturias consists of the elegant **Teatro Nacional** Ⓖ (tel: 2208 7777; Mon–Fri 9am–4.30pm and for performances), which is set in the remains of the old Spanish fortress of San José – the ancient ramparts are still evident. The views over the city and of the surrounding mountains, including Volcán de Pacaya, are excellent. The cultural complex includes a Greek-style outdoor theater and a chamber-music auditorium. Zona 4 is also home to Inguat, the tourist board headquarters, housed in a large block on 7 Avenida.

ZONAS 9 AND 10

The upscale Zonas 9 and 10 are bisected by Avenida la Reforma, an attractive tree-lined boulevard. Zona 9, to the west, is dotted with a mix of businesses, mid-range restaurants, and hotels. The main landmark in this part of the city is the **Torre del Reformador** ❤, a small-scale imitation of Paris's Eiffel Tower, erected in honor of Guatemala's liberal reformer, President Rufino Barrios (1873–85). At the southern end of the boulevard is the Parque El Obelisco, named after the huge obelisk commemorating Guatemalan independence. Zona 10 is the abode of Guatemala's wealthy elite, with a good proportion of the city's luxurious hotels, restaurants, and nightlife, as well as top museums. The **Jardín Botánico** ❶ (Botanical Garden; Avenida La Reforma; tel: 2331 0904; Mon–Fri 8.30am–3pm, Sat 8am–noon), features a diverse range of nearly 1,000 species of Guatemalan

plant life, and a small museum, the Museu de Historia Natural, with exhibits on plants, birds, including quetzals, and other indigenous animals. The two biggest attractions in the city are also in Zona 10, inside the verdant grounds of the Universidad Francisco Marroquín. **Museo Ixchel del Traje Indígena** ❶ (tel: 2331 3622; www.museoixchel.org; Mon–Fri 9am–5pm, Sat 9am–1pm), superbly set in a dramatic Maya-esque structure, is dedicated to Maya culture, especially textiles. The museum has a superb collection of *huipiles*, complete with explanations about the weaving process and the importance of Maya symbolism in the colorful patterns and designs. Looking to bring gifts for those back home? Stop by the museum shop, which has a gorgeous array of textiles, including clothing, napkins, and more. The **Museo Popol Vuh de Arqueología** ❶ (tel: 2338 7896; www.popolvuh.ufm.edu; Mon–Fri 9am–5pm, Sat 9am–1pm), adjacent to the Ixchel, houses a small range of top-quality archeological artifacts arranged into pre-Classic, Maya Classic, post-Classic and Colonial rooms. Also worth

Administrative buildings in Centro Cívico (Zona 4).

a visit, in Zona 13, just to the south, is the **Museo Nacional de Arqueología y Etnología** 🄻 (tel: 2475 4010; www.munae.gob.gt; Tue–Fri 9am–4pm, Sat–Sun 9am–noon, 1.30–4pm), in the Parque Aurora, which has some spectacular Maya art, costumes, masks, and jade artifacts.

LAGO DE AMATITLÁN AND VOLCAN DE PACAYA

About 30km (18.5 miles) to the south of Guatemala City, following the Carretera del Pacífico, is the lovely Lago de Amatitlán, which is presided over by **Volcán de Pacaya** 🄴, one of the most active volcanoes in Central America. Pacaya is an astonishing sight, especially at night when the finest sound and light show in Guatemala can paint the sky orange with great plumes of lava and gas. Tour agencies in Antigua or Guatemala City can arrange transportation and a guide for the volcano hike.

ANTIGUA

The colonial charm of tranquil **Antigua** 🄴, and its setting amid forest-clad volcanic peaks make it one of the most popular tourist destinations in Guatemala. This former capital abounds in attractions, notably its vast legacy of stunning colonial architecture. The city's compact size is another factor – walking the cobblestone streets is a pleasure, with cultural and culinary treasures around every corner. Rising over the city are three giant cones: Volcán de Agua, which destroyed the first Guatemalan capital; Volcán de Fuego, active and smoking plumes of gas; and slumbering Volcán Acatenango, the largest but least threatening of the trio.

THE PARQUE CENTRAL

The heart of Antigua is the Parque Central, the delightful main square, popular night and day with locals and visitors who come to soak up the atmosphere. The park is bounded on all four sides by graceful colonial buildings that represented the epicenter of the Spanish empire in Central America for more than 200 years, now occupied by local government offices and museums. Note the risqué fountain (where topless mermaids spurt

Children by the Arco de Santa Catalina, Antigua.

water from their nipples) in the center of the square.

The **Catedral** (tel: 7832 0909; hours vary, but generally open daily 9am–5pm) on the east of the square dates from 1669, although it was built on the ruins of an earlier structure that dated back to 1543. The Catedral survived the 1717 earthquake, but was all but reduced to rubble after the 1773 tremors. What is left today is only about a third of the original building, which measured almost 100 meters (330ft) in length and had a 21-meter (69ft) dome, twin bell towers, three naves, and eight domed bays. Inside, the Catedral sparkled in a riot of tortoiseshell, marble, and bronze. Now the building is much more perfunctory, with most of the original in ruins to the rear and the interior relatively bare. Below the Catedral are several crypts and the remains of the Royal Chapel, and supposedly the remains of many historic figures, including Pedro de Alvarado, Francisco Marroquín, and Bernal Díaz de Castillo.

On the north side of the square is the **Ayuntamiento** , the city's municipal offices, with its twin-deck facade of solid stone arches built in a Tuscan style. This has hardly changed in appearance since it was built in 1740, surviving both the 1773 and 1976 earthquakes. In the Ayuntamiento, you'll find the small but well curated **Museo del Libro Antiguo** (tel: 7832 5511; Tue–Fri 9am–4pm, Sat–Sun 9am–noon, 2–4pm), dedicated to publishing, where there is a replica of the first printing press in Central America. Facing the Ayuntamiento on the other side of the *parque* is the **Palacio de los Capitanes Generales** (tel: 7832 2868; Wed–Sun 9am–4.30pm). The two-story colonnaded building dates from 1761 and was the nucleus of power in Central America for over two centuries, home not only to the colonial rulers but also the Courts of Justice, the Mint, a prison, and barracks.

AROUND THE PLAZA

The **Arco de Santa Catalina,** one of the great Antiguan landmarks, was built in 1693 to connect the convent of Santa Catalina to orchards and gardens on the other side of the street so that the

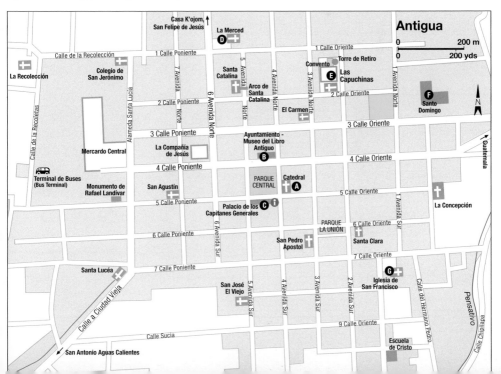

nuns could cross the street without fear of contamination by the outside world. The arch was later restored in the 19th century. Continuing up 5 Avenida is the church of **La Merced**  (ruins daily 8.30am–5.30pm, church daily 7am–noon, 3–8pm), whose 'wedding cake' facade is the finest in all Antigua, fully restored and painted a fantastic shade of yellow with white detail. Inside, at the end of the south nave is the figure of Jesus Nazarene, sculpted by Alonso de la Paz in 1650, and in the ruins of the adjacent cloisters a fountain that is said to be the largest in Central America. Perhaps the most evocative of all Antigua's ruins are **Las Capuchinas** (2 Avenida Norte and 2 Calle Oriente; daily 9am–5pm; charge), in the north of the city. The Capuchin order was an extremely strict splinter group of the Franciscans: nuns were permitted no contact at all with the outside world. The unique (and intriguing) feature at Las Capuchinas is the Torre de Retiro (Tower of Retreat), a circular courtyard of 18 tiny cells thought to have been a retreat cloister for nuns. Don't miss the fine museum, which has some

impressive religious art and ecclesiastical artifacts. **Santo Domingo** (3 Calle Oriente; tel: 7820-1220; www.casasantocomingo.com.gt; Mon–Sat 9am–6pm, Sun noon–6pm), once a monastery, is now an upscale hotel, cultural center, and museum complex. The site given to the Dominicans in 1541 was the largest occupied by any religious body, and the monastery grew to become the wealthiest order in the city. It also started up a college for the study of theology, philosophy, art, Latin, and Mayan language, which in 1676 was established as the University of San Carlos. Santo Domingo was reduced to rubble in 1773, but a superb restoration has transformed much of the site. A series of museums cover religious treasures from the Spanish era, Maya artifacts and ceramics, fascinating crypts, a re-creation of an early pharmacy, and more. Just north of the monastery is Santo Domingo del Cerro, an art and culture park featuring contemporary sculptures – and gorgeous views of Antigua.

The mighty **Iglesia de San Francisco** (1 Avenida Sur; tel: 7882 4438; daily

La Merced.

9am–5.30pm) is most notable for the tomb and shrine of Hermano Pedro de Betancourt, a teacher-friar who tirelessly cared for the sick and the poor and established hospitals and convalescent homes. Today hundreds of Guatemalans visit his shrine to ask for his help, and he is credited with many miracles. Don't miss the extensive ruins and small museum in the church.

AROUND ANTIGUA

There are some fascinating sights in the stunning countryside of pine trees, coffee bushes, and volcanoes around Antigua, and many interesting villages, both indigenous and *ladino*. It is best to explore the area as a series of day and half-day trips, using Antigua as your base. **San Andrés Itzapa** ❹ has a Tuesday market, but is best known for its shrine to the pagan saint of Maximón. It is customary to light a candle or two in Maximón's chapel (daily 6am–6pm) to ask for good fortune, but if you want to take things further, pay one of the cigar-smoking women attendants for a *limpía* (soul cleansing), which involves

you drinking *aguardiente* liquor and getting thrashed by a bundle of herbs.

North of the Interamericana there are three more villages worth a visit. **San Martín Jilotepeque** is a pleasant place with an excellent Sunday market, with beautiful local *huipiles*. At **Comalapa** to the west, there is a long-established tradition of *primitiva* (folk art) painting, with plenty of artwork on sale locally and also the spectacular crumbling Baroque facade of the village church. Market day is on Tuesday in Comalapa. Heading in the other direction toward Guatemala City along the Interamericana highway, the village of **Santiago Sacatepéquez** is famous throughout Guatemala for its giant kites, constructed by the villagers every year to be flown on the Day of the Dead (November 1). The kites, which can be up to 7 meters (23ft) in diameter, are flown in a symbolic act to release the souls of the dead.

The three spectacular volcanic peaks near Antigua – **Volcán de Agua, Volcán de Fuego,** and **Volcán Acatenango** – can all be climbed, offering unrivaled views of the surrounding landscape.

Weaving in a textile shop, Antigua.

⊘ ANTIGUA: A CATACLYSMIC HISTORY

Few cities in the world can claim such a cataclysmic past, founded on disaster and punctuated by periods of glory and seismic destruction. Antigua was actually the third capital of Guatemala. The Spanish first settled close to the modern town of Tecpán, near the ruins of their allies, the Kaqchikel Maya, at Iximché, but quickly moved to set up a permanent capital near the town of Ciudad Vieja in 1527. Disaster soon struck here, though, and after torrential rain, a massive mudslide from nearby Volcán de Agua destroyed the settlement and killed the widow of Alvarado the conquistador. The site chosen for the third capital, in the Panchoy valley, just 5km (3 miles) away, is where Antigua stands today. Originally called Santiago de los Caballeros de Guatemala, Antigua grew steadily after it was founded in 1543 to become the most important city in the Americas between Mexico City and Lima. Santiago expanded further following the 1717 earthquake, which demolished many weaker buildings and necessitated the

strengthening of those remaining. Many of Antigua's colonial structures date from this period, built in a uniquely 'squat Baroque' style with colossal walls in an attempt to resist future seismatics.

The city prospered again until 1773, its population growing to around 75,000, when a six-month long series of tremors all but crippled the capital. Damage and disease epidemics forced the government out of the city, and the king of Spain ordered it to be evacuated in favor of a new capital (Guatemala City) some 45km (28 miles) away in the valley of Ermita. But Antigua was never completely abandoned, and the fertile hillsides around the old capital proved perfect for the production of cochineal dye and coffee. Wealthy enthusiasts renovated colonial mansions, and middle-class Guatemalans again repopulated the city. Today, Antigua is one of the most international cities in the Americas, and it is estimated that at least 80 percent of its economy is dependent on the booming tourist trade and language-school industry.

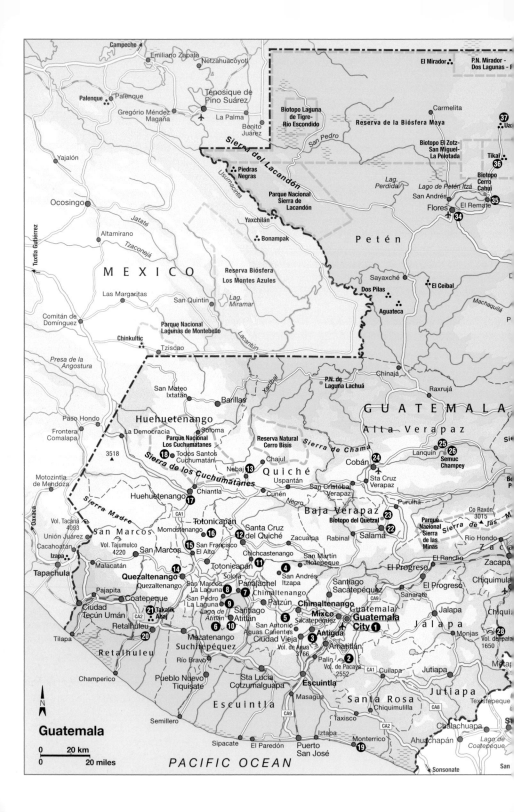

Many tour and adventure sports agencies in Antigua offer guided hikes.

Textile enthusiasts may want to head for **San Antonio Aguas Calientes ❺**, just 2km (1.2 miles) from Ciudad Vieja, which is the premier weaving center in the Antigua area. The sprawling village is mainly Maya, and is the base for a number of different collectives and stores selling textiles from all over the country, some of which also give weaving lessons. The local *huipil* design combines elaborate floral and geometric patterns on a predominantly red background.

WESTERN HIGHLANDS

This is the heartland of the Guatemalan Maya, a place of living traditions amid the most beautiful landscape in the country. The absorbing Maya culture – that's still vibrantly alive – in the rugged mountains of the Western Highlands is the apex of most visitors' experience in Guatemala. The natural setting rivals the culture, epitomized by the chain of volcanoes that strides through the heart of the land. There is Lago de Atitlán, one of the most beautiful lakes in the world, the Cuchumatanes mountain range to the north, and the hot springs and market villages around Quetzaltenango.

The strength of Guatemala's indigenous culture is apparent in the peoples' costume, fiestas, religious practice, and language – a dozen different tongues (plus Spanish) are spoken in these mountains. Visit as many markets as possible: the spectacle of Chichicastenango, the tranquility and hushed tones of Chajul, the frenetic hustle and commerce of San Francisco El Alto.

LAGO DE ATITLÁN

Of all Guatemala's natural attractions, perhaps the most beautiful is the volcanic caldera of **Lago de Atitlán ❻** and its unforgettable highland setting, which have seduced travelers for centuries. Its various bays and inlets give the lake an irregular shape, but it measures about 19km (12 miles) long by 12km (7.5 miles) at its widest point. Atitlán is transcended by three towering volcanoes, its shores are dotted with Maya villages, and its 305-meter (1,000ft) deep waters conjure up a spectrum of shifting color changes.

While Panajachel is the main resort, Santa Cruz is supremely peaceful and relaxing, San

Pedro is a backpacker haven, Santiago Atitlán has a traditional feel, and San Marcos is a 'new age' center. Santa Catarina Palopó and San Antonio Palopó are different again, both villages specializing in textile weaving, while tranquil San Juan has some excellent community tourism projects.

The Maya probably first settled the Lake Atitlán area around 2000 BC when they formed small farming and fishing communities on its shores. The region around Lago de Atitlán has likely been volcanic in character for at least 12 million years, when a colossal caldera, much larger than the present lake, extended several kilometers farther to the north. More eruptions around 9 million years ago then formed another, slightly smaller, bowl-shaped caldera.

Lago de Atitlán's present outline is the result of a third volcanic explosion 85,000 years ago. This eruption blocked all access to the sea, so that the three rivers that tumble into the newly formed crater formed today's vast, high-altitude lake, some 1,562 meters (5,125ft) above sea level.

PANAJACHEL

Dubbed *Gringotenango* by the locals because of the heavy influx of tourists and the high density of Westerner-owned bars and cafés, **Panajachel** ❼ or 'Pana' has become something of a boomtown since the turn of the millennium. Yet, despite the vast kasbah of traditional textile stores and the dozens of hotels, restaurants, cafés, and new-age services, Pana's great appeal is all about its location overlooking the lake and volcanoes, and its inimitable laid-back atmosphere. Transportation connections are also superb, with regular buses and shuttles running up to the Interamericana and a flotilla of boats linking Pana with the other lakeside villages.

AROUND LAGO DE ATITLÁN

The north shore of the lake is sparsely populated and the perfect place to head for some real relaxation. The first place the boat heading west to San Pedro stops at is **Santa Cruz La Laguna**, the main village high above the water, with a variety of lakeside hotels and outdoor activities, from kayaking to hiking.

⊘ THE CHURCHES OF ANTIGUA

Antigua's numerous churches, characterized by a unique 'squat Baroque' style, are the dazzling jewels in this colonialized city's crown. Built with immensely thick walls, and supported by colossal foundations and giant buttresses, the churches were developed in a futile effort to resist the perpetual tremors that have plagued the city since it was founded in 1543. Structurally, 21st-century Antigua is almost entirely an 18th-century city. A few earlier details have survived, but the dominant style is Iberian-American Baroque, a supremely pictorial, decorative, and flamboyant style that's expressed on virtually all Antigua's church facades. It's also called Churrigueresque, and not to everyone's taste. The Maudslays, who wrote *A Glimpse at Guatemala*, based on visits in the late 1890s, the height of the Victorian Gothic revival, considered it vulgar, garish, and ostentatious. But at its best, as witnessed at the restored La Merced, or at Santa Cruz, the depth, fluidity, and theatrical nature of Antiguan Baroque is astounding – undeniably grandiose, with dreamy facades

embellished with astonishing detail. These remarkable facades were created by applying layers of plaster over the exterior masonry, a technique called ataurique.

The sheer number of ecclesiastical buildings in Antigua is amazing: there are over 30 within a few blocks of the Parque Central. By the mid-17th century, all the main denominations and many more minor ones were established in the city. The religious orders were possibly the greatest power in Central America: free from taxation and granted huge swathes of the most productive land where sugar, tobacco, wheat, and, most lucratively, cochineal and indigo were farmed.

The orders were also allocated vast numbers of Maya laborers to work in the fields and construct the grand edifices of the capital. These laborers managed to implant indigenous imagery onto some of the great church facades: corn cobs (sacred to the Maya) at La Merced and the white water-lily (a hallucinogenic used in sacred rituals) at San Francisco.

Santa Cruz is also a hub for lively night-life, as well as a growing number of superb Spanish-language schools. Also, a new wave of eateries are resurrecting ancient Maya recipes with local, organic products. If you plan to climb **Volcán San Pedro**, this is the ideal base for an early-morning start

San Marcos La Laguna ⑧ takes the top prize for lakeside beauty. This has, predictably, pulled in the visitor crowds, particularly those on a spiritual path. The dense foliage gives way to an aromatic tangle of jocote, banana, mango, and avocado trees – the perfect setting for a meditation-yoga center and some excellent budget and mid-range hotels. In nearby San Juan La Laguna, you'll find a weaving co-op run by the locals and an excellent village-based tourism initiative designed to promote the regional arts and crafts.

San Pedro La Laguna ⑨, a short distance beyond San Juan, now often matches Panajachel in popularity, drawing scores of visitors to its lakefront hotels that make an excellent base for hiking, kayaking, and scuba-diving..

A road runs around the east side of the lake, connecting Pana with another two interesting villages. **Santa Catarina Palopó**, 4km (2.5 miles) from Pana, is famous for its weavings. You will see the turquoise and purple *huipiles* at markets all over the highlands. There's not much to see in the village itself, though as ever the volcano views are magnificent.

Santiago Atitlán ⑩, a Tz'utujil Maya village on one of the lake's inlets around the western flank of Volcán Tolimán, is 20 minutes from Pana by fast *lancha* boats. A shrine is kept here to Maximón, part evil saint, part pagan idol, said to be a combination of San Simón, Judas Iscariot, and Pedro de Alvarado the conquistador. The two other points of interest are a small weaving museum to the left of the dock, and the church.

QUICHÉ: THE MAYA HEARTLAND

The mountainous department of Quiché stretches from Chichicastenango northward as far as the Mexican border. As the name suggests, this is the heartland of the 2 million or so K'i che' Maya, the most numerous Maya group

⊙ Tip

If you are in Santiago Atitlán over Easter, you can watch the symbolic confrontation in the plaza between Jesus Christ and Maximón that always takes place on Good Friday.

Boats at Santa Cruz La Laguna, Lago de Atitlán.

☉ Fact

Highland costumes are decorated with a wide range of flora and fauna motifs as well as geometric forms. Some images, such as the horse, peacock, and chicken, are obviously post-Conquest, as these animals arrived in the Americas with the Spaniards. Others, like deer, snakes, and double-headed birds figure in Maya mythology. It is said that the zigzag patterns symbolize Chac, the god of lightning. Monkeys are associated with disaster, while the quetzal was the spiritual protector of the rulers.

in Guatemala. Quiché has had a long history of bloodshed, from the days of the Conquest when, in 1524, Alvarado's men massacred Maya warriors after a final battle at K'umarkaaj, near Santa Cruz del Quiché, to the horrors of the 'scorched earth' policy of the 1980s, when thousands of Maya civilians were massacred in a series of paramilitary operations. The department is crossed by several mountain ranges and travel to the Ixil region in the north is a long slog, taking up to three hours from Santa Cruz del Quiché on steep roads.

CHICHICASTENANGO

Chichicastenango ⑪ is a quiet highland town with an intriguing past that has become one of the chief tourist destinations of the highlands. Twice a week, the normally calm 'Chichi' hosts the most famous market in the Maya region, coming to life in a maelstrom of furious commerce. From the dead of night every Thursday and Sunday, traders arrive to set up their stands by candlelight, and by daylight the roads into town are crammed with trailers, trucks,

Wares for sale at the Thursday market, Chichicastenango.

and *camionetas* (buses). The market is a good place to buy *típica* textiles and handicrafts, short of venturing to their place of origin.

Sitting pretty in the main plaza, the whitewashed **Iglesia de Santo Tomás** (daily) is an overwhelming sight, the air around the crescent-shaped stone steps thick with the sweet, smoky aroma of smoldering pine-based incense called copal. The church, dating back to 1540, is one of the most fascinating in Guatemala, a place where Maya religious traditions have long been tolerated and fused with Catholicism. Enter by the side door (the front door is reserved for priests and *cofrades* – religious officials). The atmosphere inside is magical on Sundays, the aisles and the altar packed with Maya families and groups softly praying. Candles, *aguardiente* liquor wrapped in corn husks, and flowers are offered at different platforms spread around the church, each dedicated to the souls of the deceased.

As you leave (again through the side door), the neighboring building holds the former monastery where, in

☉ HABLAS ESPAÑOL?

Antigua has more than 50 language schools, which cater to all levels, from beginners to those seeking total fluency. It is an excellent place to learn Spanish, with highly affordable rates. Antigua's schools offer a range of classes and accommodations, including family homestays – with three meals a day – or guesthouses; prices range from US$170–$320 a week. There are also top schools in Quetzaltenango, Petén, and around Lago de Atitlán.

Antigüeña Spanish Academy, 1 C Pte 10; tel: 7832 7241; www.spanishacademyantiguena.com; **Centro Lingüístico Maya**, 5 C Pte 20; tel: 7832 0656; www.clmaya.com; **Ixchel Spanish School**, 4 Av Norte 32; tel: 7832 3440; www.ixchelschool.com; **Ixquic**, 7 Av Norte 74; tel: 7832 2402; www.ixquic.edu.gt; **San José El Viejo**, 5 Av Sur 34; tel: 7832 3028; www.sanjoseelviejo.com

about 1702, a Spanish priest, Francisco Ximénez, first discovered the *Popol Vuh*, the K'iche' sacred book, containing their story of creation involving the hero twins – it is considered one of the great literary masterpieces of the pre-Columbian Americas.

SANTA CRUZ DEL QUICHÉ

North of Chichicastenango is **Santa Cruz del Quiché** ⑫, the departmental capital. Santa Cruz is, at heart, a local's town, with far fewer tourist crowds than bustling Chichi. The market days are Thursday and Sunday, but most visitors come here to visit **K'umarkaaj** (also called Utatlán), the former capital of the K'iche' Maya, 4km (2.5 miles) southwest of the plaza. Like all the highland Maya capitals, K'umarkaaj is set superbly in a defensive position, surrounded by pine trees and ravines, and the ruins are low-rise and lack initial impact. Yet this is the fortified capital where Pedro de Alvarado and the conquistadors burned alive two K'iche' kings in 1524 and sealed their control of the highlands. Today K'umarkaaj remains an active site for Maya religious ceremonies and prayers, especially beneath the grassy plaza, where a long tunnel leads to an underground chamber.

THE IXIL REGION

One of the most compelling regions of the highlands, the Ixil region is an extremely traditional and beautiful area that also saw some of the bloodiest conflicts of the civil war during much of the 1970s and 1980s. Now that the war is over, the Ixil region (Ixil is the language spoken in these parts, region refers to the three main towns of Nebaj, Chajul, and Cotzal) is again welcoming a steady flow of visitors, especially hikers.

NEBAJ

Nebaj ⑬ is the largest of the Ixil towns, set dramatically in a broad green valley encircled by steep-sided ridges. The first thing you will notice is the startling costume worn by the Ixil women, arguably the finest in the Maya region: incredibly tightly woven white, green, and red *huipiles* and waist sashes, scarlet *cortes* (skirts) and Medusa-like headdresses of fabric and colorful woolen pom-poms. Check out the Sunday market for its colorful bustle, but you'll find better prices for textiles at the co-operatives in the main plaza or from the women who regularly visit the town's *hospedajes* to sell their wares. The town museum, Centro Cultural Kumool (tel: 7756 0273; Mon–Fri 9am–noon, 1–6pm, Sun 8am–1pm), has exhibits on local culture and history, including Maya ceramics and other artifacts. The hill-walking in the area is tremendous, and a variety of companies offer guided hikes. One hike takes you to the 'model village' of **Acul**, a strategic hamlet two hours' walk from Nebaj, where villagers were resettled under pressure from the military during the civil war. Nearby is Hacienda San Antonio (www.haciendasanantonio.webs. com), a beautiful Italian-Guatemalan farm where some of the best cheese in the country is made – and is for sale.

Colorfully-dressed woman in Nebaj.

◎ **Fact**

Maya Nobel Peace Prize laureate Rigoberta Menchú grew up in the mountains north of the town of Uspantán, in the El Quiché region, and chapters in her autobiography, *Crossing Borders*, cover the region.

QUETZALTENANGO

The department of Quetzaltenango, with its chief city of the same name, sits high in a mountain range. Also Guatemala's second city, **Quetzaltenango**  rivaled the capital for centuries as the country's most important business, banking, and cultural city. By the 20th century, Quetzaltenango (also known as Xela – pronounced 'Shella' – from its Maya name Xelajú) was an impressive city, its wealth boosted by its pivotal position as a center for the coffee trade and a direct rail track to the Pacific port of Champerico. But the stately architecture and theaters were all but destroyed by a colossal earthquake in 1902, and ever since, Quetzaltenango has been relegated to second-division provincial status as a capital of the highlands, devoid of metropolitan swagger, but retaining a friendlier, less frenetic character. Looming above the buildings is the majestic Volcán Santa María, the most perfectly proportioned cone in Guatemala.

The heart of the city, the sprawling **Parque Centroamérica** holds an impressive assortment of buildings, including the Municipalidad (city hall), the cathedral, and, in the center of the square, a strange visual cocktail of neo-Grecian columns and stone benches. The **Catedral** (generally daily) is a modern concrete building, with only the facade remaining of the original. The Bishop of the Highlands, an important post, is stationed here. Inside the cathedral is an image of El Padre Eterno (The Eternal Father) housed in a silver case. The **La Casa de la Cultura** (tel: 7761 6031; hours vary, generally Mon–Fri 8am–noon, 2–6pm, Sat 9am–1pm) on the south of the square, features a variety of museums, including the Museo de Historia Natural where there's an assortment of pre-Columbian artifacts, and the Museo de Arte, with changing exhibits local art.

The **Museo del Ferrocarril** (Mon–Fri 8am–noon, 2–6pm, Sat 8am–1pm) focuses on the railroad that connected the city to the Pacific Coast. Next door, in the same building, Museo Ixkik' (daily 9am–1pm, 3–6pm) covers Maya costume from the highlands.

Girl in traditional costume, San Andrés Xecul.

◎ THE COSTUMES OF GUATEMALA

The Maya today identify with their villages rather than with their ancestral tribes, although the languages they speak still conform to the pattern of ancient tribal boundaries. Marriages between members of different communities are relatively rare, and village identity is consolidated further by the distinctive clothes worn by the women and some men.

Costumes fall into three categories: everyday dress; more elaborate wear for special occasions; and the ceremonial garments worn by the *cofradías*. Although colors, designs, and the way of wearing particular garments differ from village to village, all women's apparel consists of the same basic articles: a *huipil* (a loose rectangular blouse), a skirt, sash, hair-ribbon, and *tzut* (multi-purpose carrying cloth) or shawl. Each item is hand-woven, either on a simple hip-strap loom or a foot-loom.

Men's traditional costumes have been preserved in only a few villages, most notably in those around Lake Atitlán, and in the mountains of Huehuetenango. You can recognize Maya men from Lake Atitlán by their striped pants decorated with village motifs and held up by sashes. Black split over-pants are used in Todos Santos and by Sololá officials, whilst the men of San Juan Atitlán wear woolen *capixays* that resemble the cassocks used by the Spanish friars. In Santiago Atitlán men embroider their own pants, copying pictures of birds or Maya hieroglyphs.

The **Teatro Municipal**, north of the park, is a solid neo-colonial edifice. The theater faces a plaza, which contains various busts of local artists, including Guatemala's first Poet Laureate, Osmundo Arriola (1886–1958).

AROUND QUETZALTENANGO

The village of **San Francisco El Alto** ⑮ hosts one of the biggest markets in the Maya region. The Friday morning market is a wonderful spectacle and a real assault on the senses, as thousands of traders descend on the small village to buy and trade everything from honking hogs to fine fabrics. Textiles are bought here to be sold around the country, and some good bargains can be found here and in the town's many textile shops.

Around 19km (12 miles) from San Francisco is the popular market town of **Momostenango** ⑯, specializing in *chamarras* (warm, woolen blankets) and carpets. Some good-quality textiles can be bought here, especially at its twice-weekly markets on Wednesday and Sunday. Momostenango is also a center for Maya religious study, with many shamans working here, attracting students from all over Guatemala.

THE CUCHUMATANES

In the far west of the country, the highland scenery becomes even more dramatic, dominated by the blunted peaks of the Cuchumatanes mountains. Above Huehuetenango there's a huge high-altitude plateau known as the *altiplano*, a dauntingly inhospitable environment where trees are stunted by the cold and little else will grow.

The Cuchumatanes have always been an isolated region, which helped shield the overwhelmingly Maya inhabitants from changes that have affected villages closer to the Interamericana. In many villages, the Maya Haab and Tzolkin calendars are still observed by prayer keepers. Travel in the mountains is tough, hotels and restaurants are simple, but the spellbinding scenery is ample compensation.

HUEHUETENANGO

The pleasant town of **Huehuetenango** ⑰ is both a transportation hub and a

⊘ Fact

San Andrés Xecul, about 8km (5 miles) to the northeast of Quetzaltenango, has a stunningly colorful church that is claimed to be the oldest in Central America (although the color scheme is 20th-century). The background color is yellow, decorated with brightly dressed angels and vines, while the dome resembles a stripy beach ball.

The church in San Andrés Xecul.

departmental capital. The main sight, however, is **Zaculeu**, Maya ruins 5km (3 miles) from the center of 'Huehue.' Zaculeu was the capital of the Mam nation, one of the main tribes that confronted the Spanish. The former capital, like the other highland Maya centers, was well fortified, and the Mam held out for six weeks before they surrendered.

Unfortunately, Zaculeu was insensitively rebuilt in 1947, the temples covered in a bland stucco finish, lacking any decorative detail. Despite this, it is still worth a visit – the ruins sit above ravines on three sides, providing tremendous views, and there's also a small museum on site with exhibits of burial pieces (daily 8am–noon, 1–6pm).

TODOS SANTOS CUCHUMATÁN

Todos Santos Cuchumatán ⑱, some 50km (31 miles) northwest of Huehue, is famous for its spectacular festival (see box), in addition to its sublime setting in a canyon-like valley beneath the 3,837-meter (12,589ft) peak of Chemal, and richly colorful evidence of Mam Maya culture throughout town. The women

wear beautiful purple and navy *huipiles* that are among the most tightly woven in the country, but it is the men who are the real peacocks – they sport an almost outrageous outfit of candy-striped pants and thick cotton shirts with huge, flapping pink or purple collars.

The countryside around Todos Santos is perfect for challenging hikes, including one route that takes you out of town, south past the minor ruins of Tojcunanchén, up on to the spine of the Cuchumatanes and on to the equally traditional Mam village of San Juan Atitlán, six hours' walk away. A variety of top-notch local guides offer guided treks from Todos Santos – ask at your lodging for recommendations and contact information. Todos Santos also has a couple of popular language schools, including Academia Hispano Maya (www.hispanomaya.weebly.com).

THE PACIFIC COAST

Glance at a map of Guatemala, and the 300km (190-mile) long Pacific coastline might appear to be the perfect place to chill out. But if you are dreaming of

Men wearing the distinctive costume of Todos Santos Cuchumatán.

palm-fringed beach resorts, try the Caribbean. Guatemala's Pacific coast is the engine room of its agricultural economy, a sultry, humid strip of land that's almost entirely dominated by vast *fincas* devoted to sugar cane, cattle ranching, cotton, and bananas.

Attractions in this area are thin on the ground, but there are a few highlights: between the sugar plantations are important (both Maya and Olmec) archeological remains at Takalik Abaj and in numerous sites around the town of Santa Lucía Cotzumalguapa, including the colossal stone heads in La Democracia. The scale of these sites cannot compete with the temples and pyramids of the Petén and Yucatán, but some of the sculpture is fascinating.

Running parallel to the coast is Guatemala's fastest highway, the Carretera del Pacífico, and it is simple to get around this route by bus. To explore the region fully, however, you will need your own transportation, as many of the sights, and all the beaches, are a considerable distance off the highway.

MONTERRICO AND AROUND

The village of **Monterrico** ⓳ is a popular base for exploring the coast, with a few casual beachfront hotels and access to the surrounding wetlands, which are protected as part of a national nature preserve, the **Biotopo Monterrico-Hawaii**. The preserve forms an important habitat for herons, egrets, and migratory birds, iguana, alligators, opossums, raccoons, and anteaters. It is the three species of sea turtles that nest on these shores that make Monterrico really special, however.

RETALHULEU AND TAKALIK ABAJ

Retalhuleu ⓴, usually shortened to 'Reu' (pronounced 'RAY-oo'), draws in visitors with its attractive, shady plaza, a relaxed air, and a good Museo de Arqueología y Etnología (Tue–Sat 8am–5.30pm), which is full of historical photographs and anthropomorphic

figurines. West of Reu, near the small village of El Asintal, is **Takalik Abaj** ㉑ (daily 7am–5pm), probably the most important ruins on the entire coast, with Maya and Olmec-style temples as well as stelae and altars, and a small but worthwhile museum.

EASTERN GUATEMALA

This varied region has some superb lakes, the wonderful carved stelae of Quiriguá and Copán, a quetzal preserve, and a fascinating Caribbean coastal culture. A network of protected preserves has been established to safeguard the region's ecosystems, and the unique habitat of species like the manatee and the quetzal, the national bird – but this preserve status is all too often poorly enforced.

Historically, the Motagua River that flows through the heart of the region to the Caribbean Sea was a crucial trade route. Close to the banks of the Motagua were the largest jade deposits in the entire Maya area, contested and controlled by the Maya settlements of Quiriguá and Copán. Today the ruins of

Boatman on the wetlands that make up the Biotopo Monterrico-Hawaii reserve.

⊙ FIESTA DE TODOS SANTOS

Guatemala is the land of festivals, but there's one that tops them all: the Fiesta de Todos Santos. At the end of every October, Todosanteros (men from Todos Santos Cuchumatán) return to the village from all over Guatemala to celebrate the festival of All Saints (Todos Santos), the most famous in the country.

The festivities start the week before the horse race, which takes place on the morning of November 1 (All Saints' Day). Music and dancing is held on October 31, in the costume of the next day's race. Riders, most of whom have been drinking hard liquor all night, must circumnavigate a course around the town, stopping to take another swig of *aguardiente* after each lap and struggling to hang on. The 'race' in reality becomes a comical stampede, with the drunken jockeys urging their long-suffering steeds like demons possessed. The winner is the one who survives, still on his mount; all the riders gain considerable kudos, however, just for taking part.

On the next day, appropriately 'the day of the dead,' everyone moves to the cemetery for a day of eating, more drinking, and commemorating the lives of their dearly departed. Marimba bands play in the town center for days, and in the cemetery itself on November 2. Many traditional dances are performed, including the dance of the conquistadors.

both sites are essential visits for their astonishing sculptural remains.

THE VERAPACES AND SALAMÁ

The twin departments of Baja and Alta Verapaz (vera paz meaning 'true peace') were the last part of Guatemala to fall under Spanish control (apart from Flores), such was the ferocity of opposition from the indigenous Achi tribes, and dominance was only established in 1538 after a successful 'softly-softly' approach pioneered by a group of Dominican priests led by Fray Bartolomé de las Casas.

The Verapaces contain some of the most beautiful scenery in the country, in places almost Swiss alpine in appearance; a large spread of cloud forest, home to the elusive quetzal; and some of the world's best coffee-growing country.

Salamá ㉒, the capital of the department, lies some 60km (37 miles) northeast of Guatemala City. The scenery around the town is a delightful mix of productive pastoral land (everything from oranges to olives are grown) and extensive pine forests. It is a historic place set in a wide river valley with an excellent Sunday market. The 17th century colonial church in the plaza is an absolute gem, with no fewer than 14 gilded altars.

BIOTOPO DEL QUETZAL

The **Biotopo del Quetzal ㉓** (daily 6am–4pm) is a sanctuary for the quetzal – once the spiritual talisman of the Maya lords, now Guatemala's national bird – a beautiful but notoriously elusive creature that these days is very rare throughout Central America.

The preserve is a permanently humid patch of forest thick with ferns, epiphytes, moss, and lichen. Dawn is the best time to spot a quetzal, which feasts on the fruit of the aguacatillo (wild avocado) tree, but there are at least another 87 species of birds to look out for. A map available onsite details the two trails that meander through the ever-dripping foliage. The season for spotting the quetzal is just before and after the nesting season, between March and June.

In the caves at Lanquín.

⊘ TURTLES

The green turtle and olive ridley nest at Monterrico between July and November, and the leatherback between mid-October and February. All the turtles crawl ashore at night to lay their clutch of 80–100 eggs, a laborious effort that sends the turtles into an exhausted state. Despite the protected status of the preserve, egg collectors seek out nesting turtles and take the eggs, considered an aphrodisiac in Central America. Conservationists have set up two hatcheries on this section of the beach, however, and have had some success in persuading the egg collectors to donate part of their cache. The collected eggs are protected until they hatch, when the baby turtles are released into the ocean. Around 10,000 baby turtles are released annually, though it is estimated only a few dozen of these will reach maturity and return here to nest.

COBÁN

The commercial center of the Verapaces is **Cobán ㉔**, which, though founded by Las Casas in 1538, remained a slumbering backwater until the late 19th century, when large numbers of German immigrants arrived. The Germans were granted authority to plant coffee bushes, which thrived in the mild, moist Verapaz climate, and business prospered until World War II, when many of the coffee barons were expelled at the USA's insistence because of their open support for Adolf Hitler.

Tranquil Cobán makes an excellent base to explore the beautiful Verapaz scenery. Though the town maintains a sleepy demeanor, there are some good-value cafés and hotels. Take a stroll up to the Templo el Calvario, a fine old church dating from 1599, which is popular with Q'eqchi' and Poqomchi' Maya worshipers. Don't miss the exquisite carvings and artifacts inside the small **Museo El Príncipe Maya** (Mon–Sat 9am–5.45pm), or the chance to take a guided tour of the **Finca Santa Margarita** (Mon–Fri 8am–12.30pm, 1.30–5pm, Sat 8am–noon), a coffee plantation southeast of the plaza. Once owned by prominent German coffee grower Erwin Dieseldorff, the guided tour takes you step by step through the coffee-making process from propagation to roasting. You also have a chance to sample the different types of Arabica coffee blends, and to buy beans direct.

AROUND COBÁN: LANQUÍN AND SEMUC CHAMPEY

One of the most popular excursions from Cobán is **Lanquín ㉕**, a lovely village around 60km (37 miles) to the east. The gargantuan **Grutas de Lanquín** (Lanquín caves; daily 8am–6pm) are a speleologist's delight, stretching for several kilometers. Numerous tour companies offer trips here. Lanquín is also the perfect jumping-off point for **Semuc Champey ㉖**, which

is, put simply, one of the most beautiful places in Guatemala. A cascade of cool turquoise and emerald-green pools surrounded by lush, tropical forest, Semuc Champey is one of eastern Guatemala's top tourist attractions. The Río Cahabón eventually flows into Lago de Izabal, but at Semuc Champey most of its current plunges underground, leaving a great limestone bridge at the surface. A little river water spills over this natural shelf, creating a series of idyllic pools perfect for swimming, and a magical place to relax and enjoy the magnificent natural setting (keep your valuables with you). Tour companies in Cobán run regular trips here.

EL ORIENTE

El Oriente unfolds south of the Carretera al Atlántico. This is the hottest part of Guatemala, a relentlessly uncompromising land where the thermometer regularly nudges 38°C (100°F). Probing the horizon are a scattering of ancient, extinct volcanoes – though much smaller in scale and more

⊙ Where

Orchid lovers, take note: **Orquigonia** (tel: 4740-2224; www.vivienteverapaz.com; Mon–Sat 9am–noon, 2–4.30pm, Sun 9am–noon) is a specialist nursery where thousands of plants, including more than 600 species of orchid, are grown. Orquigonia hosts a variety of activities, including tours and workshops, and they rent cabins.

Semuc Champey.

weathered in appearance than the chain across the western highlands.

One of the region's major towns is **Chiquimula** ㉗, which is archetypal of the region – hot, dusty, and featureless. For travelers, Chiquimula serves two key purposes: as a transit hub, and to break up the journey, as a place to stay for a night of two, thanks to its quality array of affordable lodging. The colonial church, the Iglesia Vieja, on the edge of town, was badly damaged by an earthquake in 1765 and has now been reduced to ruins.

South of Chiquimula looms **Volcán de Ipala** ㉘, a 1,650-meter (5,410ft) eroded volcano with an exquisite crater lake at its rounded summit. It is a fairly easy two-hour hike to the top from the closest village of Agua Blanca. If you have your own transportation, the most direct route is up a trail that begins at Km 26.5 on the Ipala–Agua Blanca road, near to a drinks stand in the tiny settlement of Sauce. Once here, you can walk all around the forest-fringed summit of the lake in a couple of hours.

Stela J, Quiriguá.

ESQUIPULAS

Near the border with El Salvador, **Esquipulas** ㉙ is famous as the site of the biggest pilgrimage in Central America. The object of veneration is an image of El Cristo Negro, the Black Christ, which is housed in a colossal white basilica (tel: 7943 1108; daily, hours vary). Inside the church the atmosphere is heady with incense and smoky from burning candles, while a continuous procession of pilgrims lines up to receive a blessing, many on their knees and reciting prayers. The image itself, created from balsam wood, was carved by the fabled sculptor Quirio Cataño in the late 16th century, while the origins of the pilgrimage are thought to predate the Conquest. The main pilgrimage date is January 15, and there is a smaller event on March 9, but Esquipulas is busy throughout the whole year with pilgrims and devotees paying homage and seeking cures to ailments.

IZABAL

Fringed by the Caribbean Sea, with Belize just to the north and the Honduran coastline to the south, the low-lying department of Izabal feels totally unlike the rest of the country. The population is a polyglot assortment of *ladinos*, Garífuna, Caribs, and Q'eqchi' Maya. The scenery is also different: the landscape is lush, and the heat and humidity are punishing at any time of year, creating a decidedly languid, tropical ambience.

Izabal is bounded by mountains: the Sierra del Merendón defining the Honduran border, the Sierra de las Minas to the southwest, and the Sierra de Santa Cruz to the north. In the very center of the department is **Lago de Izabal**, the biggest lake in the country, which drains into the Caribbean through the beautiful Río Dulce gorge

QUIRIGUÁ RUINS

The early Classic ruins of **Quiriguá** ㉚ (daily 8am–4.30pm), a Unesco World Heritage Site set in a beautiful clearing just off the highway, are well worth investigating for their remarkable stone carvings of fine-grained sandstone stelae and giant flat boulders. Quiriguá had always been a minor site, possibly first settled in the early Classic period by an elite group from the northern Maya lowlands. It was subsequently dominated by nearby Copán, but in AD 737, the leader Cauac Sky (or Two-legged Sky) captured and sacrificed Copán's ruler 18 Rabbit, turning centuries of Maya power politics upside down.

To celebrate this success, Cauac Sky started rebuilding Quiriguá, commissioning the carving of the largest stelae anywhere in the Maya world, which were grouped around an enormous monumental plaza, enclosed on three sides by an acropolis.

The site's largest stela is Stela E, 8 meters (25ft) tall, which depicts Cauac Sky crowned with an elaborate headdress. There are 10 other stelae in the plaza, a small acropolis to the south, and a ball court. Don't miss the six fantastic carved boulders just below the acropolis, which are decorated with images of frogs, turtles, jaguars, and snakes.

LAKE IZABAL

North of Quiriguá is **Lago de Izabal**, a huge freshwater expanse which is steadily being opened up to tourism. The western environs of the lake are protected as part of the Bocas del Polochic preserve, where there are alligators, iguanas, and a riot of colorful birdlife. Most people stay at the eastern edge of the lake at the town of **Río Dulce** ③. The town, scattered on both sides of the bridge, is no beauty, functioning mainly as a transportation hub, but unexpectedly close by there are some delightful hotels that are well placed for exploring the lake.

Back in the 16th and 17th centuries, British pirates caused mayhem around Izabal, raiding Spanish merchant caravans, and the Castillo de San Felipe (daily 8am–5pm; charge), just 3km (2 miles) from Río Dulce town, was built to combat these marauding buccaneers. There's a lot more to see around the lake, including an incredible hot

Fisherman at Río Dulce.

⊙ Fact

Boat cruises around El Golfete (usually departing from Livingston) often stop at the hot springs that empty into the lagoon, so you can take a dip in the warm, sulfurous water. It is an idyllic spot, shaded by overhanging trees and surrounded by lush jungle vegetation.

spring waterfall near Finca El Paraíso, which drops about 12 meters (40ft) into a deep pool.

LIVINGSTON

At the point where the Río Dulce meets the Bahía de Amatique is the Garífuna town of **Livingston** ㉜, sometimes known locally as La Buga (The Mouth). Livingston is one of the most interesting villages in Guatemala, its atmosphere seemingly much more in tune with Jamaica or the Honduran Bay Islands than the Central American mainland. Connections with the rest of Guatemala are somewhat tentative, and not just culturally, as Livingston can only be reached by boat from Puerto Barrios, Belize, or Honduras.

Good excursions from Livingston include the impressive series of waterfalls called Siete Altares (best in the rainy season); one of the best beaches in Guatemala, Playa Blanca; and even snorkeling trips to the edge of the Belizean reef system. A variety of tour companies offer trips – check with your hotel for recommendations.

The fishing docks at Livingston.

PUERTO BARRIOS

Puerto Barrios ㉝, in the southeastern corner of Bahía de Amatique, is today little more than a transit point for tourists picking up boats for Punta Gorda in Belize or en route for Livingston. For many years, though, the town was the country's most important port. Now it has been eclipsed by the modern facilities available at Santo Tomás de Castilla, just 11km (7 miles) to the west around the bay.

Puerto Barrios was established by President Rufino Barrios in the late 19th century, but developed by the United Fruit Company in the 1900s as the company's exclusive port for the export of its bananas. The UFC modeled the town on urban North American lines, and it retains this legacy today, with broad streets and sprawling city blocks.

Most of the old wooden Caribbean buildings are crumbling and dilapidated now, unfortunately, replaced by faceless concrete constructions. The odd reminder of more prosperous times remains, however, and the town's one real sight is the atmospheric Hotel

del Norte, right on the waterfront, an immaculately preserved – and charming – living monument, built entirely from wood.

THE PETÉN

Hidden in this vast northern jungle department are some of the most spectacular Maya cities, including the indisputable, dazzling jewel in their crown: Tikal.

Between 750 BC and around AD 900, the Maya civilization – arguably the greatest of all pre-Columbian cultures – evolved, excelled, and ultimately collapsed in the lowland subtropical forests of what is now northern Guatemala. It was in the jungles and savannas of the department of Petén, which covers a third of the country, that the Maya city-states succeeded in creating some of the greatest human advances on the continent: a precise calendrical system, pioneering astronomy, a complex writing system, breathtaking artistry, and towering architectural triumphs.

There's compelling evidence that a combination of environmental and social factors (including overpopulation, warfare, and revolt) prompted the disaster of the Maya collapse, but the exact reasons are still subject to animated academic debate. Whatever the truth, the jungle reclaimed the temples, plazas, and palaces, so that by the time the 19th century explorers arrived, buildings were choked with over 1,000 years of forest growth.

The Petén is still Guatemala's wild frontier province, and transportation, communications, hotels, and restaurants are generally pretty basic away from the main town of Flores. To get to Maya sites like El Mirador takes time (unless you take a heli-tour!), planning, and local expertise – there are a number of excellent local organizations that operate expeditions to the remote ruins. The Petén climate is perennially hot and humid. The rainy season can extend until December, and can disrupt overland travel to isolated areas. Tikal and Flores are always accessible nevertheless.

FLORES

Set on a natural island in Lago de Petén Itzá, connected via a small causeway to shore, **Flores ㉞**, is a peaceful, civilized place now largely dependent on tourism. It is a small, tranquil, and historic town that's by far the most pleasant urban center in the department. Today's town stands on the remains of the old Itzá Maya capital, Tayasal, which was first visited by Hernán Cortés in 1525, left alone, and only conquered in 1697. The Spanish had no appetite for jungle life, and Flores retained closer contact with Belize and Mexico until the road links to the rest of Guatemala improved in the late 20th century.

The best way to explore Flores is to stroll around the lane that circumscribes the shoreline – it will take you about 15 minutes to walk around the cobblestone streets and lanes of the town. Some of its architecture is delightful: the older houses are brightly painted wooden and adobe constructions, many of the hotels

⊙ Where

One of the most impressive ancient sites in Mesoamerica is Copán (see page 229), featuring some of the Mayan world's greatest treasures. This restored Mayan city sits on the banks of the Río Copán, only 12km (8 miles) into Honduras from the Guatemalan border town of El Florido. An increasing number of visitors to Guatemala make a special detour to these superb ruins, whose carved stelae are widely considered the finest as yet found in the Maya world.

⊙ THE UNITED FRUIT COMPANY

For more than half a century, all Guatemala's political and economic decisions were effectively supervised by the United Fruit Company, Central America's biggest employer, and dubbed *El Pulpo* ("The Octopus") because of its huge influence in the region. The UFC first began banana business in Guatemala in 1901, and quickly struck a deal to complete the Guatemala City–Puerto Barrios railroad track in exchange for almost complete tax exemption and land concessions. By 1930 the company was worth US$215 million, and its yellow tentacles controlled the country's railroads, the main port Puerto Barrios, and consequently had control over all the country's other exports.

This hegemony was largely unchecked until 1952, when President Jacobo Árbenz Guzman drafted new reform laws, which redistributed land to peasants at a fraction of its market value. US interests were deemed to be under threat, and a plot was hatched by the CIA (whose director Allen Dulles was also on the UFC board) to support an invading force of Guatemalan exiles from Honduras, which overthrew Árbenz in 1954.

The new CIA-backed strongman, Carlos Castillo Armas, returned all the confiscated land to the UFC, which merged with United Brands in the 1960s and finally quit Guatemala in 1972, selling its remaining land to Del Monte.

have been painted in harmonious pastel shades, and there's a fine plaza in the center of town that boasts a twin-domed cathedral.

Just across the causeway, the gritty urban sprawl of Santa Elena and San Benito could not present more of a contrast. These are rough and ready frontier towns, where the streets are thick with dust and dirt.

AROUND FLORES

The small but spread-out village of **El Remate** ㉟ is another good base for exploring Tikal, with a burgeoning number of hotels. It is 30km (18.5 miles) from Santa Elena/Flores and particularly convenient if you are approaching the ruins from Belize.

About 3km (2 miles) from the center of the village is a small nature preserve, the **Biotopo Cerro Cahuí** (6.30am–dusk). The preserve is home to a remarkable diversity of plant life (mahogany, *ceiba*, and *sapodilla* trees, orchids and epiphytes), animals (spider and howler monkeys, armadillos, and ocelots) and particularly an exceptional

Flores is a colonial town perched on an island.

quantity of birds, with hundreds of species recorded here.

TIKAL

Entombed in dense jungle, where the inanimate air is periodically shattered by the roars of howler monkeys, the phenomenal, towering ruins of **Tikal** ㊱ are one of the wonders of the Americas. Five magnificent temple-pyramids soar above the forest canopy, finely carved stelae and altars in the plaza eulogize the city's glorious history, giant stucco masks adorn monuments, and stone-flagged causeways lead toward other ruined cities lying even deeper in the jungle.

Tikal's scale is awesome. In the Classic period its population grew to almost 100,000. Trade routes connected the city with Teotihuacán (near modern-day Mexico City), the Caribbean and Pacific coasts. Temple IV was built to a height of around 65 meters (213ft), complete with its enormous roof comb. Exquisite jade masks, ceramics, jewelry, and sculptures were created. There were ball courts, sweat baths, colorfully painted royal palaces, and another 4,000 buildings to house the artisans, astrologers, farmers, and warriors of the greatest city of the Classic Maya civilization.

Most travelers concur that Tikal is the most visually sensational of all the Maya sites. To get the most out of your visit, try to stay overnight at one of the hotels close to the ruins, to witness the electric atmosphere at dawn and dusk when the calls of toucans, frogs, monkeys, and other mammals echo around the surrounding jungle. The temperature and humidity are punishing at any time of year, so make sure you take plenty of water, and also insect repellent.

TIKAL HISTORY

Tikal is one of the oldest Maya sites: only some of the Mirador Basin sites and Cuello (in Belize) predate it. It's located in the central lowland Maya zone, the cradle of Maya civilization, in a dense subtropical forest environment. The earliest evidence of human habitation at Tikal is around 700 BC, in the Preclassic period. By 500 BC the first simple structures were constructed, but Tikal would have been little more than a small village at this time and Nakbé, some 55km (34 miles) to the north, was the dominant power in the region.

By the time Tikal's first substantial ceremonial structures were built (the North Acropolis and the Great Pyramid) around 200 BC, powerful new cities had emerged, above all the enormous El Mirador, 64km (40 miles) to the north and connected by a *sacbé* raised causeway.

By the start of the Classic period in AD 250, El Mirador and Nakbé had faded and Tikal had grown to be one of the most important Maya cities, along with Uaxactún. The great Tikal leader Great Jaguar Paw and his general Smoking Frog defeated Uaxactún in AD 376, bringing on an era when Tikal and rival 'superpower' Calakmul contested dominance of the Maya region for another two centuries. Huge advances were made in the study of astronomy, calendrics, and arithmetics under Stormy Sky (AD 426–57). But disaster struck in 562 when upstart Caracol (in Belize) defeated Double Bird of Tikal and forged a crucial alliance with Calakmul that was to humble Tikal for 120 years – no stelae at all were carved in this time.

Tikal's renaissance was sparked by Ah Cacau or Lord Chocolate (682–734) and continued by his son Caan Chac, who ordered the construction of most of the temples that bestride the ruins today, which are taller and grander than earlier buildings. Caan Chac also reassumed control of the core Maya area, eclipsing bitter rival Calakmul. Tikal continued to control the region, enjoying unsurpassed stability and prosperity into the 9th century; it faded quickly by AD 900, however, along with all the other lowland sites.

VISITING TIKAL

Before (or after) you enter Tikal (tel: 2367 2837; daily 6am–8pm), have a look in the **Visitors' Center Ⓐ**, where the **Museo Lítico** has an excellent collection

Temple I at Tikal.

⊙ PETÉN WILDLIFE

Despite illegal logging and environmental damage, vast areas of the Petén forest remain intact, and this is still one of the best places in Central America to see some spectacular wildlife. A number of national parks and preserves have been established (and combined as the Maya Biosphere Reserve) to protect the subtropical habitat of over 4,000 plant species and animals that include jaguars, crocodiles, tapirs, ocelots, collared peccaries, armadillos, boa constrictors, blue morpho butterflies, and 450 resident and migratory birds. Even if you only make it to Tikal, you should hear the deafening roar of the howler monkey, glimpse toucans and parrots squabbling in the forest canopy, and perhaps spot an ocellated turkey or a gray fox in the undergrowth.

A Mayan Classic-period censer, depicting a deity holding a human head, at Museo Tikal.

of stelae and carvings; nearby is the **Museo Morley B**, where the exhibits include ceramics, jade, the burial ornaments of Lord Chocolate, and Stela 29, the oldest found at Tikal (both daily).

The **Great Plaza C** is the first place to head for, the nerve center of the city for 1,500 years. The grassy plaza is framed by the perfectly proportioned Temples I and II to the east and west, the North Acropolis, and the Central Acropolis to the south. In Classic Maya days, these monumental limestone buildings would have been painted vivid colors, predominantly red, with clouds of incense smoke smoldering from the upper platforms. Civic and religious ceremonies, frequently including human sacrifice, would have been directed by priests and kings from the top of the temples.

Temple I D (also known as the Temple of the Giant Jaguar because of a jaguar carved in its door lintel), was built to honor Lord Chocolate, who was buried in a tomb beneath the 44-meter (144ft) high structure with a stately collection of goods (now exhibited in the Morley Museum). Facing Temple I

across the plaza is **Temple II E** (also known as the Temple of the Masks), slightly smaller at 38 meters (125ft) tall, and a little less visually impressive, too, because part of its massive roof comb is missing. Both temples were constructed around AD 740.

Between the two mighty edifices, on the north side of the plaza is a twin row of stelae and altars, about 60 in all. Many date from Classic Maya times, but were moved here from other parts of the site by post-Classic people in a revivalist effort – Stela 5 has some particularly fine glyphs. Behind the stelae is the untidy bulk of the **North Acropolis F**, a jumble of disparate masonry composed of some 16 temples and an estimated 100 buildings buried underneath, parts of which are some of the oldest constructions at Tikal, dating back to 250 BC.

On the south side of the plaza is the **Central Acropolis G**, a maze of buildings thought to function as the rulers' palace, grouped around six small courtyards. In front of the Central Acropolis is a small ball court, and behind it to the south is the palace reservoir and

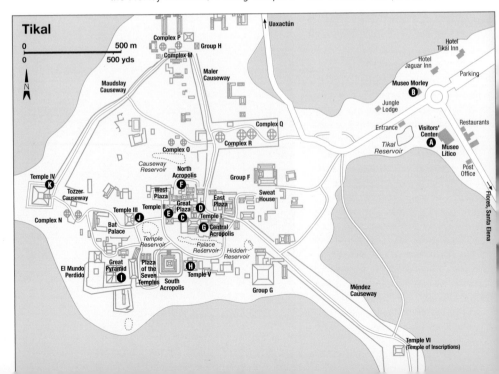

the restored 58-meter (190ft) **Temple V** . A very steep staircase ascends this temple (which may be closed following heavy rain), and from its summit there's an astonishing view of the entire site.

THE LOST WORLD

Reached by a trail from Temple V, El Mundo Perdido (The Lost World) is a beautiful, atmospheric complex of buildings, dominated by the mighty **Great Pyramid** ❶, a 32-meter (105ft) high Preclassic monument that's Tikal's oldest known structure. It is also an ideal base from which to watch sunrise or sunset. **Temple III** ❶, north from here, peaks at 55 meters (180ft) and remains cloaked in jungle, while **Temple IV** ❸, has been half-cleared of vegetation. Temple IV is the tallest of all Tikal's monuments, at around 64 meters (210ft), or 70 meters (230ft) if you include its platform, making it the second-highest pre-Columbian structure ever built – only the Danta temple at El Mirador eclipses it. Getting to the top involves a tricky climb up a ladder, but the view from the summit really is astounding – mile after mile of rainforest, broken only by the roof combs of the other temples.

For more on Tikal, see page 38.

THE NORTHERN RUINS

In the thick jungle of the Maya Biosphere Reserve in the extreme north of Guatemala, there are dozens more Maya ruins, most almost completely unexcavated. The easiest to get to is **Uaxactún** ❸, 24km (15 miles) away, and connected to Tikal by a dirt road, served by one daily bus from Flores/Santa Elena. Uaxactún rivaled Tikal for many years in the early Classic era, but was finally defeated in a battle on January 16, AD 378. Today there is an interesting observatory comprising three temples built side by side (Group E), numerous fine stelae, simple accommodation, and, of course, the jungle to explore and admire.

Just a couple of kilometers from the Mexican border, the Preclassic metropolis of **El Mirador**, matches Tikal in scale and may yet be found to exceed it. Unless you take a pricey helicopter tour, it is only accessible by foot.

Finally, way over on the other side of the Maya Biosphere Reserve on the Río Usumacinta is the extremely isolated **Piedras Negras**. The site, which towers over the Guatemalan bank of the river, can only be accessed by boat, with trips organized in Guatemala City. Some of the finest stelae in the Maya world were carved at Piedras Negras, and there is a megalithic stairway and substantial ruins to admire, including a sweat bath and an impressive acropolis, with extensive rooms and courtyards.

YAXHA

Around 73km (45 miles) east of Flores are the substantial ruins of **Yaxhá** ❸, which are steadily being restored. Structure 216, which tops 30 meters (98ft), is Yaxhá's most impressive construction. There's also a fine Preclassic temple cluster, with three large pyramids arranged in a triadic formation, and two giant stucco masks.

View from Temple V, Tikal.

The Great Blue Hole in Belize's waters.

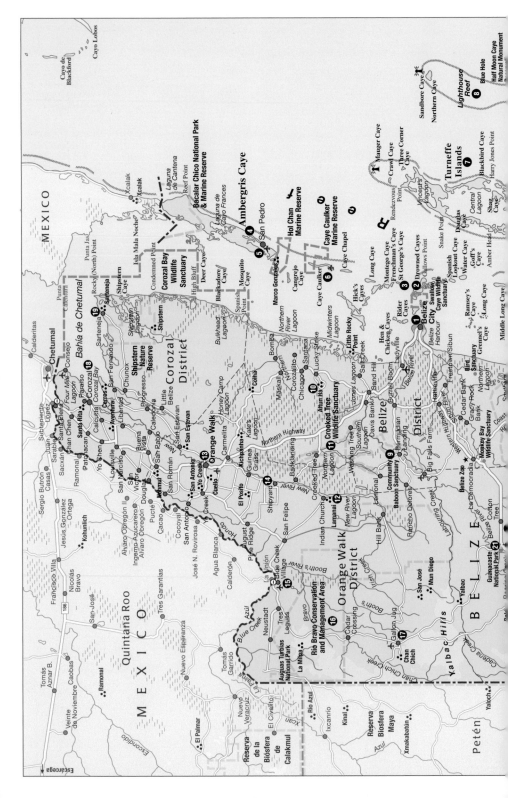

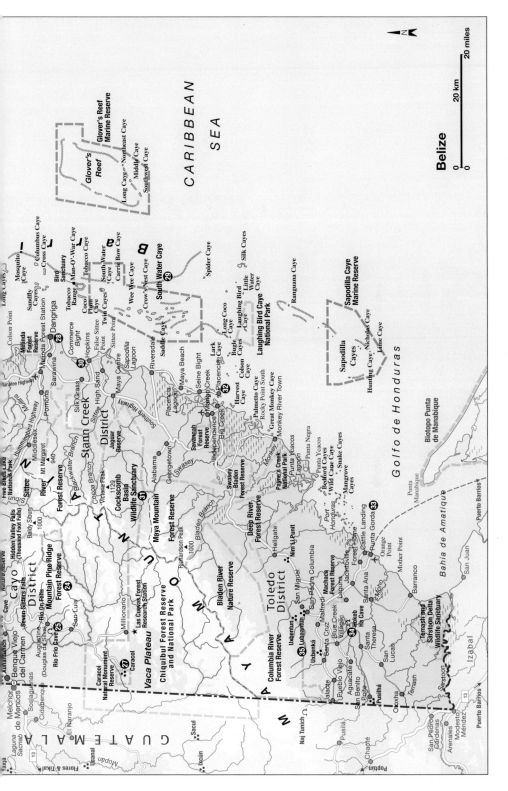

Belize

CARIBBEAN SEA

Beach at Laughing Bird Caye National Park.

BELIZE

Belize may be tiny, but it can claim plenty of superlatives, from the longest barrier reef in the Western Hemisphere to what are some of the most important Maya sites in the world.

Nature reigns supreme in Belize, from tangled rainforests crisscrossed with ancient caves, roaring rivers, and crystal pools, to the lively sunwarmed cayes, where you can sip rum cocktails with your toes planted in the sand. Spend a day or two in Belize and it's easy to see why this is a country that welcomes many repeat visitors: one taste is rarely enough.

Belize City is the cacophonous hub – the whole nation under one roof, distilled down into this bustling, ramshackle port town by the Caribbean Sea. North of the city, riverside communities left slumbering since the end of the logging industry in the 1960s are waking up and breathing new life into Belize's environmental treasure chest. Here, you'll spy more wildlife in one day than in most other parts of the world in a year. Maya cities like Lamanai are being further unearthed, their mysteries studied by teams of archeologists from around the globe.

Heading west into the hills around San Ignacio, a welcome drop in temperature is accompanied by a booming network of jungle lodges. Pump up the adrenalin by tubing down wild rivers, followed by horseback rides up to mountain summits for sweeping views of the canopy. Capped by the Mountain Pine Ridge, home of the great Maya city of Caracol, the region has become

Belize's main ecotourism hub. Toward the south, Placencia is blessed with the country's finest beaches, but even with the tourist influx, the locals retain a defiantly laid-back lifestyle. Head into the interior of the far south to explore Belize's only true tropical rainforest, where Maya villages coexist with nature in a way that has not changed in thousands of years.

Finally, the undisputed highlight for most visitors to Belize: the cayes (pronounced keys), a necklace of islands strung the length of the coral reef.

Main Attractions
Belize City
The cayes
Altun Ha
Lamanai
Corozal
San Ignacio
Caracol
Dangriga
Placencia

Maps on pages
166, 170

Lamanai ruins.

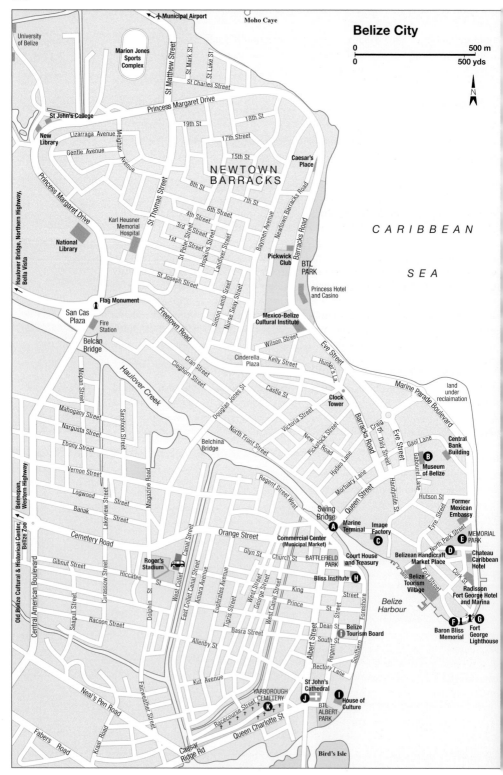

Belize City

Unforgettable islands, the cayes range from upbeat tourist spots to stranded desert isles offering the best diving, snorkeling, and fishing.

BELIZE CITY

The rough and tumble exterior of **Belize City ❶** belies its treasures, which include the country's top museums, beautifully restored historical buildings, and a premier performing arts center.

Most travelers see just one small, rather dismal corner of Belize City: the airport. They fly in to Belize, and promptly fly back out – to the cayes or elsewhere in the country. But, if you're here to experience all sides of the country, then it's worth lingering for a day or two. In addition to the city's lively streets, this is the cultural heart of the country, with several excellent museums covering archeology and the country's history.

DOWNTOWN BELIZE CITY

The city center's busiest hub – and best-known landmark – is the **Swing Bridge ❹**, one of three bridges connecting the city's south and north sides. Constructed in 1922 for what was then primarily pedestrian traffic, the bridge has the distinction of being the only manually operated swing bridge still in existence in the Americas. Using long poles inserted into a capstan, four men lever the bridge to face the harbor mouth so that boats can sail through. The bridge now operates generally only when large boats are passing through or during special events. Whether it's in use or not, it's worth stopping by for picturesque views of Belize City and the colorful fishing boats bobbing on Haulover Creek.

The star cultural sight of Belize City is the excellent **Museum of Belize ❸** (Gabourel Lane, tel: 223 4524, www. nichbelize.org, Mon–Fri 8.30am–5pm), housed in Her Majesty's Prison, which was in use until the early 1990s. The superbly curated museum showcases a variety of exhibits that explore the history of Belize City and stunning ceramics and jade jewelry from Belize's Maya culture, including a replica of the famous jade head from Altun Ha.

Swing Bridge, Belize City.

THE NORTHSIDE

The northside unfolds north of the Swing Bridge, and is dotted with city's top hotels, the breezy Memorial Park and Belize City's cruise ship port.

Near the Swing Bridge is the Marine Terminal, where boats depart regularly for Caye Caulker and San Pedro. The surrounding stands sell T-shirts, hats, beach towels, and other souvenirs. Just up the street from the Marine Terminal, heading away from the Swing Bridge is the **Image Factory** Ⓒ (91 North Front Street; tel: 610 5072; www. imagefactorybelize.com; Mon–Fri 9am–6pm). This is one of Belize's first comprehensive art galleries, and it features local artists and visiting talents, as well as educational exhibits on natural and cultural history.

On the waterfront is the Belize Tourism Village, a large shopping mall and entertainment complex that caters to the vast number of cruise ship visitors. A few blocks over, near Memorial Park, is the **Belizean Handicraft Market Place** Ⓓ (Memorial Park; tel: 223 3627; hours vary, generally Mon–Sat 9am–5pm), which is filled with Belizean hardwood crafts, such as bowls and picture frames, along with Maya basketry and hot sauces and spices.

MEMORIAL PARK AND MARINE PARADE

In 1924, an American construction company reclaimed the land and built some lovely homes – many of which still stand – on Cork Street and facing **Memorial Park** Ⓔ, which commemorates the Battle of St George's Caye in 1798 and Belizean servicemen who served in World Wars I and II. The park is used for open-air concerts and is a favorite gathering spot during the September Celebrations. The Marine Parade, which runs along the waterfront edge of Memorial Park, has been renovated over the last decade and is now a breezy boulevard and pedestrian promenade.

With several guesthouses and one of the city's largest hotels, Radisson Fort George Hotel and Marina, the tip of the northside – known as the Fort – may have more tourist accommodations than anywhere else in town. Locals also

Jade mosaic mask originating from Corozal in 150-300 AD, at the Museum of Belize.

enjoy the view from the Fort, particularly on Sunday afternoons when families and lovers take a walk out to the lighthouse, past the **Baron Bliss Memorial** **F**. The Baron, a wealthy British invalid who fished Belizean waters for several weeks and then died aboard his yacht in 1927, left the bulk of his estate to the Belizean people in gratitude for their hospitality during his final days.

The **Fort George Lighthouse** **G** is one of the last things visitors see when leaving the city by water taxi and it is still a welcome site to boaters when they approach the mouth of the Haulover Creek.

BLISS CENTRE AND HOUSE OF CULTURE

Facing the sea near the Court House rises the **Bliss Institute** **H**. Built with funds from the Baron Bliss trust, the modernized building houses the Bliss Centre for the Performing Arts (Southern Foreshore, tel: 227 2110, www.nichbelize.org, visitor center Mon–Fri 8am–5pm, performances usually 6–9pm), a state-of-the-art venue, with a 600-seat theater that features local shows, dance, and music.

The **House of Culture** **I** (Regent Street, tel: 277 3050, www.nichbelize.org, daily 9am–4pm), formerly the Government House, completed in 1812, rises over the end of Regent Street. This spacious colonial mansion was home to British governors appointed to Belize. The House of Culture offers art and music classes, and hosts art exhibitions, concerts, plays, and even fashion shows.

ST JOHN'S CATHEDRAL

The oldest Anglican church in Central America, **St John's Cathedral** **J** (southern end of Albert Street, daily 6am–6pm) looms just across the street from the House of Culture. Built by slaves using bricks brought to Belize as ship's ballast, the building was completed in 1820 and became the coronation site of four Mosquito Kings, whose

people (Native Americans who once inhabited the Mosquito Coast, in what is now Nicaragua) maintained good relations with the British government in Belize, even though they eventually came under Spanish rule.

Lying opposite the cathedral is **Yarborough Cemetery** **K**, named for the land's owner, the magistrate James Yarborough. It was used from 1781 to 1882, first as a burial ground for the colony's more prominent citizens and later opened to the masses.

Nearby is Regent Street, which is lined with the city's best-preserved examples of 19th- and early 20th-century architecture: a stroll here is like stepping back into Belize City's history.

THE CAYES

From the spectacular Blue Hole to the lively resorts of Ambergris Caye, the cayes of Belize are the country's leading tourist attraction.

Ambergris Caye may get all the glory (and the majority of visitors to Belize), but there's a lot more to the cayes than just this sun-dappled island. Each of

Sailing boats in the harbor, Belize City.

There is one place in Belize where you can sure of seeing the country's most special creatures in a natural setting.

What many people fail to realize when they come to Belize is that their chances of seeing the larger land animals are limited. The tangle of vines and thick foliage makes it difficult to see even a few feet off a forest path or road. Also, many tropical creatures are nocturnal, finding safety under the cloak of night. Except for a flash of fur dissolving into the bush, or the snap of branches and rustle of leaves, most visitors will end up experiencing the habitat where wildlife live instead of viewing the creatures themselves.

But there is one place where you are assured of seeing a jaguar or a tapir in a natural setting. Belize Zoo (www.belizezoo.org; daily 8am–4.30pm) is an oasis of ponds, forests, and flowers among the sprawling savannas 47km (29 miles) west of Belize City. More than 60 indigenous Belizean animals live here in large, natural enclosures.

If you can, try to visit the zoo first thing in the morning or late in the afternoon, when the animals

A margay cat, or 'tiger cat,' at Belize Zoo.

are more active. You will often feel that you are in the forest, peering through a tangle of vines and shrubs to catch a glimpse of a puma, jaguarundi, or ocelot. Patience and persistence are necessary to view the creatures here, but your patience will be rewarded: a glimpse of a jaguar staking out his dominion, time in the company of curious and lively kinkajous, or eye-to-eye contact with the towering jabirú stork. Other star attractions include a pair of harpy eagles, the largest eagles in the world, which are nearly extinct in Central America. They are an awesome sight, and of great conservation importance.

There's also a reptile area where you can see Belizeans snakes, including the very venomous fer-de-lance and the boa constrictor. The Belize Zoo education programs concentrate on informing visitors about snakes and their beneficial role in the ecosystem, helping to control rats and other rodents.

The animals and grounds are meticulously cared for, and fun signs spell out the natural habits of each animal and its endangered status, reminding visitors that 'Belize is my home too!' Raised gravel paths lead from exhibit to exhibit through natural savanna and pine ridge vegetation, as well as transplanted rainforest. Belize Zoo is as much a botanical garden as it is a zoo, and it is a focal point for environmental awareness in Belize. It operates on strict environmentally friendly principles, with composting and lots of recycling.

Sharon Matola, the North American founder and driving force behind the zoo, arrived in Belize after a colorful career that included time as a lion-tamer in Romania and on a circus tour in Mexico. She started the zoo to provide a home for animals that were used in a wildlife documentary she worked on. Today the focus of the zoo is on research and conservation – with projects that range from educating schoolchildren about harpy eagles to organizing a national day for the tapir.

Belize Zoo covers 12 hectares (30 acres), and is part of a larger complex that includes a Tropical Education and Research Center; you can stay here, too, in the Belize Zoo Jungle Lodge (www.belizezoo.org), which includes an unmissable night tour of the zoo. As many animals are nocturnal, including wild cats and most mammals, you have a good chance of observing them at their most active.

the cayes and atolls, from Caye Caulker to Turneffe Atoll, offer a wholly unique experience. In short: to fully experience the cayes is to travel liberally among them. Regular flights from the International Airport in Belize City serve both Ambergris Caye and Caye Caulker, and water taxis and boat charters can get you everywhere else.

CAYES HISTORY

Many of the cayes' names date back to the days of pirates and buccaneers. Near Belize City, for example, the **Drowned Cayes ❷** contain such evocative titles as Frenchman's Caye and Spanish Lookout; Bannister Bogue is a channel named after a pirate who later became a logwood cutter in the late 17th century, while Gallows Point was where criminals and freebooters were hanged. The pirate John Colson anchored his ship at **Colson's Caye** farther south, but today lobster fishermen use these mangroves to collect booty of a different sort. **Robinson's Point** was once the center of Belize's boat-building industry with a shipyard run by

the Hunter and Young families; all that remains is an old lighthouse.

Just 14km (9 miles) from Belize City, crescent-shaped **St George's Caye ❸** is the most historic of all the offshore islands. It was here that the British buccaneers established the territory's first real settlement around 1650; a century and a half later, they defeated Spanish invaders in the famous Battle of St George's Caye in 1798.

Today the only reminders of these colorful times at St George's Caye are a mounted cannon on the beach and a small graveyard near **St George's Lodge**. The one hotel operating on the island is the luxury **St. George's Caye Resort** (www.st-georgesresort.com), catering mainly to scuba divers.

AMBERGRIS CAYE

As your boat pulls up to the palm tree-shaded shoreline – or as you catch a bird's-eye view of the verdant island from the plane, ringed by sandy beaches and crystal waters – it comes as no surprise that Madonna's famous song *La Isla Bonita* was inspired by **Ambergris**

An inviting hammock, Ambergris Caye.

Caye . The hugely popular island commands more than 50 percent of all visitors to Belize – with all the attendant tourist services, from lavish resorts to hostels catering to budget backpackers to all manner of restaurants and bars. The island lies 56km (35 miles) from Belize City, and can be reached by water taxi in two hours or by small propeller plane in about 20 minutes. The main settlement on the island is **San Pedro** ❺, whose name has effectively become synonymous with the caye. San Pedro's airport has a rugged appeal to it, far removed from the crowded world of international terminals. Sometimes, you'll even see dogs snoozing beneath the parked planes.

SAN PEDRO

In the early 1980s, fishing was still the major industry at San Pedro – which is why the town and church were named after St Peter. Now many of the fishermen use their locally made mahogany boats to take tourists to the Barrier Reef that parallels the island. But although this is the most touristy part of Belize, the population is still only 5,000. If you like your tourism slick and well-orchestrated, with raging nightclubs and elegant dining, this may not be the place for you. The allure of San Pedro and the caye is its low-key charm, flanked by its stunning setting.

The heart of town is midway along Barrier Reef Drive. On one block, there is the **Town Hall** and police station. On the next block is **San Pedro Church**, an airy building whose large windows have jalousies so that the congregation can be cooled by the Caribbean breeze. On the breezy beachfront several miles north and south of San Pedro, numerous luxury resorts have been built over the last decade – with new resorts regularly popping up. Even so, life on Ambergris is still pretty mellow, and going barefoot is appropriate just about anywhere. This relaxed atmosphere has attracted more than a few resident North Americans, who now run hotels, gift shops, and restaurants. Directly down on the beach from here is the center of the caye's nightlife.

North of town is the **Boca del Rio**, known locally as The River: a bridge

Golf carts along San Pedro's high street.

joins the town to the northern part of the island, where a rugged dirt road leads to the tiny village of **Tres Cocos** and the northern resorts that lie on beautiful, though largely deserted, beaches. There are no towns here, so activity centers around several resorts and some good restaurants.

The lagoon side of Ambergris Caye has long been overlooked, with just a few restaurants and untamed swathes of land that hold pockets of residential homes. But, with the completion of the ambitious San Pedro Sunset Boardwalk and Water Taxi Terminal in 2014, which became fully operational in 2016, that's beginning to change. Although many boats and water taxis still pull up on the reef side, it is hoped that the new terminal will increase traffic to the lagoon in the future.

SOUTH OF SAN PEDRO

Ambergris Caye owes much of its physical existence to the mangrove, which can be most easily seen to the south, following the sand road from the airport. Untouched except for the occasional plastic wrapping or old shoe washed in by the gentle waves, the mangrove swamp is like a trip into the womb that gave birth to the island.

South of San Pedro, the beachfront is dotted with a number of rustic-chic resorts, such as the eco-friendly Xanadu Island Resort (www.xanaduislandresort.com) as well as the luxurious colonial-style Victoria House (www.victoria-house.com). Plenty of outdoor bars liven up the evenings.

THE LONGEST BARRIER REEF IN THE WESTERN HEMISPHERE

Like any other self-respecting tropical island, Ambergris Caye looks to the sea. The island is set in the Barrier Reef, and it is offshore that one heads for swimming, fishing, diving, and snorkeling. Most of the water between the coast and the reef is shallow and grassy – a shoreline for lounging, not surfing. It was the

Maya who discovered a natural cut in the reef, which attracted a wide range of marine life. They called it 'Hol Chan,' Little Channel. In 1987, the area around the cut was declared the **Hol Chan Marine Reserve** – only 10 minutes away by boat, it is Ambergris' principal local site for snorkeling and scuba diving.

SHARK RAY ALLEY

While San Pedro is the ideal base if you're planning to visit Hol Chan, many dive and snorkel operators from Caye Caulker will also take you there. Snorkeling along the reef is fun, but the truly adventurous will want to take the plunge at **Shark Ray Alley**. This is only 2km (1 mile) south of Hol Chan and offers the unique experience of diving or snorkeling with stingrays and sharks – well, nurse sharks. Although they seem fairly harmless (but don't look that way at feeding time) this is not a swim for the fainthearted. You may jump into the water fairly confident but suddenly start feeling a little nervous when the wings of the ray brush against you. You can only visit Shark Ray Alley with an experienced guide.

El Pescador resort, south of San Pedro.

Buy fresh coconuts at Caye Caulker.

THE BLUE HOLE

Lying just 11km (7 miles) north of Half Moon Caye is one of the world's most famous dive sites – and a stunning natural wonder: the **Blue Hole**.

Looking from the air like a dark blue pool in a field of turquoise, the site gained fame in 1972 when Jacques Cousteau maneuvered his ship *Calypso* through narrow coral channels to moor and film inside. The Blue Hole is actually a sinkhole created by a collapsed underground cavern; over 300 meters (980ft) across and 135 meters (445ft) deep, with huge stalactites hanging from offshoot caves at depths of 30–45 meters (100–150ft).

While there is not much marine life in this vivid blue shaft of water, the geological formations and encircling coral are spectacular. Sharks and turtles abound in the waters around the Blue Hole, though their presence is rarely predictable. This dive is usually reserved for the more adventurous and experienced, under the strict supervision of a dive master. It is definitely not a plunge to be attempted by the novice.

The Belize Audubon Society and the Forestry Department manage the **Blue Hole Natural Monument at Lighthouse Reef**, which covers an area of 414 hectares (1,023 acres), with the Blue Hole at the center.

CAYE CAULKER

'Go slow' is the motto on **Caye Caulker** ❻, and after a few days ambling its sunny shores, you'll understand why. The great appeal of Caye Caulker is the loose and languid rhythm – wake up late, take a leisurely sail, then a dip in the water, and finally ease into the evening with a chilled Belikin in hand and toes in the warm sand as the sun sinks into the Caribbean Sea.

This working fishing village was originally settled by mestizos (of mixed Spanish and indigenous blood) fleeing the Caste War in Mexico's Yucatán in the mid 19th century; today it has about 1,500 year-round residents, mostly of mestizo descent. The population swells considerably on weekends and holidays, when hundreds of Belize City residents descend on the island's small

⊘ DISCOVERING BELIZE'S BARRIER REEF

Immerse yourself in a spectacular underwater world of colorful corals, tropical fish, huge rays, barracudas, sharks, and turtles. The Belize Barrier Reef is a colossal epic – and was declared a Unesco World Heritage Site in December 1996 – offering some of the finest diving and snorkeling in the world.

The Belize Barrier Reef (which comprises the central section of the Great Maya Reef that stretches between the Yucatán and Honduras) is split into segments separated by relatively deep channels. Oxygen and plankton (free-floating microscopic plants and animals) carried by tides flush the Belize coastal zone twice daily through these channels, thereby feeding billions of hungry coral polyps and other reef creatures. As a result, the reef attracts large numbers of fish and is consequently superb for diving and snorkeling. Numerous companies offer diving, snorkeling, and sailing trips, making it a breeze to explore the reef.

Hundreds of species of fish are visible to snorkelers and divers over the coral reefs. Most ignore humans, unless the area has been heavily spear-fished. But there are exceptions.

Barracudas have an unnerving habit of approaching and even following swimmers. This is pure curiosity – they normally move away when approached. Moray eels can inflict a nasty bite if annoyed. Sharks will sense you long before you see them, and usually move away. However, all sharks should be treated with caution. Even the nurse shark can become aggressive if molested.

Lying as close as 16km (10 miles) off the barrier reef are three of the very finest coral atolls in the Caribbean: Turneffe Atoll, Glover's Reef, and Lighthouse Reef, whose combined reef systems comprise almost 225km (140 miles) of coral growth.

Coral reefs do not exist in isolation. Mangroves line much of the Belizean coastline, the cayes and lower reaches of the rivers. Seagrass beds, their blades swaying in the current like the long grass of spring meadows, blanket the sea floor between reef and shore. These mangrove and seagrass beds may not look as spectacular as coral reefs but, as giant marine nurseries, they form the foundation of the continuing long-term health of the country's coastal zone.

guesthouses and hotels. The winter holidays and Easter are the busiest seasons, so it's well worth making reservations in advance, though you can usually still find a few basic spots with rooms available even at the last minute.

The Split, at the north end of the village, is a channel through the island made by Hurricane Hattie in 1961. It's one of the most popular gathering places on Caye Caulker, with a nice swimming area (be careful of the strong current and speedboats, however) and an open-air bar.

Caye Caulker's big draw is, as with elsewhere on the Cayes, the accessibility to the longest Barrier Reef in the Western Hemisphere. Numerous tour operators offer diving, snorkeling, boating, and kayaking trips to the reef, where you can explore the colorful underwater world. Growing tourism has also meant growing pressure on the nearby reef. After a decade of requests from local fishermen and environmentalists, in 1999 the government gave preserve status to most of the reef in front of the caye.

At the island's northern tip is the **Caye Caulker Forest and Marine Reserve**, home to mangroves, gumbo limbo, and poisonwood. Other native inhabitants of the reserve's littoral forest include scaly-tailed iguanas (here called 'wish willies'), geckos, and multiple species of land crab. Local tour companies will offer day trips here upon request.

TURNEFFE ATOLL AND LIGHTHOUSE REEF

Diving and fishing enthusiasts may venture further into the Caribbean to Belize's three coral atolls. Although most watersport activities take place from charter boats, a surge of interest has fueled the development of a few island-based resorts. Two of these atolls, the Turneffe Atoll and Lighthouse Reef, can be reached from Belize City; the third, Glover's Reef, is off the coast from Dangriga

The **Turneffe Atoll** ❼ forms the surface elements of Belize's largest atoll running some 30 miles (48km) from north to south; it has several shallow lagoons, a couple of upscale resorts

Watching the sunset at the Lazy Lizard bar on the Spit, Caye Caulker.

⊘ Fact

The luxurious Maruba Resort and Jungle Spa (www.maruba-spa.com) is a surprising attraction in this undeveloped area. Marked at Mile 40.5 on the highway, the hotel offers a range of therapeutic cures, as well as an excellent restaurant.

Gorgonians and coral colonies growing on a shallow reef at Turneffe Atoll.

and two lighthouses. The northern-most beacon, built in 1885, is on **Mauger Caye** ('Skinny' in creole) while a second lighthouse can be found on **Caye Bokel** ('Elbow' in Dutch) at the southern tip of the atoll. Almost all the major charter boat and dive services arrange trips to Turneffe, but guests at the various fishing and vacation lodges are usually picked up by the lodge's own transportation from Belize City.

Lighthouse Reef ⑧ is another atoll with a treacherous boundary of coral. Like Turneffe, there are also two lighthouses here, one on **Sandbore Caye**; the other, first built in 1828 and replaced in 1848, is on **Half Moon Caye,** a crescent-shaped island that is easily one of the most beautiful places in Belize. The abundance of nesting sea birds and marine life made Half Moon Caye and its surrounding waters a natural choice for the nation's first Natural Monument in 1982. Around 4,000 red-footed booby birds nest on the island; the population is unusual for being white instead of the usual dull brown (the only other similar booby

colony is near the island of Tobago in the eastern Caribbean). An observation platform allows unrestricted viewing of the boobies, along with some of the 98 other species of birds that have been recorded on the island.

NORTHERN BELIZE

While the rest of Belize, from Cayo to the Cayes, is solidly on the tourist trail, Northern Belize remains largely undiscovered. And that's a big part of its appeal. This rural, quiet region nudges up against Mexico and is the territory of Latinos or mestizos – Spanish is as common as Creole and there's a distinctive Latin flair to the villages and towns. The Latin influence is also noticeable in the cuisine, which is a delicious blend of Mexican and Belizean. As for commerce: sugar cane continues to be king and just about every family is either growing it, trucking it, or processing it.

Tourism is a sideline, so you won't find the eco-lodges of San Ignacio or the lively bars of San Pedro. But if you like your Maya ruins remote and

mysterious and your towns and villages untouched and genuine, then you'll enjoy what sleepy Orange Walk, and even sleepier Corozal, have to offer.

COMMUNITY BABOON SANCTUARY

Community Baboon Sanctuary ❾ (8am–5pm) is one of the most popular and successful conservation projects in Belize. Founded in 1985, the Baboon Sanctuary is a co-operative effort between environmentalists (aided by the World Wildlife Fund under the auspices of the Belize Audubon Society) and local creole landowners to save Central America's declining population of black howler monkeys, known as baboons in Belize. Apart from Belize, this sub-species is only found in the river lowlands of Guatemala and southern Mexico, where the rainforest has been shrinking at such a rate that extinction was becoming probable.

The sanctuary's service village is **Bermudian Landing**, a British logging camp in the 17th century and today a relaxed creole outpost. Check in at the visitors' center here – there are some places to stay, some flat ground for tents, or the station manager can arrange for accommodations with local families. A small museum, opened in 1989, was Belize's first devoted to natural history, and an interpretative trail can be followed. Canoe trips, horseback riding, and crocodile-watching tours are also available.

ALTUN HA

Whether or not they know the archeologists' name for it, everyone in Belize recognizes the Temple of Masonry Altars at **Altun Ha** ❿ (www.nichbelize. com; daily 8am–5pm). The image is on the paper money, school textbooks, and perhaps even most importantly for some, it was chosen for the logo of the national beer, Belikin.

Altun Ha, Mayan for 'stone water,' was first excavated in 1957, but extensive work did not start until the discovery of

a jade pendant in 1963, which excited a great deal more interest. Archeological excavations unearthed a jade replica of the head of the Maya sun god Kinich Ahau, found in the Temple of the Masonry Altars (also known as Temple of the Sun God). At 15cm (6in) high and weighing 4.4kg (9.75lbs), it is the largest carved jade object ever found in the Maya world.

Altun Ha is made up of two plazas surrounded by temples. Plaza A is the first you come to, and beneath Temple A-1 is a magnificent temple, the Temple of the Green Tomb. More than 300 pieces were unearthed here, including jade, jewelry, flints, and jaguar skins.

Plaza B has the site's largest temple, B-4, the Temple of the Masonry Altars (which is depicted on the Belikin beer label).

CROOKED TREE WILDLIFE SANCTUARY

Due west of Altun Ha on the Philip Goldson (Northern) Highway is a dirt road to the left, leading after 19km (12 miles) to the **Crooked Tree Wildlife Sanctuary** ⓫

Altun Ha.

(8am–4.30pm). This string of four lagoons, connected by swamps and rivers, is one of Belize's richest bird habitats – nesting here are migratory flocks of egrets, tiger-herons, roseate spoonbills, and hundreds of other species. Perhaps the most impressive, although elusive, is the jabiru stork, the largest bird in the Western hemisphere, with a wingspan of up to 2.4 meters (8ft). The wildlife sanctuary was set up by the Belize Audubon Society in 1984 and is now managed by wardens from the village. Before entering, sign in at the tidy visitors' center, just outside the village of **Crooked Tree**, one of the first logging camps, founded by British logwood cutters in the 17th century. Before the causeway was built in the 1980s, the only way to get to Crooked Tree was by boat. The lagoon is a natural reservoir in the Belize River Valley and regularly floods in the rainy season.

The managers of the sanctuary can give you a little local history as well as provide information on nature trails and birdlife. The ideal way to visit is by taking a hired boat trip into the swamps

Fishing on the New River Lagoon, Lamanai.

and lagoons (call the visitors' center or any of the resorts in Crooked Tree). Peak birdwatching season is between April and May, when hatching begins (most migratory birds arrive in November, and many leave before the rainy season starts in July). As usual, start at dusk. There are three daily buses from Belize City, in the morning and afternoon.

LAMANAI

The trip to **Lamanai** ⑫ (daily 8am–5pm) is often as memorable as the impressive ruins themselves, thanks to the adventurous journey required to get there, via a rugged dirt road or a dreamy river trip through the sinuous waterways of a remote jungle river. Located on the banks of the New River Lagoon, it can be reached by easy day trips from Orange Walk. In addition, numerous tour companies offer trips to Lamanai from Belize City and the Cayes.

The river and surrounding swamp is teeming with wildlife, including a healthy population of Morelet's crocodiles. These gave Lamanai its name – Maya for 'submerged crocodile' – and make the prospect of swimming, while safe, rather nerve-racking. Apart from pointing out birdlife, most boat drivers will bump up against gutted tree trunks on the shoreline, waking up a mass of tiny, sleeping bats, and sending them in a cloud over passengers' heads.

By the time you reach the ruins, you feel like Indiana Jones, and since you may well have the place to yourself, there's nobody to destroy the illusion. A few thatched-roofed houses have been built at the dockside for the ruin's guards, along with an open-air picnic hut and a small museum piled high with Maya artifacts.

Lamanai was first settled some 3,000 years ago and its most impressive temples were built in the Preclassic period around 100 BC. Several centuries later, in the Classic period, the population had increased from 20,000 to 50,000. What makes Lamanai unique is that it was still inhabited when the first Spanish conquistadors arrived in search of gold here in the 16th century. The population was about a quarter of what it had once been and its most spectacular temples were untended. How Lamanai survived the cataclysm that devastated the other Maya cities is unknown. In any case, Spanish missionaries quickly set about building a church to convert the heathens. The Maya rebelled and burned it in the 1640s, but European-imported diseases soon decimated the community. Even so, there were a few Maya inhabitants here when British settlers arrived in the 19th century; the new colonialists drove them out to Guatemala so the land could be cleared for sugar.

Lamanai's best-known and most impressive pyramid is **N10-43**, a steep, 34-meter (112ft) high edifice. It reached its present height by around 100 BC, making it the largest Preclassic structure in the whole of Mesoamerica (although not as tall as the Classic pyramids at Xunantunich and Caracol, it is still considerably higher than any modern Belizean building). Like most Maya structures, it was modified heavily.

If you'd like to stay near the ruins, one of the best spots is the Lamanai Outpost Lodge (www.lamanai.com), which has thatched cabanas with private decks and a lagoon-facing restaurant that serves excellent local cuisine.

ORANGE WALK

Forming the hub of northern Belize's main roads, **Orange Walk** ⑬ is still the most convenient, if not the most interesting or comfortable, base for exploring the north. Although this is the largest town in the north, it's a dusty, quiet place, with just a handful of sights. The **Banquitas House of Culture** (www.nichbelize.org/houses-of-culture; Mon–Fri 8.30am–5.30pm), a small museum and cultural center just north of the town, has exhibits on the history of Orange Walk and the logwood industry, and some Maya artifacts on display.

Orange Walk is fondly called 'Sugar City' by residents because it is smack in the center of the northern sugar industry. Orange Walk has a variety of breezy,

Climbing the high temple at Lamanai.

inviting accommodations, including El Gran Mestizo Riverside Cabins (www. elgranmestizo.com), which also feature one of town's best restaurants, Maracas Bar & Grill, where you can feast on shrimp ceviche and tropical cocktails while looking out at the New River.

While it may not have the mass appeal of Lamanai, the **Cuello** archeological site on the property of the Cuello rum distillery, some 5km (3 miles) to the west of Orange Walk, is believed to be the oldest Maya ceremonial site in the area, dating back some 2,600 years. Permission must be obtained from the distillery to go onto the property.

The still-unpaved road from Orange Walk to Blue Creek was settled by mestizos and Yucatec Maya fleeing the Mexican Caste Wars, and many villages still bear Maya names like Yo Creek and Chan Pine Ridge. In the 1950s they were joined by a new immigrant group: the Mennonites (see box), who have ended up in two settlements, each representing opposite ends of their philosophical spectrum. The most conservative sect lives in **Shipyard** ⑭.

Known as the Old Colony, this is where the Mennonite women wear long, dark dresses and large beribboned straw hats in a style brought from Europe, while taciturn men wear suspenders or overalls rather than belts.

Along the Río Bravo escarpment in northwestern Orange Walk District is the more progressive Mennonite community of **Blue Creek Village** ⑮.

RÍO BRAVO CONSERVATION & MANAGEMENT AREA

In the far reaches of northwest of Orange Walk District is the **Río Bravo Conservation and Management Area** ⑯, established by the Program for Belize, which was founded in 1988 by the Massachusetts Audubon Society, This enormous tract of land – about 121,000 hectares (300,000 acres) – is designated for research and conservation, and is held up as one of Belize's most successful environmental conservation projects. The lands were acquired through donations inspired by its distinctive 'sponsor an acre of rainforest' fund-raising appeal.

Mennonite boys in Orange Walk district.

With more than 240 species of trees, 390 species of birds, and over 70 known species of mammal, Río Bravo represents one of Belize's highest concentrations of biodiversity. To generate further income, the program has entered the ecotourism industry and offers on-site accommodations and meals at two field stations: La Milpa and Hill Bank, located at opposite ends of the reserve.

Accommodations include *cabañas* and 'green dormitories' near La Milpa (5km/3 miles from the ruins) and Hill Bank field stations. For information and to make reservations, contact the Program for Belize Office (www.pfbelize.org).

CHAN CHICH LODGE AND GALLON JUG

Just south of the Río Bravo Area lies the **Gallon Jug** ⑰, a parcel of land covering some 52,000 hectares (130,000 acres) of tropical forest retained by Barry Bowen as a private preserve. Intensive farming is carried out in a small area, with corn, soybeans, coffee, cacao, and cardamom being grown. But Gallon Jug is best known for the spectacular **Chan Chich Lodge**, which is located – with the Archeology Department's blessing – in the lower plaza of an ancient Maya site. Chan Chich Lodge was carefully planned to have a minimum impact on the surrounding tropical forest and the Maya plaza (it also protects the site from robbers). It features luxurious thatched *cabañas* and a cozy dining room and bar, paneled in a variety of local hardwoods. There is also a screened swimming pool and Jacuzzi.

As a private preserve protected from hunting, Chan Chich enjoys some of the most abundant concentrations of tropical forest wildlife in Central America. Various tame animals wander around the site, including deer and foxes; there is a wealth of birdlife and jaguar sightings are not uncommon.

COROZAL DISTRICT AND TOWN

Tucked up in the northern limit of Belize, Corozal District looks like it has changed little since colonial days – or, by a further stretch of the imagination, the days of the Maya. The district is still only sparsely populated and scattered

Bedroom at Chan Chich Lodge.

⊙ THE MENNONITES IN BELIZE

Belize's Mennonite community is a resilient, religious sect that traces its roots to the 16th century Netherlands. They stand out in any Belizean crowd: blond, blue-eyed men in denim overalls and cowboy hats; modestly dressed women whose home-made outfits – ankle-length, long-sleeved frocks and wide-brimmed hats tied down with black scarves – defy the tropical heat. Polite and reserved, they talk quietly among themselves, not in Spanish, English, or Creole, but in guttural German.

These are part of Belize's Mennonite community, who take their name from a Dutch priest, Menno Simons. Mennonites live in isolated farming communities, calling themselves *die Stillen im Lande*, the Unobtrusive Ones. They reject state interference in their affairs and are committed pacifists.

Belize is the latest stop in a three-century odyssey – their beliefs have often led to persecution, driving them from the Netherlands to Prussia in the 1600s, to southern Russia, and, when the Russian government suggested military conscription in the 1870s, to Canada.

After World War I, the Canadian government demanded that only English be taught in Mennonite schools and, spurred on by anti-German feeling, reconsidered conscription. Again, many of the Mennonites moved on, this time to Mexico – only for the Mexican government then to try to include them in a new social security program.

Around 80,000 Mennonites remain in Mexico, including a community in Campeche, but others have moved to Belize, where their farming skills have proved successful. In colonial times few Belizeans farmed the land – even eggs were imported from abroad. The Mennonites are today the most successful farmers in Belize. They supply much of the country's food, including chicken, dairy products, and eggs, and make most of the country's furniture.

There is one important rule to remember: strict Mennonites object to having their photographs taken, believing no memory should be left of a person after they die.

with small, sleepy villages. Its entire eastern half is swampy savannah, accessible only by an uneven road that roughly traces the New River and Freshwater Creek; the western coast is dominated by sugar cane, and is one of the most intensely cultivated agricultural areas in the country.

The district's urban hub, **Corozal Town** 🔞, overlooks Chetumal Bay. A sea wall winds its way around the edge of town, and you'll often see the locals splashing in the waters here.

For an overview on Corozal and the region, head to the **Corozal House of Culture** (1st Avenue; tel: 422 0071; www.nichbelize.org; Mon–Fri 8am–5pm), housed in a renovated market dating back to 1886. The well-curated museum features a wide range of exhibits, including local art and Maya artifacts.

SARTENEJA AND SHIPSTERN NATURE RESERVE

The name of **Sarteneja** 🔟, a lazy fishing village on the **Sarteneja Peninsula**, means 'hole in a flat rock,' referring to a *cenote* or well. This must have been an attraction to the ancient Maya in this low rainfall district, with levels of precipitation well below the rest of Belize. Sarteneja is a pleasant enough place to pass an afternoon. The buildings' pastel colors are drained by the fierce sun, and you can go swimming right off the main pier in waters that range from milky to clear.

Just outside Sarteneja – and the main reason for coming to this remote corner – is the **Shipstern Conservation & Management Area** (tel: 632 7467; www.visitshipstern.com; daily 8am–5pm), founded in 1988. The reserve features an extensive, shallow, brackish water lagoon system, home to breeding colonies of many varieties of birds like the reddish egret and the wood stork.

WESTERN BELIZE

When travelers talk about visiting the interior of Belize, they are usually referring to the lush, mountainous rainforests around the town of San Ignacio, long the heart of the country's ecotourism trade. The region is a nature-lover's fantasy come true. Spread out across a remote subtropical wilderness are dozens of *cabaña*-style lodges, many of them quite luxurious. Within striking distance – by car, horseback, canoe, or foot – are secluded, jungle-rimmed swimming holes, enormous limestone caverns, Belize's most significant Maya ruins and Central America's highest waterfalls. The background music is the shriek of tropical birds, while iguanas, gibnuts, and skunks habitually stroll across the well-marked nature trails.

Meanwhile, the rainforests are surprisingly free of Belize's least popular life form, the mosquito – the higher altitude makes days around San Ignacio hot without being overwhelming, while evenings can almost be described as cool.

On the frontier with Guatemala, this is also one of the more Hispanic parts of Belize, populated largely by Spanish-speaking mestizos, and Maya

Cable ferry crossing New River on the way from Corozal Town to Copper Bank.

farmers; second in numbers come creoles, followed by a classically Belizean smattering of East Indians, Chinese, and Lebanese. Several large communities of Mennonites farm the rich land and can be seen clattering along the highways in horse-drawn buggies.

Across the Belizean western border in Guatemala lie the remains of one of the most magnificent ancient cities anywhere in Central America – Tikal (see page 38). A wide variety of tourist companies offer trips to Tikal from Belize; inquire at your hotel, which can often supply a list of recommended outfitters. Note that Crystal Auto Rental (see page 344) is one of the few car rental companies that allow you to take their vehicles across the border.

BELMOPAN

Founded in 1971, **Belmopan** ⑳ is the Brazilia of Belize: an artificial capital that has never quite caught on. Government departments are based here, but most politicians would rather commute from Belize City than take up permanent residence.

Belmopan has few historical monuments, and most of the buildings are administrative offices – in 10 minutes on the **Ring Road**, you can take in all the sights, including **Market Square**, which at any given moment is usually the busiest place in town: buses serving destinations all over Belize stop here and there are several banks and restaurants. Central American street vendors sell tasty corn and chicken tamales, and other local goodies.

GUANACASTE NATIONAL PARK

Guanacaste National Park ㉑ makes a good place to freshen up, right at the intersection of the George Price (Western) Highway. Not only does Guanacaste have magnificent trees and nature trails, but not too far from the main road there is an incredible swimming spot on the river. The current is very slow here as the water cascades gently over the rocks; locals wade right in with their clothing on, so there's no need to miss the refreshing cold water just because you forgot a bathing suit. A bus from Belize City, Belmopan or points south

The National Assembly building in Belmopan.

can drop you right at the entrance to the park making it one of the most accessible natural reserves in Belize.

BLUE HOLE NATIONAL PARK

Heading west from Belmopan, 21km (13 miles) down the Hummingbird Highway is the **St Herman's Blue Hole National Park** ㉒. There is one entrance near the Blue Hole itself (at the bottom of a long flight of steps) and another at the visitors' center near St Herman's Cave. The blue hole is an astonishing sight: it's truly blue, with just a touch of green at the edges of the 9-meter (30ft) diameter pool. The natural wonder is actually a collapsed karst sinkhole, estimated to be about 31 meters (100ft) deep. In the dry season the water is extremely cold because it is cooled by the underground limestone. The Belize Audubon Society manages the park, which also contain more than 250 species of birds and other animals.

CAYO DISTRICT

Cayo is the heart of Belize, embracing all the country's landscapes and

cultures and a perfect antidote to the heat and bustle of Belize City; the air is cooler, the people calmer, the pace gentler. And a short journey south from western Cayo into the Mountain Pine Ridge opens a world of environmental treasures here in the foothills of the majestic Maya mountains.

Cayo received its name after the Spanish word for cayes – coral islands off Belize's coast – while San Ignacio itself is also known as **El Cayo**. The name may be a reflection of the isolation early settlers felt from the rest of the world before a roadway was first pushed through in the 1930s. Until then, boat trips to Belize City took about 10 days, horseback journeys anywhere from two weeks to a month.

SAN IGNACIO

Built in a spectacular valley, on the edge of a ravine above the Macal River, the town of **San Ignacio** ㉓ is separated from the neighboring village of **Santa Elena** by the **Hawkesworth Suspension Bridge** – a miniature model of the Brooklyn Bridge.

San Ignacio was the last frontier in

Eva's restaurant and tourist information point, San Ignacio.

one of the most obscure corners of the British Empire, and several of its buildings retain a faded colonial charm. The narrow streets are quiet to the point of somnolence – although the combined population of San Ignacio and Santa Elena is around 14,000, making this the largest metropolis of western Belize. It's worth timing your visit to be here for Saturday, when local farmers flock to the **market** with their produce.

San Ignacio is dotted with welcoming restaurants and bars, and also has a wide range of accommodations. It draws many international travelers and Belizeans from other parts of the country, which translates into a boisterous bar scene, particularly on the weekends.

Just off Buena Vista Road, around a mile south (1.6km) are the ruins of **Cahal Pech** (tel: 824 4236; generally open daylight hours), one of the oldest Maya sites in the area – it was populated around 1,000 BC until AD 800. The name means 'Place of the Ticks' – given in the 1950s when the area was used as a cow pasture. Various tour companies offer trips here from San Ignacio.

MOUNTAIN PINE RIDGE FOREST RESERVE

The most popular excursion in the region is due south of San Ignacio to the **Mountain Pine Ridge Forest Reserve ㉔**. The sudden appearance of the pine forest, looking as if it is straight out of Vermont, is one of Belize's more peculiar geological anomalies. Geologists explain that the unique granite base and nutrient-poor soil content of the area was either thrust up from below Central America countless millennia ago or was a Caribbean island that was effectively pushed on top of the rest of the isthmus during its formation. **Actun Tunichil Muknal** (also known as ATM) is one of the country's grandest underground sights, consisting of a subterranean river with soaring chambers that are strewn with astonishing Maya archeological finds, including calcified skeletons of human sacrifice victims. ATM is only accessible via guided tour, the majority of which depart from San Ignacio or Belmopan; inquire at your hotel or the tourist office. One of the best ways to see ATM is Ian Anderson's Caves Branch Adventure

A traditional Creole meal, comprised of chicken, rice, beans, and fried plantain at Eva's restaurant, San Ignacio.

⊘ BELIZE: THE PATH TO INDEPENDENCE

It took Belize many years to win its independence. After the decline of the local Maya settlements, it was British settlers – known as 'Baymen' – and their slaves from the Caribbean who occupied the territory in the 17th century. These new inhabitants were interested in the lumber from Belize's forests, and they founded the settlement on St George's Caye.

Relations with the Spanish rulers of neighboring Guatemala were frequently tense throughout the 17th and 18th centuries, as British pirate ships used Belize's sheltered waters as harbors from which to attack Spanish ships. As a result of the American War of Independence, Spain declared war on Britain and in 1779 a sizeable Spanish force attacked St George's Caye. The settlement was rebuilt, but in 1798 the Spanish attacked again. Despite the fact that the Spanish had far superior firepower, a decisive sea battle was fought at St George's Caye, and the Spanish were soundly defeated.

In 1862, Britain finally recognized Belize as the Colony of British Honduras, and in 1871 it became a Crown Colony. In 1992, the Guatemalan Congress officially ratified the decision to recognize Belize, which led to a final pull-out of the British

garrison in 1993. The struggle within Belize to gain independence from Britain had begun in earnest after World War II. The People's United Party (PUP) was founded in 1950 under leader George Price; in 1961 he became First Minister.

On October 31, 1961, Belize was devastated by Hurricane Hattie. This particularly affected Belize City, which had been the capital since the 18th century. The authorities decided to build a new inland capital: Belmopan, named in honor of the Mopa, the Maya tribe who had resisted the Spanish conquistadors, and 'Bel' for Belize. Belmopan soon became a symbol of the new, independent Belize, though it has struggled to evolve from an administrative center to a thriving city.

The long-sought independence from Britain was eventually won in 1981, and George Price was elected as the first prime minister of the newly independent country, now officially Belize. Since then the PUP and rival United Democratic Party (UDP), a more conservative political grouping, have battled it out with the electorate. Dean Barrow was elected the nation's first black prime minister in 2008, and repeated his success in 2012 and in 2015, when he won a record third term.

Company & Jungle Lodge (www.caves-branch.com), where you can stay in wonderful treehouses, complete with hot tubs, and opt for a variety of adventures, including exploring ATM, rock-climbing, and more. At **Green Hills Butterfly Ranch** (tel: 820 4017; http://green-hills. net; daily 8am–4pm; guided tours available, final tour 3.30pm), you can walk through a butterfly enclosure and view an impressive botanical collection

Hidden Valley Falls are also known as the 'Thousand Foot Falls,' although they happen to be 480 meters (1,600ft) high. From the picnic ground you can watch the thin plume of water stream down a cliffside and disappear into the lush forest below. In the vicinity are many smaller but arguably more beautiful falls, including **Big Rock Falls** and perhaps the most charming, **Butterfly Falls**. Eighteen kilometers (11 miles) farther southwest (marked on the left) are the **Río On Pools**, natural rock pools and little waterfalls formed by enormous granite boulders, in a serene open setting – also ideal for a swim. Eight kilometers (5 miles) south is the turn off

to the **Río Frío Cave** ㉕, the largest cave in Belize and the most accessible. During the dry season, it is possible to follow the river into the cave's enormous mouth and out the other end. The rocks are a little slippery, but not unmanageable; inside are unusually colored rock formations, stalactites, and the odd colony of bats. There is also a 45-minute outdoor nature trail for the energetic.

A variety of accommodations have been set up in the area, including Blancaneaux (www.coppolaresorts.com), a luxury lodge and resort owned by the Hollywood film director Francis Ford Coppola.

XUNANTUNICH

San José Succotz, a village a few km/ miles southwest of San Ignacio, is the jumping-off point for the Maya ruins of **Xunantunich** ㉖ (www.nichbelized.com; daily 8am–4pm), one of the biggest attractions in the Cayo District, and one of the most impressive Maya sites in all Belize. The ruins are reached by crossing the Mopan River on a hand-winched ferry. In contrast to Cahal Pech, the Maya site of Xunantunich is inspiring, and the view from the top of the highest structure is breathtaking. The view of the Mopan River from the ferry on the way over is itself memorable. Xunantunich is best known for the towering pyramid known as **El Castillo**, or **A-6**. At around 40 meters (130ft), this was considered the highest structure in Belize until the pyramid at Caracol was found to top it by a few feet. In 2016, a great Maya treasure was discovered at Xunantunich: one of the largest royal tombs ever found in the country. The burial chamber revealed a male corpse, as well as jade, animal bones and ceramic vessels.

CARACOL

The main attraction for most travelers in the **Chiquibul Forest Reserve and National Park** is the ruined Maya city of **Caracol** ㉗ (www.nichbelize.com; daily 8am–5pm). Until 1993, Caracol was only accessible by one of the worst roads in

El Castillo at Xunantunich.

Belize, but a paved highway cut the driving time down to two hours. Even so, the going can be rough, particularly when it rains. The route runs into the **Vaca Plateau**, with a return from pines to the more familiar rainforest foliage and some spectacular views over mountains and river valleys.

Beneath the Vaca Plateau are a series of great cave complexes, including the Chiquibul, which may be the largest in the western hemisphere. It was only found by modern spelunkers in the 1970s and remains little explored – although tales of prehistoric fossils being discovered there have sparked interest. The road becomes progressively more bone-shaking until the ruins suddenly appear – a Maya pyramid, hacked from the jungle, glimpsed through a gap in the vines.

DANGRIGA AND THE STANN CREEK DISTRICT

Stann Creek District is the home of Garífuna culture, famous for its arts, dance, and punta rock music. You'll also find some superb caves inland and idyllic cayes out on the reef.

The Hummingbird Highway, running from Belmopan to Dangriga, has a beautiful name, amply justified by the surrounding scenery, which is among the most spectacular and tropical of southern Belize. The road passes through a magnificent forest of cohune palm: Cohune Ridge, as it is known locally. The largest town in Stann Creek District, **Dangriga** ㉘, which takes its name from the local Garífuna language, loosely meaning 'standing waters.' It lies peacefully along the banks of the North Stann Creek River, whose water is legendary: the town's drinking supply is refreshingly cool and arguably the best-tasting water in Belize. A well-known Belizean saying warns that once you drink from *gumaragaru* (the Garífuna name for the North Stann Creek River), you must come back to Dangriga.

Dangriga was settled in the early 19th century by the Garífuna, also known as Garínagu or Black Caribs, a cultural hybrid of escaped African slaves and Caribbean Indians. The town's dreamy atmosphere still harks back to a past

Traditional stilt houses, Dangriga.

Ø SETTLEMENT DAY

A carnival atmosphere consumes Dangriga during the celebration of Garífuna Settlement Day on November 19, which commemorates the landing of Garífuna leader Elijio Beni and his followers at the mouth of the North Stann Creek River. This is the most important local holiday, when the town swells with Garífuna from all over Central America and the United States. Singing and dancing crowds, all in traditional Garífuna costume, follow drummers from house to house until sunrise, when everyone gathers at the riverside for a re-enactment of the Landing. This is followed by a procession to the Sacred Heart Roman Catholic Church, to attend the special Mass performed entirely in Garífuna to the rhythmic beat of the drums. Many restaurants and bars also offer special meals and drinks in honor of Garífuna Settlement Day.

⊙ Tip

Tables across the country have one thing in common: bottles of trademark Marie Sharp's hot pepper sauce. This is Belize's most beloved hot sauce, and near Dangriga, you can go to its source. 12 kilometers (8 miles) northwest of Dangriga, near Melinda Forest Station, is the **Marie Sharp's Factory** (www.mariesharps-bz.com; Mon–Fri 7am–4pm) set on a 162-hectare (400-acre) estate. Guided tours take in the fields, orchards, and factory, and you can pick up a bottle (or five) to take home.

age. The houses are made of weathered wooden planks and raised on stilts. Old-fashioned wooden fishing dories are tied up along the banks of the river, beside canopied ferries with hustling fishermen unloading their day's catch.

At heart, Dangriga is a celebration of Garífuna culture, marked by one important landmark – the **Drums of Our Fathers** monument, in the southern part of town, that pays homage to the key role of drumming in Garífuna history. Dangriga is bisected by North Stann Creek, crossed by a bridge; on the north side are the town hall and small market, on the south the post office. For an excellent overview of Garífuna culture, head to the **Gulusi Garífuna Museum** (www.ngcbelize.org; Mon–Fri 10am–5pm, Sat noon–8pm), on Stann Creek Valley Road, which features in-depth exhibits tracing Garífuna history, as well as artworks, traditional dress, and more. There are budget hotels, lively restaurants, and raunchy bars in the center of town, if you're up for some local color. Just north of town is the Pelican Beach Resort (www.

pelicanbeachbelize.com), which maximizes its beachfront perch with breezy rooms and a restaurant with views out to sea.

TOBACCO REEF

Some 20km (12 miles) offshore from Dangriga lie a row of tiny coral cayes, including Carrie Bow Caye, South Water Caye, and Tobacco Caye, all perched on top of **Tobacco Reef** like gems on a necklace. All are lined by perfect sands and dotted with coconut palms, and can be easily reached in an hour's boat ride from Dangriga. There are some beautiful clusters of coral in the shallow waters off these cayes, offering great snorkeling opportunities. In addition to the usual kaleidoscopic array of tropical fish, there is also a good chance of spotting moray eels, turtles, and nurse sharks.

The most accessible of the cayes in this area is **South Water Caye** ㉙, a small and beautifully maintained caye, with a superb array of accommodations, such as Glover's Atoll Resort (www.glovers.com. bz), with breezy thatched *cabañas* on the beach, and a welcoming restaurant that serves fresh seafood; and Pelican's

⊙ GARIFUNA ARTS AND CRAFTS

The Garífuna have a long legacy as artists and craftsmen. Primitivism dominates in their painting, with great elaboration of detail, flat colors, and unreal perspective. Dangriga local Pen Cayetano, an acclaimed punta rock musician, is also an accomplished artist, having displayed at many art exhibitions in the United States and Europe. Pen's work is more realistic than other Garífuna painters, but it still retains the attractive aspects of primitivism.

To view Cayetano's works, pay a visit to the **Pen Cayetano Studio Gallery** (www.cayetano.de; hours vary), near Ecumenical Drive, which also features historical exhibits on Garífuna culture, drumming demonstrations, and more. Throughout town, you'll also find a colourful array of other crafts, including drums made with cedar and mahogany, and deer and cow hides; stuffed cotton dolls in traditional Garífuna dress; coconut-leaf baskets and hats; and maracas made of dried calabash gourds.

Ask at any of the local restaurants, and they'll point you in the direction of craftspeople who are selling their wares.

Pouch Resort (www.pelicanbeachbelize.com), the sister resort to the Pelican Beach Resort in Dangriga, which is set on a gorgeous private beach, where you can swing in a hammock under palm trees, soaking up the sun.

HOPKINS

While Dangriga is the largest Garífuna settlement in Belize, smaller colonies lie scattered farther down the coast, including **Hopkins** ㉚. It can be reached by sea from Dangriga across the **Commerce Bight Lagoon**, or from the west along a 7km (4-mile) road linked to the Southern Highway. The seashore at Hopkins is lined by scores of tall coconut trees sprouting from mountains of soft sand. Nets, draped over palmetto poles, lie drying in the sun beside fishing dories pulled up on the beach. Clumps of Maya-style homes – palmetto walls and palm-frond roofs – sit perched on stilts with magnificent views of the azure Caribbean to the east and jungle covered mountains to the west. Perhaps more than any other of the villages in the south, Hopkins has enthusiastically embraced tourism, with a growing number of guesthouses and *cabañas*, along with colorful restaurants, bars, and craft shops.

COCKSCOMB BASIN WILDLIFE SANCTUARY

Seen from satellite photographs, the Cockscomb Basin looks like a huge meteor crater blasted from the center of the Maya Mountains. From closer to earth, it is a lush mountain basin, full of pristine tropical forest and riddled through with jungle streams. It has one of Central America's densest concentrations of jaguars, and was the site of the world's first jaguar reserve, the **Cockscomb Basin Wildlife Sanctuary** ㉛ (www.belizeaudubon.org; daily 8am–4.30pm). This rugged sanctuary supports a profusion of endangered wildlife. The bird list for the sanctuary stands near 300 species, including the brilliant scarlet macaw, the great curassow, the colorful keel-billed toucan, and the king vulture. The sanctuary is predominantly known to be a safe haven for the largest raptors,

The versatile cassava is an integral part of Garífuna heritage, and is used for a variety of foods, including baked round loaves and, after mixed with ginger, sugar, and sweet potatoes, a favourite drink called Hiu.

Tobacco Caye.

such as the solitary and white hawk eagles. Besides the jaguar, four other species of wildcat prowl the basin's forests – the puma, ocelot, margay, and small jaguarundi. The signature howl of black howler monkeys has also returned to the Cockscomb Sanctuary, which established a new home for the baboons, as they're called in Belize, in the early 1990s.

PLACENCIA

In recent years, **Placencia** ㉜ has become second only to Ambergris Caye as a coastal tourist hotspot, thanks to its sparkling sandy beaches, a vibrant social life, and a growing arts scene. The town is a mix of traditional wooden stilt-houses that are juxtaposed with an ever-expanding number of swanky new villas and hotels. Aside from the tourist boom, this is still a working fishing village, and the annual Lobsterfest in July celebrates both a bountiful harvest and fishing as a way of life. The Sidewalk Arts Festival, held in February around Valentine's Day, is a popular showcase for artists from all over Belize.

Relaxing on the beach at Placencia.

TOLEDO DISTRICT

The residents of the Toledo District, to the far south of Belize, often refer to their home as 'the forgotten land.' But it's precisely the fact that Toledo is less touristed than elsewhere that makes it an exciting destination for adventurous travelers: This is a land that's rich in primary rainforest, monstrous caves, and jungle-covered ruins. Outside of Punta Gorda, the only town of any size, restaurants are quite basic. The Toledo District is also, first and foremost, Maya country: more than half the population belongs to one of two Maya groups: Mopan or Kekchi.

PUNTA GORDA

Known locally as PG, **Punta Gorda** ㉝ is the southernmost town in Belize, and is the capital of the Toledo District. These days, although the town receives fewer visitors than most other parts of the country, more people are venturing south to seek out the genuine atmosphere of a frontier outpost. The air is crystal clear here, possibly due to the annual 400cm (160ins) of rain continuously washing the dust from the air. Perched on a limestone escarpment, much of Punta Gorda lies only 4.5–6 meters (15–20ft) above sea level. The long, narrow town only stretches back a few blocks from the coastline, which slopes to pebbly, dark sand beaches where fishing dories lie pulled up on shore. Farther south, the Caribbean ceaselessly nibbles away at the land, dragging old houses and graveyards into the sea.

The pace of life is slow in PG, even by Belizean standards. The town is charmingly overgrown: huge mango trees tower majestically along the streets, providing welcome midday shade; flowering bushes and potted plants decorate the verandas of lichen-stained clapboard homes; and tall grass flourishes in most yards. That said, the town also has a good collection of accommodations and restaurants, as well as an excellent tour infrastructure in place

– you can easily find quality guides to take you out to the Barrier Reef or on inland adventures.

BLUE CREEK PRESERVE AND HOKEB HA CAVE

One of the most impressive natural sites in Toledo is the **Hokeb Ha Cave ㉞**. The huge cave entrance is carved from the summit of a hill where the Blue Creek gurgles up from underground. After leaving the cave, the creek cascades over limestone boulders, under the towering shadows of the surrounding rainforest. Archeologists have found inside many Late Classic ceramics and an altar, leading them to theorize that the Hokeb Ha cave was used specifically for ceremonial purposes. The cave lies within the Blue Creek Preserve, a private sanctuary, with cabins by the riverside and various amenities, including an excellent canopy walkway strung between the trees, 24 meters (80ft) above the river.

LUBAANTUN

Lubaantun ㉟ (Place of Fallen Stones; 8am–5pm), one of the largest Maya sites in Toledo, lies high on a ridge above a valley cut by the Columbia River, near the village of San Pedro Columbia. The ruins were first excavated in 1915, and subsequent archeological study suggests that Lubaantun was built completely without the use of mortar; each stone was precisely cut to fit snugly against its neighbor. The slim, square-cut stones are one of the distinctive features of Lubaantun; it is also exceptional among Maya ruins for the complete absence of carved stelae, particularly in contrast with those of nearby Nim Li Punit.

Uphill from nearby Indian Creek village is the ceremonial center of **Nim Li Punit** (Big Hat; 8am–5pm), with splendid views and 26 stelae, eight of them carved, and among them the tallest ever found in Belize. The site's name comes from a detail of a figure carved on one of the site's stelae (Stela 14), which is the longest such ancient monument found in Belize. This stela, together with several others, is on display in the attractive visitors' center at the entrance to the site.

The Maya site of Lubaantun.

ECOTOURISM IN BELIZE

For centuries, Belize's small population and lack of industry caused it to be left behind in the development race. When it comes to ecotourism, however, this has worked to its great advantage.

Belize has long been the region's ecotourism titan, with some of the world's most accessible tropical wilderness and the longest Barrier Reef in the western hemisphere, which lures travelers from across the globe. In the mid-1980s, the government recognized that small-scale, low-impact tourism was the way to provide stable economic growth while still safeguarding the environment. Rather than mimic the mass-tourism path of Cancún, 400km (250 miles) to the north, Belize decided to follow one that would allow as many Belizeans as possible to participate in the tourism industry as stakeholders.

Belize's rainforests support by far the greatest diversity of wildlife. They are the result of optimal conditions for life on land in this area – abundant sunlight, warmth, and moisture. For birders and all wildlife watchers, the best time to visit such a forest is at sunrise, when the air is cool and filled with the sounds of birds feeding and declaring their territories.

The jaguar is probably the most celebrated creature of the rainforest – Belize created the world's first jaguar sanctuary at Cockscomb Basin (see page 193) to protect it. Roaming beneath the rainforest canopy and along the banks of mountain streams, four other wildcats share the territory: jaguarundi, margay, ocelot, and puma. All are endangered throughout their ranges, but Belize supports healthy populations. Other celebrated inhabitants of the forest include Baird's tapir, known locally as the 'mountain cow,' and the black howler monkey, whose aggressive roar is frequently mistaken for that of a jaguar. Howlers often begin and end their days with a roar – a noise that can carry for several kilometers. Belize supports one of the last strongholds of baboons in the region: at the Community Baboon Sanctuary (see page 181), landowners have agreed to manage their properties in ways that will not be detrimental to the baboons.

Unesco has awarded World Heritage status to the Belize Barrier Reef, and miles of these delicate ecosystems have been designated as marine reserves.

Many local fishermen benefit from tourism by using their boats to conduct snorkeling trips to the nearby reefs. Don't remove any of the shells and coral, though.

Belize's numerous national reserves and parks make it an eco-tourism paradise.

Belize Audubon Society

The Belize Audubon Society (BAS; www.belizeaudubon.org), formed in 1969, is Belize's foremost environmental organization. It aims to maintain a balance between the needs of the nation's people and the environment through sustainable management of natural resources and public education programs. The society manages more than 77,000 hectares (192,000 acres) of protected land in nine separate areas, including Crooked Tree Wildlife Sanctuary, Guanacaste National Park, St Herman's Blue Hole National Park, Cockscomb Basin Wildlife Sanctuary, Blue Hole Natural Monument, and Victoria Peak National Monument. Looking to do your part for the environment? The BAS offers volunteer opportunities throughout the country – sign up via the website.

With the help of a guide, trail systems can be explored throughout Belize on horseback, mountain bike, or on foot.

...e great appeal of birdwatching in Belize isn't just the ...onishing variety – at last count, 574 different species – ... the fact that these winged creatures are readily visible ...oughout the country, from egrets to pelicans to ...cans, the national bird.

...sk falls over Tobacco Caye.

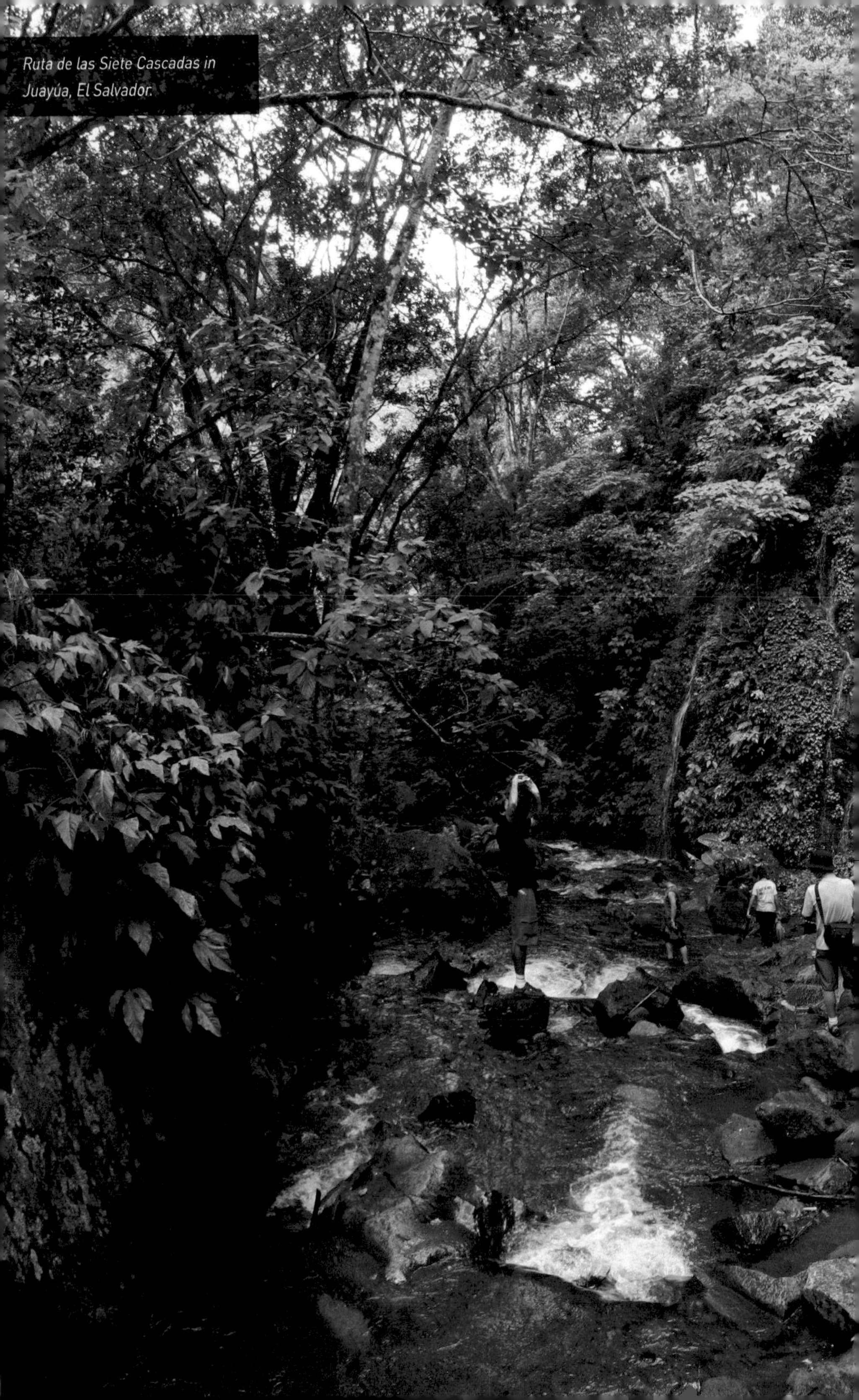

Ruta de las Siete Cascadas in Juayúa, El Salvador.

Playing frisbee in the shadow of Concepción volcano on Punta Jesus Maria beach, Nicaragua.

THE CENTRAL REGION

Pristine cloud forests burst with wildlife, mist-covered coffee plantations, and lively tropical isles, yet the once-turbulent central region countries remain virtually unexplored.

Copán ruins in Honduras.

Central America's mid-isthmus nations have landscapes as diverse as Costa Rica, a flora and fauna as rich as Panama, and beaches as dreamy as Cancún, yet the world has yet to fully take notice. Tied together by years of civil war and corruption, much of it influenced by exterior forces, El Salvador, Honduras, and Nicaragua are less developed than their neighbors, but that shouldn't deter your visit by any means. These countries have plenty to offer the intrepid visitor.

On the Pacific coast, white sand beaches and some of the world's most reliable surfing can be found. There's no sense of mass tourism here, although luxe resorts have established themselves north of San Juan del Sur. In the Caribbean, the English-speaking Bay Islands and Corn Islands have a completely different vibe than the mainland, with reggae blasting in the streets and a culture that revolves around diving, fishing, and tourism. Intersected with banana plantations and mangroves, Honduras' north coast is starting to come into its own, with one-of-a-kind ecolodges and a mega-resort project that have changed the way people travel to the country.

Beach life at Roatán, Honduras.

There are ruins here too, like the Mayan city of Copán, with its carved stelae and hieroglyphic staircase, as well as El Salvador's Joya de Cerén, a farming village covered in volcanic ash after an eruption, giving it the moniker of the 'Central American Pompeii.' Lake Nicaragua, with its double volcano island of Ometepe, and lesser known Yojoa, are two biodiversity hotspots in a region full of them.

Then there's La Mosquitia, the vast, undeveloped region of tropical rainforest and pine savannah that is Central America's largest area of wilderness. Natural areas like the Río Plátano Biosphere Reserve have some of the region's highest concentrations of flora and fauna, making it one of the more likely settings for spotting bucket list species like jaguars and harpy eagles. Little known ethnic groups like the Miskito, Pech, and Sumo live along isolated rivers and lagoons, while the remnants of lost cities are slowly being carved out of the jungle.

EL SALVADOR

Famed surf breaks, hikes through untrammeled cloud forests, and exploring the Mayan Pompeii await the traveler looking for Central America's next big thing.

Despite frequent earthquakes and a tumultuous history that includes a brutal civil war, the tiny nation of El Salvador, smaller than Massachusetts, has one of the most robust economies in the region. A growing middle class is being fueled by the presence of multinational companies' call centers. These are opportunistically hiring English-speaking deportees who have been affected by the US's stepped-up immigration control efforts, a policy which, more soberingly, has also brought along an increase in gang activity.

Central America's smallest country has two distinct regions: the highlands, which make up most of the landscape; and the swelteringly hot Pacific lowlands along the coast. With a good network of roads, getting around is quite easy.

The country's vibrant capital San Salvador can be found on the hot central plateau. It's a city of contrasts, where the image of luxury shopping malls and American fast-food chains conflict with the rough, often crime-ridden barrios on the outskirts of town. Just to the north is the Salvadoran version of Antigua, Suchitoto, a laid-back, colonial country town with cobblestone streets, yet only a fraction of the tourists found in similar locations in neighboring countries.

Heading west from the capital, along the Ruta de las Flores and toward the Guatemalan border, a cluster of volcanoes such as Santa Anaz and Izalco have provided rich soil that provides ideal conditions for coffee plantations. The surrounding mountain ranges are dotted with small crater lakes and natural reserves like the Los Volcanoes and Montecristo national parks, which offer superb hiking and wildlife watching. The region can also claim the country's most famous ruins at Joya de Cerén, a preserved 1,400-year old Mayan village long covered in ash, similar to Italy's Pompeii.

Along the coast, the mountains roll right into the ocean in places, while in

Main Attractions

San Salvador
Joya de Cerén
Los Volcanoes National Park
Suchitoto
Montecristo National Park
Balsamo Coast

Maps on pages 204, 207

Local man in Perquín.

others there are coastal plains, mangrove forests and estuaries. The Salvadoran Pacific is perhaps the region's most underappreciated strip of sand and the golden and black volcanic beaches have attracted a growing surf community who take advantage of the breaks at Punta Roca and El Sunzal. The coast has it all, from large all-inclusive resorts to no-frills beach hostels with hammocks strung up between two palms.

A military marching band parades along the city streets during Salvadoran Independence Day celebrations.

THE POST-WAR ERA

In the Chapultepec Peace Accords that marked the end of El Salvador's civil war in 1992, the size of the army was reduced and the National Police force was dissolved, as was the National Guard and other security forces. The former insurgent group known as the Farabundo Martí National Liberation Front, or FMLN, became one of El Salvador's political parties, though they failed to gain much traction other than a strong showing in the capital. Three consecutive National Republican Alliance, or ARENA, candidates have pushed for the privatization of large state enterprises and other neoliberal policies.

Despite strong support, the FMLN's continuing losses in presidential elections caused them to pick, a former journalist, Carlos Mauricio Funes Cartagena, to run as their candiadate in the 2009 election. He won, becoming the first president of a leftist party in El Salvador's history. His administration had some success; however, after FMLN candidate and former guerrilla leader Salvador Sánchez Cerén won the 2014 election, Funes came under scrutiny for corruption and sought asylum in Nicaragua.

A CYCLE OF MIGRATION

One of the drivers of El Salvador's burgeoning economy are the remittances sent by Salvadorans living abroad in the US, Canada, Mexico, Guatemala, Costa Rica, Australia, and Sweden. Estimates suggest that the two million Salvadorans living outside the county send an estimated $2 billion back to the country each year. However, during the administration of President Barack Obama,

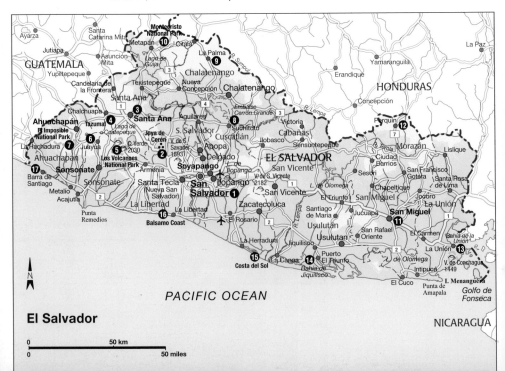

the US deported an estimated 150,000 undocumented Salvadorans who had been living in the US, a move that has shaken the already fragile nation.

The move has led to increased crime from the *maras*, or gangs, which had already been showing their teeth throughout the country. Law enforcement programs like *La Mano Dura* and *Mano Superdura* have done little to stop the violence. Then there are the deportees who had been living in the US since they were young children and have known no other life. They are strangers in their own land, though many who are perfectly bilingual are finding work in the call centers set up to service international corporations that have opened over the past decade. Earning higher wages than they could otherwise anticipate, they are participating in developing El Salvador's domestic economy.

SAN SALVADOR AND AROUND

Nowhere are the divisions in Salvadoran society as clear as in **San Salvador ❶**. Set at the base of green San Salvador volcano in the pleasant-sounding Valle de las Hamacas – so named by the Spaniards for the tectonic activity in the region – El Salvador's sprawling capital is home to one third of the country's entire population. Leafy suburbs where the nation's wealthy live and the dizzying collection of multinational chains almost seem out of place compared to grittier parts of the city, like the sketchy eastern districts that should be avoided by tourists. For many, San Salvador is simply the port of arrival, a place for a nice dinner and a comfortable night's sleep before heading out to the coast or into the mountains, neither of which are far away.

CENTRO HISTÓRICO

The city was founded in 1545 after resistance from the Pibil people stopped a capital from forming in Suchitoto to the north. Growing up around Plaza La Libertad, the city heard the first cries of independence from Spain in Central America in 1811 and 1814. Over the following decades, the city's progress was fueled by profits from a rapidly growing

Plaza La Libertad in downtown San Salvador.

coffee industry and many of the most famous palaces, churches, and theaters were built.

San Salvador's historic center would not fare as well as those of other Central American capitals, with the natural disasters that plagued the city preventing it from reaching its full potential. In 1873, an earthquake wiped out much of the city, and the San Salvador volcano erupted in 1917 while it was still being rebuilt. By the 1960s El Salvador had become the third-largest coffee exporter in the world, but a 1986 earthquake caused mass destruction and shifted much of the wealth away from the center and into the suburbs. Violence during the civil war kept the country's middle class away from this district for years and what's left is a crumbling, congested grid of streets where the Central Market has all but taken over.

Bordering the attractive **Plaza Barrios Ⓐ**, you will find many of the city's most impressive monuments. The Palacio Nacional is built of Italian marble and dates to the early 20th century, though government offices moved out

At a street market in San Salvador.

after the 1986 earthquake. A courtyard and some rooms with artifacts are open to the public. The hulking **Catedral Metropolitana Ⓑ** (tel: 2221 0003; daily 6am–6pm; free), with its blue and yellow dome, is one of the symbols of the city and replaced an earlier church that was destroyed by an earlier earthquake. It's here that Archbishop Oscar Romero, who was assassinated after criticizing the government during the height of the civil war, lies buried. More attractive is **Iglesia Rosario Ⓒ** (tel: 2222 2171; daily 8.30am–4.30pm; free), built by sculptor Ruben Martinez in the 1970's inside an airplane hanger-like structure that hides a dramatic stairway of rainbow colored light that projects itself onto the altar. To the east, the French Classical **Teatro Nacional Ⓓ** (tel: 2222 5689; www.cultura.gob.sv; Mon–Fri 1–4pm), Central America's oldest theater, has undergone extensive renovations and regularly hosts concerts.

To the southwest is the **Mercado Central Ⓔ** (tel: 7442 2557; daily 7am–5pm), a sprawling commercial complex that is anchored by a traditional produce market with food stands, but fans out into the streets into a maze of mass produced goods like clothing, footwear, and homewares.

COLONIA ESCALON AND THE ZONA ROSA

Several of the best museums are found just west of the center, en route to the suburbs. Near Colonia San Benito, the Museo Nacional de Antropología Dr. David J. Guzmán, or **MUNA Ⓕ** (tel: 2243 3750; http://muna.cultura.gob.sv; Tue–Sat 9am–5pm, Sun 10am–6pm), has artifacts from the Maya and other pre-Colombian cultures. The **Museo de la Palabra y la Imagen** (http://museo.com.sv) focuses on the work of Salvadoran writers and journalists and their efforts during the civil war.

Farther west is the suburb of **Colonia Escalón Ⓖ**, an enclave that's home to the city's elite. The neighborhood, along with nearby Colonia San Francisco and Colonia Maquilishuat, were mostly untouched by the civil war, aside from the 1989 battle known as the 'Final Offensive.' This area is the most secure part of the city and many of the older houses have been converted into condos, restaurants, and art galleries. The best hotels, like the Crowne Plaza, can be found here and to the south in the **Zona Rosa**  and Santa Elena, home to the modern **La Gran Vía** and **Multiplaza** malls, and the US Embassy.

OUTSIDE OF SAN SALVADOR

In the southwest of San Salvador is **Santa Tecla**, a large suburb with a village feel. The town was briefly the capital of the country from 1855 to 1859, as San Salvador rebuilt after an earthquake. At Paseo El Carmen, a pedestrian-only walkway, cafés, and restaurants line the street, making it a favorite weekend escape for those in the city center. Food vendors selling traditional snacks and sweets can be found everywhere, while at Plaza de la Música there's usually some sort of informal live music jam going on.

North of Santa Tecla the road climbs 13km (8 miles) to 1,800m (5,905ft) at the top of the San Salvador volcano, to **El Boquerón National Park**. The highlight is the crater, 5km (3 miles) in diameter and 558 meters (1,830ft) deep, which is intersected by walking and bicycle trails through the pine forests. Armadillos, deer and other mammals can occasionally be seen. There are a few restaurants and cafés at the park visitor center.

Ten kilometers (6 miles) to the southeast of San Salvador is **Los Planes De Renderos**, a popular green space in the hills with sweeping views of the city. Small eateries and pupusa stands can be found near Parque Balboa, plus there are opportunities for rock climbing.

El Salvador's largest crater lake, **Lago Ilopango**, is 22km (14 miles) east of San Salvador. The 28 sq km (11 sq miles) lake is a favorite spot for adventure sports. Here, divers can explore the caves, hot water vents, and volcanic rock formations with San Salvador based El Salvador Divers (www.elsalvadordivers.com). One dive site known as Las Tres Virgenes,

Iglesia Rosario's colorful interior.

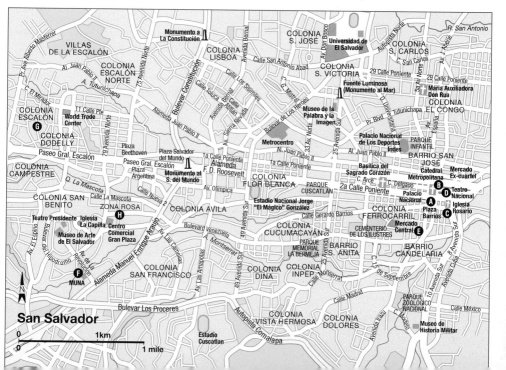

San Salvador

features three 3-meter (10ft) -high hand carved stone statues. From April to November, paragliding is also offered.

JOYA DE CERÉN

Just off the Pan American Highway, **Joya de Cerén ❷** (tel: 2401 5748; Tue–Sun 9am–4pm), 33km (20 miles) north-west of San Salvador, is one of Central America's most fascinating archeological sites. While it's not nearly as visually attractive as other ruins in the country, the site offers a glimpse into what life was like in a small Mayan farming community 1,400 years ago. Like Italy's Pompeii, Joya de Cerén was buried beneath ash during an eruption of the Laguna Caldera volcano around AD 600. The residents had time to flee before the seven meters (23ft) of ash fell on their village, but items like garden tools and ceramics still filled with legumes were frozen in time. A shaman's house, a community temezcal sauna, and various other buildings have been preserved at what is now a Unesco World Heritage site. It was rediscovered in 1976 when a bulldozer dug up a building during the construction of a grain silo. Extensive excavations didn't begin until 1988, after the civil war, and are still ongoing. There's a viewing platform and an air-conditioned museum beside the site and free English or Spanish language tours can be arranged.

WESTERN EL SALVADOR

Moving west from San Salvador, the landscape transitions from the hot, flat plateau to a more scenic, mountainous terrain lined with coffee plantations and charming rural villages. Along the Ruta de las Flores, artisan towns with cobblestone streets and perfectly manicured gardens make for a quick escape from the heat of the capital. Closer to the Guatemalan border, the landscape gets more rugged, with jungle-clad hillsides and what many claim is the country's best national park, aptly named El Imposible.

SANTA ANA

Sixty-five km (40 miles) west of San Salvador is the country's second largest city, **Santa Ana ❸**. With its tree-lined streets and air of general order that seems lacking in the capital, many travelers prefer to base themselves here and take day trips to nearby attractions like the Tazumal ruins or the Ruta de las Flores.

Coffee wealth in the early 20th-century helped fund a building boom in the city, with barons building haciendas in the surrounding hills and some of the country's best architecture within a few blocks of the main plaza, **Parque Libertad**. The neo-Gothic Cathedral, completed in 1913, is the most imposing monument, while the neo-colonial **Teatro de Santa Ana** has frequent performing art performances, some of which are free. While coffee is still important here, the city's economy primarily revolves around the foreign-owned factories in the north of the city.

South of town is **Lago Coatepeque**, a deep blue crater lake surrounded by

⊘ LA BORN, SALVADOR RAISED

While the criminal gang Mara Salvatrucha, or MS-13, originated in Los Angeles, California, the majority of its members are ethnic Salvadorans. National Geographic went as far as to call them the World's Most Dangerous Gang in a 2005 documentary. They have expanded across urban areas of North America and their reach goes as far as Australia. Named after guerrilla fighters during the Salvadoran Civil War, the gang is so large, with 30,000 to 50,000 members worldwide, that it has its own subculture of sorts, with members speaking in their own form of sign language. The most popular hand sign, learned from heavy metal concerts, is the 'devil's head' which, when displayed upside down, forms an 'M.' Tattoos are a distinguishing element of most MS-13 members, who often cover their bodies and sometimes faces, although it's believed some members are moving away from the trait in the attempt to go unnoticed.

The gang is known for their violent ways and connection to the drug trade and sex trafficking, which has caused increased concern in the US, where stepped up immigration efforts have pushed for more members – as well as those who have minor associations with them – to be deported to El Salvador. The thousands of MS-13 members returning to the country in recent years has led to higher crime rates and instability in El Salvador's urban areas.

forests and the mansions of the wealthy. Most of the lakeshore is privately owned and inaccessible aside from a small public section that is lined with restaurants and small hotels, many of which rent kayaks and other watercraft.

TAZUMAL AND CASA BLANCA

El Salvador's most important Mayan ruin is **Tazumal** ❹ (Tue–Sun), 13km (8 miles) west of Santa Ana. Mostly excavated, the ruins cover 10 sq km (4 sq miles), encompassing a pyramid, ball court, and other examples of classic Mayan architecture. Believed to be an important trading center, Tazumal, which translates to 'the place where the victims were burned,' dates as far back as AD 100. It's believed that construction at the site was abandoned for many years after an eruption of the Ilopango volcano, though picked up again in the Early to Middle Classic period from AD 250–650 until about AD 1200. Artifacts in the small site museum reveal that the city has contacts with communities as far away as southern Mexico. Nauhtl Tours (http://nahuatours.com) runs day trips here, though the site can easily be visited with private transportation and will take about an hour to explore.

A little more than 1km (0.6 mile) north, on the other side of the town of Chalchuapa, is the archeological site of **Casa Blanca** (Tue–Sun). There are several Maya Late Pre-classic and Classic pyramids and other structures. There's a small site museum and, more interesting, an indigo dye workshop.

LOS VOLCANOES NATIONAL PARK

Within the Apaneca-Llamatepec Biosphere Reserve, **Los Volcanoes National Park** ❺, aka Cerro Verde National Park, is home to three volcanoes: Iazalcom, Santa Ana, and Cerro Verde. The park, just southwest of Lago de Coatepeque, is filled with lush cloud and tropical forests and is a hotspot for migrating bird species. Emerald toucanets and numerous species of hummingbirds can easily be seen on a short hike from the visitor center at Cerro Verde, located in the center of the park. From the visitor center, there are 4-hour round-trip hikes to the summits of either Volcán

Tazumal's ruins.

In the early 20th century, a collapse in the price of coffee lead to an uprising of mostly Nahuatl coffee farmers along the Ruta de las Flores. On January 22, 1932, government forces stepped in to suppress the rebellion and an estimated 30,000 were killed in the aftermath. The event became known as the Peasant Massacre.

Bathing in Los Chorros de la Calera waterfalls.

de Izalco or Volcán Santa Ana, the latter one of the most active volcanoes in El Salvador and the second highest peak. Both hikes are steep, challenging climbs up a barren landscape and leave once per day with a guide (who works for tips) from the parking lot at 11am.

RUTA DE LAS FLORES

West of San Salvador along Highway CA-8 is a 36km (22-mile) stretch of scenic roads known as the Salvador Ruta de las Flores, or Route of the Flowers, which connects a string of quaint mountain villages.

The first village on the route is Nahuizalco best known for its hand-crafted furniture. The most visited village, **Juayúa** ❻, pronounced 'why-ooh-ah,' features cobblestone streets and a renowned black Christ statue carved by Quirio Cataño in the late 16th century. Originally a Nahuatl settlement, Juayúa was the epicenter of indigenous uprisings in the region in 1932, which were quickly put down by government forces backed by the coffee barons. Los Chorros de la Calera, a natural area with

waterfalls and a swimming hole just outside of town, is a popular distraction in the summer.

At 1,450 meters (4,757ft), **Apaneca** is El Salvador's second highest town and is a base for hiking in the surrounding Sierra Apaneca Ilamatepec mountains. With a more authentic feel than Juayúa, the colorful adobe houses and handicraft shops seem surprisingly undiscovered by day trippers from San Salvador. While Iglesia San Andres was mostly destroyed in a 2001 earthquake, it has been rebuilt. Just south of town is Finca Santa Leticia (www.hotelsantaleticia.com), a hotel and coffee farm with a small archeological park.

At Ataco, the adobe walls are splashed with brightly colored murals that blend indigenous and contemporary styles. The town has seen an influx of unique stores and cafés in recent years, giving it something of a bohemian feel. Located near the Guatemalan border, Ahuachapán is the birthplace of Salvadoran poet Alfredo Espino and a good base for hikes in El Imposible National Park.

EL IMPOSIBLE NATIONAL PARK

The 3,800-hectare (9,400-acre) **El Imposible National Park** ❼, the largest in El Salvador, was named for a dangerous gorge that often claimed the life of farmers transporting coffee to the Pacific. The birthplace of eight rivers and home to extensive rare tropical dry forest, the park ranges in altitude from 250 meters (820ft) to 1,425 meters (4,675ft), allowing for a stunning array of flora and fauna, including pumas, wild boars, and nearly 300 species of birds. You can enter near the town of Tacuba, which has basic accommodations. From here trails lead into the green hills, past waterfalls and caves etched with Pre-Colombian petroglyphs. All visitors must first register with park administrator in San Salvador (www.salvanatura. org), who can help arrange transportation and guides into the park. Imposible Tours (www.imposibletours.com) in Tacuba can also help set up guided hikes into the park, as well as cycling trips and tours of coffee plantations.

NORTHERN EL SALVADOR

North of San Salvador the hills become mountains, hiding former rebel villages that are now prime tourist attractions. One the shores of Lago de Suchitlán, one of the country's top birdwatching spots, is the attractive art-centric village of Suchitoto, the preferred base for hikes to the surrounding volcanoes and forests. Handicraft centers like Concepción de Quezaltepeque and La Palma are here, as is Cerro El Pital, El Salvador's highest peak, and the cloud forest of Montecristo National Park.

SUCHITOTO

Often called just Suchi, **Suchitoto** ❽ is a former rebel village that has become the preeminent tourist destination in the northern reaches of the country. Overlooking Suchitlán lake, Suchitoto has a vibrant history, having briefly been the capital of the country and a focal point of the civil war. Still, the colonial city has escaped the natural disasters of other cities, with its well-preserved white-washed houses and cobblestone streets.

Plaza Centenaria, the city's main plaza, and the surrounding blocks are where much of the finest architecture can be found. The post-colonial **Santa Lucía Church** (tel: 1049 2335; daily 8am–noon and 1–6pm), built in 1853, is topped with three towers and features a facade with molded arches and six columns. Several of the centuries-old buildings have been turned into boutique hotels, such as **Los Almendros de San Lorenzo** (http://losalmendrosdesanlorenzo.com), with corridors lined with original wood columns and a fresco by Salvadoran master painter Luis Lazo.

To the west, the **Centro Arte para La Paz** (tel: 2335 1080; http://capsuchitoto. org; hours vary; free), opened in 2000 in a former Dominican convent, is a gallery and museum that donates proceeds to victims of domestic violence. It's a hub of cultural activity in the city. Nearby is the gallery of Argentine sculptor Miguel Martino, known as

Santa Lucía Church, Suchitoto.

○ Tip

Founded by renowned cinematographer and Suchitoto resident Don Alejandro Cotto several decades ago, Suchitoto's International Permanent Festival of Art and Culture is held on weekends throughout February. Fine arts performances from national and international artists take place at venues around town for the duration of the festival.

Detail of a La Palma, wall painting.

Casa del Sculptor (tel: 2335 1836; www. miguelmartino.com; Sat–Sun 9am–5pm; free), which holds feasts for guests every Sunday from noon–4.30pm, utilizing his wood fired grill and lots of Argentine wine.

On the road to the lake is the **Casa-Museo Don Alejandro Cotto** (hours vary), the former home of the Salvadoran filmmaker and writer of the same name. The house, with its spectacular views of the lake, acts as something of a city museum, displaying Suchitoto's cultural history, as well as boasting an extensive network of gardens and trails.

OUTSIDE OF SUCHITOTO

A short walk to the east of the center is **Los Tercios**, a 9-meter (29.5ft) high waterfall and swimming hole. The face of the falls are made up of nearly uniform vertical rocks, believed to have been created from lava that cooled very rapidly, which are covered in moss. On weekends vendors come here to sell pupusas and drinks.

On the lakefront at **Puerto San Juan**, there is a public swimming pool and a few traditional restaurants that fill up on weekends. Boats line up here to sell tours of the 135-sq-km (52-sq-mile), man-made **Lago Suchitlán**, which was created in 1973 when the government dammed the Río Lempa. Most of the tours stop at **La Isla de los Pájaros**, a resting point for the many migrating birds that pass through here.

About an hour east of Suchitoto is the tiny village of **Cinquera**, where the bullets and bomb damage have been preserved to showcase the rebel town's history. Murals around the main plaza depict the war and the tail of a downed government helicopter sits on display. A 4,000-hecatre (9,884-acre) ecological park outside the town is open daily and has a small network of trails and a waterfall that are worth exploring on a day visit.

CONCEPCIÓN DE QUEZALTEPEQUE

North of the lake, opposite Suchitoto, the landscape is made up of rugged hills dotted with patches of dry forest and farmland. The civil war impacted this area hard and a cave network that once housed rebel hospitals and even a radio station can still be seen. Many come to this region to visit the village of **Concepción de Quezaltepeque**, which is devoted to the production of colorful hammocks. Nearly the entire town is involved in the *hamaca* industry in some form, either weaving the tapestries that hang from them or selling the final product in the stores that surround the main plaza. The town gets busiest on weekends, when hammock sales are in full swing and there's a festival-like atmosphere.

LA PALMA

High on the mountainside, 50km (31 miles) west of Chalatenango, the remote village of **La Palma** ❾ is best known for its murals, created and influenced by renowned artist Fernando Llort, who moved to the village in 1972. The naïve-style murals of religious figures and mountain villages are noted for their colorful, geometric designs. Before moving away, Llort taught local residents to paint in much the same way and La Palma has become a driving force in the modern Salvadoran art movement. The murals cover the galleries along the center of town. Llort's cooperative, **La Semilla de Dios**, is open daily and is where many of the town's artists can be found at work.

About 30-minutes outside of La Palma is El Salvador's highest peak, **Cerro El Pital**, which rises to 2,730m (8,957ft) above sea level. The road takes visitors most of the way up to the summit, with only a 2–3 hour round-trip hike required. One stretch of the trail is privately owned and someone will usually ask for a small fee to pass.

MONTECRISTO NATIONAL PARK

Northeast of the country town of Metapán is the cloud forest-covered national park of **Montecristo ⑩**, which straddles the border with Honduras (where it is known as Montecristo-Trifinio National Park). Within the humid park are giant ferns, lichens and mosses that provide cover for spider monkeys and anteaters. Cypresses, oaks, and pines can reach up to 30 meters (98ft) in height, attracting nearly 300 bird species, including green toucans and white-faced quails that are rarely seen in other parts of the country. Basic trails intersect the park and a four-wheel-drive vehicle is necessary to reach the entrance. Within the park are several attractions, such as an orchid garden and a museum (both daily) with a collection of oddities inside an historic hacienda. It's best to visit the park during the dry season from December to April.

EASTERN EL SALVADOR

Off the radar for most visitors, this rural, undeveloped region with its hodgepodge of cattle farms and sugarcane plantations is for many the real El Salvador. Eastern El Salvador is noticeably poorer than the west and saw some of the most brutal incidents of the civil war. As the scars continue to heal, the region is opening up, with friendly, country towns planting themselves firmly on the tourist trail.

Cloud-shrouded valley below Cerro El Pital.

ALEGRÍA

Between San Salvador and San Miguel, the hilltop town of **Alegría** is considered the flower capital of El Salvador. The cooler climate at 1,200m (3,937 ft) above sea level affords the village sweeping views of the surrounding countryside and coffee plantations. Activity centers around the town square, where a kiosk can help arrange tours to a crater lake and plantations, as well as map out the hundreds of flowers displays in town.

A former volcano crater is now a turquoise lake near Alegria.

SAN MIGUEL

The largest city in the eastern half of El Salvador is traffic-clogged and chaotic, with high crime and crowded marketplaces. However, just when you think there is nothing in **San Miguel ⓫**, founded in 1530, you come face to face with some of the finest colonial architecture in the country, seemingly lost within the disorder. On the main plaza, the **Catedral Nuestra Señora de La Paz** (daily), which dates to the 18th century, and the neoclassical **Teatro Nacional** (Mon–Sat), which has a storied history as a silent film movie theater and later a hospital.

Mortars at the Museo de la Revolución Salvadoreña in Perquin.

A small museum, the **Museo Regional de Oriente**, is attached.

Eight kilometers (5 miles) west of San Miguel, just off the Pan-American Highway, is the archeological site of **Quelepa**, a Lenca site with several dozen ceremonial platforms that are mostly unexcavated.

Roughly 40km (24 miles) to the southeast is the **Laguna de Olomega**, where you can arrange trips with local fisherman around the lake and to Los Cerritos Island.

PERQUÍN

In the mountainous, forested Morazán region 53km (33 miles) north of San Miguel near the Guatemalan border, **Perquín ⓬** was the headquarters for the FMLN. There are a few small artisan shops around the plaza, but the main attraction here is the **Museo de la Revolución Salvadoreña** (tel: 2634 7984; Tue–Sun 8.30am–4.30pm), which recounts the guerrilla movement with pride through artifacts and photos. One of the highlights is a recreation of Radio Venceremos, an opposition radio

station that was broadcast throughout the country during the 1980s and is now is a commercial radio station (la RV).

NORTH OF SAN MIGUEL

The community of **Cacaopera**, about 9km (6 miles) east of Delicias de Concepción, is something of a mystery. The village's residents are believed to be the very last of the Ulua ethnic group, which linguistic evidence points to having originated south of El Salvador. The residents still cling to their ways of farming, architecture and clothing, which is detailed briefly in a small ethnographic museum.

One of the most infamous moments of the civil war occurred in the village of **El Mozote**, 8km (5 miles) south of Perquín. On December 11 and 12, 1981 the army rounded up nearly 1,000 people from the village around the square and church, many of them children, and executed them. Much of the town was burned after and the massacre was kept hidden for years. The United Nations truth commission formally recognized the incident in 1992 when the bodies were excavated, drawing international condemnation. Today, guides in town show visitors a memorial on the plaza where the names of those who died are written.

LA UNIÓN AND AROUND

Founded as Puerto San Carlos, the grimy port town of **La Unión** ⑬ is little more than a transit hub for those en route to Honduras or to explore the beaches and islands in the Gulf of Fonseca. While there are a few interesting colonial buildings in the city, there's little reason to make an extended stop here.

Along the coast southwest of town, beyond the Conchagua Forest, is a string of unspoiled beaches, many of which rarely see any visitors outside of the occasional surfer. The first pair of beaches, moving east to west along CA-2 are **Playa Jaguey** and **Playa El Tamarindo**. There are few amenities

and private homes take up much of the beachfront.

A few kilometers west, **Playa Esteron** and neighboring **Playa El Cuco** have the most to offer. Many weekenders from San Miguel come here regularly and there are plenty of small restaurants and hotels scattered out along the wide beachfront. The best hotels are closer to El Cuco, such as the upscale 15-room Las Flores Resort (www.lasfloresresort. com), designed by Salvadorian architect Rodrigo Barraza Dominguez and taking up 2.8 hectares (7 acres) of beachfront, and the more laid back Las Olas Surf Resort (www.lasolassurfresort.com). The surf is good here, and for much of the year pros gather near Las Flores and Punta Mango.

BAHÍA DE JIQUILISCO

More wild and raw than points east, the **Bahía de Jiquilisco** ⑭ is closed off from the Pacific by the San Juan del Gozo Peninsula. The bay is ringed by mangrove forests and coconut groves cover many of the islands. The Pacific side of the peninsula, one seemingly

⊘ MONSEÑOR ROMERO

Born August 15 1917 in Ciudad Barrios, El Salvador, the Roman Catholic priest Óscar Arnulfo Romero y Galdámez has become a symbol of the struggle for human rights in Central America. After witnessing various abuses of power against the poor at the hands of the military as an archbishop, Romero began speaking out against US military support in El Salvador and called on soldiers to disobey orders to fire on innocent civilians. The violence began to undermine his trust in government officials and he feared that religion itself was under attack in the country. In 1977, after the murder of his long-time friend, Jesuit Father Rutilio Grande, he suspended masses in the capital's churches the following Sunday and demanded the punishment of those responsible. Over the coming months his following grew larger and larger. With no more room in the church to hear his sermons, many listened to YSAX, the archdiocesan radio station. Not only did he denounce the violence of the civil war, but he denounced the injustice that helped start it. In 1980, while celebrating mass in the chapel of the cancer hospital where he lived, he was assassinated by members of Salvadoran death squads, including two graduates of the infamous School of the Americas. Romero suspected that he could be a martyr, once stating: 'I do not believe in death without resurrection. If they kill me, I shall rise again in the Salvadoran people.'

endless white beach with rough surf, is home to a few small fishing villages like **Corral de Mulas**, which has a small hotel and restaurant facing the bay. Tour companies in San Salvador, such as Eco Maya Tours (www.ecomayan-tours.com), can help set up kayaking and birdwatching trips in the bay.

PACIFIC COAST

While well known to Salvadorans, the beaches of El Salvador's Pacific coast are only beginning to appear on the radar to other travelers in Central America. The waves are among the best in Central America and both pros and beginners come here by the busload, shacking up in low-key surf camps on the coves of the Balsamo Coast. To the east, the Costa del Sol is a favorite escape for non-surfers indulging in large, gated resorts.

COSTA DEL SOL

At just 25-minutes from the airport, visiting the **Costa del Sol** ⑮ is how to come to El Salvador and head right to the beach without experiencing much

Children surf the waves off Playa El Tunco.

else of the country. This roughly 20km (12.5 mile) strip of land between the Pacific and an enclosed bay has been developing since the end of the Civil War and many wealthy Salvadorans have snatched up real estate here and dock their yachts along the inlet. While most other beaches in the country tend to be rocky with strong waves and currents, the Costa del Sol's beaches are sandy and calm.

Large and midsize yet reasonably priced resorts like the Bahia del Sol (www.bahiadelsolelsalvador.com), Tortuga Village (www.tortuga-village.com) and Hotel Pacific Paradise (www.hotelpacificparadise.com) are scattered along the strip in gated compounds. There's no central town to speak of and just a few restaurants dotted around, so many visitors tend to confine themselves within the resorts. An easy day trip from the capital, many tour operators offer transportation there and back, bundled with the use of the pool and other amenities at some of the resorts.

THE BALSAMO COAST

This bustling port town of La Libertad is the easternmost point of the **Balsamo Coast** ⑯, a 32km (20 mile) string of black sand beaches known for some of the best waves in all Central America. Once considered quite dangerous, the city has cleaned up its image in recent years, though there's really no reason to spend the night here. While passing through, stop to walk along the long fishermen pier and maybe have lunch at the decades old Italian seafood spot, La Dolce Vita (www.ladolcevita.com.sv).

The Balsamo Coast, named for the balsam trees once found here in abundance, begins west of La Libertad at **Playa El Tunco** and neighboring **El Sunzal**. The rocky ocean is rich with sea turtles, dolphins, and other marine life, though it's better known for the consistent surf. There are dozens of small surf hostels and surf shops around town and surf guides like Cadejo Adventures (www.cadejoadventures.com) can set up visits to more remote breaks like Punta Roca or La Bocana, as well as paragliding trips off of the coastal cliffs. On weekends, the bars and beach clubs come alive with residents of San Salvador, who make the 45-minute drive back to the capital after the sunrise. Several dozen small hotels cluster together within a 10-minute walk of town.

Weekend homes of wealthy Salvadorans line the green hillsides in the attractive village of **Atami**, 8km (5 miles) to the west of Playa El Tunco, which rises above a small cove surrounded by a handful of nice seafood restaurants. More relaxed is **Playa El Zonte**, a fishing village with a wide beach and little nightlife. The waves are less intense here, making for surfing suitable for beginners. Aside from a few small villages, the beachfront is quite empty all the way to **Los Cóbanos** on the western end of the Balsamo Coast, where there's excellent snorkeling and diving on the reef just offshore. Between Los Cóbanos and the port of **Acajutla** is where you'll find the all-inclusive resort, Royal Decameron Salinitas (www.decameron.com).

BARRA DE SANTIAGO

Northwest of Acajutla, sandwiched between the Pacific and a mangrove-filled estuary, is **Barra de Santiago** ⓱, a remote sandbar lined with coconut palms and a few tourist facilities. A two-hour trip from San Salvador, few make the effort to reach this unspoiled beach town backed by the green hills of Imposible National Park off in the distance. From August to November, however, the area is one of the most active sea turtle nesting sites in Central America and the amphibians can be seen laying their eggs on the wide beach, as well as the hundreds of hatchlings making their way to the sea. Hotels in town can arrange guided turtle-spotting trips, as well as surf lessons and boat trips through the mangroves.

The beach of Los Cóbanos.

Cocalto Beach in Parque National Jeanette Kawas in Honduras.

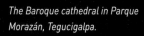
The Baroque cathedral in Parque Morazán, Tegucigalpa.

HONDURAS

Rainforests, cloud forests, beaches, jungles, lakes, islands, Mayan ruins, colonial cities, and buzzing metropolises come together in Central America's least discovered country.

Despite its large size – its 111,369 sq km (42,999 sq miles) make it second only to Nicaragua in the region – Honduras remains a mystery to many travelers to Central America. Political instability and high crime in recent years has steered what were promising investments in tourism off course, leaving the fate of many projects in the air. Still, no country in the region has more potential.

This is a country with a profound wealth of fascinating destinations. What it lacks in volcanoes, it makes up for in pine-covered mountains and lush cloud forests, 965km (600 miles) of coastline dotted with resorts and Garífuna villages, and a mini-Amazon with impenetrable jungles.

The sprawling cities of Tegucigalpa, the capital, and San Pedro Sula, the commercial center, are the main points of entry into the country and are home to fine museums and bustling nightlife. They demand no more than brief stops in transit, as to appreciate real Honduras requires you to get away from the often chaotic, sometimes dangerous centers of population.

Most tourism is concentrated in the Bay Islands of Roatán, Utila, and Guanaja, three idyllic little English-speaking Caribbean isles with some of the world's best – and most inexpensive – diving. They are a place where escaped slaves, pirates, and now a growing

number of expats have created a distinct cultural makeup. The North Coast, with its wildlife-rich national parks like Pico Bonito, Spanish forts, and family friendly beach resorts is a close runner up, attracting adventure sports enthusiasts, birdwatchers, and a growing number of North American retirees.

In the interior, there's the ancient city of Copán, perhaps the most spectacular Mayan ceremonial city in all of Mesoamerica, and the majestic Lago de Yojoa, flanked by two different national parks. Not far away is Comayagua, one

Main Attractions
The Bay Islands
Pico Bonito National Park
Comayagua
Cayos Cochinos
Tela
Lago Yojoa
Gracias
Copán

Maps on pages
222, 225

Copán.

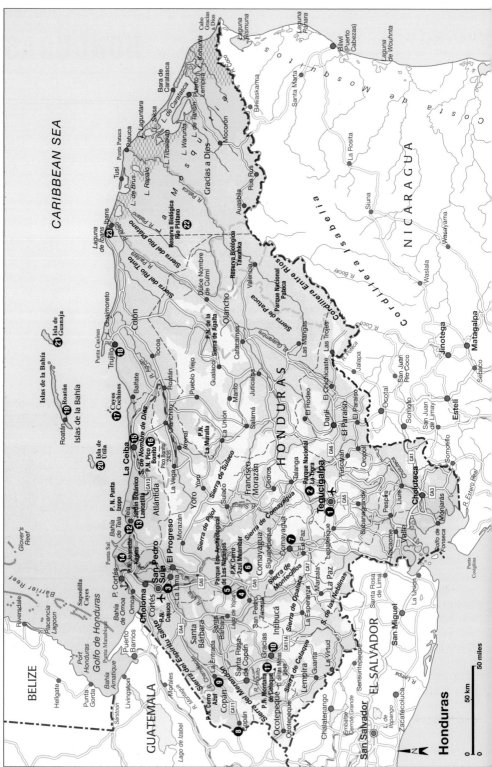

CARIBBEAN SEA

BELIZE

GUATEMALA

EL SALVADOR

NICARAGUA

HONDURAS

Honduras

0   50 miles

of the region's best preserved colonial cities, and sleepy Gracias, once the capital of Central America and now a jumping off point to explore a string of Lenca villages. Lastly, there's La Mosquitia, where the thick jungle hides raging rivers, indigenous communities, and the remains of a mysterious civilization that's slowly being revealed.

THE MODERN ECONOMY

Carlos Roberto Flores Facussé became president in 1988 and initiated widescale currency reforms to slow the rapid inflation that was sinking the value of the lempira against the dollar. After decades of instability, things were beginning to look up, until Hurricane Mitch, the most powerful Atlantic storm ever recorded at the time, came along in October 1998 and caused billions of dollars worth of damage. More than 6,000 people were killed and 1.5 million displaced in the aftermath. The following years were spent trying to get the country back on its feet and repairing much of the damage. Even today the country's infrastructure still has not fully recovered.

In 2006, Olancho rancher Manuel Zelaya Rosales was elected president on a platform of doubling the police force and lowering gas prices. The Central America and Dominican Republic Free Trade Agreement (CAFTA-DR) went into effect not long after, which led to increasing costs for food and energy. Zelaya turned to controversial Venezuelan President Hugo Chavez for help, allowing him to make modest economic and social reforms, like nearly doubling the monthly minimum wage from $157 to $289 and resolving longstanding land conflicts between peasant farmers and agribusinesses. However, his reforms didn't always go over well, as many factory owners could no longer afford to pay their employees and laid them off.

HONDURAS TODAY

Despite low approval ratings, Zelaya called a referendum to reform the constitution and allow presidents to stand for re-election. On June 28, 2009, a few days before the vote was to take place, the army forced him on a plane, still in his pajamas, and took him to Costa

Cruise ship docked at the Mohogany Bay Cruise Center.

⊘ US INTERVENTION

While Honduras somehow avoided political upheaval like its neighbors in the second half of the 20th century, the US military used it as a base for the counter-insurgency movement against the Sandinistas in Nicaragua. Aid was provided to Honduras in exchange for space to train and equip the Contras, though many Hondurans were displeased. Mass protests against the US military broke out, and even as the Honduran military responded by kidnapping and killing protestors, they didn't lose momentum. In 1988, after it was revealed that the Reagan administration had sold arms to Iran to support the Contras, the government ended its military agreement with the US. By the time the Contra war ended in 1990, the Contras were already gone from the country.

⊙ Where

To the southwest of Tegucigalpa, across of the Río Choluteca, is the neighborhood of Comayagüela, which doubled the size of the capital when the cities merged in 1938. While there are still some interesting colonial buildings here, mostly neglected, plus some of the city's bus terminals, this area can be unsafe and should mostly be avoided.

View of Tegucigalpa from above.

Rica. Amid mass protests, a five-month curfew imposed by the new government cost the economy $50 million a day. In the weeks following the coup, Zelaya made three attempts to re-enter the country, but was stopped each time. New elections, boycotted by much of the country and many opposition candidates, took place that November. The right-wing National Party's Pepe Lobo Sosa took office in January 2010, initiating a series of mining, logging, and agri-business projects, to the dismay of environmentalists.

The coup set the country on a downward spiral from which it is still trying to recover. Wages have dropped, public education and social security systems were destroyed, and tourism took a nose dive. Organized crime began taking advantage of weak institutions. The murder rate surged and by 2010, Honduras had become the world's most violent country outside of a war zone. The drug trade flourished and it is estimated that 80 percent of cocaine-smuggling flights bound for the US passed through Honduras.

Elected in 2013, current president Juan Orlando Hernández has pushed forward with an overhaul of the country's political system, creating a new militarized police force and installing figures loyal to his party in the supreme court and congress. Violent crime and government corruption remain serious problems in the country. Nevertheless, after years on the decline, tourism has picked back up as new beach resorts have opened and cruise ship traffic to Roatán has exploded. While development has been uneven at best and Honduras is not going to become the next Costa Rica anytime soon, there's some hope in the air.

TEGUCIGALPA AND AROUND

Founded on September 29, 1578, **Tegucigalpa ❶**, sitting in a valley surrounded by mineral-rich hills, lingered in obscurity until 1880 when then president Marco Aurelio Soto moved the capital here from Comayagua. While the commercial center of the country has moved to San Pedro Sula, 'Te-goose,' as it's sometimes called, remains the

political and intellectual center of the country. While it lacks major attractions, Honduras' best museums and cultural institutions are found here.

THE CITY CENTER

The colonial center of Tegucigalpa a grid of 7 by 20 blocks, is at **Parque Morazán** Ⓐ, or Parque Central. On the square's eastern edge is a baroque Cathedral, built between 1765 and 1782, that honors Saint Michael the Archangel, while the pedestrian-only Calle Peatonal leads west from the square, sided by clothing stores and inexpensive restaurants. A few blocks northwest is **Iglesia de Nuestra Señora de los Dolores** Ⓑ (daily 7am–noon and 3–6pm; free), dating to 1732 and featuring an impressive carved altar. On a small plaza beside the Iglesia la Merced is the **Galería Nacional de Arte** Ⓒ (tel: 2222 0250; www.galerianacionaldeartehonduras.org; Mon–Sat 8.30am–4.30pm, Sun 9am–3pm), Honduras' most important art museum. The museum, housed in a former convent, displays exhibits chronologically, from the art of pre-Mayan cultures to the

religious art of the colonial period and modern paintings from contemporary artists like Pablo Zelaya Sierra.

At Parque Herrera, there's the stunning **Teatro Nacional Manuel Bonilla** Ⓓ (tel: 2222 4366), which was modeled on Paris' Plaza Athenée. The finest performing arts in the country, from opera to the ballet, are staged here throughout the year. Just up Avenida Barahona is the **Museo para la Identidad Nacional** Ⓔ (tel: 2238 7412; www.min.hn; Tue–Sat 9am–5pm, Sun 11am–5pm), which opened in 2006 in what was previously the Palace of Ministries. Honduran history is laid out from its pre-Columbian origins to modern times though photos, historical documents, and artifacts.

On Paseo Soto, inside the former Presidential palace, is the **Museo Histórico de la República** Ⓕ (Mon–Fri 8am–4pm, Sat–Sun 9am–4pm), which focuses on the independence era, with exhibitions displaying portraits, documents, and other paraphernalia of past presidents.

Not a residential area and lacking hotels, the center seems deserted after dark and is best avoided.

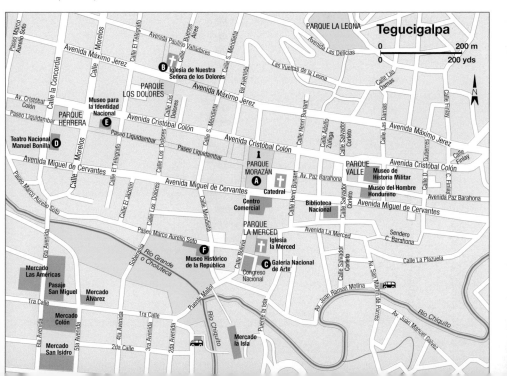

OUTSIDE THE CENTER

The rest of the city spreads out to the south and east. Along Boulevard Morazán is **Colonia Palmira** and **Colonia San Carlos**, middle- and upper-class residential communities where many of the best hotels and restaurants can be found. Most tourist amenities such as embassies, airline offices, and travel agencies are located here as well. Near the boulevards of Juan Pablo II and Suyapa is the most modern part of the city, where many upscale residents live. The **Multiplaza Mall** complex, a North American-style shopping complex with international chain stores, is beside top hotels like the Intercontinental.

Farther east is **Suyapa**, a small town that was swallowed whole by Tegucigalpa's urban sprawl. Most tourists come here to visit the **Santuario Nacional** and **Basílica de Suyapa** (grounds open daily, interior of the basilica only during mass) the largest cathedral in the country. At this gothic cathedral, the Virgin of Suyapa, famous throughout Honduras for its healing powers, is brought out for special events like the Feria de la Virgen de Suyapa.

PARQUE NACIONAL LA TIGRA

Twenty-two kilometers (14 miles) from Tegucigalpa is **Parque Nacional La Tigra ❷** (daily 8am–5pm), a 238 sq km (92 sq miles) tract of cloud forest that has been a national park since 1982. While much of the forest was cut down by loggers and the El Rosario Mining Company, it is slowly being recovered. Hiking trails run through the park, mostly from the western entrance at Jutiapa, where there is a small campground, cabins, and a visitor center. The 6km (3.7 miles) **Sendero Principal** is the primary route across La Tigra, though a handful of other trails in various states of maintenance branch off it. Even though the park is so close to Tegucigalpa, it has a surprisingly rich collection of flora and fauna. Mammals like pumas and armadillos are rare, though more than 350 species of birds have been identified, including the resplendent quetzal and wine-throated hummingbird. The non-profit Amitigra (tel:

Equestrian statue of Franscisco Morazán in Plaza Morazán.

504 232 6771; www.amitigra.org) controls access to the park and can help make arrangements for visiting.

VALLE DE ÁNGELES AND SANTA LUCÍA

On weekends, day trippers from Tegucigalpa head to a pair of colonial mountain villages east of the city. The first you will come to is **Santa Lucía**, where small rural inns, country restaurants, and nurseries are strung out along the road. **Valle de Ángeles**, 8km (5 miles) east of Santa Lucía, has a cooler climate and many wealthy *capitalinos* have houses here. The 16th-century village is filled with artesania shops selling items from every part of Honduras. While most items are from elsewhere in the country, jewelry made from silver and other metals that once came from the area's mines are made locally. You'll find better prices and variety here than in Tegucigalpa. There's a good hike through the pine forests to the Las Golondrinas Waterfall, about 1km (0.6 miles) outside of town on the road to San Juancito.

WESTERN HONDURAS

For many, the mountainous western region of Honduras is the real Honduras. As you move away from the urban sprawl of San Pedro Sula, cowboys and indigenous groups like the Lenca and Chortí Maya have learned to coexist amidst the pine covered hills. Much of the cigar industry is based here, near Santa Rosa de Copán, and must see attractions like the ruins of Copán, the intellectual capital of the Mayas, and the breathtaking Lago de Yojoa, are here too.

SAN PEDRO SULA

Many travelers tend to skip **San Pedro Sula ❸**, the economic and transportation hub of Honduras, especially given its violent reputation of recent years. San Pedro lacks a connection to the past in the way Tegucigalpa does, as it lingered as a rural backwater until the

1920s when the United Fruit Company set up here. Today the population is around 500,000, making it the second largest conurbation in the country.

The country's busiest airport is well outside of town and therefore many don't even get a glimpse of the rather laid-back city center and all of the amenities it holds. The core of San Pedro Sula lies within the Circunvalación, a beltway lined with flashy malls, international chain hotels, and fast food restaurants that give it the feel of a typical American city. In the very center of the Circunvalación is **Parque Central**, a rather quaint main square surrounded by restaurants and store. A few blocks to the north is the **Museo de Antropologia e Historia de San Pedro Sula** (tel: 2557 1874; Mon, Wed–Sat 9am–4pm, Sun 9am–3pm), which has a chronological display of the region's history from pre-Columbian times to the modern era.

Farther north is the sprawling **Mercado Guamilito** (daily 10am–5pm) an excellent destination for exotic produce and handicrafts from all of the country, like Garífuna coconut carvings, Lenca

The charming streets of Valle de Ángeles.

pottery, and hammocks. Don't miss the row of stands with women making tortillas and *baleadas* (a popular Honduran tortilla dish, folded in half and filled with mashed fried beans) by hand; a great photo opportunity.

LAGO DE YOJOA

Surrounded by misty pine-covered mountains and coffee *fincas*, the 89 sq km (55 sq mile) **Lago de Yojoa** ➍ is a premier eco-destination that somehow isn't swarming with tourists. It's the country's largest natural lake and a hotspot for birders who come from around the world hoping to glimpse some of the 400 or so species that have been identified here. Along the lakeshore are several fine hotels, which mostly attract Honduran families, and even a small craft brewery, the American owned **D&D** (http://ddbrewery.com), which also runs guided boat excursions on the lake. Along the highway bordering the lake are dozens of fish restaurants, selling freshwater fish that are fried whole and served with *patacones* (fried plantain).

Boat on Lago de Yojoa.

On the lake's northern edge, 3km (1.9 miles) from the town of Peña Blanca, is **Parque Eco-Archeological de Los Naranjos** ➎ (daily 8am–4pm), a Lenca archeological site that dates back to approximately 700 BC. More interesting than the few mounds and piles of stones there are the 6km (4 miles) of stone paths, trails and observation towers scattered throughout the site where you can observe birds and other wildlife. A small museum and visitor center is at the entrance.

Covering 478 sq km (297 sq miles) along the rugged eastern side of the lake is **Parque Nacional Cerro Azul Meámbar** ➏. The forested landscape rises to a height of 2,047m (6,714ft) and is quite pristine with waterfalls and elfin forests. Several hundred bird species have been identified here, including keel-billed toucans and resplendent quetzals. As few humans reach the higher altitudes, larger mammals like monkeys, jaguars and tapirs thrive here, though are not easily seen. There are three primary trails ranging from 1.2km (0.75 mile) to 8km (5 miles) that extend from the visitor center in Los Pinos. Guides can be hired at the visitor center.

Near San Buenaventura, about 10km (6 miles) from Peña Blanca, are the 43m (141ft) high **Pulhapanzak Falls** (daily 6am–6pm) on the Río Amapa. While few tourists visit, these thundering falls are plastered on tourism posters all over the country.

COMAYAGUA

The capital of Honduras for more than three centuries before being moved to Tegucigalpa, **Comayagua** ➐, 71km (45 miles) south of Lago de Yojoa, has the best-preserved colonial architecture in the country. Founded in 1537 by the Spanish explorer Alonso de Cáceres, much of the original city grid remains, along with palaces, churches, and squares

At the north end of Parque Central, the **Catedral de Santa María** (tel: 2772 7672; daily 8am–6pm; free), dates to the late 17th century and is a masterpiece of colonial architecture. Four of the original 16 hand-carved wooden altars have been immaculately maintained. Outside in the tower, the clock dates to around 1100 and was built for the Alhambra in Granada, but given to Comayagua by King Phillip III. It was originally was placed in the **Iglesia La Merced** (daily 8am–6pm; free), four blocks to the south and the oldest church in Comayagua. It was built in 1550, but badly damaged in a 1774 earthquake and is partially reconstructed. Set in a 1558 building that once housed Central America's very first university, the **Museo Colonial de Arte** (tel: 2772 0386; daily 8am–4pm) maintains a collection of religious art and artifacts that have been created or donated to the city over the past five centuries.

COPÁN

Near the Guatamalan border is the Maya ceremonial city of **Copán** ⑧ (daily 8am–4pm). The area around the ruins has been inhabited since at least 1400 BC. There were 16 consecutive kings who saw the rise and fall of the city, beginning with the Great Sun Lord Quetzal Macaw in 426 AD, as the history carved into the stone dictates. Adventurer John L. Stephens discovered the ruins in 1839, as described in his book *Incidents of Travel in Central America, Chiapas and Yucatan* (1841).

The town of **Copán Ruínas** is about 1km (0.6 mile) from the archeological site. Tourism runs the town and within a few blocks of the cobblestone plaza are dozens of small hotels, ex-pat restaurants, and handicraft shops. There are few attractions in town, other than the small **Museo Regional de Arqueología** (tel: 2651 4108; daily 8am–4pm), aka the Copán Museum, with some pottery and artifacts from the ruins.

On entering the grounds of the archeological site, a path leads to the claustrophobic **Rosalia and Jaguar tunnels**, which partially opened to the public in 1999 and are subject to an additional fee beyond regular park admission.

Gran Plaza, Copán.

The tunnels give an idea of how the Maya layered construction, building one temple over another. The trail continues to the **Acropolis** and **Temple of Inscriptions**. On the Great Plaza, diagonal from the Temple of Inscriptions, is where the city's most important symbol can be found: the **Hieroglyphic Stairway**. Built by King Smoke Shell, the stairway features 64 steps, each carved with hieroglyphs that recount the history of Copán's kings and their line of succession. Many of the carvings have faded and the necessary covering makes them difficult to make out, though collectively they read like a giant book. Carved stelae, originals, and replicas, beside the stairs depict various rulers and mythical beasts.

Near the main entrance is the **Museum of Maya Sculpture**, which contains some of the most important stelae and carvings found at the archeological site. At the center of the museum is a full-scale replica of the Rosalia Temple. The museum also contains the reconstructed original facade of one of Copán's ball courts. Admission is

Mayan Rosalila temple replica at the Museum of Maya Sculpture.

included with your ticket to the park. The Copán Guides Association has a booth near the entrance, where bilingual guides offer 2-hour tours of the site.

About 2km (1.2 miles) from the main archeological site, **Las Sepulturas** was a residential area for Copán's ruling elite. It was once connected to the Great Plaza by a broad path causeway, identified by NASA through satellite imaging, though it's now reached on a leafy jungle trail. Admission is included.

OUTSIDE OF COPÁN

Outside of town are forest-covered mountains hiding waterfalls and hot springs, plus superb birdwatching and other attractions. On the road to the border is **Alas Encantadas** (daily 8am–4.30pm), a butterfly garden and breeding project, plus a botanical garden with more than 200 species of orchids.

There are a few carvings of frogs and the figure of a pregnant woman at a small site called **Los Sapos** (daily 9am–5pm), across the river from Copán near the excellent country inn, **Hacienda San Lucas** (www.haciendasanlucas.com),

which is known for its multicourse dinners using native techniques and ingredients. Several agencies in town offer horseback-riding tours here.

LA ENTRADA AND EL PUENTE

At the intersection of highways CA 4 and CA 11, **La Entrada ❾** is an otherwise uninteresting town that you would bypass if it weren't for one spectacular attraction: **El Puente** (daily 8am–4pm). The ruins, 10km (7.5 miles) out of town, are of a Mayan city built between the 6th and 9th centuries and it is Honduras' second most important archaeological site after Copán. Still, few actually visit it outside of the occasional tour bus. Several hundred stone buildings are scattered around the park and only a fraction have been excavated. There's a small visitor center and museum at the entrance, from where it's a walk of about a kilometer (a half mile) to the site's primary attraction, a rather large pyramid.

GRACIAS

For a short time, the sleepy colonial village of Gracias a Dios – named after conquistador Juan de Chavez's reaction after finding flat land after weeks in the mountains – was the capital of all of Central America. Eight years after being founded in 1536, **Gracias ❿** was home to the Spanish Royal courthouse with a jurisdiction that extended from Mexico to Panama. Four years later the court moved to Antigua and everyone forgot about Gracias for centuries.

Today, with nearby Lenca villages and national parks luring visitors, the town has been capitalizing on its stock of 500-year-old churches and cobblestone plazas. Much of the original Spanish grid, topped by a small fortification on a hillside called **El Fuerte de San Cristóbal**, has been reconstructed, with boutique hotels and cafés filling the whitewashed houses. Once the home of a wealthy colonial family, **Museo Casa Galeano** (daily 9am–6pm) is a restored colonial house from the

1840s stocked with artifacts, old photographs, and a folk art collection. It's adjoined by a botanical garden, one of the oldest in the region.

The **Balneario Aguas Termales** (daily 8am–8pm), 6.5km (4 miles) south of Gracias, is a public hot springs amenity popular with locals and tourists alike. Surrounded by pine forests, the pools range from 33–35.5°C (92–96°F) and are relatively quiet outside of the weekend rush.

PARQUE NACIONAL MONTAÑA DE CELAQUE

One of the largest tracts of cloud forest remaining in Central America, **Parque Nacional Montaña de Celaque ⓫** is the birthplace of 11 rivers that supply freshwater to villages as far away as El Salvador. Hidden within its pines and endless fog are resplendent quetzals, ocelots, and all sorts of rare flora and fauna. It's not easy though. The trails through the park are rather steep and are often muddy. The difficult hike up the mountain of **Cerro El Gallo** takes about 3 or 4 hours, while other trails

In the Parque Nacional Montaña de Celaque.

⊙ LA RUTA LENCA

A string of Lenca villages outside of the highland town of Gracias, each with an impressive colonial era church, have banded together to market themselves as **La Ruta Lenca**. Surrounding Celaque National Park, a circuit pieced together by mostly rough, unpaved roads connects the mountain villages of La Campa, Belén Gualcho, San Manuel de Colohete, San Sebastián, Corquín, and Mohaga. In each town you are rewarded with an unspoiled adobe village where an artisan or two specializes in Lenca crafts, such as the iconic black and white earthenware ceramics. Sundays are the best day of the week to come, when families come to town to sell produce and socialize, and churches are open. In La Campa, one of the first villages, the **Centro de Interpretation de Alfarería Lenca** (daily 8am–4.30pm) gives some background on the significance on Lenca pottery, especially the giant urns called *cántaros* that the village is known for. From La Campa the road gets too rough to drive without a 4x4 and slowly winds its way to a fork. Take the road to **San Manuel de Colohete**, where you'll find the area's most impressive church, with a facade from 1721 and frescoes and altars that date back more than 400 years. A lively outdoor market is held on the 1st and 15th of every month (6am–noon).

lead to waterfalls and mountain lakes. For the summit of **Cerro de las Minas**, the tallest peak in Honduras at 2,849m (9,344ft), camping on the mountain is essential for at least one night, with a guided hike requiring at least 2 days. Tour agencies lead guided excursions into the park, though some trails can be hiked independently.

NORTHERN HONDURAS

With smart new beach resorts in Tela Bay and a growing number of North American retirees settling down, the North Coast has a sense of momentum that hasn't been around since Standard Fruit entered the area. There are several important national parks, a good highway and all around good infrastructure, while away from the zipline tours, Garífuna villages and Spanish forts remain to be discovered.

TELA

Conquistador Cristóbal de Olid founded the city of Triunfo de la Cruz on May 3, 1524, though its name was eventually shortened to just **Tela** ⑫. Beginning in the early 1800s, the Garífuna came from Roatán and began settling here; many of their communities can still be found all around Tela Bay. For much of the 20th century, Tela was a company town, formed around the banana plantations of the Tela Railroad Company, a subsidiary of the United Fruit Company. When operations moved to La Lima in 1976, Tela took a hit. It wasn't until the start of the next century, when plans were introduced to turn the bay into the next Cancún. Efforts were made to clean up the city and roads were paved through fragile ecosystems to the dismay of many environmentalists. The megaproject is still not fully developed and may never fully materialize, though a golf course and one luxury resort has opened.

Split in two by the Tela River, the city center is on the southernmost point of Tela Bay. **Tela Veija**, a small colonial grid with most city amenities, is to the east, while **Tela Nueva**, where the old Tela Railroad buildings and Telamar Resort (www.telamarresort.com), a hotel created from the skeletal remains of company houses, are to the west.

Roughly 5km (3.1 miles) north of Tela is the **Jardín Botánico Lancetilla** ⑬ (www.lancetilla.org; daily 7.30am–3pm), one of the world's largest and most important botanical gardens. Established in 1926 by American botanist William Popenoe, Lancetilla was created so he could help United Fruit research and test new varieties of fruit, as well as treat diseases in the plantations. He brought in plants from all around the world, including the African Palm, which would eventually become a major cash crop, albeit a destructive one. The Honduran government took control in 1974 and now manages research here. From the visitor center, trails lead through the 1,680-hectare (4,151-acre) park, passing a large bamboo forest and hundreds of varieties of palms and fruit trees. Many visitors who come here are birders, taking advantage of the estimated

Boats moored up on Tela's shores.

400 species that can be spotted, including trogons and toucans.

OUTSIDE OF TELA

On the outskirts of the city around the bay are a string of traditional Garífuna communities, such as **Triunfo de la Cruz** to the east and **Tornabé, San Juan**, **La Ensenada**, **Río Tinto**, and lastly **Miami** to the west. Tensions have risen in these communities as the resort project as has been seen as a threat to their way of life; however, many are now employed by the resort. Miami, on a sandbar between a lagoon and the ocean, is the most interesting. It lacks running water and the residents still live in thatched huts, much in the same way they have for the last 200 years. For a small fee, local boatmen can paddle visitors out on dugout canoes or ride in motorized boats into the mangroves. The beach area is also quite pleasant and informal restaurants can prepare simple meals just off the sand.

Originally called Punta Sal, the 782km (484 miles) **Parque Nacional Jeannette Kawas** ⑭ was renamed after the environmental activist Jeannette Kawas Fernández, who was killed after establishing the park. Two distinct ecosystems are found here: the lagoon and the peninsula. Protecting the bay from strong winds called *nortes*, the peninsula is home to a combination of unspoiled coral reefs, dense jungle filled with howler monkeys, and stunning beaches. Los Micos Lagoon is separated by a small sandbar near Miami, and canals here weave through the rich landscape where hundreds of species of migratory birds can be seen. Outside of driving to Miami and hiring a boat to enter the lagoon, private transportation here is difficult. It's recommended to use a Tela-based tour operators like Garífuna Tours (www.garifunatours.com), which have regular trips to the lagoon and peninsula.

On the opposite end of Tela Bay is **Punta Izopo**, where the Lean and Hicaque rivers flow into the ocean amidst thick mangrove forests. Caimans, manatees, monkeys, and hundreds of species of birds can be seen. Kayak trips here are offered by

Tropical paradise on Cocalto Beach in Parque National Jeanette Kawas.

Garifuna Tours, otherwise boatmen in the village of Triunfo de la Cruz west of the park will negotiate trips.

LA CEIBA

The transportation hub of the North Coast is **La Ceiba** ⑮, the capital of the department of Atlántida. Fronting the Caribbean Sea and backed by the jagged mountains of Pico Bonito National Park, Honduras' third largest city sprawls out along Highway CA-13, where Americanized malls and fast-food chains have firmly entrenched themselves. Two main avenues, San Isidro and 14 de Julio, run parallel to the beach and the city center, surrounding a leafy **Parque Central**, is not entirely without charm. Barrio La Isla, to the northeast is where you will find the **Zona Viva**, where the city's best hotels, restaurants, and nightlife can be found. The city's beaches tend to be polluted, so it's best to go to the **Playa de Peru** east of the pier, or better yet outside of town, for bathing. More than a destination within itself, La Ceiba is better used as a jumping off point to explore nearby national

Garífuna people on the beach near La Ceiba.

parks or to catch flights and ferries to the Bay Islands.

Protecting the estuary of the Cuero, Salado, and San Juan rivers, the **Cuero y Salado National Wildlife Refuge** (daily 6.30am–6pm) is 30km (18 miles) west of La Ceiba. Rich with flora and fauna, sloths, otters, and white-faced monkeys, inhabit this mangrove ecosystem, best explored by boat from the visitor center at Salado Barra, where there is a café and dorm amenities. Omega Tours (www.omegatours.info) runs wildlife focused trips here that include about two hours on a boat plus transportation.

PICO BONITO NATIONAL PARK

La Ceiba's crown jewel is the 100,000-hectare (247,105-acre) **Parque Nacional Pico Bonito** ⑯. Ranging in altitude from sea level to more than 2,000m (6,500ft), there's more biodiversity here than in any other natural reserve in Honduras. Seven different ecosystems can be found within the park, which contain large tracts of virgin rainforest and cloud forest, not to mention waterfalls and rivers. The range of species living here is staggering. Big cats like jaguars and pumas can be found in more remote corners of the park, though there are also tapirs, several species of monkeys, and hundreds of species of birds, butterflies, and reptiles.

The park is divided into two parts. On one side is The Lodge at Pico Bonito (www.picobonito.com), an upscale ecolodge that regularly ranks among the world's best, with a gourmet restaurant and highly trained guides. From the lodge, guests and non-guests who come on day trips can access a network of immaculately maintained trails, bird-watching towers and swimming holes in the Coloradito River. A butterfly sanctuary and serpentarium can also be found on the grounds. The other section of the park is along the buffer zone of the park at the Cangrejal River, up the mountain from the village of Las Mangas, west of La Ceiba, just beyond Sambo Creek. Upon

crossing a hanging bridge over the river, there is one primary trail that leads to the 60 meter (196ft) **El Bejuco Waterfall**. This section of the park is more active, with a dozen or so small ecolodges. Adventure tour operators like Jungle River Tours (www.jungleriverlodge.com) set up rafting trips on the Class II-V Cangrejal that pass through pristine forests and over giant granite boulders.

CAYOS COCHINOS

Also known as the Hog Islands, the **Cayos Cochinos** ⑰ are a cluster of tropical islands, cartoonish coral cays, and sandbars 30km (19 miles) northeast of La Ceiba. Part of the Mesoamerican Barrier Reef System, there are strict conservation rules, such as no commercial fishing within the 489 sq km (189 sq miles) reserve. The reef here, with 60 or so dive sites, is as good, if not better, than any you will find in the Bay Islands and includes walls, drifts and small wrecks. There are good chances of seeing manta rays, bottlenose dolphins, whale sharks, and hawksbill turtles. The two main islands, **Cayo Menor** and **Cayo Mayor**, provide accommodations in a small hotel and a few private homes, plus a hiking trail, and a research station. The only permanent settlement belongs to the Garífuna community of Chachauate Cay, which lacks running water and electricity. Here, small restaurants serve typical dishes to daytrippers and rent out hammock space for those that want to stay longer.

TRUJILLO

At the end of the north coast highway CA-13, 165km (102 miles) east of La Ceiba, is the town of **Trujillo** ⑱. It was here, on August 14, 1502, that Christopher Columbus – on his fourth and final voyage – set foot on the American mainland for the first time. There have long been rumblings about turning Trujillo into a major beach and cruise destination, and with its wide beaches and

unspoiled forests it still might achieve its potential, but since Hurricane Mitch hit in 1998 and caused considerable damage, those plans have been on hold.

The colonial center of town is on a hilltop, guarded by a row of canons at the **Santa Bárbara fort** (daily 8am– noon, 1–4pm), erected in the 17th century to guard against pirate attacks. There is a small museum with muskets and other relics from British rule on display. One of the only other attractions in town is the old **cemetery**, where the three-centuries-old graves are usually overgrown with weeds. The most notable grave belongs to American adventurer William Walker, who, after a failed attempt of taking over Costa Rica, fled to Trujillo and took over the fort before surrendering to Honduran authorities and being swiftly executed.

Unpaved roads from the town along the coast lead to the Garífuna communities of **Santa Fe** and **Guadalupe**. Santa Fe, 12km (8 miles) to the west, has some nice beaches and **Comedor Caballero**, better known as Pete's Place, a traditional Garífuna restaurant

Chachahuate Cay on Cayos Cochinos is a Garífuna community.

Cruise ship in Roatán.

Roatán Port.

with some of the best seafood on the North Coast.

The 4,500-hectare (11,119-acre) **Capiro y Calentura National Park**, occupying the mountainous jungle behind Trujillo, has very little infrastructure and is understaffed. A dirt path on the southern end of town will lead to the Calentura mountain summit in about three hours.

THE BAY ISLANDS

For several centuries, as the Spanish raided the New World for gold, the Bay Islands were used as hideouts for French and English pirates, including famous buccaneers like Henry Morgan and John Coxen. After war broke out between England and Spain in 1739 the British took control of the islands and set up forts at Port Royal in Roatán; however, battles until the end of the 18th century left the islands uninhabited. At Punta Gorda in 1797, the British dumped a few thousand Garífuna, many of whom settled on the east end, where their culture is widely celebrated. New waves of settlers arrived

from the Caymans in the following centuries and, even though Honduras was granted sovereignty to the islands in 1859, there is a completely different air than on the mainland.

ROATÁN

Most tourism to the islands rotates around **Roatán ⑲**, the largest of the Bay Islands at 64km long (40-mile). It's here that the cruise industry has sunk about $100 million into modern ports, **Mahogany Bay** and the **Port of Roatán's Town Center**, which have attracted waves of oversized cruise ships that come to the island as part of longer Caribbean itineraries. When cruise ships are in town, much of the island loses its charm, filling roads with tour buses and crowding West Bay beach.

Most development has taken place on the Western half of the island. The crystal clear waters of **West Bay Beach**, the best in Honduras, has seen a surge in development over the past decade and resorts and condo projects have bought up every last hectare. In the hills above West Bay is **Gumbalimba Park** (www.gumbalimbapark.com; daily 8am–4pm) an island adventure park with watersports, a monkey island, and a canopy tour that's often visited by cruise travelers. **West End**, reached by road or water taxi from West Bay, is the older center of tourism here and the main hangout for the dive community. Hotels are smaller and less polished here than in West Bay and many of the restaurants and bars are owned by expats.

Sandy Bay is dominated by the all-inclusive resort at **Anthony's Key** (www.anthonyskey.com), which is set up on the shore and an adjoining cay. At attached **Bailey's Key**, operated by the Roatán Institute for Marine Sciences, there is a dolphin encounter and dolphin training program. **Carambola Gardens** (www.carambolagardens.com), also in Sandy Bay, has several trails that weave through the island's native flora and fauna.

Coxen Hole, in the center of the island, is home to the majority of the population and is the transportation hub of Roatán. Aside from cruise tourists arriving at the nearby Port of Roatán, there's little reason to come here. Mahogany Bay, the other cruise port, which was formerly known as Dixon's Cove, has a white sand beach, but it's still not West Bay.

The town of **French Harbour** was once the home of the island's fishing fleet, but now the marinas are filled with yachts and the town filled with expats. It's more of a residential area, though there's one large resort, **Pristine Bay** (www.pristinebayresort.com), with the Pete Dye-designed Black Pearl golf course.

Connected along the coast through canals, the eastern towns of Oakridge and Jonesville are mostly Afro-Antillean, with people residing in traditional-style stilt houses. Boatmen line the road offering short tours through the mangroves, stopping at the famous restaurant Hole in the Wall, reached only by boat. Punta Gorda, where the paved road ends, is where the Garífuna

first arrived from St. Vincent in 1797, though there is little beyond here other than the excellent beaches of **Camp Bay** and **Paya Bay**, which has a small resort (www.payabay.com).

ÚTILA

Despite being the smallest of the Bay Islands, **Útila** ❷⓪ might be the most interesting. It's not really a beach island, though there are a few sandy stretches. There are no large settlements other than **East Harbour**, where the ferries dock. Residents are mostly descendants of pirates and Garinagu from the Caymans, plus a mix of expats who came diving here and just never left. Much of the island is covered by mangroves and there are even tales that Captain Morgan buried treasure from a 1671 raid in Panama somewhere in the hills.

There are two beaches within walking distance from town, **Bando Beach**, which is privately owned and rents snorkel and kayak gear, and **Chepes Beach** near Sandy Bay. For a more paradisiacal experience, there's **Water**

Divers off Roatán.

⊘ BAY ISLANDS DIVING

With easy access to the world's second largest barrier reef, the Bay Islands of Roatán, Utila, and Guanaja, not forgetting Barbareta and 60 or so other cays, are best known for diving. Nearly every resort found on these mostly English speaking islands offers a dive package. Aside from the low prices for certification courses, what makes the Bay Islands so good for scuba diving is the variety of dive sites you can find just off shore of the three islands. On Roatán there are wrecks, reef sharks that get together in the deep waters at Cara a Cara Point, and dramatic crevices like Mary's Place. On Útila, Duppy Waters is home to barrel sponges and whale sharks. On Guanaja, the Pinnacle offers gorgonian and black coral where seahorses play and the *Jado Trader*, a wreck that is one of the region's best artificial reefs.

Cay, essentially a sand bar with a few palm trees, ringed by turquoise water.

Diving here is spectacular and prices for dives and certification courses are lower than almost anywhere. Dive shops like Útila Dive Center (www.utila divecenter.com) and the Bay Islands College of Diving (www.dive-utila.com), line the main drag in East Harbour and every hotel can help set you up with an all-inclusive rate. There are nearly 100 permanent mooring buoys that give access to various reefs and wrecks within a short boat ride of the shore. Whale sharks are commonly seen in March and April and most dive shops will run snorkeling trips.

GUANAJA

On July 30, 1502, Christopher Columbus landed on **Guanaja** ㉑, 12km (7 miles) east of Roatán and the least developed of the Bay Islands. Like Utila, Guanaja was a pirate hideout and many of the residents descend from these buccaneers. In 1998, Hurricane Mitch winds blew over the main island's pine trees and wiped away many of the

stilted houses. Much of the main island remains untouched by development, apart from a few houses, hotels, and an airstrip; however, tiny **Bonacca Cay** just offshore is perhaps the most densely populated place in Honduras, where five thousand people crowd in a maze of pastel colored houses, many of them hanging off the land on stilts. There are a few beaches on the main island, all of them quite empty and raw. Diving is good here and many boats come from Roatán on day trips.

LA MOSQUITIA

The largest tract of virgin tropical rainforest in Central Americas remains almost entirely unexplored. Only recently have archeologists and explorers uncovered stone cities, revealing a lost civilization that remains a mystery. Covering the entire northeastern part of the country, La Mosquitia is sparsely populated, with the exception of a few small towns and isolated Pech, Tawahka, Garífuna, and Miskitos villages. The region is only loosely controlled by the government and drug traffickers have taken

Enjoying the sunset from a waterfront dock in Útila.

advantage, disrupting what was beginning to look like a blossoming ecotourism industry.

RÍO PLÁTANO BIOSPHERE RESERVE

Named a Unesco World Heritage Site in 1980, the 525,000 hectares (1.3 million acres) **Río Plátano Biosphere Reserve** ㉗ is home to a diverse set of rare ecosystems including wetlands, pine savannas, and tropical forest. The only inhabitants are a few Pech and Miskito communities who live in much the same way as they have for hundreds of years. The array of flora and fauna is dazzling, with bucket list species after bucket list species: jaguars, harpy eagles, Baird's tapirs, and many others.

Despite its natural wonders, most of the park is almost inaccessible. For much of the rainy season, travel here is impossible, while during the dry seasons, running from February to May and August to November, it requires a series of air, boat, and overland connections to get into the interior, which begins to pile on costs, especially for solo travelers. The easiest way is to fly to airstrips in the northern end of the park, such as Raista or Brus Laguna, where there's lodging and tours can be arranged deeper into the reserve. One option is the 10- to 14-day rafting trip down the Río Plátano, which are run once or twice a year by tour operators in La Ceiba.

LAGUNA DE IBANS

The large lagoon of **Laguna de Ibans** ㉓, separated by a narrow sandbar from the Caribbean, has been to focus of numerous tourism projects in recent years. Along its shores are several Miskito and Garífuna villages that have launched conservation initiatives. In **Plapaya**, the Sea Turtle Conservation Project helps protect the green, loggerhead and leatherback turtles that nest on nearby beaches from February

to September. In the adjoining Miskito towns of **Raista** and **Belén**, which share an airstrip utilized by charter flights organized by tour agencies in La Ceiba, there are a few small ecolodges and a good beach. Community run tours explore the Parú, Ilbila, and Banaka creeks to spot monkeys and caimans.

LAS MARÍAS

Inland from Raista and Belén, **Las Marías** is as far upriver as you can get by motorized boat. The traditional Pech community on the Río Plátano is the base for many travelers coming to the reserve. With the help of NGOs the village has trained dozens of guides and naturalists to lead various guided hikes, like the 3-day round trip ascent to the top of **Pico Dama**, and canoe trips to the Walpaulban Sirpi petroglyphs. Additionally, they've built a few surprisingly comfortable guest rooms for those who come. All profits are split among the community. Upon arrival tourists are introduced to the *sacaguia*, a head guide elected for a six-month period, who coordinates all tours and rooms.

Traditional house in Las Marías.

WEIRD AND WONDERFUL WILDLIFE

Central America harbors magnificent natural treasures – hundreds of species of birds, mammals, and colorful marine life, forming a paradise for the wildlife enthusiast.

Visitors to the Central America often spend their time clambering over its awe-inspiring Maya ruins, sunning themselves on its gorgeous beaches, or exploring old colonial towns, but many birders, divers, and wildlife enthusiasts flock here above all for its uniquely rich and diverse natural environment.

A biodiversity hotspot with migrations running in both directions, the sheer array of different species found within the region is astounding. There are seven species of monkeys found in Central America, which includes Geoffroy's spider monkey, found in every country in the region, as well as the mantled howler and the white-headed capuchin, not to mention sub-species like the Coiba Island howler. There are healthy jaguar populations, as well as ocelots and other big cats, in undeveloped regions like La Mosquitia and the Darién Gap, while other mammals like tapirs, sloths, anteaters, capybaras, and pacas can also be seen. Reptiles like poison dart frogs and coral snakes often stand out for their bright colors.

The Caribbean coast is one of the richest regions on earth in coral formations. Reefs, in turn, harbor an incredible variety and density of marine life. Over 50 species of coral, 400 of fish, and 30 gorgonians have been identified along Central America's reefs, along with hundreds of mollusks, crustaceans, sponges, and algae. Both coasts are major nesting sites five species of sea turtles, including leatherback, Olive Ridley, and hawksbill.

An emerald basilisk lizard found in Sarapuiqi, Heredia Province, Costa Rica.

A spider monkey hangs from its prehensile (capable of grasping) tail, which acts as a fifth limb, in the Osa area, Costa Rica.

The blue-jeans frog or strawberry poison dart frog, native to Costa Rica.

Belize is home to a good population of jaguars.

Habitat threats

Despite the efforts to protect Central American forests, habitat destruction has had a serious effect on some of the birds. The quetzal is particularly vulnerable because it largely depends for survival on one special *aguacatillo* tree, found only in cloud forest. The three-wattled bellbird shares this habitat, and is equally threatened when forests are converted to pasture. Great green macaws are the most threatened species of macaw. Conservation efforts on the Caribbean coast, where they exclusively live, include honoring farmers who maintain the *dipteryx* trees upon which the macaws feed. There are only 30 active nests recorded in the protected breeding area straddling Costa Rica and Nicaragua.

Even higher on the critical list is the region's biggest raptor, the American harpy eagle. This giant monkey-eating bird is known to breed in the forests of the Osa Peninsula and Darién Gap, but sightings of it have become extremely rare. A handful of species, such as the cattle egret and roadside hawk, have actually benefited from man-made changes to the environment, because they need open ground on which to feed.

*...chool of tropical fish, including painted sweetlips,
...ench grunt, and schoolmaster circling coral in Hol Chan
...rine Reserve, Belize.*

*...sta Rica's most famed creature, the three-toed sloth,
...Manuel Antonio National Park.*

A beautiful male resplendent quetzal with a long uppertail preens in Monteverde Cloud Forest, Costa Rica.

The resort of San Juan del Sur on the Pacific coast of Nicaragua.

Looking out over the roofs of Granada and the Cathedral from the bell tower of Iglesia La Merced.

NICARAGUA

A land of contrasts, Nicaragua is Central America's sweet spot with all of the culture and nature, yet few of the tourists.

Word is quickly getting out about Nicaragua, long off the radar for all but the hardiest of travelers to Central America.

With 78 protected areas covering over 20 percent of the country, which is even more than Costa Rica, and home to seven percent of the world's biodiversity, there is masses to explore here. While the effects of the Sandinista insurrection and several natural disasters will linger for the foreseeable future, the country's tourism infrastructure has been on the up for years.

Along the Pacific coast, luxe resorts north of the former fishing village-turned-surf hangout San Juan del Sur can now be accessed by an airport, Costa Esmeralda, a name that follows a new marketing strategy. The faded architecture of colonial cities like Granada and León is being given a facelift, with boutique hotels and cafés moving in by the dozen. Expats, priced out of Costa Rica, are finding their way here, taking advantage of the inexpensive healthcare, not to mention the excellent rum and cigars.

Ecotourism continues to be an important enticement, with sandboarding down the slopes of Cerro Negro and the smoking crater of Masaya major geological attractions. Hikes through cloud forests, dry forests, and lowland tropical forests reveal a country swarming with wildlife. If you get tired of canopy tours, which are now a dime a dozen, there are organic farms reached only by horseback and kayaking excursions with caimans to sample.

While a potential canal may one day cut through the Caribbean coast and turn Lake Nicaragua into a major shipping route, for the time being Isla de Ometepe remains a place for volunteerism and excellent coffee. Other corners of the lake, like the artist colony on the Solentiname Archipelago and the wild islets in the north, remain much as they were decades ago. Along the Caribbean

Main Attractions
Léon
Granada
Isla de Ometepe
Solentiname Archipeligo
San Juan del Sur
Corn Islands
Costa Esmeralda

Maps on pages
246, 248, 255

Concepción volcano and Ometepe island.

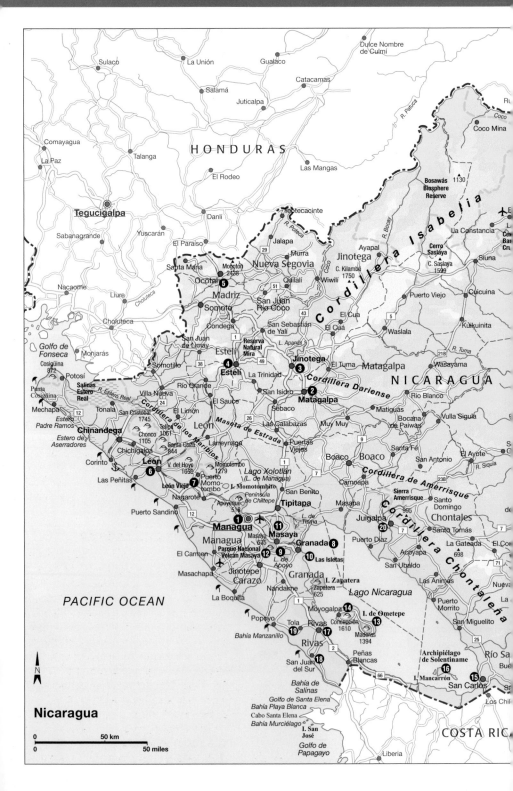

HONDURAS

Sulaco
La Unión
Gualaco
Catacamas
Dulce Nombre
de Culmí
Salamá
Juticalpa
R. Patuca
Coco
Comayagua
La Paz
Talanga
El Rodeo
Las Mangas
Coco Mina
Tegucigalpa
Danlí
Teotecacinte
Bosawás 1130
Biosphere
Reserve
Sabanagrande
Yuscarán
R. Poteca
R. Bocay
La Constancia
Cer
Bar
Cru
El Paraíso
Jalapa
29
Ayapal
Cerro
Saslaya
Santa María
Mogotón
2438
Murra
Jinotega
C. Kilambé
1750
C. Saslaya
1599
Siuna
Nueva Segovia
Ocotal 5
51
Quilalí
Wiwilí
Cordillera Isabelia
Madriz
San Juan
Río Coco
Puerto Viejo
Cuicuina
Somoto
43
El Cua
Condega
San Sebastián
de Yalí
El Quá
Waslala
Kukuinita
San Juan
de Limay
1
Reserva
Natural
Mira
5
R. Tuma
21B
Esteli
L. Apanas
Jinotega
Estelí
49
El Tuma
Matagalpa
Wasayama
La Trinidad
Cordillera Dariense
NICARAGUA
Rio Grande
Somotillo
38
San Isidro
2
Matagalpa
Río Blanco
Villa Nueva
El Sauce
Sébaco
Matiguás
Bocana
de Paiwas
Vulla Sigula
San Cristóbal
1745
El Limón
26
Las Calabazas
Muy Muy
Tonala
Maseta de Estrada
Telíca
1105
León
Larreynaga
Puertas
Viejas
9
Santa Fé
San Antonio
El Ayote
R. Siquia
Chonco
1105
Santa Clara
844
1
Boaco
Boaco
Cordillera de los Maribios
Chichigalpa
León
6
V. del Hoyo
1050
Momotombo
1279
Lago Xolotlán
(L. de Managua)
7
Camoapa
Cordillera de Amerrisque
23B
Las Peñitas
León Viejo
7
Puerto
Momo-
tombo
L. Momotombito
San Benito
Sierra
Amerrisque
995
Santo
Domingo
Nagarote
Peninsula
de Chiltepe
Masapa
Juigalpa
20
Chontales
Cordillera Chontaleña
Santo Tomás
7
Puerto Sandino
12
Apoyeque
V. de
518
Tipitapa
7
L. de
Tisma
Managua
1
Masaya
635
Masaya
11
Puerto Díaz
La Gateada
698
El Cor
7
Managua
Masaya
9
Granada
8
Acoyapa
San Ubaldo
71
El Carmen
Parque Nacional
Volcán Masaya
12
10
Las Isletas
Masachapa
Jinotepe
Carazo
L. de
Apoyo
Granada
I. Zapatera
Lago Nicaragua
Las Animas
Nueva
La Boquita
Nandaime
Zapatera
625
Puerto
Morrito
La
Popoyo
Tola
1
Moyogalpa
14
I. de Ometepe
San Miguelito
Bahía Manzanillo
19
Rivas
17
Concepción
1610
13
25
Río Sa
Bue
Rivas
2
Maderas
1394
San Juan
del Sur
18
Peñas
Blancas
Archipiélago
de Solentiname
16
I. Mancarrón
15
San Carlos
66
Los Chil
Bahía de
Salinas
Golfo de Santa Elena
Bahía Playa Blanca
Cabo Santa Elena
Bahía Murciélago
I. San
José
Golfo de
Papagayo
COSTA RIC

PACIFIC OCEAN

Golfo de
Fonseca
Cosigüina
872
Potosí
Monjarás
Punta
Cosigüina
Salinas
Estero
Real
R. Estero Real
Mechapa
12
Estero
Padre Ramos
Tonala
Cordillera de los Maribios
24
Chinandega
Estero de
Aserradores
Corinto

N

Nicaragua

0   50 km
0   50 miles

Liberia

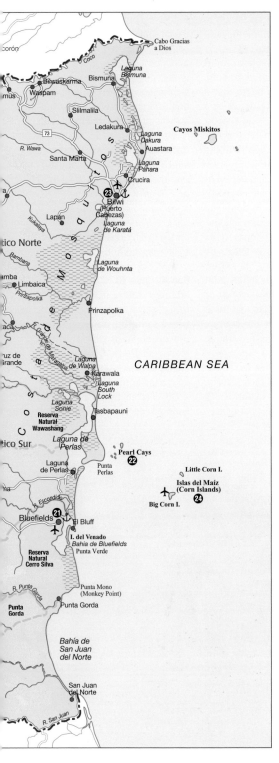

coast and farther afield on the Corn Islands, the vibe is even more relaxed, with days filled with swaying palms and snorkeling and nights vibrating to the beat of an African drum.

THE POST-WAR PERIOD

Weary of war, Nicaraguans voted out the Sandinistas in 1990 in a surprise victory for Violeta Chamorro, the widow of journalist Pedro Joaquín Chamorro Cardenal, who became Nicaragua's first female president. With the economy devastated and a series of natural disasters unfolding shortly after, such as a 1992 earthquake and 1998's Hurricane Mitch, Nicaragua saw few major improvements in the years subsequent to Sandinista rule.

In 2006, Sandinista Daniel Ortega returned to power and was reelected in a landslide in 2011. In 2014, the congress adjusted the constitution so he would be able to run for a third term, which he won by a large margin in 2016. The general economic stability from Ortega's social programs and business-friendly environment has been widely popular among Nicaraguans who are eager to put the past behind them. With an economy growing at double the Latin American average and a society avoiding the violence of Honduras to the north, Nicaragua appears to be in better shape than it has ever been. Still, many opponents claim that the election was a farce and that the growing autocracy, pushed by Ortega's vice president and wife, Rosario Murillo, are keeping it from becoming truly democratic.

MANAGUA AND AROUND

Named Nicaragua's capital in 1852, ending the rivalry between León and Granada and setting up extensive urbanization for the next 80 years, more than two million people call **Managua ❶** home. Set on the shores of **Lago Xolotlán**, aka Lake Managua, parts of the city feel like the apocalypse has hit, with empty lots filled with rubble and swaths being overtaken by jungle. Much of this disorder can be traced back to December 23, 1972, when an earthquake flattened 8 sq km (3 sq miles) of the city, killing an estimated 10,000 people. Before anything could be rebuilt, revolution came and bombings knocked down buildings and sent the city's wealthy fleeing to Miami. Only in the 21st century, as the economy has begun to stabilize, has Managua seen efforts to bring it into the modern era.

While most travelers hightail it out of the city immediately upon landing, especially with Granada being just a short drive away, those who do spend a day or two in Managua will find a major Central American city that is essentially free of tourists. The center of the city, the **Zona Monumental**, is where the majority of attractions and government buildings can be found. However, this neighborhood was badly damaged in the 1972 earthquake and can be dangerous outside of daylight hours.

Managua's center is the **Plaza de la Revolución Ⓐ**, with its 1933 monument honoring the Nicaraguan poet Rubén Darío. The Catedral Vieja, or at least what is left of it, is less than a block to the east. While the church, which dates from 1929, is too fragile to enter, visitors can still glimpse at the frescoes and statues inside. To the south, attached to the National Library, is the **Palacio Nacional de la Cultura Ⓑ** (tel. 2222 2905; as Mon–Fri 8am–5pm,

Sat 9am–4pm, Sun 10am–5pm), where Sandinista rebels staged a hostage siege in 1978, resulting in the release of political prisoners. Today the building is home to the National Museum, with a collection of Pre-Columbian ceramics and artifacts, as well as various pieces and displays from the revolution.

Built in 1969, the **Teatro Nacional Rubén Darío Ⓒ** (www.tnrubendario.gob.ni), to the north of the plaza near the malecón (pier), was one of the few buildings to survive the 1972 earthquake and continues to be an integral part of Managua culture with regular dance exhibitions and concerts.

The sprawling lakefront complex in the old port area, **Puerto Salvador Allende Ⓓ**, stretches for several kilometers and is lined with restaurants, playgrounds and beach access. Opened in 2008, it has quickly become the preeminent tourist attraction in Managua. There is live music and roving performers on the weekends, and boat trips to the Island of Love.

Discovered by miners in 1874, the **Huellas de Acahualinca Ⓔ** are the

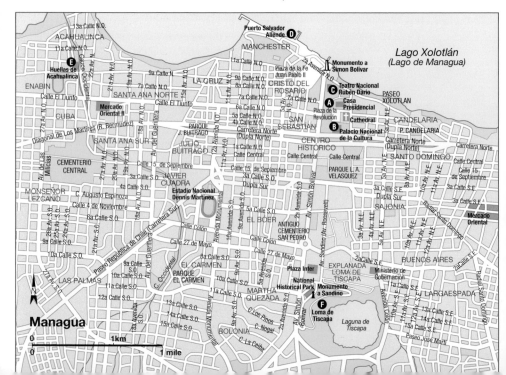

fossilized tracks on the shore of Lake Xolotlán of a small group of people, as well as various animals and birds that date back an estimated 6,000 years. It's believed that volcanic ash covered the footprints, perfectly preserving them. There is a small site museum (Mon–Fri), with an exhibition of Pre-Columbian ceramics. It's in a rough neighborhood near the Mercado Oriental, so it's best to take a taxi in and out.

A national historic park southeast of the center on the edge of **Volcán Tiscapa, Loma de Tiscapa** , looks out over a small crater lake and is home to Managua's most recognizable landmark, a statue of revolutionary hero Augusto Sandino. The site was once the home of Somoza's presidential palace; it's now home to a collection of Sandinista monuments, such as a tank donated by Mussolini. There are stunning views of the lake and center, as well as a canopy tour (tel: 8872 2555).

OUTSIDE OF MANAGUA

The 184-hectare natural preserve of **Chocoyero-El Brujo**, 23km (14 miles)

south of Managua, protects one of Managua's primary water sources. Dissected by a network of hiking trails, the park contains two waterfalls, El Brujo and Chocoyo, both around 25 meters (82ft) in length. At around 3pm each day, flocks of chocoyos, a variety of the Pacific green parakeet, can be seen flying around the cliffs of the canyon near the Chocoyo falls. Also within the lush green park are toucans, two types of monkeys, and other small mammals.

In the town of **Tipitapa**, about 22km (16 miles) east of Managua along the shore of the lake, you will find the **El Trapiche** hot springs, a basic thermal pool overlooking the Tipitapa River.

NORTHERN NICARAGUA

Despite being well removed from the tourist trail, the mountainous northern half of Nicaragua has some of the country's most interesting attractions. Dotted with patches of picturesque farmland and cloud forest dripping with waterfalls in the east, and volcanoes and hot lowlands toward

Managua, Nicaragua's capital.

⊘ THE POTENTIAL CANAL

Conceived by Ortega's administration, Nicaragua's Grand Interoceanic Canal project was pushed through parliament in 2014 with almost no debate. Backed by HKND, a Chinese company that few know anything about, the proposed $50 billion waterway is the hope of many to finally develop a Panama-like economy and modern infrastructure in Nicaragua.

The designers say it will be the biggest earth-moving operation in the history of the world and it will clear a 286km (178-mile) -long, 30-meter (98ft) -wide channel so that the world's largest ships can pass through the isthmus between the Pacific and the Atlantic. Additionally, developers want to add a large hotel on Isla de Ometepe and further ports, providing jobs for hundreds of thousands who sorely want them.

Despite the promises, there are serious doubts that the canal will ever be built. While ground was broken on the project in 2014, no work has been completed. Landowners have railed against the appropriation of their property and environmentalists oppose the destruction of some of the world's most biodiverse ecosystems. Others bring up the fact that what became the Panama Canal was once considered for construction in Nicaragua, but engineers determined that the location would be too prone to natural disasters. Additionally, the Chinese telecom tycoon behind HKND lost 85 percent of his fortune in a stock market crash.

the Pacific, waves of colonists, from pirates to the Spanish to revolutionaries, have all made their mark here.

For much of the past century the region has been plagued with wars and natural disasters. The turbulence began in the early days of Spanish settlement, when a volcanic eruption destroyed the original setting for León; emerged in the conflicts of the 1930s, when General Sandino battled American marines; continued with the Sandinista struggle in the 1970s; the Contras a decade later; and culminated with Hurricane Mitch in 1998, which left countless towns devastated.

Today the north is one of the most industrious parts of the country as the setting for coffee farms around Matagalpa and the tobacco plantations near Estelí. There's also cycling through the pine-filled valley that surrounds the colonial town of Ocotal, and hiking through the gorges outside of Jinotega. More of a DIY Nicaragua than Granada or the Pacific coast, the north is full of authentic rural character.

Matagalpa.

MATAGALPA

Surrounded by green hills, the valley town of **Matagalpa** ❷ is an important economic engine for Nicaragua, being the heartland of the country's coffee industry. The country's fourth largest city, nicknamed the 'Pearl of the North,' was originally an indigenous settlement of the Matagalpa culture, fierce warriors known for their stone statues that disappeared in 1875. The Spanish arrived here in 1528, but it wasn't until gold was discovered that Matagalpa really began to grow, attracting mestizo settlers and many German, American, and British immigrants, including Ludwig Elster and his wife Katharina Braun, who planted the first coffee plants.

While many visitors spend much of their time outside of the city, there are several interesting pieces of colonial architecture in town, like the neoclassical **Iglesia San Pedro** fronting **Parque Morazán**. The church dates to 1874 and features a wood altar and whitewashed exterior. To the east of Parque Dario is the humble adobe

birthplace of Carlos Fonseca Amador, who founded the FSLN and is widely regarded as Matagalpa's most famous son. Now a museum, the **Casa Museo Comandante Carlos Fonseca** (Mon–Fri), the house displays various pieces of revolutionary history.

OUTSIDE OF MATAGALPA

Finca Esperanza Verde (http://fincaesperanzaverde.com) is an ecolodge on a coffee farm with various cloud forest trails. Set at 1,200 meters (4,000ft) above sea level near the town of Yúcul, east of Matagalpa, it has stunning views of the green hills. Open to the public during the day, it's a popular day trip from Matagalpa.

Founded in 1891 by German immigrants, the **Selva Negra Ecolodge** (www.selvanegra.com) 11km (7 miles) outside of Matagalpa was a coffee estate that became a tourist resort in 1976. Arguably the most famous hotel in Nicaragua, the cool highland resort has long been a favorite escape of the country's elite who come to hike, wander through the organic farm, or look for birds such as tanagers or manakins in the surrounding forest.

JINOTEGA

Beyond Selva Negra, the road continues north to **Jinotega ❸**, which is one of the most scenic drives in Nicaragua. The mountain highway hovers above 1,500m (5,000ft) for much of the way, an ideal setting for coffee plantations and lush, green farmland. Set in a misty valley ringed by granite ridges and thick cloud forest, Jinotega's quaint cobblestone streets are perpetually covered with rain. An easy yet sweaty hike for a birds-eye view of the city is to **Cerro La Cruz**, marked by a cross placed here in 1703 by Franciscan Fray Margíl de Jesús. A pilgrimage site, the mirador hosts the Fiestas de la Cruz from April 30 to May 16 each year, the city's biggest party.

To the northeast, en route to Estelí, is **San Rafael del Norte**, one of the highest towns in Nicaragua. Dating to the late mid-17th-century, the rural village has opportunities to hike deeper into the mountains, as well as to visit coffee fincas.

East of Jinotega is the **Reserva Natural Cerro Datanlí-El Diablo**, a 10,000-hectare (24,710 acre) cloud forest reserve with a rich array of flora and fauna. A network of trails enters the reserve from the communities surrounding it. The solar-powered **La Bastilla Ecolodge** (http://bastillaecolodge.com), with all profits invested back into a jointly-run agricultural and tourism school, offers guided hikes and horseback riding to waterfalls and coffee fincas within the reserve.

ESTELÍ

Near the border with Honduras, just off the Pan-American highway, **Estelí ❹** is a university town that gave rise to the Sandinistas. Set in a broad valley surrounded by forested hills, the highland city is Nicaragua's third largest. Beyond the shady main plaza and adjacent whitewashed cathedral, which dates

A colorful bus in Matagalpa.

⏀ A UNICYCLIST TURNED REVOLUTIONARY

A California-born engineering graduate named Benjamin Ernest Linder, inspired by the Sandinista Revolution, moved to Nicaragua in 1983 to help the country's poor. After several years in Managua he moved to the northern highland town of El Cuá, in the middle of a war zone where the Sandinistas were fighting the US funded Contras. Linder helped build a hydroelectric plant, bringing electricity to the village of San José de Bocay, and launched vaccination campaigns against measles. However, Linder will always be remember for his talents as a clown, who amidst the horrors of war, entertained village children as he juggled and rode his unicycle.

In 1987, Linder and two Nicaraguan friends were ambushed by Contras while walking through the forest, an incident that raised international headlines, leading to questions about the US role in Nicaragua. Congress withdrew support for the war a year later. Linder is fondly remembered throughout the north as the juggling ambassador, with murals plastered around the region. President Ortega posthumously awarded him the country's highest civilian honor and served as a pallbearer at his funeral. Numerous books and songs have been dedicated to Linder, including Sting's *Fragile* on the 1987 album, ...Nothing Like the Sun.

⊙ Tip

Every Saturday on the north side of León's main plaza, Parque Juan José Quezada, a community fiesta called Tertulia Leonesa is held to showcase the best of the city's cultural traditions. Micro-artisans sell traditional handicrafts and foods, while folkloric musicians and dancers perform for onlookers.

to 1823, are multiple tributes to the revolution, such as a series of murals and the **Galería de Héroes y Mártires** (Tue–Fri 9.30am–4pm), with photos and various artifacts from the battles against the Somoza government in the late 1970s, which destroyed much of the city and killed an estimated 15,000 people. Bullet holes can still be seen in many of the buildings around Estelí. Rural Estelí comes alive on Saturdays, when farmers from the surrounding countryside come to the sprawling produce market to sell their harvests. A modern commercial complex with a hotel, mall, and movie theaters is a symbol of the town's progress.

After the Cuban Revolution in 1959, Cuban cigar makers flocked to Estelí to take advantage of the ideal tobacco growing conditions in the surrounding countryside. Today, some of the best cigars in the world come from the city and it remains one of the primary local industries. While most cigar factories do not offer tours, some do, and these can be set up through any hotel or tour agency in town. The tours reveal how the leaves are dried and the tobacco rolled, though some are more elaborate with multi-day itineraries that include extensive sampling and visits to farms, such as at **Drew Estate** (www. cigarsafari.com).

Roughly 30km (19 miles) northeast of Estelí is the **Miraflor Cloudforest Reserve**, notable for the tourist-friendly organic farming community that adjoins it. The reserve centers on a mountain lake ringed by primary forest that is transected by hiking trails to several waterfalls.

OCOTAL

The Spanish began settling in what is the scenic Nueva Segovia region in 1534, though pirates sailing up the River Coco from the Caribbean in search of gold repeatedly attacked. The settlers moved to what is now **Ocotal** ❺ in 1654, quickly developing an important source of timber for the growing nation. In 1927, Augusto Sandino and his army seized the city in their first major blow to government forces, which resulted in a devastating air raid by the US marines. Today, the city of 30,000 is home to a lovely central plaza filled with tropical foliage, pine trees, and flowers, and sided by a neoclassical church.

The surrounding countryside, chock-full of cattle ranches and coffee fincas, makes for fine cycling and several tour agencies and hotels in town will rent bikes.

Southwest of Ocotal on the Pan-American Highway, not far from the Honduran border, is the **Somoto Canyon**, a rugged gorge with unusual rock formations.

LEÓN AND AROUND

Closer to the Pacific coast, near the Honduran border, **León** ❻ is the country's second largest city with a population of 200,000. Founded in 1524 by Francisco Hernández de Córdoba, it was abandoned in 1610 after earthquakes turned much of it to rubble.

Working at a cigar factory in Estelí.

The settlement was then moved about 30km (20 miles) east to where the present-day city now stands. Long the liberal and intellectual capital of the country, León was the political capital too from colonial times until the mid-1800s, when this title moved back and forth from more conservative Granada before finally landing in Managua. During the revolution the city was a stronghold of the Sandinistas, leading to a brutal backlash from the Somoza regime, which burned down the city's central market.

The swelteringly hot lowland city has maintained its colonial core, with more than a dozen 18th-century churches, many of which are connected by underground tunnels once used to escape pirate attacks and now part of the sewer system. The colonial baroque **Basilica Catedral de la Asuncion** (tel: 2311 4820; Mon–Sat 8am–noon, 2–4pm; free) was built between 1747 and 1814 and is the largest cathedral in Central America. Having endured earthquakes and bombings, it has become a symbol of the city itself: proud and resilient. Within the crypts are the tombs of some of the most important figures in Nicaraguan history, such as the poets Rubén Darío and Salomón de la Selva, the father of independence Miguel Larreynaga, and composer José de la Cruz Mena.

Founded in 1639 by Friar Pedro de Zúñiga, the church and convent of **San Francisco** (hours vary; free), two blocks west of the plaza, is one of the oldest in the country. With its plateresque altars, courtyard lined with lemon trees, and porticoes covered in red bougainvillea, it's one of the most attractive examples of Leónese colonial architecture. Dating to 1786, the **Iglesia de la Recolección** (hours vary; free), three blocks north of the plaza, features a Mexican Baroque facade and altarpieces. Opposite the cathedral is the **Museo de la Revolucion** (daily), dedicated to the Nicaraguan revolutionaries who stood up to the Somozas, while the **Museo Rubén Darío** (daily) is where the country's favorite poet spent his first 14 years and is filled with various relics from his life. A block away, the **Centro de Arte Fundación Ortíz-Gurdián** (www.

León's cathedral is the largest in the region.

fundacionortizgurdian.org), set in two colonial houses, holds Nicaragua's best art collection, with contemporary works of Nicaraguan painters and even works from Rembrandt and Picasso.

OUTSIDE OF LEÓN

The ruins of the original León, a Unesco World Heritage Site known as **León Viejo** ❼ (daily 8am–5pm), were laid buried in ash from the 1610 eruption of the Momotombo Volcano. The ruins were lost for 300 years until the late 1960s; excavations have revealed brick walls and the general layout of the city, as well as the cathedral and plaza, with the headless remains of founder Francisco Hernández de Córdoba beneath it. The site can be visited on a day-long guided tour through any agency in León, such as Vapues (www.vapues.com), and are usually combined with a hike to the top of the **Cerro Negro Volcano**, with options for sandboarding down the black volcanic slopes.

On the coast, the **Reserva Natural Isla Juan Venado**, 18km (11 miles) long, is an uninhabited barrier island with wide, desolate beaches and mangrove forests in the interior reaches. Kayak trips through the canals can be arranged in León, as can turtle tours from July to December, when Olive Ridleys, leatherbacks, and other turtles arrive in their thousands to lay their eggs in El Vivero, close to Las Peñitas. Just north of Las Peñitas is **Poneloya**, the far north's most popular beach destination. A fishing village with seafood restaurants fronting the beach, there are several small hotels here and there is regular bus service from the Mercadito Subtiaba in León.

GRANADA AND THE MASAYA REGION

The short distance between Managua and Lake Nicaragua is one of the most visited in Nicaragua. For many travelers, the cobblestone streets and colonial townhouses-turned-boutique hotels in Granada serve as a base from which they explore the rest of the country. Easy day trips from the city allow for hikes on the forested slopes

The skyline of Granada at sunset.

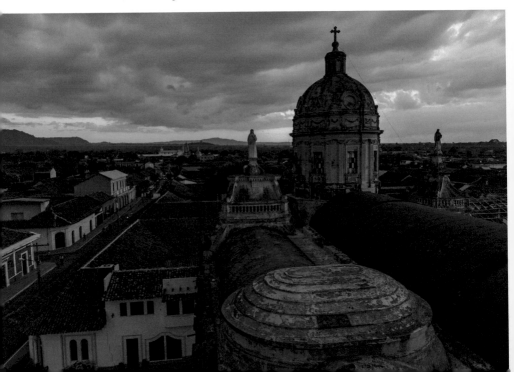

of the Mombacho Volcano or for soaks in the hot springs below it. Options for extended stays in the wilderness can be found in the ecolodges along the turquoise waters of the Laguna de Apoyo or on the islands in the tranquil Isletas de Granada on the lake.

GRANADA AND AROUND

Founded in 1524 by Francisco Hernández de Córdoba, **Granada ❽**, near the base of the Mombacho Volcano, was the first official European city in mainland America. La Gran Sultana, nicknamed for its Moorish and Andalusian architecture, was an important port city on Lake Nicaragua throughout the colonial period, making it a target for English, French and Dutch pirate attacks. In 1856 American adventurer William Walker, after taking up residence in the city, set it on fire while surrounded by opposing forces, planting a sign declaring 'Here was Granada.' Despite the tumultuous history, Granada has some of the best preserved colonial architecture in all of Central America.

ORIENTATION

The center of Granada's historic core is at **Parque Colón ❹**, a vibrant central square where parrots squawk in the tall palms and food stands sell *vigorón*, a traditional snack of pork and cabbage wrapped in banana leaf. Surrounding the plaza are many colonial buildings, like the ritzy **Hotel Plaza Colón** (http://hotelplazacolon.com) and the **Catedral de Granada ❺** (hours vary; free), which was originally built in 1583, though it has been destroyed and rebuilt multiple times. Also on the plaza is the **Casa de los Leones**, an elegant house that dates to 1720, now a cultural center.

At Real Xalteva and 14 de Septiembre, the Baroque **Iglesia La Merced ❻** (daily 11am–6pm) dates to 1534 and has undergone several rebuilds and renovations, although it has maintained its beauty. Inside, a spiral staircase leads up to a bell tower with some of the best views of the city. The pale blue **Convento San Francisco ❼** (tel: 2552 5535; Mon–Fri 8am–4pm, Sat–Sun 9am–4pm), one of Nicaragua's oldest buildings, is a block farther east of the cathedral.

Dancers perform in the shade of the Granada's Catedral.

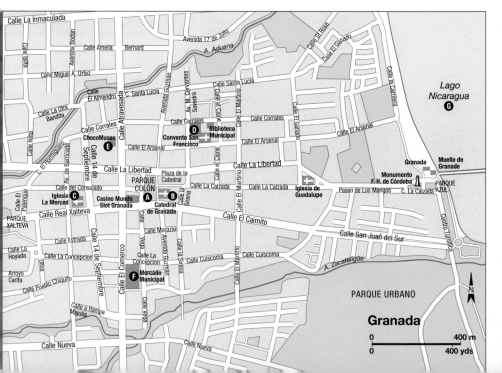

Having been famously destroyed by both the pirate Henry Morgan in 1679 and then by William Walker in 1856, the galleries now contain a museum (daily) with a collection of pre-Columbian basalt statues from Zapatera Island.

On Calle Atravesada northwest of the plaza is the **Choco Museo ❺** (www.chocomuseo.com; daily 7am–6.30pm), a chocolate store with chocolate-making workshops and farm tours. East of the plaza, along the pedestrian-only Calle La Calzada, is the primary concentration of stores, restaurants, and nightspots in the city. Several hip boutique hotels like the **Hotel Dario** (www.hoteldario.com) and **Tribal** (www.tribal-hotel.com) are found here as well. To the south is the neoclassical **Mercado Municipal ❻**, constructed in 1892, which spills out into the surrounding streets, while farther west is the **municipal cemetery**, with stone tombs that date to the late 19th-century and contain the remains of six Nicaraguan presidents. There's also the neoclassical **Capilla de Animas**, modeled after a French chapel.

Market day in Granada.

On the eastern end of Calle La Calzada is the shore of **Lake Nicaragua ❼** where there are a few bars and a waterfront boardwalk that gets crowded on weekends.

OUTSIDE OF GRANADA

Twenty-minutes west of Granada is the **Laguna de Apoyo ❾**, Nicaragua's largest volcanic lagoon. More than 200 meters (656 ft) deep and 6km (4 miles) in diameter, the caldera is ringed with lush forests where toucans and white-face monkeys can easily be spotted on a short hike. A few restaurants and ecolodges, some of which rent kayaks, can be found on a strip along the northwestern shore of Apoyo, though the majority of visitors come on a day trip from Granada.

The archipelago of 354 jungle clad islands called **Las Isletas ❿** are easily reached from Granada's waterfront. While many of the islands have been purchased by wealthy residents of Managua, who have built mansions on them, others – often just the length of a fishing line away – are quite humble, with rustic yet charming wooden shacks. From the southern end of the **Complejo Turístico Cocibolca** near Granada, boat tours explore the islands, stopping at the small Spanish fort of **San Pablo**. Another way of experiencing Las Isletas is to stay at the eco-friendly Jicaro Island Lodge (www.jicarolodge.com), the premier hotel in Las Isletas and built using local materials. The lodge helps fund an organic farm on one of the islands and supports several schools.

Managed by the Fundación Cocibolca – which has built a network of trails, a butterfly garden and organic coffee farm – the **Mombacho Volcano Natural Reserve** (www.mombacho.org) south of Granada along the lake is a popular day trip from Granada. Home to three species of monkeys and nearly two hundred species of birds, the lush jungle here has been well preserved. Treks go up to the lip of the crater and around, though the steep, sweaty trails are not for the unfit.

MASAYA

Nicaragua's capital of folklore, **Masaya** , is just 9km (5.5 miles) from Granada. Surrounded by hissing volcanoes and tiny rural villages known for their handicrafts, Masaya is where to come to buy souvenirs. While the city of 100,000 was badly damaged in the 2000 earthquake, the markets, craft workshops, and old churches here remain in good condition. Most head straight for the **Mercado de Artesanías de Masaya**, an artisan market selling hammocks, pottery, woodcarvings, and leather good, among other things.

It's also possible to go direct to the source of the handicrafts, which are mostly created in a string of mountain villages called the **Pueblos Blancos**. Scattered within 15 km (9 miles) of the city are Nindiri, Niquinohomo, Masatepe, Catarina, Diria, and Diriomo, each with their own specialty.

VOLCÁN MASAYA NATIONAL PARK

Nicaragua's first and largest national park, the 54 sq km (34 sq miles) **Parque Nacional Volcán Masaya** is the home of five craters and two calderas. The extremely active Masaya caldera, known as the 'Gates of Hell' to the Spanish, exploded as recently as 2001, allowing a new vent to form; ash and steam regularly shoot out into the sky above. While the situation is always changing depending on the level of activity, and the park is often closed to visitors, the standard tour allows for about 30 minutes at the viewpoint overlooking the crater, where steam and bubbling lava can be seen. The road runs nearly to the top of the crater, with the visitor center halfway up, while a network of 20km (12 miles) of hiking trails branches out from it.

LAKE NICARAGUA AND AROUND

Lake Nicaragua, also called Lake Cocibolca, is nearly the same size of South America's Lake Titicaca, which is why the Spanish nicknamed it the 'Mar Dulce,' or Sweet Sea. There are plans to make the lake the centerpiece of a canal project that would rival the one in Panama, likely causing serious

The Masaya volcano is highly active.

environmental degradation, though it might never become a reality. For now, the lake is an ecotourism hotspot, with the island of Ometepe – made of two volcanoes and the narrow strip of land between them – as the focal point. Farther afield is the Solentiname archipelago, an artist colony, and the Rio Coco, which runs parallel to the Costa Rican border and gives access to the Caribbean coast.

ISLA DE OMETEPE

The world's largest volcanic island within a freshwater lake, **Ometepe** ⑬ is one of Nicaragua's primary attractions, even though it's quite rugged and lacks much infrastructure. Seeing the island's twin volcanic peaks from the lake – the perfectly conical Concepción and forest covered Madera, connected by the Istián isthmus – is one of the most majestic sights in the country or anywhere else, for that matter. Primarily used for agricultural purposes, nearly anything will grow in Ometepe's rich volcanic soil, including coffee, bananas, and avocados. Pre-Columbian

petroglyphs and rock carvings are found across the island, though there is likely much more to be discovered beneath the thick jungle. Most visitors arrive via the hour-long ferry ride from San Jorge near Rivas, though the airstrip occasionally has flights from Managua. There have long been rumors of a luxury resort being built, but many simply prefer to leave Ometepe as it is.

MOYOGALPA AND AROUND

With a regular ferry service from San Jorge, **Moyogalpa** ⑭ is the gateway to Ometepe for most travelers. From the terminal, a road lined with stores, tour agencies, and seafood restaurants runs uphill several blocks to the main ring road that circles the Concepción volcano and the northern half of the island. The largest town on the island and most active, it is rather charming, with a small grid of whitewashed houses with tile roofs and Concepción looming above from every angle.

Moyogalpa makes a good base for a hike up the 1,610 meter (5,282ft) high **Concepción**, with the trailhead 4km (2 miles) north of town at La Concepción. The ascent takes about three hours up and allows for plenty of time to spot monkeys and birds.

Southeast of Moyogalpa is the **Reserva Charco Verde**, a green lagoon surrounded by jungle and a windy, black sand beach facing the lake. A few simple hotels, a restaurant, and a butterfly farm are just west of the lake.

On the opposite side of the volcano from Moyogalpa is **Altagracia**, close to where the ferries from Granada dock. The second largest town on Ometepe, it has a small museum with Pre-Columbian ceramics discovered on the island, though it opens at will.

AROUND VOLCÁN MADERA

The southern half of Ometepe, on the isthmus and surrounding the **Madera Volcano**, is less developed and has more variety in terms of ecotourism. **Playas**

Isla de Ometepe rises from Lake Nicaragua

Santo Domingo and Santa Cruz on the eastern side of the isthmus are the best beaches on the island, with black sand and the green jungle creeping up right to the shore. A few rustic hotels and restaurants dot the shoreline.

The road from Santa Cruz to Balgüe, as well as south to San Ramon, has improved dramatically in recent years, opening up the tropical and cloud forests and coffee farms on the northern slopes of Madera to tourists. Several organic and permaculture farms in the area have tourism and/or volunteering projects, including **Zopilote** (http://ometepezopilote.net), **Totoco** (www.totoco.com.ni), **Finca Magdalena** (www.fincamagdalena.com), and **Café Campestre** (www.campestreometepe.com).

SAN CARLOS AND AROUND

On the southern eastern shore of Lake Nicaragua, where it meets the San Juan River, **San Carlos** ⑮ is a bustling port town that isn't much to look at. However, the strategic setting was recognized centuries ago as a place to control a waterway that nearly connects two oceans. After being founded in 1526, the town developed quickly, though pirate attacks and feisty natives upset about rubber tappers encroaching their land kept San Carlos from becoming too powerful.

Most travelers pass through here on their way to the **Solentiname Islands**, using their time while waiting for boats to hang out at the string of bars and restaurants located in stilted wooden houses over the water. San Carlos has a small, yet impressive, Spanish built **fort** that dates from 1724 and offers stellar views of the river from a hill above town, as well as a lively waterfront promenade.

Agencies in town can arrange tours east along the San Juan River, where there are several unique hotels like **Sabalos Lodge** (www.sabaloslodge.com), which has a private reserve and handful of stilted cabins, plus options for sport fishing. A Spanish-built fortress can be seen at **El Castillo** (daily), which is much stronger than the one in San Carlos. It dates from 1673 and was commissioned after Granada was repeatedly sacked by

Kayaking Lake Nicaragua at sunset.

⦿ LAKE SHARKS

The relatively shallow waters of Lake Nicaragua are the last place anyone would expect to find a shark. Their appearance surprised scientists who believed they were a unique freshwater species – until 1976, when a tagging exercise revealed that highly adaptable Caribbean bull sharks were able to swim the 193km (120 miles) span of the San Juan River from the Atlantic coast. The sharks have adapted to the freshwater of the lake and can grow up to 3 meters (11ft) in length. A Japanese shark-fin factory was established near Granada during the Somoza regime, and even though it closed in 1970, the population of bull sharks has yet to recover. With increasing habitat destruction and a potential canal cutting through the middle of the lake, it's highly likely that the sharks could completely disappear from here.

pirates. A 20-minute drive farther east takes you to the 2,606-sq-km (1,006 sq mile) **Reserva Biológica Indio-Maíz**, the second largest tract of rainforest in Nicaragua. While most of the reserve is off limits to all but scientists, some portions are accessible to tourists, including from the all-inclusive **Rio Indio Ecolodge** (http://therioindiolodge.com), which has a resort atmosphere.

LOS GUATUZOS WILDLIFE RESERVE

On the south side of the lake on the Costa Rican border, where it connects with the Caño Negro Wildlife Refuge on the other side, the **Los Guatuzos Wildlife Reserve** is one of the most pristine ecosystems in Nicaragua, with more than 400 species of birds and a healthy population of jaguars. Descendants of the Zapote and Guatuzo people live within a few small fishing communities hidden in the mangroves and can provide rustic rooms and meals, usually set up through the CANTUR office in San Carlos, which can arrange boat transportation into the preserve.

The Solentiname islands are located towards the southern end of Lake Nicaragua.

ARCHIPIÉLAGO DE SOLENTINAME

In the quietest corner of Lake Nicaragua, the 30-plus small tropical islands that make up the **Archipiélago de Solentiname** ⓰ have been the unlikely center of the internationally renowned primitive art movement. In the 1960s, the poet and priest Ernesto Cardenal helped inspire the islanders to paint the flora and fauna around them. Other artists came, as did television crews to capture the phenomenon, and today many of the roughly 1,000 residents here make a living painting and carving sculptures of local fauna out of balsawood. Most tourist amenities, which are few, are concentrated in **Mancarrón**, the largest island and where Cardenal based his colorful parish in the whitewashed **Iglesia Nuestra Señora de Solentiname**. There's a small archeological museum and a couple of small guesthouses here as well.

THE PACIFIC COAST

Much of the attention Nicaragua has received in recent years has been focussed on the south of the country, particularly the narrow stretch of land

between the Pacific coast and Lake Nicaragua. Many travelers coming up from Costa Rica looking for the next great beach destination found it long ago in San Juan del Sur and the collection of surfing and fishing villages, isolated coves, and bays up and down the coast. With improving highways and the Costa Esmeralda airport – offering regular flights to Managua – much more development is expected in the coming years. Closer to the lake, the old colonial town of Rivas, long faded into memory, is taking on a new lease on life as the transportation hub of the region.

RIVAS AND AROUND

Located on the Pan-American highway along the shore of Lake Nicaragua is **Rivas** ⓱, 110km (68 miles) south of Managua. While many passing through Rivas only see a highway lined with modern buildings and gas stations, its charming Parque Central and 18th-century church is surrounded by a Spanish-designed grid of streets that are still full of original architecture. It's where tyrant William Walker failed to penetrate and also the birthplace of former president, Violeta Chamorro, who is credited with reuniting the war-torn country in the 1990s.

East of Rivas, opposite the highway is **San Jorge**, with a long windswept beach and a bustling port offering with regular ferry services to Ometepe. There are a few traditional restaurants and B&Bs within walking distance of the port.

SAN JUAN DEL SUR

A little more than a couple of decades ago, word started to get out about a sleepy fishing village with great surf breaks called **San Juan del Sur** ⓲. The surfers came, then the backpackers, and then the wealthy Nicaraguans and North American retirees, looking to take advantage of the inexpensive beachfront real estate, snapping up whatever they could. Prices have since ballooned, both to the pleasure and dismay of locals. Some found themselves getting rich, while others were priced out of their once-tranquil neighborhoods. Local anger reached a boiling point in 2006 when an American realtor was

San Juan del Sur's beachfront.

⊘ TRAVERSING AMERICA

During the California gold rush, thousands of would-be prospectors from the east coast of the United States came by ship to Nicaragua, where they were able to cross the country via the San Juan River to Lake Nicaragua and then overland to the Pacific, where they could catch a ship up to the north. In the years shortly after this, one famous American traveler who crossed Nicaragua en route to New York from California was the writer Mark Twain, who published a series of dispatches about his adventure in San Francisco's newspaper, the *Alta California*. Twain's 1866 journey has since been immortalized in his posthumously published 1940 book Travels *With Mr. Brown*.

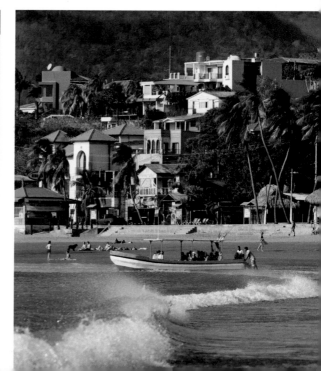

convicted of murdering his Nicaraguan ex-girlfriend and sentenced to 30-years in prison. The verdict was overturned a year later after it was proved to be a miscarriage of justice, but an outraged public had wanted to place blame on the gringos that had been disrupting their community. Things have since calmed down and the development on the beaches surrounding San Juan del Sur has spread up and down the coast.

San Juan del Sur's main attraction, the beach, encircles a crescent shaped bay where the San Juan River empties into the Pacific Ocean. Aside from a few beachside restaurants, most amenities are set back from the beach's south-eastern corner, in a seemingly thrown-together grid packed with surf stores, a microbrewery, an artisanal donut shop, taquerias, and dozens of small hostels and hotels. The more upscale resorts, like Pelican Eyes (www.pelicaneyesresort. com), with three pools and a day spa, are set back from the bay in the hills above town.

On the southern end of the bay is a lookout point where humpback and occasionally blue whales can be seen from November to April. On the highest hill on the north side of the bay, a 25 meter (82ft) statue of Jesus, **Cristo de la Misericordia**, can be reached on a one-hour hike from the beach, giving spectacular views of the bay.

BEACHES OUTSIDE OF SAN JUAN DEL SUR

While San Juan del Sur is the hub of activity along the Pacific, its beach is only so-so. Small coves hidden within the dry hills to the north and south of town have more attractive sand, better waves, and are seeing a speedy influx of new resort communities. Reached by water taxi or along a bumpy, partially paved road from Highway 72 north of San Juan del Sur, **Playa Marsella** is one of the most accessible good beaches from the town. The road comes right up to the beach and there are a few simple restaurants and guesthouses within a short walk of the waterfront.

A couple of kilometers north is **Playa Madera**, with a long white sand beach that is popular with both surfers and sunbathers. Clustered in the jungle-clad hills above the beach are a mix of budget surf hostels and upscale hotels like Hulakai (www.hulakaihotel.com) and the Buena Vista Surf Club (http://buena vistasurfclub.com). At **Playa Ocotal**, where the beach road ends, is the luxe Morgan's Rock Hacienda and Ecolodge (www.morgansrock.com), set on a 4,000-acre private reserve.

The beaches south of San Juan del Sur are less developed, though no less spectacular. The first good beach is **Playa Remanso**, which is home to a gated vacation home community and a few palapa (open-sided structure with thatched roof) restaurants on the sand. **Playa Hermosa**, 20-minutes south, is where the US competitive reality television show *Survivor* once filmed a season. It has a long white beach popular with surfers and there's little development, other than the solar powered

The view from the Cristo de la Misericordia of San Juan del Sur bay.

Playa Hermosa Ecolodge (www.playahermosabeachhotel.com). The **Refugio de Vida Silvestre La Flor**, 20km (12 miles) south of San Juan del Sur, is an important nesting area for Olive Ridleys, as well as hawksbill, leatherback, and green turtles. They arrive en masse from July to January and groups come nightly from San Juan del Sur to protect the eggs.

TOLA AND BEACHES

Looking for a more authentic scene than the cookie cutter communities being built around San Juan del Sur, developers started carving out the even more dramatic, 30km (18 miles) stretch of coastline west of the tiny town of **Tola** ⓳. The town, located between Rivas and the coast, is little more than a service hub with a shady central plaza and a smattering of stores. The Costa Esmeralda airport, which opened close to the beach in 2016, offers direct flights from Managua with the Nicaraguan La Costeña airlines, as well as from Liberia in Costa Rica with Sansa Airlines.

The southernmost of Tola's beaches is the private **Playa Manzanillo**, where

Guacalito de la Isla, a 1670-acre (675-hectare) luxury resort community, is located. Owned by the billionaire Pellas family, who also own Flor de Caña rum and Toña beer, the Mukul hotel (www.mukulresort.com) offer Nicaragua's most luxurious accommodations, with a David McLay Kidd signature oceanfront 18-hole golf course, full service spa, and rooms with private plunge pools.

Next is **Playa Redonda**, home of the luxe Aqua Wellness Resort (http://aquanicaragua.com). More accessible to the public is **Playa Gigante**, a popular beach with weekenders from Rivas, only an hour away. Backed by thick jungle, the crescent-shaped beach has a few seafood restaurants and small hotels. Fishing boats bob in the bay, while world-class breaks attract a steady stream of surfers.

North of the long, mostly undeveloped beaches of Playa Amarilla and Playa Colorado is **Playa Santana**, which is really five beaches. The 1,100-hecatre (2,700-acre) Rancho Santana (https://ranchosantana.com) is an intentionally rugged, private complex

How the other half live; the penthouse suite at the Mukul hotel.

with multiple residential communities that share a beach club, organic farm, and surf center. A clubhouse and hotel complex on the northern end of the property is the hub of activity.

The road is still being paved to **Playa Popoyo**, which is one of the premier surfing destinations in Nicaragua. Farther north is the **Refugio de Vida Silvestre Río Escalante-Chacocente**, a remote wildlife refuge where thousands of Olive Ridley turtles, as well as four other types, come to nest from July to December.

THE CARIBBEAN COAST

The Caribbean coast of Nicaragua, formerly known as the Mosquito Coast, takes on a character that is more like the Bay Islands and coasts of Honduras and Belize than the rest of Nicaragua. Fierce Miskito resistance, plus British support of Mosquito kings from 1655 until 1860 – claiming the region as a protectorate in exchange for access to isolated bays and coves – prevented the Spanish from conquering the region. It wasn't until 1894 that Nicaraguan president Zelaya

Dancing in Bluefields during Palo de Mayo.

marched into Bluefields to lay claim to the coast, but even today, amidst calls for autonomy and after so many years apart, it feels like a land joined in name only with the rest of Nicaragua.

Many in the region speak creole and still have English surnames, the same ones as the pirates that once frequented the area, such as Morgan and Dampier. Along the lagoons and muddy rivers surrounded by thick tropical forests are communities of indigenous Miskito, Mayangna, Rama, and Garífuna, who maintain their own way of living in the wild terrain. There is real, unabashed culture here that doesn't know air-conditioned malls or cable TV. The entertainment in gritty towns like Bluefields involves colorful parades fueled by sugarcane liquor and calypso.

MANAGUA TO THE CARIBBEAN

From Managua, Highway 7 runs parallel in spots to the Mico River, passing through **Juigalpa** ⑳, where there's a small archeological museum, the **Museo Arqueológico Gregorio Aguilar Barea** (tel: 2512 0784; Tue–Sat 8am–noon,

1–5pm, Sun 9am–noon, 1–3pm), which is home to the most important of Pre-Columbian stone stelae in Nicaragua. More than 100 of the basalt statues were carved between 800 and 1500 AD. Finally, the road comes to **El Rama**, a town of 50,000 that's six hours from Managua. This isolated port on the Escondida River is as far east as you can go by road. From here, tiny prop-planes and riverboats run to the coast at Bluefields.

BLUEFIELDS

Named after a Dutch pirate named Blewfeldt, the port town of **Bluefields** ㉑ is a mish-mash of cultures, from West Indian and Miskito to mestizo. Crime is high here, partially because of the influx of money from the transit of cocaine passing from South America to the north. The town itself, set between docks and jutting out into the bay on floating restaurants, is not particularly attractive at first glance, with ramshackle buildings and a murky bay. The town's most interesting attraction is the wood-paneled **Moravian Church** near the municipal pier, which dates from 1848, although it's been mostly rebuilt since Hurricane Juana in 1988, which wiped out many of the Victorian buildings that once lined the brick streets. Attached to the church is a **cultural museum** with Miskito artifacts, including a sword that belonged to the last Miskito king.

The nightlife in Bluefields is raucous, even legendary, and is reason enough to make a trip here. They call Bluefields the Jamaica of Nicaragua, and 'Maypole,' a style of tropical calypso with raunchy lyrics and dance moves, is the town's claim to fame, with the beat blasting at full volume in grungy discos like Four Brothers and Fresh Point. Things get even crazier during **Palo de Mayo**, a festival that takes place throughout the month of May. The event celebrates when a maypole was erected in the center of town, decorated with ribbons in flowers, during the town's early days to mark the coming of spring. Today, the festival is an excuse to party, with drunken parades and dancing that goes on until the wee hours of the morning.

LAGUNA DE PERLAS

Reached by pangas (small boats) through a network of canals each day from Bluefields (three hours), the town of **Pearl Lagoon** was once considered to be the second capital of the Miskito Kingdom, after the last Miskito king took up residence after being deposed in Bluefields in 1894. Today, it's a relaxed fishing village with dirt roads where reggae wafts through the air. Visitors chill in over-water wooden restaurants with thatched roofs, sampling soulful plates of seafood and cheap beer. There are no beaches here; for those, travelers will need to hire a boat to the Pearl Cays (see below). You can visit the Miskito community of **Awas**, 3km (1.8 miles) west, or the Garífuna village of **Orinoco** on the other side of the lagoon, reached by boat. The fishing is good here, with opportunities to catch tarpon and snook in the lagoon, plus yellowtail and bonefish in the open sea.

A Creole woman in Pearl Lagoon.

⊘ BEISBOL, NICARAGUAN-STYLE

In the 1880s an American businessman named Albert Addlesberg was living in Bluefields, at the time part of autonomous Mosquito territory, which had a strong British influence. Cricket was widely popular in Bluefields at the time and Addlesberg convinced two of the clubs to switch to baseball, giving them equipment he had shipped in from New Orleans. The game caught on and spread all along the Caribbean coast. When the region was incorporated into Nicaragua, the sport spread all around the country.

The first official game was played between Managua and Granada in 1891 and US marines stationed in the country during the early years of the 20th-century helped bring it to the masses. In 1956, La Liga Nicaragüense de Beisbol Profesional (LNBP) was formed and enthusiasm for the sport grew, pushed along by the success of the country's national team on the world stage and the emergence of Nicaraguan players in the American leagues. The league shut down in 1967 amid economic and political problems in the country. After the civil war, the game picked up again and in 2004 the league was reestablished, with teams in Managua, Masaya, Rivas, Granada, and Chinandega. While stadiums lack funding and players often have second jobs, baseball is considered Nicaragua's national sport.

PEARL CAYS

Just off the Caribbean coast, 35km (22 miles) northeast of Pearl Lagoon, the **Pearl Cays** 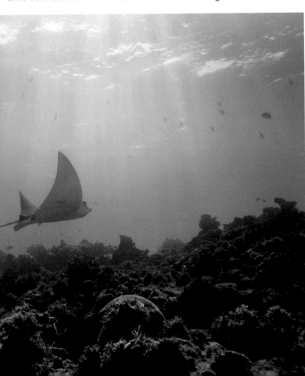 are the isolated tropical paradise many hope to find in the Corn Islands. Most of the 18 cays – several of which disappear during high tide – amount to nothing more than a patch of palm trees sticking out of white sand, fringed by coral reefs that can be seen through the crystal-clear water. Several of the islands are privately owned, a touchy subject among the Miskito and Creole islanders who live there and claim them as their own. Some of the cays, like **Pink Pearl**, can be rented out entirely, although the rest can be visited on day trips from Pearl Lagoon.

From May to November the cays are an important nesting site for the endangered hawksbill turtle, which have traditionally been hunted for their shells. The Wildlife Conservation Society now helps with managing the wildlife on the islands, having trained ex-poachers to protect the nests, from an office in Pearl Lagoon.

BILWI

In the far north of Nicaragua's Caribbean coast, not far from the border with Honduras, **Bilwi** is an impoverished port town of 50,000 people, half of which live in the dozens of Miskito communities outside of the center. Also known as Puerto Cabezas, the ramshackle town is surrounded by rivers and lagoons, which make for great exploring.

In town, there are a handful of good seafood restaurants, although the most interesting place to eat is the **Mercado Muncipal**, where there are stands with traditional dishes like *rondón* (see margin) and coconut bread. The **Muelle Viejo**, the old pier, which extends 420 meters (1,378ft) into the sea, is worth a sunset stroll. It's here that the Contras once received smuggled arms; the Somoza government allowed it as a launch point for the failed, US-funded Bay of Pigs invasion. Today, it's better known as a launch point for artisanal lobster fishermen. Opened in 2001, the Casa Museo Judith Kain (tel: 2792 2225; Mon–Fri 8am–3pm, Sat 1–2pm) is set in a colorful wooden house once owned by a local painter. It now features cultural and historical displays.

THE CORN ISLANDS

Two tiny blips of land 83km (52 miles) off of Nicaragua's Caribbean coast, the chilled out islands of Big Corn and Little Corn are a world of their own. With white sand beaches fringed with palm trees and turquoise water offering the country's most pristine coral reefs, the **Corn Islands** sound as if they are a fictional place. The creole-speaking islanders get by on lobster fishing and harvesting coconuts, with tourism not far behind. Reached by short La Costeña airline flights from Bluefields and Managua to Brig Bay, or a weekly, 5-hour ferry trip from Bluefields, they are just remote enough to avoid an onslaught of tourists. There are no large resorts here and no ultra-luxury rooms whatsoever. Just simple

An eagle ray flies across a coral reef off Little Corn Island.

beachside bungalows and no-frills eateries where the kitchens are, more often than not, exposed to the breeze.

BIG CORN

A single paved road runs the length of **Big Corn Island**, which is where most tourism in the Corn Islands is concentrated. **Brig Bay** is home to more than half of the total population of the islands, with nearly 4,000 residents who mostly live in the colorful wooden houses that ring that waterfront. It's the transportation and commercial hub of the islands.

Many come to Big Corn for the beaches, the most famous being **Picnic Bay**, in the south. It's a long, white sandy beach with calm blue water and a couple of simple restaurants. **Arenas Beach**, home of the 29-room Arenas Beach Hotel (www.arenasbeachhotel.com), is smaller, while **Sally Peaches Beach** on the northeastern shore features pink sand and shallow pools filled with marine life.

With warm water, undisturbed reefs and year-round good visibility, diving is one of the most popular pastimes in the Corn Islands and prices are as inexpensive as those in the Bay Islands. On Big Corn, the PADI-certified Corn Island Dive Center (www.cornislanddivecenter.com) runs inexpensive dives to sites like Blowing Rock, a pinnacle of giant boulders where nurse sharks are usually spotted, and a 19th-century Spanish galleon off Waula Point.

LITTLE CORN

For those that think there is too much going on over on Big Corn Island, they will love **Little Corn**. Less than 2km (1.2 miles) long, the tiny isle is accessible by speedboat several times a day from Big Corn Island, an approximately 30-minute ride. There are no cars here, just a patch of jungle circled by clean, clear beaches and one well-trodden footpath. Electricity is scarce here and most accommodations are limited to thatched cabanas. One exception is the chic Yemaya Boutique Hotel (www.yemayalittlecorn.com), on the northern shore, with its own spa and farm to table restaurant.

⊘ Eat

On Nicaragua's Caribbean coast, one of the most famous traditional dishes is *rondón*, a anglicism of the words 'run down,' describing the search for the ingredients. The slow-cooked stew simmers coconut milk with anything else that is lying around, which usually includes plantains, yuca, fish and shellfish. It was a traditional African dish that was adapted with local ingredients by slaves brought to the region by the Spanish.

A quiet beach on Little Corn Island.

Caribbean life in Costa Rica.

Remains of a Spanish fort at Portobelo, Panama.

SOUTHERN CENTRAL AMERICA

Discover the most cosmopolitan cities and the best infrastructure in Central America, plus laid-back Caribbean vibes, upscale ecolodges, and superb surfing and sport-fishing.

Sarchí ox-cart detail, Costa Rica.

Having avoided much of the turmoil that has disrupted the progress of their northern neighbors, Costa Rica and Panama can seem like another part of the world at times. The tourist infrastructure is better developed here, with regional airports and luxe accommodations in even the most remote areas.

In San José, the metropolitan area is newly invigorated by a growing number of expats, who have turned rural towns on the city's periphery into modern suburbs. Panama City, with its growing skyline that resembles Dubai more and more each day, is the region's most dynamic metropolitan area, with the region's first subway system, the best restaurant scene, and a rapidly gentrifying colonial core where new boutique hotels and rooftop bars open with the wind. Not far away, the Panama Canal – the country's economic motor – has been newly expanded to allow an extra lane of traffic and expanded locks that can let through the world's largest ships.

There's a rivalry brewing between the Caribbean and Pacific coastlines of the two countries. On the Caribbean side, it's more laid back, even in the steamy port towns of Puerto Limón and Colón. For the true experience, head to the rainforest-covered island of Bocas del Toro or the easy-going village of Cahuita. To get off the beaten path, try the homeland of the Kuna , the Kuna Yala (San Blas) Islands, the tiny cartoonish cays that have thus far avoided any large-scale development. Tourism on the Pacific is more beach-oriented with an array of all-inclusive resorts, ultra-luxe hotels on their own nature reserves, and no-frills B&Bs only steps from the sand. The surfing is big here, as is the fishing and the yoga.

Bocas del Toros, Panama.

Throughout the region, coffee fincas and hot springs attract more adventurous travelers, who are willing to go it alone with their own transportation. In remote areas, indigenous tribes like the Bribrí and Emberá still maintain their ways in the Talamanca Mountains and within the Darién Gap. This region has preserved its natural diversity better than anywhere else, with hikes on the Osa Peninsula and in Manuel Antonio National Park putting tourists in touch with capuchin and spider monkeys, amongst other wildlife, with little effort.

Manzanillo on Costa Rica's
Caribbean coast.

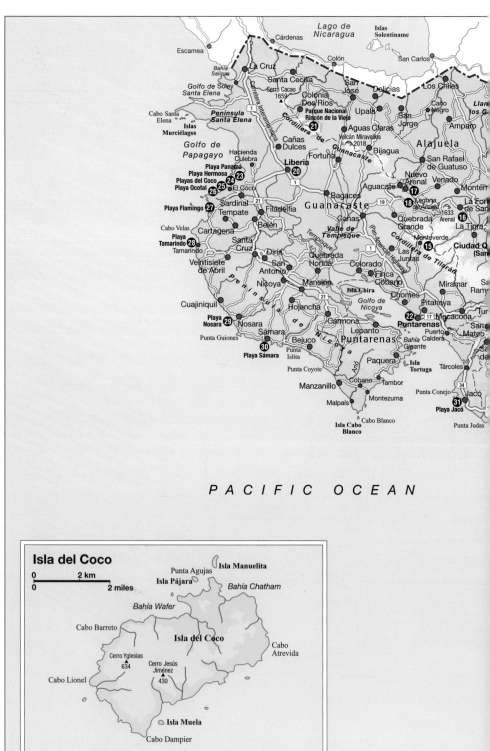

PACIFIC OCEAN

Isla del Coco

0   2 km
0   2 miles

Punta Agujas
Isla Pájara   Isla Manuelita
                                   Bahía Chatham

Bahía Wafer

Cabo Barreto

                          Isla del Coco
Cerro Yglesias   Cabo
634   Cerro Jesús   Atrevida
               Jiménez
                430

Cabo Lionel

                        Isla Muela
Cabo Dampier

Costa Rica

0   20 km
0   20 miles

N

NICARAGUA

Indio

Caño Negro

Deseado

San Juan

San Juan del Norte

Punta Castilla

Barra del Colorado

CARIBBEAN SEA

Trinidad

a de arlos

Heredia

Las Medias

Llanura de Tortuguero

11 Tortuguero

Puerto Viejo de Sarapiquí

Suerte

La Virgen

4

19

Las Horquetas

Limón

Cariari

Parismina

STA RICA

Rita

Río Jiménez

na

Parque Nacional Braulio Carrillo

6

32

Guápiles

Batán

Matina

Puerto Limón

Charrizal

Cordillera Central

Florida

Siquirres

32

12

Isla Uvita

San José de la Montaña

Parque Nacional Volcán Irazú

2

Heredia **3**

9

Santa Cruz

10

Peralta

Limón

San José **1**

Turrialba **10**

Petróleo

Desamparados

Tucurrique

Pavones

7

Cartago

8

Platanillo

Finca Banaga

Aserrí

Lankester Jardín Botánico

Pejibaye

San Gabriel

San Andrés

Cartago

Vesta

Punta Cahuita

Cahuita **13**

12

San Marcos de Tarrazú

Cordillera

Chirripó

Valle de la Estrella

Puerto Viejo de Talamanca **14**

José

Parrita

San Lorenzo

2

Telire

Shiroles

Bibrí

Manzanillo

Punta Uva Punta Mona

renas

San Gerardo de Dota

Cerro Ukán 3333

Valle de Talamanca

Bratsi

Sixaola

I. Colón

32 Naranjito

Río Nuevo

Rivas

3819

Cerro Chirripó

Coén

Changuinola

rue Nacional anuel Antonio

Savegre

33

San Isidro de El General

General Viejo

Cerro Ele 3097

Teribé

Cajón

2

de

Matapalo

Barú

San Pedro

Volcán

Almirante

Punta Uvita

Pejibaye

General

Buenos Aires

Cerro Kamúk 3549

Talamanca

Djochal

Valle de El General

Térraba

Potrero Grande

Colinas

34

Boruca

Valle de Coto Brus

Santa Elena

Alturas

PANAMÁ

Bahía de Coronado

Cortés

Palmar Sur

Chánguena

San Vito

Río Sereno

Boquete

Valle de Diquís

2

Puntarenas

Limoncito

Sabalito

Hato del Volcán

Agua Buena

Isla del Caño

34 Bahía Drake

Drake

Aguijitas

Golfo Dulce

Golfito

Ciudad Neily

Pueblo Nuevo

Gualaca

35

Punta San Pedrillo

14

Zancudo

Portón

Punta Llorona

Parque Nacional Corcovado

Peninsula de Osa

Puerto Jiménez

Canoas

La Cuesta

La Concepción

36

Punta Salsipuedes

Carate

Punta Pavones

Banco

David

Cabo Matapalo

Banco

Puerto Armuelles

I. Sevilla

Peninsula de Burica

Bahía de Charco Azul

Yerbazales

I. Boca Brava

Punta Burica

Isla Burica

Treetop walkways, Selvatura
Park, Monteverde.

COSTA RICA

Amidst the turmoil that sometimes characterizes Central America, Costa Rica is a land at peace with nature and itself.

Nestled between Nicaragua and Panamá, Costa Rica is a small, democratic country, famous for its natural environment and a peaceful political climate that is unusually stable for this historically troubled region.

Since the armed forces were abolished in 1949, the government has been able to devote a large percentage of its resources to education, health, and conservation. About a quarter of the country is protected in national parks, biological reserves, wildlife refuges, and private reserves. With more than 850 species of birds, 250 mammals, and some 6 percent of the world's total identified species, Costa Rica is a paradise for anyone who delights in the unspoiled natural world.

A land of dense jungles, active volcanoes, and pristine beaches on two coasts, this tiny country is full of geophysical contrasts that make it seem much bigger. More than half the population (total 5 million) live in the temperate Central Valley that houses the modern capital of San José. But as any Tico (Costa Rican) will tell you, the 'real' Costa Rica will only be found in the campo, or rural areas.

An official at the World Bank first called Costa Rica the 'Land of the Happy Medium.' And while its economy is far from perfect, the high standard of

living and social development belie its 'Third World' status.

For over two decades, tourism has been one of the country's leading industries. More than 2.6 million visitors now arrive every year, the vast majority of them coming from North America and Europe. Eco- and adventure tourism are the buzz words that distinguish tourism here, encompassing such diverse activities as birdwatching in the Monteverde Cloud Forest and whitewater rafting on the Río Pacuare. Costa Rica has come a long way from the sleepy, agricultural

Main Attractions

San Jose
Coffee Country
Tortuguero National Park
Monteverde Cloud Forest
Arenal Volcano
Pacific beaches
Osa Peninsula

Maps on pages 274, 278

Jesus Christ lizard, so-named becase they can walk on water, in Tortuguero National Park.

UNIÓN
SANTA TERESA
La Trinidad ↑
Centro Costarricense de Ciencias y Cultura
Museo de Los Niños, National Gallery
TOURNON
Spirogyra Jardín de Mariposas (Butterfly Garden) **H**
Torres
108

PASO DE LAVACA
Avenida 11
AMON
PARQUE ZOOLÓGICO SIMÓN BOLÍVAR

Avenida 9
Avenida 7
Avenida 9
Avenida 7
Avenida 5
Hospital Calderón Guardia
Ferrocarril al Atlántico

Mercado de Borbón
Avenida 3
Correos, Museo Filatélico
Radiográfico Costarricense
Instituto Nacional de Seguros INS
Casa Amarilla (Foreign Ministry)
Avenida 7

Banco Nacional de Costa Rica **F**
Club Unión
Iglesia El Carmen
Galería Namu
Edificio Metálico
PARQUE ESPAÑA
Fábrica Nacional de Licores, Museo de Arte y Diseño Contemporáneo **I**
Biblioteca Nacional

Mercado Central **G**
Avenida 1
Avenida 3
PARQUE MORAZÁN
Avenida 1
PARQUE NACIONAL

Banco Central
Avenida Central
Banco de Costa Rica
Teatro Melico Salazar
Gran Hotel Costa Rica **B**
Plaza de la Cultura **i**
Musei del Oro Precolombino **A** **C**
Palacio Nacional, Asamblea Legislativa (Parliament)

Iglesia La Merced
Avenida 2
PARQUE CENTRAL **D**
Teatro Nacional
Museo Nacional del Jade
Avenida Central
San Pedro

Avenida 4
Catedral Metropolitana **E**
Avenida 2
Mercado Nacional de Artesanías (National Crafts Market)
Plaza de la Democracia
Centenario
Museo Nacional (Bellavista Fortress)

Avenida 6
Teatro Rex
Avenida 4
Archivos Nacionales
Iglesia La Soledad
Av. 2

Avenida 8
Avenida 6
Av. 6

Estación General de Bomberos (Fire Station)
Avenida 8
Tribunales de Justicia
Av. 8

Avenida 12
Rep. de Chile
Iglesia La Dolorosa
Avenida 10
Paseo de Los Estudiantes
San
Martín
Av. 10
Av. 10 bis

Avenida 14
Avenida 12
BARRIO CHINO
Av. 12 bis
Av. 12

Avenida 16
Avenida 14
Paseo
Sarmiento
DOS FINOS
Av. 14

Avenida 18
Avenida 16
Av. 16
Av. 16 bis

República de Panamá
Avenida 18
CERRITO

Ferrocarril Eléctrico al Pacífico
214
Avenida 20
Estación de Plaza Viques
Av. 18

Av. 22
Ministerio de Obras Públicas y Transportes
Plaza Gonzales Viques
Instituto Geográfico Nacional IGN
Dr. Carit

Avenida 24
Avenida 24
Autopista Estado de Israel
Desamparados

Avenida 26
Avenida 26

Calle Central Alfredo Volio
Av. 30
Avenida 28
209
Avenida 28
SAN DIMAS

N

San José
0   250 m
0   250 yds

MONGITO
INVU
175
Av. 32
Av. 34
Av. 34 bis
Desamparados

COLOMBARÍ

land it once was, but it retains a laid-back charm, especially in the more remote areas.

THE POST-WAR ERA

Modern Costa Rica began to take shape in the late-1940s, after a disputed election resulted in The War of National Liberation. During the 44-day war, some 2,000 men – one in every 300 Costa Rican at the time – had been killed, but afterward a junta headed by Don Pepe Figueres drafted a new constitution that expanded the social-security system, enacted full voting rights for all women, created a minimum wage, established low-cost national health care services for all, passed legislation on child support, and proposed nationalizing the banks. The new constitution also abolished the military. This was perhaps Figueres' most celebrated and memorable achievement. In a public ceremony, he delivered the keys of the Bella Vista military fortress to the minister of public education, and told him to convert it into a national museum. Don Pepe knew how to exploit the moment:

with photographers standing by, he raised a sledgehammer and symbolically smashed at the wall of the fortress.

CALM BEFORE THE STORM

The 1960s and 1970s were essentially peaceful and prosperous decades. The development of a welfare state and bills protecting indigenous peoples were just two highlights of a progressive regime. But in 1979, the anti-government Sandinista forces in neighboring Nicaragua toppled the Somoza dictatorship. Costa Rica became a fallback area for guerrilla groups and anti-Sandinistas, largely at the behest of the US, to whom Costa Rica was financially indebted.

Equally bad news, if not worse, was the collapse of both the banana and coffee markets, reaching a peak in the early 1980s. Throughout the decade debt continued to mount. The silver lining on the cloud was provided by its president, Oscar Arias Sánchez, who was trying to mediate a peace settlement in the escalating regional conflicts. By now El Salvador, Honduras, and Guatemala were

Monument to Costa Rican Workers in front of the Central Bank building, San José.

also embroiled in various types of war or disputes. Costa Rica, for all its economic problems, was at least an oasis of peace. In 1987, Arias was awarded the Nobel Prize for his efforts to bring peace to Central America.

AN ERA OF CORRUPTION

In 1998 the Social Christian Unity Party (PUSC) won the election under conservative economist Miguel Angel Rodríguez, who pledged to liberalize certain key economic sectors and slash government spending. Despite attracting foreign investment and signing free-trade deals with Canada and Mexico, critics accused his government of lack of transparency, triggering the largest street demonstrations since the 1948 revolution.

In April 2002, the PUSC retained power with the election of Abel Pacheco, who placed much emphasis on tourism as the country's greatest economic priority. His tenure, however, was plagued by incompetence, an uncooperative Congress, and a plethora of scandals. In 2004 two ex-presidents were arrested on corruption charges, including Rodríguez, who had to step down from his post as the first-ever Central American Secretary General of the Organization of American States.

The 2006 election was won by the National Liberation Party (PLN)'s Oscar Arias Sánchez with the slimmest of margins. Some 20 years after his first term started in 1986, Arias returned to the Casa Presidencial to preside over the passing, in 2008, of CAFTA, the US-Central American Free Trade Agreement, which had violently polarized the nation. He soon dumped Costa Rica's long-standing trading partner Taiwan in favor of China.

The 2010 election made history when Laura Chinchilla, former vice-president in the Arias administration, became the first female president of Costa Rica. It was made yet again in October 2010 when former President Rafael Angel Calderón Fournier was found guilty on corruption charges, and became the first president to be sentenced to a prison term. Luis Guillermo Solís of the center-left Citizen's Action Party

Passing by murals promoting racial harmony, San José.

(PAC) on a platform of reducing income inequality and eliminating corruption.

POSITIVE CHANGE

Despite social and economic problems, recent years have seen a string of positive developments in Costa Rica. Since 2012, the country has been investing more in education and health and the government has been taxing the sale of fossil fuels to pay for environmental protection. In 2015, the country produced 99 percent of its electricity from renewable sources and has set an admirable goal to become the first carbon-neutral country by 2021. Meanwhile, the country's fortunes on the international sporting stage garnered attention in 2014 when the national soccer team (La Sele) made history by reaching the World Cup quarter-finals for the first time. In 2012 and 2016 the UK-based New Economics Foundation, which ranks countries on the basis of life expectancy and ecological footprint, named Costa Rica the happiest place on earth.

SAN JOSÉ

San José's metropolitan area, which includes and parts of Cartago, Alajuela and Heredia, probably won't win any beauty prizes. With modern high-rises ranked alongside faded 19th-century buildings, Costa Rica's capital may seem a jumble at first. Yet visitors soon discover that it possesses a certain Tico charm.

Although traffic pollution and congestion are constant irritants, there are some conservation efforts under way, including restoring notable buildings and turning downtown streets into pleasant traffic-free zones. Some barrios still possess a certain charm: Barrio Amón has some grand mansions, many of them now converted into attractive boutique hotels; Barrio Mexico retains an Art Deco ambiance; and Parque d'España is like a tiny, urban rainforest.

ORIENTATION

Before you embark on the following tour of the city, or indeed go looking for any address within **San José ❶**, sit down with a map and familiarize yourself with the city's grid system of numbered streets (*calles*), which run north to south, and avenues (*avenidas*), which run east to west. The northern avenues and eastern streets have odd numbers; the southern avenues and western streets have even numbers. Confusingly, however, buildings are not numbered and, for the most part, only in downtown San José do any streets have names. Addresses are often given in the following format: Metropolitan Cathedral, Calle Central, Avenida 2–4, meaning that it is on the Calle Central between Avenida 2 and Avenida 4. Alternatively, and more commonly, addresses are given in terms of distance in meters (*metros*), north, south, east, or west from known landmarks.

THE CITY CENTER

The Plaza de la Cultura marks the heart of the city. The area around this

The Correos, or Central Post Office, San José.

large square is a popular meeting point for peddlers, artisans, street musicians – in fact, just about anybody and everybody. The pride of the square is the neoclassical **Teatro Nacional** Ⓐ (www.teatronacional.go.cr), modeled after the Paris Opera House and without doubt the finest building in San José, if not all Costa Rica. The country's top-quality National Symphony Orchestra performs here with illustrious international guest artists; their season begins in March. There are also daily tours where you can admire the marble, gold, bronze, tropical woods, crystal chandeliers, velvet drapes, and statuary. The ceiling fresco is famous and features an idyllic, if improbable, scene of coffee and banana pickers. Across from the National Theater is the **Gran Hotel Costa Rica** Ⓑ, restored to its 1930s glory and renowned as a meeting place for tourists who gather in its outdoor café, where musicians often entertain with marimbas.

Beneath the Plaza de la Cultura is the **Museo del Oro Precolombino** Ⓒ (www.museosdelbancocentral.org; daily 9.15am–5pm). On the east side of the square in cool, darkened, cavernous rooms, the collection features more than 2,000 brilliant pre-Columbian artifacts made by the indigenous peoples from the southwestern part of the country. Highlights include tiny half-man, half-bird figures, and erotic statuettes. Farther east, between avenidas 2 and 14 and calles 7 and 11, lies the **Barrio Chino** (Chinatown), the only one in Central America.

WEST OF THE PLAZA

A short walk west of the Plaza de la Cultura along Avenida 2 is the **Parque Central** Ⓓ, another great place for people-watching. The Gaudí-like kiosk in the center of the park was donated by the Somoza family of Nicaragua and sometimes hosts open-air concerts on weekends. At the northern end of the Parque Central, look out for the restored neoclassical facade of the Teatro Popular Melico Salazar.

Directly in front of the park is the huge **Catedral Metropolitana** Ⓔ (Mon–Sat 6.30am–6pm, Sun 6.30am–9pm). Notice the finely carved wood ceiling of the Chapel of the Holy Sacrament and its walls, so carefully adorned with flower motifs that it almost looks as if they have been tiled. The cathedral provides a refuge of peace from the hot bustling city, and the microphone-amplified midday Masses are always well attended.

Due north of Parque Central, along Calle 2, is the **Correos** Ⓕ (Central Post Office), in a grand old, ornate building that also houses the **Museo Filatélico** (Philatelic Museum; Mon–Fri 8am–5pm) and a pleasant café. Three blocks west of the post office, walking along pedestrian-only Avenida 1, you will find the renovated and much brightened up **Mercado Central** Ⓖ (Mon–Sat 6.30am–6.30pm), the city's best market since 1881, where there are more than 200 vendors selling everything from old kitchen utensils to saddlebags, fresh

Exihibits in the Museo del Oro Precolombino.

fish, coffee and spices by the kilo, to religious icons.

NORTH AND EAST OF THE PLAZA

To get a feeling for the San José of old, take a walk in Barrio Amón, where some vestiges of elegance survive. Start at the **Casa Amarilla** (Yellow House), the ornate, Spanish-colonial-style home of the foreign ministry. Walk a block north to Avenida 9 and head west (left). You will pass by some elegant Victorian mansions, complete with gingerbread trim and stone lions guarding walled gardens.

For an urban view of Costa Rican wildlife, visit the enchanting **Spirogyra Jardín de Mariposas** ⓗ (Spirogyra Butterfly Garden; www.butterflygardencr.com; daily 8am–2pm). One of the main aims of Spirogyra is to help rural women find alternative sources of income from field labor, by exporting butterfly cocoons to Europe and the US instead. Go on a sunny day when the butterflies are most active.

Across the street from the INS building is the former **Fábrica Nacional de Licores** ❶ (National Liquor Factory), which now houses an arts and cultural center, as well as the Ministry of Culture. Pop into the pretty courtyard and amphitheater (a venue for plays and concerts) which lead to another part of the complex, the **Museo de Arte y Diseño Contemporáneo** (www.madc.cr; Mon–Sat 9.30am–5pm; free on Mon), which mounts changing exhibitions with the latest in avant-garde art, sculpture, and photography.

THE CENTRAL VALLEY

The Central Valley (Valle Central), or Central Plateau (Meseta Central), as it is often called, is strictly speaking neither a valley nor a plateau since it contains both kinds of landscape. The Central Highlands might be a more apt name for this area, only 24km by 64km (15 miles by 40 miles), where two mountain ranges meet. You will find rich, volcanic hills and river-filled valleys, with altitudes reaching up to 1,500 meters (4,500ft).

The countryside is beautiful and variable. The climate is salubrious. The air

Fish stall, Mercado Central.

is sweet and soft. The people are generally friendly, dignified, and independent. Volcanoes, some still active, others dormant or extinct, rise up above the hills around the valley. Above them, a big sky is constantly changing – dark, charcoal rain clouds; intense, searing patches of blue; fluffy white cumulus; and rainbows galore. All come and go in quick succession. Day trips by bus or car, or with tour groups, can easily be arranged.

ALAJUELA AND HEREDIA

As you descend by some 200 meters (660ft) into **Alajuela ❷**, the country's second-largest city, it becomes noticeably warmer. To relax, you can join the old-timers in the central park, amid an orchard of mango trees. Alajuela is the birthplace of Juan Santamaría, the young Costa Rican whose courage in helping to rout William Walker and his *filibusteros* from Costa Rica in 1856 is enshrined in national legend. The expanded **Museo Histórico Cultural Juan Santamaría** (www.museojuansantamaria.go.cr; Tue–Sun 10am–5.30pm;

free), one block from the central park, tells his story.

Heredia ❸ (pop. 123,000) lies 11km (7 miles) north of San José, and is known as *La Ciudad de las Flores* (The City of Flowers). The city was first settled in 1706 by the Spanish, long before San José was even thought of. Historically a bastion of coffee wealth, the city today is even more prosperous, with trendy new stores popping up, fueled by affluent suburbs housing professionals and Costa Rica's burgeoning middle class.

SARCHÍ

For a half-day excursion of craft shopping and sightseeing around typical Central Valley coffee towns, head north through Alajuela toward **Sarchí ❹**. The approach to the mountain town is unmistakable. Swirling, colorful decorative designs adorn practically every bus stop, bar, bakery, restaurant, and house. In the town's central park in front of the wedding-cake white church, there is a giant painted ox-cart, weighing in at 2 tons and delighting camera-toting tourists. Sarchí is a crafts center

Characteristic Sarchi ox-cart designs.

heavily geared toward the tourist trade, where you can see artisans painting traditional ox-cart designs and creating household furnishings out of tropical hardwoods. There are pleasant little roadside stands on the outskirts of Sarchí selling homemade candied fruits, honey, and fudge.

POÁS VOLCANO NATIONAL PARK

The most developed of all the parks is **Parque Nacional Volcán Poás** ❺ (tel: 2482 2165; daily 8am–3.30pm), a popular stop on the tourist trail. It is only 37km (25 miles) from San José on good roads leading through the city of Alajuela. Poás can become crowded and cloudy, so it is best to visit early in the day when views are better and before the throngs arrive. The cool freshness of the air as you ascend the mountain is invigorating, although it can get chilly and rainy.

A map of the nature trails is available at the Visitors' Center, where there are nature exhibits, a gift shop, a cafeteria, and restrooms. If the weather closes in, as it often does up here, at almost 2,740 meters (9,000ft)

above sea level, the Visitors' Center is a good place to hunker down and warm up. From a lookout point above the crater, there is an overview of the volcano, which in 1989 shot ash well over a kilometer (a half-mile) into the air. The main crater, which is 1.5km (1 mile) wide and 300 meters (1,000ft) deep, is one of the largest in the world. Poás rarely has violent eruptions and is one of the more accessible active volcanoes on the continent. It is active in 40-year cycles and is currently producing acid-like rain and sulfurous gases.

Descend from the park to one of the nearby restaurants and enjoy the local specialty of *fresas en leche*, strawberries with cream. Alternatively, continue to the nearby **La Paz Waterfall Gardens** (www.waterfallgardens.com; daily 8am–5pm) and set off on 3.5 km (1.5 miles) of trails past hummingbird and orchid gardens, a huge butterfly observatory, aviaries and animal exhibits, en route to five impressive waterfalls. To spend more time in the mountain air, consider an overnight stay at Peace Lodge or Poás Lodge (www.poaslodge.com).

Coconuts for sale at San Raphael de Heredia's Sunday market.

⊘ SARCHÍ'S OX CARTS

Around 1910, as legend has it, a *campesino* (peasant) was crossing the Beneficio la Luisa when it occurred to him to decorate his ox-cart wheels with colorful mandala-like designs inspired by ancient Moorish decoration. The art form caught on and each district in Costa Rica had its own special design. Locals could tell just by looking at the cart where the driver was from. Each cart also had its own *chirrido*, or song of the wheels, by which people could identify who was passing by, without even glancing upward. As late as 1960, the ox-cart was still the most typical mode of transportation, able to handle the rugged Costa Rican terrain. Things have changed, but you will still see the occasional ox-cart on country roads.

BRAULIO CARRILLO NATIONAL PARK

Only 45 minutes from San José is **Parque Nacional Braulio Carrillo** ❻ (daily 8am–3.30pm), a true wilderness. Occupying 445 sq km (170 sq miles) of mostly primary forest, the park was founded in 1978, thanks to pressure exerted by environmentalists who feared that the opening of a highway between San José and Guápiles would provide loggers and developers with access to rapidly vanishing virgin forest.

Braulio Carrillo contains five distinctly separate forest habitats, dominated by the wet tropical forest. Hundreds of varieties of orchids and ferns, and the majority of the bird species native to Costa Rica, are found here. The lingering impression of Braulio Carrillo is of vastness: huge canyons, misty mountains, and the ubiquitous broad-leaf plant, called the Poor Man's Umbrella, covering the hillsides. The easiest way to experience the forest is to walk the trails at the **Quebrada Gonzales** station, about 17km (11 miles) past the tunnel. The

Basílica de Nuestra Señora de los Angeles, Cartago.

Las Palmas Trail, starting from the parking lot, gradually climbs up from the highway, quickly immersing you in the forest.

For a bird's-eye view of the forest canopy adjacent to Braulio Carrillo, you can ride on the **Rainforest Aerial Tram** (tel: 2257 5961; www.rainforestad-venture.com; charge includes tram ride, video, and a short hike; reservations recommended). This is an 80-minute, 2.6km (1.5-mile) trip through the forest's treetops, 35 meters (100ft) above the forest floor. The 'tram' is an open, metal gondola, big enough for five passengers and a naturalist guide, who is equipped with a walkie-talkie to pass along information on wildlife sightings.

CARTAGO AND AROUND

Cartago ❼, 22km (14 miles) south of San José, was the capital of Costa Rica until 1823, when it lost its status to San José. Most of its illustrious colonial past is lost, however, since repeated earthquakes and eruptions of Volcán Irazú have destroyed most of the colonial-era buildings.

Cartago, once the center of Costa Rican culture, is still her religious center. The enormous **Basílica de Nuestra Señora de los Angeles** (Basilica of Our Lady of the Angels), a domed, Byzantine structure that dominates the landscape for many kilometers, was built in honor of Costa Rica's patron saint, *La Negrita*, the Black Virgin. It is worth a look inside to see the lovely stained-glass windows and the wood columns painted to look like marble.

From Cartago it is a short trip to the **Lankester Jardín Botánico** ❽ (www.jbl.ucr.ac.cr; daily 8.30am–4.30pm) in Paraíso de Cartago, named, so legend has it, by weary Spaniards moving inland from the Atlantic coast who found its cooler weather and lack of malarial mosquitoes paradisiacal. English botanist Charles Lankester, sent to Costa Rica by a British company to work on coffee planting, arrived in 1900 at the age of 21. The coffee venture failed, but he decided to stay and bought 15 hectares (37 acres) of land to preserve local flora, especially orchids and bromeliads, and to regenerate a natural forest. Today, Lankester Gardens is run by the University of Costa Rica. Hundreds of species of orchids attract orchid fanciers from all over the world, particularly in the peak flowering months of January through April.

Easily accessible from Cartago is **Parque Nacional Volcán** ❾ (tel: 2200 5025; daily 8am–3.30pm), atop the massive volcano that dominates the landscape on the eastern side of the Central Valley. From the 3,800-meter (11,000ft) summit, it is possible to see both the Caribbean and the Pacific on a clear day. More often, you will climb above the clouds on your way to the top. Irazú, Costa Rica's highest volcano, also known as El Coloso, broke a 30-year period of silence with a single, noisy eruption on December 8, 1994.

Nearby **Turrialba**'s ❿ reputation as a whitewater river-rafting center is growing, and rafters and kayakers from all over the world are discovering the Reventazón and Pacuare rivers. Looming above the town is **Volcán Turrialba**, spectacularly active since 2014, when the first magma eruption in 100 years took place followed by strong eruptions of ash and rocks.

CARIBBEAN COAST

The three-hour drive from San José to the Caribbean coast is on a paved, slow-moving highway winding past the canyons, mountains, waterfalls, and virgin forests of Parque Nacional Braulio Carrillo. Descending from the cool cloudiness into the tropical lowland forests of the Caribbean, the temperature rises and the air becomes heavy.

TORTUGUERO

Travel on the **Tortuguero canals**, up through the area north of Limón, has been likened to a trip on the *African Queen*, or to floating dreamily down the Amazon. It is certainly one of the most wonderfully lyrical trips to be taken anywhere in the world. As you drift

Volcán Turrialba smokes.

COSTA RICAN SNOW

When white coffee blossoms blanket the fields of the Central Valley, filling the air with a sweet jasmine-like fragrance, the Ticos call it 'Costa Rican snow.'

You might well surmise that coffee is indigenous to Costa Rica; however, it was brought by the Spanish, French, and Portuguese from Ethiopia and Arabia. In the early 1800s, when seeds were first planted in Costa Rica, coffee plants were merely ornamental, grown to decorate patios and courtyards with their glossy green leaves, seasonal white flowers, and red berries. Costa Ricans had to be persuaded, even coerced, into growing them so the country might have a national export crop. Every *Tico* family was required by law to have at least a couple of bushes in the yard. The government awarded free plants to the poor and grants of land to anyone who was willing to plant coffee on it.

The Central Valley has the ideal conditions for producing coffee: altitude above 1,200 meters (4,000ft); temperatures averaging between 15°C and

Shade grown coffee plantations, Central Valley.

28°C (59°F and 82°F); and the right soil conditions. Coffee estates quickly occupied much of the land, except for that needed to graze the oxen that lugged the coffee-laden carts. As the only Costa Rican export, the country's financial resources were organized to support it. By 1840, coffee had become big business, carried by ox-cart through mountains to the Pacific port at Puntarenas, then by ship to Chile and on to Europe. By the mid-1800s an oligarchy of coffee barons had risen to positions of power and wealth, for the most part through processing and exporting the bean, rather than growing it.

ECONOMIC DEPENDENCY

Despite its early successes, Costa Rica's coffee industry has been a mixed blessing at times. The country incurred a heavy debt borrowing US$3 million from Great Britain to finance the Atlantic railroad so coffee could be exported from the Caribbean port of Limón. And when coffee hit a low on the international market in 1900, the result was a severe shortage of basic foods in Costa Rica that year. This dependency on an overseas market has left Costa Ricans vulnerable on many occasions. Throughout the 20th century, coffee prices fluctuated wildly and the health of the nation's economy varied accordingly.

Traditionally, banana, citrus, and poro trees were planted in the coffee fields to provide nutrients and shade for coffee plants. Later coffee hybrids did not need shade, and treeless fields produced more yield per hectare. These varieties, however, depleted the soil more rapidly and required fertilizer to enrich it, adding to the cost of production. Today, many coffee-growers have returned to the traditional shade-loving plants, pleasing environmentalists who advocate shade-grown coffee.

Since coffee grows best in a mountainous climate, many of the hillsides in the Central Valley are covered with rows of the bright green bushes, reflecting the sun with their shiny, luxuriant leaves. Today, coffee growers are concentrating on producing shade-grown and certified organic beans, along with only the best high-altitude, top-quality specialty coffees from highland regions around Poás, Barva de Heredia, Tres Ríos, and Tarrazú, rated by many aficionados among the best in the world.

lazily along, awash in the fragrance of white ginger blossoms, lavender water hyacinths, and the ylang ylang flower, the tranquility here soothes all your cares away.

With the help of a naturalist guide, you may catch glimpses of sloths, crocodiles, caimans, and basking freshwater turtles. High up in the exuberant vegetation, multicolored parrots squawk noisily, while cranky howler monkeys shake the branches. Around 19,000 hectares (47,000 acres) of the coast and hinterland have been designated as the **Parque Nacional Tortuguero** (Tortuguero National Park; tel: 2709 8086; Mon–Fri 6am–4pm). There are many ways to navigate its maze of waterways, including renting a dugout canoe or kayak. The best way to tour the canals is on a boat with an electric motor, guided by an expert naturalist. Note that you cannot enter the land portion of the park without wearing rubber boots, which you can rent at the park office or in the village. Or take a package tour that includes a room at one of the jungle lodges that range from modest to luxurious, plus meals, naturalist guides, and the trip through the canals. All of the Tortuguero hotels offer guided river trips and transportation either by bus and boat or by small plane from San José. Launches going up to Tortuguero also depart from Moín, just a few kilometers north of Limón. NatureAir and SANSA have short, scheduled flights from San José to Tortuguero.

Farther north, up the canals, the village of **Tortuguero** ⓫ sits on a very narrow spit of land bordered by the Caribbean Sea and the Tortuguero River. The best thing about this village is that there are no cars, just narrow paths winding through exuberant greenery, with palm trees rustling overhead. Wooden houses sit on stilts, amid a growing number of restaurants, stores, and *cabinas* catering to tourists.

PUERTO LIMÓN

Puerto Limón ⓬ (pop. 61,000) is pure Caribbean. With its rich, ripe jumble of sights and sounds and smells, it is a hot, steamy, laid-back place. Most middle-class *Ticos* who live in the Central Valley consider it something of a disgrace, crime-ridden and poor. But multimillion-dollar plans are afoot to give Limón a facelift and make it more visitor-friendly. The main tourist focus here is the huge cruise-ship dock that disgorges thousands of visitors every year. In the center of Limón you won't find the usual cathedral or soccer field facing a plaza such as you see in all the towns of the Central Valley. Instead **Parque Vargas**, named after a local governor, is filled with huge banyan trees with buttress roots that the townspeople use for seats. Most travelers stay at the Hotel Park (tel: 2798 0555; http://parkhotellimon. com) or more upscale hotels north or south of the city center. Beware, however, that theft (particularly from cars) and muggings are a problem in the city.

Wildlife watching from the water, Tortuguero National Park.

CAHUITA

Cahuita ⓮ is a small scruffy town of faded but dignified-looking wooden houses, once painted bright colors that are now soft pastels, with a touch of Caribbean whimsy in the gingerbread details. Young travelers from Europe, Canada, and the US, oblivious to more modest local sensibilities, amble along the beaches and roadways in bright, scanty beachwear.

The main activities in Cahuita are snorkeling and eating. You can find both, side by side, at The Snorkeling House (tel: 8361 1924; www.snorkelinghouse.com), right next door to Miss Edith's restaurant, famous for its spicy Afro-Caribbean cuisine and Sunday-only *rondon*, a hearty stew based on fish and root vegetables. For tours and excursions farther afield, Cahuita Tours (tel: 2755 0101; www.cahuitatours.com) is an experienced, reliable tour operator in Cahuita.

To the immediate south of Cahuita is **Parque Nacional Cahuita** (tel: 2755 0302; daily 8am–4pm), famous for its fine, sandy beach and coral reef. The reef extends 500 meters (1,500ft) out to sea from **Punta Cahuita** and offers great snorkeling, although the point of the reef was severely displaced during an earthquake. There are many species of tropical fish, crabs, lobsters, sea fans, anemones, sponges, seaweed, and innumerable other marine creatures to observe amidst the coral formations. You can admire it all and keep your feet dry aboard a glass-bottomed boat, or you can swim from the main entrance to the park at **Puerto Vargas**, 5km (3 miles) south of town. Camping is permitted in the Puerto Vargas sector, which has restrooms, showers, and picnic tables.

PUERTO VIEJO

Heading south toward Puerto Viejo, along a partially paved road that runs parallel to the beach, you pass houses of every style and class, but there is something magical about the Caribbean air that gives even the humblest shack a picturesque quality when it is set amidst tall coconut trees. **Puerto Viejo de Talamanca** ⓮ is a hodgepodge of dilapidated wooden houses amidst tall grass. At the entrance to the town

Traditional wooden architecture, Cahuita.

you pass a rusted-out barge anchored just off the black-sand beach.

Puerto Viejo is famous in surfing circles for the Salsa Brava, a hot, fast, explosive wave that breaks over the reef from December through April and again in June and July. It attracts surfers from all over the world. At other times of the year the sea is quiet, particularly inside the reef, and good for snorkeling.

If you want to stay near town, where the action is, especially at night, try the Casa Verde Lodge (tel: 2750 0015; www.cabinascasaverde.com), a tidy, Swiss-run collection of colorfully decorated *cabinas* set in a lush garden. It's cheap and cheerful and in great demand, so make a reservation well in advance. To catch the reggae beat, head to Johnny's Place on a Friday or Monday night. For salsa and merengue, The Lazy Mon at Stanford's, practically on the beach, is the place to go on weekend nights.

South of town there are *cabinas* and sophisticated hotels and restaurants lining the road across from beautiful stretches of white sand beach edged by palm and beach almond trees, like the award-winning Cariblue (tel: 2750 0035; www.cariblue.com) at Playa Cocles, and the chic boutique hotel Le Cameleon (tel: 2750 0501; www.lecameleonhotel.com).

NORTH-CENTRAL COSTA RICA

The region to the northeast of San José corresponds roughly to the area known as the Northern Zone, where the landscape is lush and agricultural for the most part. The main attractions for visitors are the spectacular Arenal Volcano with its surrounding hot springs and spas, and some remote rainforest reserves.

MONTEVERDE CLOUD FOREST

From lowland, dry tropical forest to the misty, mountain cloud forests of **Monteverde** ⑮ isn't far as the crow flies. By road, you turn off the Interamericana Highway at the Rancho Grande exit at Km 133, heading for

Sardinal. Monteverde sits atop the Continental Divide, and, despite some road improvements, the last 37km (21 miles) are still challenging, allow up to an hour to make the slow, winding ascent up a mostly unpaved road.

Despite the ordeal to get here, every year tens of thousands of people make the climb, primarily to visit the **Reserva Biológica del Bosque Nuboso de Monteverde** (tel: 2645 5122; www.reserva monteverde.com; daily 7am–4pm; night tours by reservation). To protect the flora and fauna and the trails of this popular preserve, visitors are limited to 220 at any given time – which means you may have to wait your turn. You should book at least one night's accommodations in advance; to get the best out of the area you need to stay three days.

Monteverde is much more than an opportunity to spot a resplendent quetzal, the most colorful and spectacular bird in the tropics. This misty, verdant, high-altitude cloud forest is home to a multitude of diverse creatures: 448 species of birds identified so far, about 700 species of butterflies, 3,000

⊙ CARNAVAL IN PUERTO LIMÓN

For many people, Puerto Limón's annual *Carnaval* (Carnival) is the best reason to visit the place. This week-long jubilant event is held every October (rather than in February, the usual carnival month elsewhere). It is not an ancient Puerto Limón tradition: Carnival first began here in 1949, under the leadership of a barber called Alfred Henry King, who timed the festivities to coincide with the anniversary of Christopher Columbus's landing near Limón on October 18, 1502. *El Día de la Raza*, 'The Day of the People,' which falls during Carnival Week and traditionally includes the participation of the indigenous peoples who live in the region, has been renamed *Día de las Culturas* (Day of the Cultures) in recognition of the fact that not everyone remembers Columbus with equal affection. It is also a tribute to the contributions made to Costa Rica by people of various different cultures.

The highlight of Carnival Week is the parade, when local people joined by thousands of visitors take to the streets to revel in a glorious music and dance spectacle. The drums, the heat, the dancers and drummers in bright costumes, urge spectators to abandon their inhibitions and to surrender to the Caribbean beat. And so they do, *Limonenses* and tourists alike, filling the streets, shimmying, shaking, singing, and carousing, while the irresistible rhythms of steel drums fill the warm, humid air.

species of plants, and 130 species of mammals, of which 70 are bats. Pick up a checklist and map at the Visitors' Center. Tours with excellent naturalist guides are available.

Opposite the Hotel Heliconia, on the road to Santa Elena, follow the signs to **El Jardín de las Mariposas** (Butterfly Garden; tel: 2645 5512; daily 8.30am–4pm; www.monteverdebutterflygarden.com), which exhibits all the butterfly species of the region. Reptile-lovers won't want to miss the **Serpentarium of Monteverde** (tel: 2645 6002; daily 9am–8pm) where you can safely observe more than 40 species of reptiles and amphibians.

One of the most popular Monteverde attractions is the Monteverde Park, with its **Sky Walk** (tel: 2479 4100; www.skyadventures.travel), a 2.5km (1.5-mile) series of trails and five hanging bridges suspended Indiana Jones-style from platforms in the tree canopy. The park also offers **Sky Trek**, a high-speed, high-adrenaline canopy tour that involves donning mountain-climbing harnesses and zipping through the trees

Hiking in Monteverde cloud forest.

suspended on strong cables. A more relaxing experience is the **Sky Tram** gondolas, which take visitors smoothly up into the rainforest for amazing views accompanied by and informative commentary from a knowledgeable guide.

Around 5km (3 miles) northeast of Monteverde village is an outstanding local initiative, the **Reserva Santa Elena** (Santa Elena Rainforest Reserve; www.reservasantaelena.org). Comprising some 310 hectares (766 acres) of mixed montane and elfin forest, the reserve was created in 1992 as a local high-school project and includes several kilometers of well-kept paths and a visitors' center. On clear days, you are treated to views of magnificent Arenal Volcano to the north. Tours are well organized and cheaper than at Monteverde, yet the flora and fauna (including quetzals and howler monkeys) are every bit as impressive. There are four principal trails, all short enough to be done in a day.

VOLCÁN ARENAL AND AROUND

La Fortuna de San Carlos ⑯ is a busy, sun-baked village near the base of Arenal Volcano that's the center for local tours, accommodations, and eateries.

Some 5km (3 miles) east of La Fortuna is the turnoff to the **Cataratas del Río Fortuna**. These falls are accessible in an hour's easy horseback ride from La Fortuna through pastures and fields of corn, bananas, and peppers. If you are going to drive, the trip requires a four-wheel-drive vehicle. Once at the falls, a muddy hike down a slippery slope to the swimming area at the base of the falls makes the clear, fresh water all the sweeter. Closer to the volcano, between La Fortuna and Lake Arenal, **Tabacón Grand Spa Thermal Resort** (tel: 2479-2099; www.tabacon.com) is one of Costa Rica's most popular tourist destinations. From here you can look directly up the volcano's lava-rock slopes. Volcanologists have predicted that if Arenal erupts, Tabacón Springs will likely be in the path of the lava flow. For the moment the volcano is heating Tabacón's therapeutic waters to a perfect temperature. Tiled slides, waterfalls, and pools of varying temperatures are surrounded by tumbling warm-water creeks and exquisitely landscaped gardens. Although the springs are often crowded with day-trippers, hotel guests can enjoy volcano views at night from quiet pools under a starry sky.

Just west of La Fortuna, you can luxuriate in the warm mineral waters of the more affordable **Baldi Hot Springs** (tel: 2479 8811; www.baldihotsprings.cr). For US$57 you get a day pass with dinner, and adults can enjoy a warm soak in a plethora of pools with varying temperatures with a volcano view, while children can play on a variety of water slides.

Down the highway, past the Tabacón Hot Springs Resort, is a dirt road to the left leading 9km (5 miles) to **Arenal Observatory Lodge** (tel: 2290 7011; www.arenalobservatorylodge.com) formerly a volcano research facility for the Smithsonian Institution. It is the only lodge in the national park and the closest accommodations to the volcano, only 2.7km (1.7 miles) away. The lodge has comfortable rooms in bungalows, set on a huge estate with primary and secondary forest, waterfalls, and hiking and horseback trails.

Nuevo Arenal ⑰ is a town reborn from the old village of Arenal, in the valley that was flooded in 1973 to create the lake and the huge hydroelectric project here. Along the road to Nuevo Arenal there are some very pleasant small hotels and bed-and-breakfasts. The scenic road winds around the edges of the lake, but drivers need to be aware that although it is paved, it is often washed out, especially during the rainy season.

Laguna de Arenal ⑱ offers some of Costa Rica's most challenging freshwater fishing. Whether or not you choose to fish, do charter a boat and a guide to take you sightseeing on the lake. Better still, set off in a rented kayak. Go in the early morning, when, for much of the year, the lake's surface is like glass, and the volcano can be viewed as a crystalline reflection.

Tabacón's hot springs are a major reason to visit the area.

From December through April, usually in the afternoon, northeasterly winds blow almost daily, and the lake is anything but calm and glassy. Between 40 and 50 knots of sustained breeze whips the west end of the lake into a sea of whitecaps, making it a favorite destination for experienced windsurfers.

THE SARAPIQUÍ REGION

The lush, tropical jungles of the **Río Sarapiquí** region, on the Caribbean side of the Cordillera Central, are less than 100km (60 miles) east of San José. La Selva Biological Station, Selva Verde Lodge, and Rara Avis, private reserves with lodging, are all accessible via the Braulio Carrillo Highway east of San José, through the spectacular Parque Nacional Braulio Carrillo. Beware of driving the highway after sunset, since thick night fog blankets this steep, winding route.

The small, colorful port town of **Puerto Viejo de Sarapiquí ⑲** is where river boats loaded with tourists take scenic trips on jungle waterways with naturalist guides to point out the monkeys, birds, and other riverside animals along the way. You can also take a full-day trip up the Sarapiquí to the **Río San Juan**, on the Nicaraguan border; be sure to bring along your passport because the river crosses into Nicaraguan territory.

Oasis Nature Tours (tel: 2766 6108; www.oasisnaturetours.com) organizes both kinds of river trips.

Rara Avis Rainforest Lodge (tel: 2764 1111; www.rara-avis.com) is a pristine, 600-hectare (1,500-acre) rainforest preserve adjacent to Braulio Carrillo National Park. Established in 1983, it was Costa Rica's first ecolodge. The main office and departure point for the reserve is in Las Horquetas, a village 17km (11 miles) south of Puerto Viejo de Sarapiquí.

GUANACASTE

The province of Guanacaste includes both the northern part of the Nicoya Peninsula, attached to the mainland, and a huge tract of mainland set between mountains draped in cloud forest and the Pacific Ocean. This is Costa Rica's Big Country, where vast grasslands are punctuated by huge spreading guanacaste trees and bony, white Brahman cattle. During the rainy season, the landscape is a sea of green, but in the dry season, the savannahs become sun-baked tracts of gold. Traditionally cattle country, Guanacaste is better known nowadays as the gateway to controversially large hotel resorts for sun-starved visitors who arrive at Daniel Oduber International Airport south of the province's capital, Liberia, by the thousands. Overdevelopment in some areas has even engendered a new word: *Guanacasteficación*, signifying unsustainable development.

LIBERIA

The capital city of Guanacaste province, **Liberia ⑳** was established more than 200 years ago. It is also known as Ciudad Blanca, the White City, owing to the traditional whitewashed adobe houses,

---

⊙ LAND OF FIRE

Until early July 1968, Arenal was a heavily wooded low hill, similar to many others in the area, near the village of La Fortuna. One morning local people began feeling a few earth tremors. Suddenly, the forest started smoking and steaming. Women washing their clothes marveled at the sudden warm water that flowed in the creeks. Then, on July 29, Volcán Arenal exploded. Rolling clouds of gas and fountains of red-hot boulders and molten lava hit the countryside. Official estimates put the death toll at 62, but locals claim that more than 80 people were killed. More than 5 sq km (2 sq miles) of land near the volcano was abruptly changed from pastoral farmland to a landscape out of *Dante's Inferno*. Arenal remained continuously active from then until October, 2010, when it just as suddenly stopped spewing and spitting out fiery rocks. In 2013 it awoke again to send a column of steam high into the air. The Arenal is officially still active, but in a 'resting phase;' no one can predict when it may start performing again. Even without the pyrotechnics, Arenal is still everyone's concept of a volcano: conical, rising abruptly out of flatland vegetation. But do not attempt to climb the upper reaches. Although it's in a resting phase, the volcano still occasionally belches dangerous gases. A sign at the base of Arenal Volcano reads 'If you notice abnormal activity, run away from the area and report it to the nearest authority.'

built in the *Puertas del Sol* – 'Doorways of the Sun' – style, designed to let both morning and afternoon sunlight into north-facing corner houses. A few of these lovely old adobe homes can still be seen along the city's narrow streets. The easiest way to get a first-hand look at one of these grand houses is to drop into the **Café Liberia** (http://sdevenelle4.wix.com/cafe-liberia) on Calle Real. It's an excellent café/restaurant in a beautifully restored mansion with painted cupids cavorting amongst flowers on the ceiling mural in the main dining room, and a garden courtyard that doubles as an art gallery.

RINCÓN DE LA VIEJA NATIONAL PARK

About 5km (3 miles) north of Liberia along the Interamericana Highway, you will reach the turnoff for **Parque Nacional Rincón de la Vieja ㉑** (tel: 2666 5051; Tue–Sun 7am–3pm). This spectacular park contains two towering volcanic peaks, the slightly higher one reaching a height of 1,916 meters (6,286ft), plus four complete ecosystems within its 14,000 hectares (35,000 acres). The name, which applies to both the park and the volcano it protects, derives from the legend of an old woman who once lived on its slopes. The volcano is intermittently quite active now and some hiking trails are off limits, owing to noxious gas emissions. Check current conditions with the park office before heading to the park.

At the Las Pailas ranger station, you sign in and pick up a map of the park and the hiking trails. Just steps away is the park's most spectacular volcanic area, **Las Pailas**, Spanish for 'the kitchen stoves.' There is a well-marked, 3km (2-mile) self-guided loop tour of hot springs, boiling mud pots, sulfur streams, and vapor geysers that color the surrounding rocks red, green, and vivid yellow.

The two closest lodges to the park are Rincón de la Vieja Lodge, a collection of rustic cabins and comfortable bungalows; and Hacienda Guachipelín (tel: 2690 2900; www.guachipelin.com), a working ranch turned upscale lodge, with first-rate horses and many

Arenal volcano spews steam.

Playing in the surf at Playa Conchal.

kilometers of hiking and birding trails and adventure activities, including canopy tours and river tubing.

PENINSULA DE NICOYA

By far, the most popular beach destinations in Costa Rica cluster round the shores of the Nicoya Peninsula. The outer, western beaches rim the Pacific coast, while the inner beaches face the Gulf of Nicoya. This boot-shaped peninsula straddles two provinces: the northern part branches out from the Guanacaste mainland, then morphs into Puntarenas province in the south. In the days before there were any roads on most of the peninsula, the mainly coastal communities were accessible only by boat from the nearest port, Puntarenas. So, rather anachronistically, the Nicoya Peninsula remains part of Puntarenas province today.

PUNTARENAS

Stretched along a narrow spit of sand – *punta de arenas*, or point of sand – **Puntarenas ㉒**, the capital and the largest city of the province of Puntarenas, is the jumping-off spot for car ferries to the Southern Nicoya beaches. The growth of the Caribbean port of Limón and the more recent opening of the deep-water port at nearby **Puerto Caldera** put a major dent in the commercial viability of Puntarenas. Today, fishing is the main industry of Puntarenas and a visit to the busy fish market is the best entertainment in town.

Car ferries, as well as a smaller, passenger-only *lancha* (launch), cross from Puntarenas to Paquera on the Nicoya Peninsula. The one-hour trip across the gulf passes by 40 or so islands, including **Isla San Lucas**, Costa Rica's former prison island.

PAPAGAYO TO PLAYA OCOTAL

The Papagayo Peninsula project is home to an 18-hole golf course and an ultra-expensive hotels like the Four Seasons Costa Rica Resort (tel: 2696 0000; www.fourseasons.com/costarica) and the Andaz Peninsula Papagayo Resort (tel: 2690 1234; https://papagayo.andaz.hyatt.com), with more hotels and private villas planned. Around **Playa Panamá ㉓**, half

a dozen all-inclusive resorts are packed in the high season with budget-minded package travelers who rarely leave the manicured hotel grounds.

To the south is **Playa Hermosa** ㉔, a sparkling half-moon cove with gentle surf. Despite some large-scale development at the northern end, this beach still has some charm and some excellent small restaurants and hotels. It is also a major diving center, with the long-established Sirenas Diving Costa Rica (www.sirenasdivingcostarica.com) based here.

Nearby **Playas del Coco** ㉕ is a working beach town with a large fishing fleet. The swimming isn't great, but Coco is the launching point for myriad diving, surfing, and sport-fishing trips. The town itself has lots of character, albeit a little honky-tonk, with plenty of open-air bars, discos, and tacky souvenir stands. But there are also some excellent seafood restaurants to suit every price range. In town on the main street, Papagayo Seafood (tel: 2670 0298) has reliably fresh seafood daily.

Just a couple of kilometers south of Coco lies dramatic **Playa Ocotal** ㉖, a black-sand beach fringed with steep cliffs.

PLAYA CONCHAL TO PLAYA FLAMINGO

Playa Conchal, once a deserted slice of beach composed of bottomless drifts of pink, orange, mauve, and sunset-colored seashells, lies just south of Flamingo. Although it is an ideal place to snorkel and beachcomb, the huge Westin Golf Resort & Spa looms over the beach, blocking access from the main road. But you can still reach the public beach by walking south for a kilometer (0.6 miles) along the shore from **Brasilito**, a bustling little town with a few interesting restaurants and the vintage Hotel Brasilito (tel: 2654 4237; www. brasilito.com), which has modest rooms in an old wooden building close to the beach. Good seafood restaurants here

include El Camarón Dorado (tel: 2654 4028) practically on the beach.

About 7km (4 miles) north of Brasilito you will find **Playa Flamingo** ㉗, one of Costa Rica's loveliest, longest, white-sand beaches.

PLAYA TAMARINDO AREA

From the Flamingo area, go through Brasilito to Huacas and continue for 13km (8 miles) south, where you will need to make a right turn for **Playa Grande** and **Playa Tamarindo** ㉘, which was made famous by the classic 1960s surfer movie *Endless Summer*. Tamarindo does have a national wildlife refuge, though you would scarcely realize it. The wildlife seems more concentrated in the town's many bars and clubs than it is in the nearby estuary. Some relatively inexpensive lodging is still available in the village of Tamarindo, where commercial centers and condominium developments have popped up everywhere over the past 10 years.

Parque Nacional Marino Las Baulas (tel: 2653 0470; daily 6am–6pm, night tours in turtle season; free during the

⊙ CROSSROADS OF THE AMERICAS

Costa Rica, it appears, was a kind of mercantile and cultural crossroads of the Americas. Linguistic and cultural influences, not to mention a wealth of artifacts and materials, were being exchanged both within the country and without, from as far north as Mexico and as far south as Ecuador.

The native Costa Ricans were skilled in the arts of ceramics, of goldwork and metalwork, fine weaving, and stone carving. They were also enthusiastic traders and prized jade pieces and ceramics, as well as gold and stone carvings from Meso-america and South America. The Nicoya area, with its quiet Pacific bays and safe anchorages, provided pre-Columbian commercial ports. Merchant marines from ancient Ecuador, making ports of call all along the Pacific coast of Mexico, Central and South America, frequently stopped at sites in Nicoya, bringing with them the crafts and arts of places they had visited. The influence of the Olmecs was evident in the Pacific Northwest in the impressive range of pottery styles; utilitarian articles such as grinding stones; and the practice of filing human teeth into points.

The pottery of Nicoya developed into a vigorous hybrid style that for centuries would be traded around Central America and southern Mexico. A collection of such work, ranging from mysterious effigies of man-birds to haunting funerary masks, is on view at the National Museum.

day), which incorporates Playa Grande, was created in 1991 to protect the world's most important leatherback turtle (*la baula*, in Spanish) hatching area, and was expanded in 1995. It was estimated at that time that there were only about 35,000 leatherbacks left in the world and approximately 900 of them came to Playa Grande to lay their eggs each year. Sadly, the population has subsequently fallen into a dramatic decline despite concerted efforts by the National Park Service and scientists to protect them.

During the long nesting season from August to February, you may see one or two turtles struggling up the beach to dig a nest. Visitors must join a guided group since beach access is strictly limited. On the beach at Playa Grande is Hotel Las Tortugas (tel: 2653 0423; www. lastortugashotel.com), a congenial, turtle-friendly hotel, with low lighting at night to avoid disorienting nesting turtles.

SOUTH OF TAMARINDO

Playa Langosta, immediately south of Tamarindo, is separated on the ocean side by a rocky headland that is impassable at high tide, but connected by the dirt road that runs south from Tamarindo. This beach is also frequented by surfers who ride waves just in front of the estuary at the southern end. The shore is rockier here and the surf crashes dramatically, sending sprays high into the air. More sedate than its noisy neighbor, Playa Langosta is home to two lovely bed and breakfast establishments and to the excellent Playa Langosta Beach Club (tel: 2653 1127; www.langostabeachclub.com), a French-run restaurant where you can lunch on lobster and fish carpaccios on the beach or dine in romantic splendor, poolside under palm trees twinkling with fairy lights.

Directly south from Tamarindo, along a bumpy, dusty road, **Playa Avellanas** and **Playa Negra** are popular surfers' turf. So far, these two beaches have escaped the over-development of the Tamarindo area. At the popular **Hacienda Pinilla Beach Resort and Golf Club**, (tel: 2680-3000; www.hacienda pinilla.com), 10km (6 miles) south of

Surf's up at Playa Grande.

Tamarindo, where golfers can tee off with ocean views, on a par-72, Mike Young-designed championship course.

PLAYA NOSARA

Nicoya is the gateway to the beaches of nearby Sámara and the more remote Nosara, both popular destinations for North American and European vacationers who prefer a calmer alternative to the high-octane tourist scene in northern Guanacaste. The road is paved south from Nicoya, until the turn-off for **Playa Nosara** . Then it's a very bumpy ride along an alternately dusty or muddy road for 18km (11 miles), depending on the season. During the worst of the rainy season, this road is sometimes impassable, so many visitors fly directly to Nosara from San José. The star attractions here are idyllic **Playa Pelada** and **Playa Guiones**, two long white-sand beaches with excellent surfing waves and many kilometers of beach bordered by shade trees and tendrils of green sea grape edging the sand.

At the far northern edge of Nosara, the **Nosara Biological Reserve** is a private nature reserve with hiking trails leading down to the mangrove-lined shores of the Nosara River. It's part of the Swiss-run Lagarta Lodge (tel: 2682 0035; www.lagarta.com), which occupies an eagle's aerie, high above the ocean. There are guided nature tours daily or you can take a self-guided tour of the reserve. About 7km (4.5 miles) north of Nosara, the **Refugio Nacional de Vida Silvestre Ostional** is an important turtle-nesting site for Olive Ridley turtles, which arrive by the thousands to nest on the beach. To witness an *arribada*, as it is called, you must join a guided tour organized by a village cooperative (tel: 2682 0428).

PLAYA SÁMARA AND SOUTH

Playa Sámara is just an hour south of Nicoya along a beautifully paved, scenic road. Or you can take a regular flight from San José to Sámara. This is a beautiful white sand beach, with a reef that's good for snorkeling, but more importantly, also protects the beach from direct waves. Swimming here is safe in crystalline, shallow waters with minimal surf. Off season, there is a feeling of dramatic isolation.

Diving, snorkeling, fishing, bicycle and horseback tours, and kayaking can be arranged by all the local hotels. The waves are small for surfing, but just right for beginners. To the north of the beach are some basic *cabinas*, small hotels, and some excellent restaurants. A block north of the beach, bougainvillea-draped Hotel Giada (tel: 2656 3232; www.hotelgiada.net) has a lot of Italian style, and excellent pizza. Walking west along the beach, you'll find El Lagarto (tel: 2656 0750; www.ellagartobbq.com), a dinner-only hotspot right on the sand, famous for its of barbecued beef and seafood.

CENTRAL PACIFIC COAST

If you are anticipating the white-powder beaches washed by gentle, clear

⊙ Tip

Riptides are a danger in Costa Rica and kill several visitors every year. Ask around first whether a beach is safe for swimming. If you are caught by a riptide, don't panic and do not swim against it. Try to swim parallel to the shore, and eventually the breaking waves will carry you back in.

Horseback tour, Playa Sámara.

waters of tourist brochures, then the beaches of the Central Pacific could be something of a disappointment (Jacó sand is a dirty gray). The lure of these places is their proximity to San José, their big waves for surfers and their lively nightlife, not their picture-postcard perfection. Still, with a bit of exploration off the main road, away from the density and hustle of the central beach scene, you will find some clean and appealing beaches.

JACÓ BEACH

Playa Jacó ㉛, once famous for its year-round surfing waves and raucous, party-time ambience fueled by plenty of cold beer, has morphed into a concrete collection of high-rise hotel chains, condominiums, and outposts of trendy San José sportswear stores and restaurant chains. There are still a few inexpensive *cabinas* to rent near the beach, but most accommodations are in hotels, with swimming pools, bars, air-conditioning, and tour packages to other points of interest in this coastal province. Jacó has no shortage of amusements: horses, bikes, scooters, and kayaks are available for rent. Chuck's W.O.W. Surf Shop (tel: 2643 3844; www.wowsurf.com) rents and sells surfboards, gives lessons, and posts a daily surf report. Along the coast some 3km (2 miles) from Playa Jacó is **Playa Hermosa**, a world-class surfing spot with very strong beach breaks.

MANUEL ANTONIO NATIONAL PARK

Once an important banana-shipping port, **Quepos ㉜** is now something of a dormitory town and business center for Manuel Antonio, 7km (4 miles) away. There are some good accommodations, restaurants, shops, banks, and nightlife, a regular bus service, and the flavor of an old-time fishing and banana town. The sport fishing here is excellent. Hotel reservations are essential during the vacation season at both Manuel Antonio and Quepos.

The **Parque Nacional Manuel Antonio ㉝** (tel: 2777 5185/5155; Tue–Sun 7am–4pm) encompasses three long strands of magnificent white sand,

Playa Manuel Antonio is accessible via a hike.

fringed by jungle and the Pacific Ocean, along with 7 sq km (3 sq miles) of forest. The beaches are clean and wide. Above them are tall cliffs covered in thick jungle vegetation. This park is one of the few places in the country where the primary forest comes down to the water's edge in places, sometimes allowing bathers to swim in the shade. In order to protect the ecosystem of the park, rangers allow a daily maximum of 600 visitors on weekdays and 800 on weekends.

Playa Espadilla is the very popular public beach just outside the north end of the park. It is beautiful but it has unpredictable riptides. From Playa Espadilla, you enter the park across an estuary, which at high tide often requires a boat ride. To get to **Playa Espadilla Sur**, the first beach in the park, follow the jungle path across a long sandspit called a *tombolo*. **Playa Manuel Antonio** and **Playa Puerto Escondido** require more hiking but the latter, accessible only at low tide, is less crowded. There are excellent trails for hiking and wildlife sighting. Keep an eye out for all four of Costa Rica's monkey species – the aggressive, white-faced (or capuchin) monkeys that may steal your picnic (or bite you, so don't feed them); the larger, acrobatic spider monkeys *(colorados)* that keep their distance; the sedentary leaf-eating howler monkeys *(mono congo)*; and the tiny squirrel monkeys *(titís)* that tumble through the tree tops. Birdlife encompasses more than 350 species, including boobies, frigate birds, pelicans, and terns.

Just outside the park to the north, in the hills that rise up from the beach, there is a garish profusion of signs advertising an ever-growing number of hotels, restaurants, and *cabinas*. One of the best views is from Hotel Sí Como No (www.sicomono.com), a luxury eco-hotel that has won international prizes for its sustainability in both design and services.

SOUTHERN COSTA RICA AND PENÍNSULA DE OSA

The Zona Sur, or Southern Zone, rises in the highlands around Cerro de la Muerte, the highest point in the country, then falls away into the agricultural lands of the Valle de El General and ends in the tropical lowlands at the Panamanian border. This is an unbeatable destination for hikers and nature-lovers with a sense of adventure, who like exploring off the beaten path. Jutting out more than 50km (30 miles) into the Pacific, the Osa Peninsula shelters the **Golfo Dulce** from ocean swells and creates a magnificent natural harbor. It is sculpted with picturesque beaches and rocky headlands, and dissected by streams and rivers that cascade over volcanic cliffs on their way to the sea. The most majestic forests in all Costa Rica cover the hillsides and line the valleys of the Osa Peninsula and, in many cases, represent the last stronghold of nature and endangered animals and plants, endemic to the South Pacific. The most famous attraction is Corcovado

White faced capuchin monkey in Parque Nacional Manuel Antonio.

National Park, the jewel in the crown of Costa Rica's national park system.

DRAKE BAY

On the northern coast of the Osa Peninsula, **Bahía Drake** ❸ is reputedly where Sir Francis Drake, the first English navigator to sail around the world, landed in 1579. Until recently, this outpost, surrounded by crystal-blue waters, pristine beaches, and jungle, was accessible only on foot, by water or by charter plane. Now there is a dirt road from Rincón, built by the national power company to bring electricity to the village, as well as direct flights from San José to the Drake airstrip. A trio of upscale lodges in Drake Bay tops the wide choice of accommodations. The most romantic is La Paloma Lodge (tel: 2293 7502; www.lapalomalodge.com), built on a breezy bluff with sweeping views of the ocean; its elegant and comfortable cabinas, with thatched roofs and private decks, blend unobtrusively into the jungle environs. Just south of Drake Bay village, the Coastal Footpath begins. This easy-to-walk scenic trail cuts between dense jungle on the landward side, and crashing surf on the Pacific side. There are also calmer sandy coves along the way. The path leads south all the way to Punta Marenco Lodge (tel: 2292 2775; www.lodgepuntamarenco.com), in the 500-hectare (1,200-acre) **Refugio Nacional de Vida Silvestre Río Claro**.

ISLA DEL CAÑO

The **Isla del Caño** ❸ biological reserve sits low on the horizon, about 19km (12 miles) seaward of the Corcovado coastline, a pleasant one-hour boat ride from either Marenco or Bahía Drake. Spotted dolphins ride the boat's bow wave, and flying fish sometimes escort boats to the island. Between December and April, 40-ton humpback whales come from their feeding grounds in Alaska. The island is ringed with turquoise water, tiny beaches, and acres of coral-covered rock reefs. Brilliantly colored tropical fish are easily seen by snorkelers and scuba divers within 15 meters (50ft) of the shore at the park headquarters. Steep, well-manicured trails lead through a rich forest drooping with epiphytes and

⊘ MYSTERY OF THE SPHERES

The Diquis region is the site of one of the great pre-Columbian riddles. Spheres made of granite, andesite, and sedimentary stone have been found in their thousands along river beds and arranged in cemetery sites. Some are as small as oranges while others weigh up to 14 metric tons, and measure up to 2 meters (7ft) in diameter. They are perfectly spherical to within a centimeter or two and are perhaps the finest example of precision stone carving in the ancient world.

The stone spheres are unique – none have been discovered elsewhere in the world. How were they made? How were they made so perfectly spherical? How were they transported more than 30km (20 miles) from the source of the stone to the ceremonial sites where they were arranged? And what do they mean? Today, they stand in their new locations, at the National Museum and in the gardens of expensive homes throughout the Central Valley. You can also see them in their original habitat, Isla del Caño, near Corcovado National Park.

In addition to the enigma of the country's lithic spheres, there is another pre-Columbian riddle in Costa Rica that continues to perplex historians and archeologists: it is the source of jade for the many pieces found throughout the country, as no jade quarries have ever been found in Costa Rica. Guatemala is believed to be the principal source, although some jade may have come from Mexico.

Many of the objects appear to have been treasured for years, passed down as heirlooms; others seem to have arrived in one form, and to have been re-sculpted to the tastes of their new owners.

One interesting theory holds that some of the jade was brought to Costa Rica by pre-Columbian looters of Mayan burial sites, and this would help to explain the presence of Mayan hieroglyphs inscribed on the stone – which apparently had no value or significance to the Costa Ricans.

The Jade Museum in San José (see page 281) has the largest display of jade in the Americas, with more than 6,000 pieces. Many of the pieces are *colgantes* (amulets or pendants), generally in the form of birds, animals, or humans, but there is a great variety of other exhibits, including notable oddities such as a tooth with a jade inset, and jade breast supports, thought to have been worn by high-ranking women.

enormous philodendrons to a clearing with ancient stone spheres. Thousands of spheres like this have been found in the south of Costa Rica, and a few also in northern Panamá. They pose one of the country's great riddles. Though their exact origin and significance have defied explanation, it is speculated that they were made in villages on the Osa Peninsula near Palmar Norte, brought to Caño in canoes, and then possibly rolled to the cemetery at the highest point of the island. The best place to see las bolas, as they're locally known, is the **Finca 6 Archeological Site** (tel: 2100 6000; Tue–Sun 8am–4pm), 6km (4 miles) south of Palmar Sur, where the stones can be seen in their natural surroundings. A small museum has displays exploring the history and significance of these baffling spheres.

PARQUE NACIONAL CORCOVADO

Covering 445 sq km (172 sq miles), **Parque Nacional Corcovado** ㊱ (tel: 2735 5036; Tue–Sun 7am–4pm) is Central America's largest lowland Pacific rainforest. It's the most important sanctuary of biological diversity and endangered wildlife in the country, and one of the most important in the world. Because Corcovado Park is inundated with nearly 6 meters (20ft) of rain a year, it is technically known as a 'tropical wet forest.' But the simplicity of that classification belies the ecological complexity of the park. Thirteen distinct habitats here are each characterized by unique assemblages of plants, animals, and topography. Five hundred species of trees – one quarter of all the species in Costa Rica – more than 6,000 kinds of insects, almost 375 species of birds, plus frogs, butterflies, and many of the world's most endangered and spectacular mammals, including tapirs and jaguars, live in this place.

One of Corcovado's blessings is its inaccessibility. It is a park only for those who are prepared to make a considerable commitment in time and energy. Camping with your own tent (make reservations well in advance) can be more comfortable than staying at the shabby Sirena facilities. But there are other ways to sample the beauties of Corcovado and the Osa Peninsula, from day trips by boat or charter flights, to accommodations at nearby luxury ecolodges. The ideal time to hike and camp in Corcovado is during the dry season, from December through April. A visit might include a night at each of the three park stations, with days spent hiking from one station to the next. (Stations are joined by trails, each of which requires from three to 10 hours of hiking time.)

A pleasant alternative to sleeping in a tent in Corcovado National Park is to bed down at one of the nearby ecolodges. At one end of the scale is **Lapa Ríos** (tel: 2735 5130; www.lapa rios.com), set in its own primary forest preserve, with super-comfortable thatched-roof bungalows perched on a hillside overlooking the ocean. It's as luxurious as it gets here, but like all lodges this far south, it's off the electrical grid – no TV, no air-conditioning, and few cellular connections.

Walking in the rainforest.

📷 MOUNTAINS OF FIRE

Vulcanologists are always busy in Costa Rica, which has five active volcanoes and some 112 dormant and extinct ones. Visitors can explore volcanic peaks and soak in thermal waters.

Costa Rica is a land of earthquakes and volcanoes, where hikers and mountaineering enthusiasts can climb the Central Valley's four active cones in just two days. Visitors should remember, though, that an active volcano demands respect; proper equipment is essential. Taking a guided tour will ensure the greatest safety. Local people are proud of their explosive geology, and have made Poás and Irazú volcanoes the country's most visited parks.

The most dynamic and majestic of Costa Rica's active volcanoes is Arenal, a nearly perfect cone. The 1,633-meter (4,950ft) -high volcano rises above farmlands, adjacent to its own lake, and offered a spectacular show of clouds of gas and steam spewing out of the top. Arenal is still considered active, but it is currently in a resting phase.

Tourists looking for active volcanoes won't be disappointed, however, as two other 'resting' volcanoes have suddenly come back to life – Volcán Rincón de la Vieja, to the northwest of Arenal; and Volcán Turrialba, east of the Central Valley. The latter has been spewing ashes, rocks, and gases since late 2014 and entered a new phase in September 2016, shooting columns of ash up to 4,000 meters (13,000ft) above the crater. Poás Volcano has also shown more activity lately and the popular national park surrounding it sometimes closes temporarily when the sulfurous gas levels get too high.

On its best daytime behavior, Arenal Volcano is picture-perfect with its cone-shaped profile etched against the sky. But the pointy tip often catches passing clouds, disappointing many a photographer.

When Arenal spewed out streams of red-hot rocks and lava at night, visitors were treated to spectacular pyrotechnic shows.

A short hike along a forest trail leads visitors to the placid crater lake in Poás Volcano National Park.

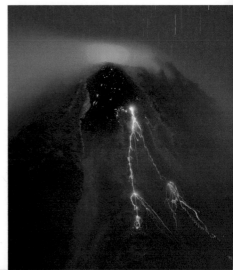

Thermal hot springs are heated up by Arenal.

Volcano stays

To observe Arenal in true luxury, pamper yourself at the Spanish colonial-style Tabacón Grand Spa Thermal Resort, built on the site of a 1975 hot avalanche deposit that provides the source of heat for the thermal waters.

Although vulcanologists feel there is a risk of future hot avalanches, this hasn't stopped the Ticos and tourists who flock here to exclaim excitedly over the activity of the volcano and soak their aching muscles. A dip in the waters is also supposedly beneficial for anyone suffering from skin problems and arthritis.

Twelve pools of varying depths and temperatures (the warmest is a sizzling 102°F/38°C), a Jacuzzi, hot waterfall, slides, and an individual tub tucked deep in the beautifully landscaped tropical gardens mean fun for everyone from children to senior citizens. A spa offers mud facials in open air bungalows, and the resort has lockers, towel rental, and showers. The hotel here is elegant and expensive. Make reservations well in advance.

If you are on a budget, try the Baldi Hot Springs, though renovations have upped the prices there significantly, or the low-key Titoku Hot Springs, both just west of La Fortuna.

Poás Volcano has the world's largest active crater.

e vast craters of Volcán Irazú look deceptively peaceful, since 1723 this very active volcano has erupted more n 20 times.

Punta Paitillia's skyscrapers, Panama City.

PANAMA

The isthmus of Panama is where Central America comes to its wild conclusion, from a modern metropolis to untouched rainforests and endless beaches.

No country in Central America has entered the 21st century quite as boldly as Panama. The zigzagging economy, still anchored by the canal, which fell under Panama's complete control on the last day of 1999, is being pushed along by its status as a tax haven, some of it on the shady side, as the Panama Papers revealed in 2016.

In Panama City, the skyline has gone from a few skyscrapers to hundreds. The region's first metro has been installed here and glitzy malls and restaurants are as cosmopolitan as anything in New York or Paris. At first glance, you might mistake the city for Dubai or Hong Kong, but the rainbow-colored buses blasting reggaeton assure you that this metropolis is Latino without a doubt.

Tourism here is quickly catching up to Costa Rica, though thus far there's no threat to authenticity or to the rich flora and fauna. The canal is bigger than it once was and sees more cruise traffic than ever before, but much of the country remains free from crowds. Coffee farms around Boquete and hiking trails along the canal zone attract the same birders and java geeks as they always have, while Afro-Caribbean towns like Portobelo and fishing lodges in the Gulf of Chiriquí have remained decidedly low-key. Still, wherever you go, the amenities have

gotten better, and a bit nicer. While the Pan-American Highway remains the most popular way to travel from the capital in the east to David in the west, low-cost airlines have cut travel time to remote destinations like Bocas del Toro and the Azuero peninsula, where new beach hotels and eco-chic resorts are opening by the handful.

Culturally, the country of 4 million is also rich. In remote mountain ranges and tropical isles, indigenous groups like the Emberá and Kuna carry on their traditions. Elsewhere,

Main Attractions

Panama City
The Panama Canal
Portobelo
Azuero Peninsula
Boquete
Bocas del Toro
Comarca Kuna Yala
The Darién

Maps on pages 308, 311

Panamax container ship in the canal.

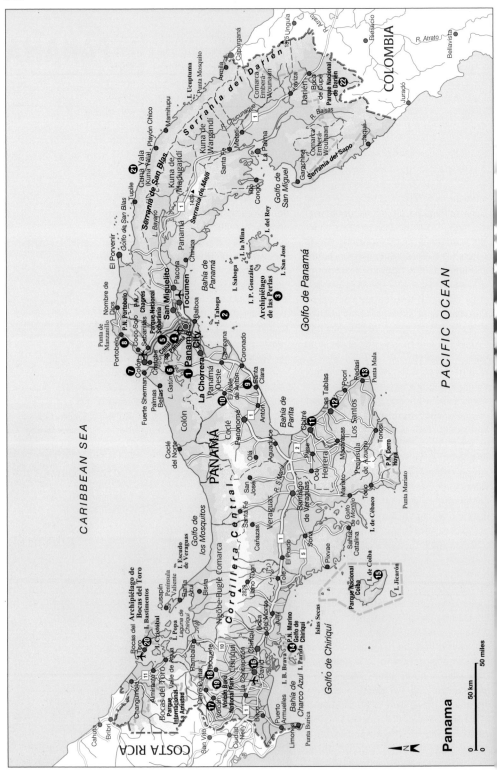

Panama

the country's genetic make-up has been altered by waves of immigrants, from the Spanish conquistadors to the Jamaicans and Italians and Americans that came for the canal to the recent surge of retirees and Venezuelans seeking better opportunities.

A NEW ERA BEGINS

A new era in Panama began on December 31, 1999, when the US formally transitioned all operations of the Panama Canal to Panama, as well as turned over all military bases. The act was more than 20 years in the making, beginning in 1977 when US President Jimmy Carter signed the Torrijos-Carter Treaty that gave Panama increasing control of the canal until the date of a complete US withdrawal.

While there were fears that the Panamanians would not be able to maintain operations and security on the strategic waterway, the Panama Canal Authority (ACP) have eased all concerns. From the first year under Panamanian control to 2016, income increased from $769 million to $2.6 billion. Accidents have dropped, traffic has increased, and expenses have increased less than revenue. In 2016, the canal completed a $5.25 billion expansion that took 10 years to build, giving it the ability to accommodate many of the world's largest cargo vessels (see page 314).

THE RETURN OF CORRUPTION

In 2004, the Democratic Revolutionary Party's Martin Torrijos won the presidency, campaigning on promises of ending corruption. Torrijos immediately went to work passing laws that made the government more transparent, though there was little follow through when high profile cases appeared.

Succeeding Torrijos was Conservative supermarket magnate Ricardo Martinelli, who won a landslide 60 percent of the vote in 2009. Voters had feared that the world financial crisis was already slowing Panama's rapid growth rate of previous years and Martinell's business experience could come in handy. His pro-business policies helped the annual GDP to

Panama City has a thriving financial center.

increase by more than 10 percent each year, turning Panama into one of Latin America's fastest growing economies, projected to be the fastest-growing in 2017. However, Martinelli proved to be far from perfect. Many in his administration, including his sons, have been investigated or charged with accepting millions in bribes from Brazilian construction firm Odebrecht S.A., which became an important government contractor during that time.

Martinelli was followed by his former political partner Juan Carlos Varela in 2014, amidst a sudden dip in the economy. Not long after being sworn in, the Panama Papers scandal broke. The vast data leak from the Mossack Fonseca law firm detailed how the world's wealthy stashed assets in offshore companies. While the Varela administration claimed to be strengthening controls over money laundering in Panama and appointed an independent investigation, they have refused to make the final reports to be public. As investigations into Mossack Fonseca continue, the extent of the political

fallout might not be understood for some time.

PANAMA CITY AND AROUND

Founded in 1519 by Pedro Arias Dávila, **Panama City** ❶ is the oldest Spanish settlement on the mainland of the Americas. The original settlement was where gold and silver being raided from South America was unloaded at sea and then transported over the isthmus by road to the Caribbean, attracting the attention of treasure-hungry pirates. By 1673 the settlement had been destroyed by attacks and then rebuilt in in present day Casco Viejo, which became heavily fortified, ensuring the city could withstand any further attacks. It lingered in obscurity until Panama seceded from Colombia and was designated the capital in 1903. When the canal was built in 1914, it became the center of trade and commerce in the Americas.

CASCO VIEJO

Bordered by the Pacific Ocean to the southeast and the Panama Canal to

Casco Viejo's colorful streets.

the west, Panama City sprawls out in a maze of congested neighborhoods that rarely follow any sort of order. While few parts of the Panamanian capital are walkable, **Casco Viejo** Ⓐ, also called Casco Antiguo, is an exception. Declared a World Heritage Site in 1997, Casco is the oldest part of the city and by far the most atmospheric. Over the past two decades, the neighborhood's stock of centuries-old Spanish, Italian, and French-influenced architecture has been gradually restored, transforming it from a gritty barrio to one of the most gentrified areas of the city. While some parts of Casco still can be quite dangerous, the bulk of the peninsula is home to boutique hotels, pulsating rooftop bars, and a wide range of upscale stores and restaurants.

Plaza de la Independencia, where Panama declared its independence from Colombia, is flanked by several interesting sights: the neoclassical **Catedral Metropolitana** (hours vary; free); the **Museo del Canal Interoceánico** (tel: 211 1649; http://museodelcanal.com; Tue–Sun 9am–5pm), which was built

in 1875 and was used as offices for the French and later US canal, and now contains historical documents and artifacts related to the construction of the canal; and the **Hotel Central** (tel: 309-0300; www.centralhotelpanama.com), once the most luxurious hotel in the region before being neglected for decades and finally restored to glory in 2016. Down Calle 6a Este is the **Presidential Palace**, a stunning Spanish mansion with a Moorish interior patio, inaccessible to tourists.

A few blocks to the northeast is Plaza Bolívar, home to the **Palacio Bolívar**, which contains the **Salón Bolívar** (Tue–Sat 9am–4pm), a room that hosted the 1826 congress organized by liberator Simón Bolívar to discuss the unification of Colombia, Mexico, and Central America. The building is now the home of the Ministry of Foreign Relations. Next door is one of the oldest buildings in Casco, the **Iglesia y Convento de San Francisco de Asís** (hours vary; free), although much of it was destroyed in a series of fires in the mid-1700s. At the corner of the plaza is the **Teatro Nacional** (tel: 262

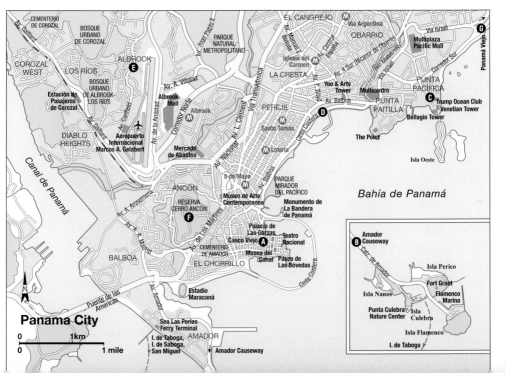

3525; hours vary; free), dating to 1908 and designed by Italian architect Genaro Ruggieri, which hosts opera, theater, and other performance art. Inside are frescoes by renowned Panamanian painter Roberto Lewis.

Plaza de Francia, on the southeastern corner of Casco, is sided by **Las Bóvedas**, a series of jail cells that have been restored and now contain several upscale stores and cafés. Leading from the plaza is the colonial-era stone promenade Paseo Esteban Huertas, where several Kuna women sell handcrafted molas.

Plaza Herrera on the western side of Casco is home to several important hotel projects, including the **American Trade Hotel** (www.acehotel.com/panama) that was created in the 1917 neoclassical headquarters of the American Trade Developing Company.

THE AMADOR CAUSEWAY

South of Casco, extending into Panama Bay, is the **Amador Causeway** , which connects the four tiny islands of **Naos**, **Culebra**, **Perico**, and **Flamenco**.

Aerial view of Amador Causeway.

These islands, connected with the dirt and rock that was excavated during the Culebra Cut, form a protective harbor for ships waiting to enter the Panama Canal. It was a military zone used by the US until the handover in 1999, when the government opened it to the public. It's now a popular walking and jogging trail and the home of several major projects.

First and foremost is the Frank Gehry designed **BioMuseo** (www.biomuseopanama.org; Tue–Fri 10am–4pm, Sat–Sun 10am–5pm), a $100 million biodiversity museum that took a decade to build. It is notable for its multicolored roof plates and eight different interior galleries, each displaying a different piece of the formation of the Panamanian isthmus. Farther down the causeway, at the Smithsonian's Tropical Research Institute, is the **Punta Culebra Nature Center** (www.stri.si.edu/english/visit_us/culebra; Tue–Sun 10am–6pm, Mar–Dec Tue–Fri 1–5pm), where visitors can explore the marine and coastal environment on trails through the tropical dry forest and various exhibitions of native flora and fauna.

THE MODERN CITY

To the northeast of Casco Viejo, running along the coast, are a string of neighborhoods like **Marbella**, **Bellavista**, **Punta Paitilla**, and **Punta Pacífica** that are nearly indistinguishable from each other. They are dominated by a sea of glitzy glass and steel skyscrapers where the city's wealthiest residents live, and which seems to grow more dense every month. Running along the waterfront is the **Cinta Costera**, a green space with a cycling and jogging path.

The interior neighborhoods of **El Cangrejo**, **Obarrio**, and the **Area Bancaria** form much of the city's business and financial district, though residential and hotel projects are also concentrated here. **San Francisco** to the north is where the city's best dining can be found, such as at renowned contemporary restaurant Panamanian Maito (www.maitopanama.com). **Albrook** 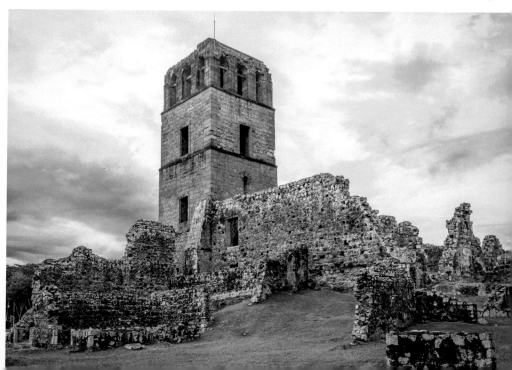, to the south, is home to the domestic airport and bus terminal and more residential, home to wooden houses with wide verandas that were built during the days of US control of the canal.

Cerro Ancón ⑤, a jungle-clad hill close to Casco, has a 360-degree view of the city. Aside from the more residential lower slopes, the reserve is mostly undeveloped and it's possible to encounter animals like sloths, armadillos, coati, and Geoffrey's tamarins.

PANAMA VIEJO

The original settlement of Panama City, **Panama Viejo** ⑥ (www.patronatopanamaviejo.org; Tue–Sun), founded by the conquistador Pedrarías Dávila in 1519, was burned down after being sacked by Henry Morgan in 1671. At the time, there were as many as 10,000 people living there, though thousands died in the attack. When the settlement was moved a few kilometers west to present day Casco Viejo, which could be better defended, much of the stone went with it.

The ruins today, a Unesco World Heritage Site, are hidden within the encroaching jungle and are largely surrounded by modern suburbs. The restored Plaza Mayor and a bell tower from what was Panama's original cathedral form most of what remains today, along with a few walls and minor buildings. The visitor center has a model of the city before it was destroyed, as well as a few colonial artifacts.

ISLA TABOGO AND LAS PERLAS

Reached by daily ferries from the Amador Causeway, **Isla Taboga** ②, known as the 'island of flowers,' is the nearest offshore island to Panama City. Just 19km (12 miles) off the coast, it's an easy day trip with a few good beaches like **Playa Restinga** and laid back restaurants.

Farther out is the **Archipiélago de Las Perlas** ③, 64km (40 miles) from Panama City, reached by ferry or a 20-minute flight. There are more than 200 small islands here, the majority of which are uninhabited. Fine snorkeling, big game fishing, and unspoiled beaches are all

Ruins of Panama Viejo.

THE EXPANDED PANAMA CANAL

The Panama Canal is now even bigger than before. A $5 billion-dollar expansion added a new lane and room for the world's largest ships, allowing for nearly double the amount of traffic.

For much of the past century the shipping industry has built ships to fit through the Panama Canal, often referred to as the 8th wonder of the world. Mostly oil tankers, they're called Panamax ships. However, by the 1990s, the size of the canal was becoming outdated as ships grew bigger and bigger. Many were far too large to enter the canal, resulting in a significant loss of market share to the Suez Canal. And so, to avoid the risk of the canal becoming obsolete, the Panama Canal Authority began work on an expansion project in 2007. A national referendum to ratify the plan was approved by a 76.8 percent majority.

The larger canal, which began operations in June 2016 (after being more than two years behind schedule and $1 billion over budget), added an entire new lane of traffic, doubling the capacity of the canal. It took roughly 40,000 workers nearly 10 years to complete the massive infrastructure project,

Cruise ship passing through Gatun Locks.

which rivals the statistics of the original canal build that took place a century before. Enough earth was dredged to fill the Great Pyramid at Giza 25 times over and there was enough steel used that they could have built 29 Eiffel Towers.

Parallel to the old locks, two new locks were built: one east of the existing Gatún locks, and one southwest of the Miraflores locks. These new locks are wider, at 54.8 meters (180ft) versus 33.5 meters (110ft), and deeper, at 18 meters (60ft) versus 12.8 meters (42ft), allowing larger ships to transit. These are called New Panamax and are about one and a half times the previous limit, with the ability to carry twice as much cargo. As the canal was expected to hit capacity between 2012 and 2014, the expansion was designed to allow for an anticipated growth in traffic from 280 million PC/UMS tons in 2005 to nearly 510 million PC/UMS tons in 2025. The total cost of the project is estimated to have been $5.25 billion. As a result of the increase in traffic, ports around the world – from the east coast of the US to the UK and Brazil – expanded their capabilities in preparation for the new, larger ships.

TRANSITING THE CANAL

While many are content to watch these colossal New Panamax ships pass through the canal at the Miraflores Locks, a quick jaunt from Panama City, many choose to transit the canal. Moving from the Atlantic to the Pacific Coast and vice versa, it takes between 6 and 8 hours to transit the entire canal, passing through all three locks: Miraflores, Pedro Miguel, and Gatún. While many passengers traverse the canals on cruise ship itineraries, partial tours of the canal are an alternative for visitors in the country. As transiting each lock can take upward of two hours, it grows tiresome for the full journey, so many tours simply offer excursions passing through the Pedro Miguel and Miraflores locks, followed by sailing under the Bridge of the Americas and into the Pacific Ocean. The 300-passenger *Pacific Queen* runs frequent trips from Gamboa to the Pacific via Panama Marine Adventures (www.pmatours.net), while the 100-person wooden *Isla Morada* and 500 passenger steel *Fantasía del Mar* run between the Flamenco Marina and Gamboa or Gatún.

found here and while there have been rumblings about development in recent years, it hasn't happened yet.

The most developed island is **Contadura**, which has dozens of small hotels and B&Bs. The island has gained a reputation for its celebrity guests, which include models, fashion designers and even the former Shah of Iran, who have built luxe mansions here. Contadura boasts 13 beaches like the popular **Playa Galeón** and **Playa Ejecutiva** on a quiet cove.

THE PANAMA CANAL

Extending 77km (50 miles) from the Port of Colón on the Caribbean Sea to the Port of Balboa near Panama City, the **Panama Canal** ❹ is the world's most strategic waterway. More than 14,000 vessels pass through it annually, representing around 5 percent of global trade. Considered one of mankind's grandest feats of engineering, the canal is without a doubt Panama's major attraction.

Aside from sailing through the canal, as many cruise passengers do, the easiest way to see the canal in action is at the **Miraflores Locks**, a 20-minute drive from Panama City. The **Miraflores Visitors Center** (tel: 276-8325; www.visitcanaldepanama.com) overlooks the locks from four levels, each with different exhibitions and interactive displays, including a 3D movie theater with films detailing the history of the canal. The best time to visit is around 11am or around 3pm, when enormous Panamax ships can be seen rising and falling as they traverse the locks. Crowds gather on the observation decks as an announcer details information about the ship, such as where it is registered and where it is going. The Atlantic & Pacific Co. Restaurant (www.atlanticpacificrestaurant.com; daily 9am–4.30pm) serves a pricey buffet where you can drink champagne and watch as the ships move through the locks.

Overlooking Gatún Lake and the new Atlantic-side locks closer to Colón,

which were built during the expansion of the canal, the **Aguas Claras Visitor Center** (daily 8am–4pm) is less formal than its Miraflores counterpart. There is no site museum and just a small theater, but most come here simply for the view of the ships passing through.

ELSEWHERE IN THE CANAL ZONE

Along the edge of the eastern side of the Panama Canal is one of Panama's most astounding natural areas, the 19,425 hectares (48,000 acres) of **Parque Nacional Soberanía** ❺ (daily 6am–5pm). Just 40 minutes from the city, Soberanía is one of the most accessible natural areas in Central America and it's been extremely well preserved. More than 100 species of mammals have been identified here, including jaguars, sloths, and monkeys, not to mention more than 500 species of birds. From the park ranger station there are several trails into the park of varying levels of difficulty. Closer to Gamboa is the renowned birdwatching spot, **Pipeline Road**.

There are several ecolodges within or on the border of the park, such as

Rainforest aerial tram, Gamboa Rainforest Resort.

> Fact

While Panama hats were popularized by Ferdinand de Lesseps during the French canal effort, and later Theodore Roosevelt during the American one, they aren't actually Panamanian. Rather, they're made in the Manabí Province of Ecuador, using fibers from the toquilla palm, and have been a cottage industry since the 1600s. Lightweight and breathable, the hats were given to canal workers and have become associated with tropical locales.

Cargo ship on Gatún Lake.

Canopy Tower (www.canopytower.com), which opened in 1999 in an ex-US-military radar station on top of Sema-phore Hill. Topped by a 9 meter (29.5ft) high dome, views of the rainforest canopy give phenomenal access to bird watchers, making the lodge one of the region's top destinations.

Gamboa, once a residential area for American workers in the canal's dredging division, is on the shore of the Chagres River and home to the Gamboa Rainforest Resort (www.gamboaresort.com), a family-friendly lodge surrounded by the pristine forests of Soberanía. Less ecolodge than posh hotel, it's a sprawling property that includes multiple pools and res-taurants, plus a full range of in-house excursions like boat trips on Gatún Lake and guided hikes with natural-ist guides.

Gatún Lake ❻ was created in 1913 when the Gatún Dam was built on the Chagres River, flooding 425 sq km (164 sq miles) of forest. The lake is home to several Emberá villages, which resettled here near the mouth of the Chagres River from the Darién Province. The villages of Parara Puru, Emberá Puru, and Emberá Drua have opened to tourism and visits have become a popular shore excursion for cruise visitors and other travelers in Panama. Most trips are half-day visits that include a typical Emberá lunch, a folkloric dance show, dugout canoe rides, and the chance – or pressure, some might say – to purchase indig-enous handicrafts. Most tour agencies in Panama City, including Ancon Expe-ditions and Advantage Panama, run tours here.

COLÓN PROVINCE

Running along Panama's central Car-ibbean coast, the province of Colón seems to have a culture all of its own. The Afro-Panamanian influence is strong here, deriving from workers who arrived to work in the canal and those who then arrived during the days of slavery. The gritty capital is the city of Colón, the largest duty-free zone in the Americas, which has undergone a series of makeovers that have yet to truly clean it up. More remote are attractions like the Spanish Fort of San Lorenzo and the historic seaside vil-lage of Portobelo.

COLÓN AND AROUND

Founded in 1850 during the California Gold Rush, when crossing the isthmus via the Panama Railroad saved a trip around Cape Horn, Colón ❼ has seen its ups and downs. The city grew large in its early days, until its progress was halted by the establishment of the US transcontinental railroad in 1869. It then saw another bump thanks to French and later, American, canal work. It was during this period that much of the city was built, although the city has lingered in obscurity as Panama City has grown.

The city's biggest industry is the Colón Free Zone on the southeast-ern edge of town. Here, nearly 2,000

showrooms sell a variety of goods tax-free, although it's of little interest to passing tourists as it's primarily aimed at wholesalers. Along the eastern shore is the cruise-ship port, **Colón 2000**, which has a few restaurants, a duty-free store, and handicraft shops. Much of the rest of the city can be dangerous and is best avoided.

Along the lake shore outside of town is the former Escuela de las Americas, a notorious military school known for training Manuel Noriega. It's now an upscale Meliá hotel (www.meliapanamacanal.com).

Near the Caribbean entrance to the canal, 10km (6 miles) west of Colón, are the **Gatún Locks**, which have their own visitor center (daily 9am–4pm). While the facility lacks the amenities of the Miraflores Locks (see page 315), the viewing platform gives a great look at Panamax ships and tankers rising to the level of Lake Gatún. About 2km (1.2 miles) farther on is the Gatún Dam across the Chagres River, which was the largest in the world at the time it was built.

Passing over the Gatún Locks, the road leads through the dense jungles of the Sherman Forest Reserve to Fort Sherman, a former US military base that has been partially dismantled. The rough road continues 8.9km (5 miles) until the mouth of the Chagres River. Nearby, you will find **Fort San Lorenzo** (daily 9am–4pm), a Spanish fort that was first built in 1595, but sacked several times in pirate attacks. The current incarnation, a Unesco World Heritage Site, dates from 1761 and is in a relatively good condition, with a collection of rusty cannons and a grass covered moat.

PORTOBELO TO ISLA GRANDE

Approximately 43km (27 miles) east of Colón lies the sleepy seaside town of **Portobelo** ⑧, which was one of the wealthiest ports in the Spanish Caribbean from the 16th to early 18th centuries, thanks to much of the silver and gold from South America passing through here before being shipped off to Europe. Portobelo today is relaxed as they come, a small grid of cobblestone

The ruins of Castillo Santiago de la Gloria, Portobelo.

streets fronting the yacht-filled bay, with jagged, rainforest covered mountains towering behind it.

Buccaneers like Henry Morgan and the British Admiral Edward Vernon made their mark on the city, and as a result, defensive fortifications were built around the bay. Much of the original architecture has been well preserved, helping Portobelo attain Unesco World Heritage Status in 1980. Fronting the plaza is the **Customs House**, dating to 1630 but partially rebuilt after cannon attacks and a fire over the centuries. It is said that one third of the gold in the world once passed through its door, and today it's a small museum. Beside the Customs House is **Fuerte San Jerónimo**, which dates back to 1664 and features a row of cannons facing the bay.

The **Iglesia de San Felipe** (hours vary; free), a block from the plaza, is home to the celebrated 'Black Christ' statue, which is honored with a festival each October 21. The statue was, as legend has it, left behind by a ship en route to Cartagena and after residents prayed to it during a cholera epidemic they were miraculously spared.

The quaint village is as rich culturally as it once was economically. The residents are descendants of African slaves brought during the Spanish colonial era, who call themselves 'congos.' They maintain rich expressions of dance, music, and art, which come alive during festivals throughout the year. An art gallery and cultural center called **La Casa Congo** (www.fundacionbp.org), which is associated with the luxury hotel El Otro Lado (www.elotrolado.com.pa) across the bay, helps organize performances for visitors and rents kayaks, to explore the mangroves and fortifications that can only be accessed by water.

Roughly 20km (13 miles) east of Portobelo in La Guaira, just beyond Adriana's Afro-Panamanian seafood restaurant, boats run offshore to **Isla Grande**, a relaxed island escape with a few good beaches and decent snorkeling. There are a few small hotels and restaurants, which open and close with the seasons. Amenities here are quite basic.

A traditional congo dance in Portobello.

THE PACIFIC COAST

West from Panama City, the Pan-American highway runs parallel to the Pacific coast, passing a string of beaches that become progressively more attractive the farther away you get from the capital. Many wealthy Panamanians and ex-pats have beach houses or condos here, which usually remain empty during the week. Seaside golf courses and a few mega-resorts are scattered about as well. The landscape becomes more rugged at the Azuero Peninsula, a cowboy country known for wild parties, that's seeing its first signs of major development on its more remote beaches. At the Gulf of Chiriquí, the coast is at its most dramatic, with wild islands and fine whale-watching.

NEAR PACIFIC BEACHES

The nearest beach to Panama City is **Playa Bonita**, just beyond the Bridge of the Americas, where there is a mega-resort, the Westin Playa Bonita Resort & Spa (www.starwoodhotels.com), though little else. The lengthy beach at **Playa Coronado**, 83km (51 miles) from the city, is one of the most developed on the coast, with supermarkets and lots of residential units. Coronado feels older, yet not nearly as cookie cutter in style as some of the developments farther west.

Santa Clara 9, 113km (70 miles) from the city, and neighboring **Farallón** are the prettiest beaches on the coast and attract more tourists than locals. Santa Clara is more public, with condo towers and mostly small hotels, aside from the all-inclusive Sheraton Bijao Resort (www.starwoodhotels.com). Farallón, which is better known as Playa Blanca, is home to the massive, 852-room Royal Decameron Beach Resort, Golf, Spa & Casino (www.decameron.com), as well as the Buenaventura complex, anchored by a JW Marriott hotel and a Jack Nicklaus-designed golf course that is one of the best in Central America.

EL VALLE DE ANTÓN

Inland, 28km (17 miles) from the Pacific, is **El Valle de Antón 10**, aka El Valle, which sits within the crater of the world's second-largest extinct volcano. With an altitude peaking at 762 meters (2,500ft), El Valle has year-round cooler conditions than the coast, making it an attractive weekend escape from Panama City, less than two hours away. On Sundays, vendors from around the region come to town to sell handicrafts and produce, including Ngäbe and Emberá people, who sell traditional cloths and baskets.

Lush and green, the town and surrounding forests are a biodiversity hotspot and more than 350 species of birds have been recorded here. **Cerro Gaital National Monument**, on the northern hillside of town, has good hiking trails, including a 2–3 hour loop, where you can see both the Atlantic and Pacific Oceans from certain points.

There are dozens of B&Bs and ecolodges on the outskirts of town, including Canopy Lodge (www.canopy-lodge.com), which runs a zipline track

Tourists on the beach at Santa Clara.

farther up the hill, and the more resort-like Los Mandarinos Hotel and Spa (www.losmandarinos.com). For dining, there's La Casa de Lourdes, (www.lacasadelourdes.com), set inside an upscale Tuscan-style manor house, run by Lourdes Fábrega de Ward, a chef who studied with Martha Stewart and Paul Prudhomme and is something of a Panamanian culinary celebrity.

AZUERO PENINSULA

Roughly 100km (60 miles) wide and 90km (55 miles) long, the Azuero peninsula is located just southward off the Pacific Coast, splitting the Gulf of Panama and the Gulf of Chiriquí. The rugged interior is defined by bare, rolling hills with grazing cattle and the occasional Spanish colonial house, while the pristine coastline is relatively undeveloped, although that is quickly changing. This is the folkloric capital of Panama, with a hard partying Carnaval and the finest makers of *Pollera* dresses.

The largest town on the Azuero peninsula is **Chitré ⑪**, which has a small airport with daily flights to Panama City. The town is of little interest, outside of amenities such as modern hotels and grocery stores that are severely lacking in other parts of Azuero. Outside of town is **La Arena**, an artisan village known for its ceramics, particularly the painted pots called *tinajas*.

Comprised mostly of whitewashed adobe houses with clay tile roofs, **Las Tablas ⑫** is one of the most atmospheric towns in Azuero. For much of the year it is a sleepy place where there is little to do other than soak up the atmosphere...until Carnaval comes along. While the holiday is celebrated all over Azuero, in Las Tablas it is downright maniacal. Beginning on the Saturday before Ash Wednesday and continuing for four days of parades, *pollera* contests, pageants, and, of course, heavy alcohol consumption. Throughout the event, the battle lines are drawn between Calle Arriba and Calle Abajo, which choose their own queens and try to out-do each other with floats and costumes. Water pistols, hoses, and buckets have become quite common, so visitors should plan on getting wet, whether they would like to or not.

The cowboy town of **Pedasí ⑬**, driven by a young mayor who has encouraged the community to spruce up the local colonial houses, is becoming increasingly gentrified. There are new cafés and boutique hotels, although horses still far outnumber BMWs here. The town is the jumping-off point for the sudden surge of development on **Playa Venao**, about 12km (7 miles) away. With its long, curved beach and consistent waves, a new community is beginning to form, much of it from Israeli investments that are pumping cash into modern hotels like Villa Marina (www.villamarinalodge.com) amidst the surf camps and yoga retreats. On the south end of the beach, there's the renowned restaurant Panga, run by an ex-Top Chef contestant who cooks over

Girls marching in a parade in Chitré wearing traditional pollera costumes.

a wood fire, forages for local produce, and works with sustainable fisherman to create surprisingly sophisticated yet affordable meals.

GOLFO DE CHIRIQUÍ

Founded in 1994, the 14,730 hectares (36,400 acres) of **Chiriquí Chiriquí Gulf National Marine Park**  is where Panama is found in its most raw and wild form. The land, much of it displayed on uninhabited islets, is jagged and green, hiding big game fishing lodges and tiny resorts. In and along the water are mangroves, coral reefs, and white-sandy beaches. Huge schools of tropical fish, whales, and white-tipped sharks all come here to play in the sea, while migrating seabirds share the thick vegetation with howler monkeys and other wildlife.

The isolated fishing community of **Boca Chica** provides the best access to the park. Here, small hotels like Bocas del Mar (www.bocasdelmar.com), and nearby fishing lodges such as the Panama Big Game Sportfishing Club (www.panama-sportfishing.com) on Boca

Brava island, set up packages where you can fish, kayak, whale-watch, or just lie on the beach.

ISLA COIBA

Panama's largest island, **Coiba**  (www.coibanationalpark.com) is one of the most pristine natural areas anywhere in Central America. The **Coiba National Park** encompasses 38 islands and islets, not to mention the waterways between them, extending to 270,128 hectares (667,500 acres), leading some to call it the region's Galapagos. Primarily reached on day trips from the town of **Santa Catalina**, the park is home to the second-largest coral reef in the eastern Pacific, which is teeming with whales, hammerheads, nurse sharks, manta rays, crocodiles, and sea turtles, plus another 36 species of mammals on land. For almost 90 years, until 2004, there was a penal colony on Isla Coiba, which kept most tourists and developers away. Now that it's gone, tourists are slowly arriving to dive the waters at Granito de Oro and hike the jungle trails of Coiba.

Looking out over the Coiba archipelago.

⊙ POLLERAS OF AZUERO

The complexly designed *pollera* costumes are widely considered to be one of the world's most beautiful forms of traditional dress. While the Spanish colonial dress was common in haciendas throughout Latin America, the most famous *polleras* come from the Azuero peninsula. Worn during special occasions, these *polleras* consist of a one-piece skirt layered with petticoats, which are intricately embroidered with floral designs and trimmed with lace. Accessories include gold and pearl jewelry called *mosquetas* and *tembelques*, which are passed down from one generation to the next. Each dress takes months to make and they can cost thousands of dollars. Panamanian women generally own two *polleras* in their life: one before they are 16 and another in adulthood.

THE CHIRIQUÍ HIGHLANDS

Adventure seekers, bird-watchers, and coffee geeks are quickly discovering Panama's highest mountains. The Chiriquí region, which has seen a surge of expats buying homes and opening businesses, is quickly becoming one of the most exciting destinations in Panama. It is rich in biodiversity, with the region's unspoiled forests home to hundreds of rare birds, such as the resplendent quetzal and blue cotinga, while raging rivers are ideal for rafting and cloud forest trails that few have trodden await.

DAVID

The transportation hub of western Panama and the country's third largest city, **David** ⑯, a 45-minute drive from the Costa Rica border, is surprisingly flat. Set in the sweltering heat of the coastal plain, many only fly here or get off a bus before heading straight up the mountain to explore the cooler climate. Still, the town, while spread out, has a few blocks of colonial charm at Barrio Bolívar, and there are fine dining restaurants like Cuatro (www.restaurantecuatro.com) and swanky old hotels like the Gran Hotel Nacional (www.hotelnacionalpanama.com), which has added a quirky casino and movie theater complex.

VOLCÁN AND AROUND

On the lower slopes of the Barú Volcano, the town of **Volcán** ⑰ is characterized by its alpine-like climate and patches of small farms that surround a modern, bustling center. It's a good base for exploring the highlands and sits in close proximity to several major attractions.

About 5.5km (3 miles) southwest of Volcán is **Sitio Barriles** (daily 7am–5pm), one of Panama's few Pre-Colombian archeological sites. Discovered on the private land of the Landau family as they were building a coffee plantation, the site was once home to the Barriles culture, which was based in the area from 600–300 BC until the eruption of Barú forced them out. Hundreds of tools, ceramics, and a burial tomb with funerary urns have

Finca Lerida, a coffee plantation in Boquete.

been found here, although only some of the finds are on display.

The rich volcanic soil surrounding Volcán has turned it into a haven for coffee farmers, and several offer tours of their plantations. Just west of town, the **Janson Coffee Farm** grows eco-friendly, organic beans that are hand-picked and roasted in small batches, a process that can be seen on several short tours, run by Lagunas Adventures (tel: 6569-7494; www.lagunasadventures. com), of their plantation and production facility. More remote is **Finca Hartmann** (tel: 6450-1853), near the town of Santa Clara, 27km (17 miles) from Volcán. The stunning setting within the dense forests is a favorite for its bird-watching, as it sits in the north–south corridor of migrating birds. Short tours of the coffee production facilities are offered, though bird-focused visitors will often stay for a few days to camp out in the finca's rustic cabins and hike through an extensive network of trails through the plantation.

BOQUETE AND AROUND

The major tourist destination in Panama's highlands is without a doubt, **Boquete 18**, which has attracted a diverse population of North American and European expats who have moved here by the planeload to take advantage of the year-round, spring-like climate. On the shore of the Caldera River and backed by the steep slopes of the Barú volcano, the town itself is quite charming and provides easy access to numerous adventure activities and coffee fincas.

Boquete and its immediate surroundings are full of interesting amenities like the **Boquete Brewing Company** (www.boquetebrewingcompany. com), the Café Kotowa coffee shop, and **Boquete Bees** (www.boquetebees.com), a coffee farm and honey plant that produces gourmet honeys from native pollinators. There is a better selection of accommodations in Boquete than just

about anywhere in Panama, ranging from the rustic Panamonte Inn & Spa, which dates from 1914 and is home to renowned chef Charlie Collins, to the posh Finca Lerida (www.fincalerida.com), on one of the region's most historic coffee estates.

Some of Boquete's most spectacular scenery is located on the hills above town, best reached by car. The paved **Bajo Mono Loop**, taking a left past the church at the end of town, gives phenomenal views of town below, as does the **Volcancito Loop**, reached by making a right after the CEFATI visitor center. On the main highway heading toward the Caribbean coast, the route winds through the lush forests to **Finca La Suiza** (www.fincalasuizapanama.com), set out over 81 hectares (200 acres). The property is intersected by three lengthy hiking trails through cloud and tropical forests that are home to waterfalls and spectacular vistas.

OUTSIDE OF BOQUETE

What Panama lacks in volume in terms of coffee, it makes up for it in quality.

The small but popular town of Boquete.

Shade-grown varieties grown in the rich volcanic soil have given Panama a name in the premium coffee market, surging past the better-known Costa Rica. In particular, it's the varietal called Gesha, or Geisha, a plant of Ethiopian origins that mutated in Boquete's climate, giving it tea-like qualities that have helped make it the most expensive coffee in the world. One of the oldest producers in the region, **Casa Ruiz** (www.caferuiz-boquete.com), offers guided tours led by Ngäbe-Buglé guides on Mon–Sat. It's the largest operation in the area. **Café Kotowa** (www.kotowacoffee.com) was founded more than a century ago by a Scottish immigrant whose original water-powered mill is now where they hold their cuppings at the end of the tour. Finca Lerida, mentioned above, also offers tours to non-guests.

The Chiriquí Highlands offer some of the best whitewater rafting in Central America, ranging from intense Class III to V kayaking and rafting to relaxed floats, to take in the mountain landscape. The Chiriquí River, and more remote Chiriquí Viejo River, feature the most technical whitewater, with Class III to Class V rapids. These rivers can only be rafted from July to November when water levels are high. The Class II Esti River is the tamest experience, suitable for families with young children, while the Class II-III Gariche River is slightly more technical. Two rafting agencies run trips: Chiriquí River Rafting (tel: 720-1505; www.panama-rafting.com) and Boquete Outdoor Adventures (tel: 720-2284; www.boqueteoutdoor adventures.com).

VOLCÁN BARÚ NATIONAL PARK

Covering the Pacific side of the 3,475m (11,500ft) extinct Barú Volcano, the highest point in Panama, the **Volcán Barú National Park** is one of the most well-trodden in Panama, for good reason. Encompassing 14,000 hectares (34,600 acres) of primary and secondary forest, the park is a biodiversity hotspot with rare flora and fauna that includes more than 250 species of birds, like the resplendent quetzal and the three-wattled bellbird, plus giant

Car with tourists on a trail to the top of Volcán Barú.

oak trees that are hundreds of years old, and dozens of species of orchids that aren't found anywhere else. Entrance fees are paid at the ranger stations of the Los Quetzales trailhead 8km (5 miles) from Boquete at Alto Chiquero, as well as on the other side, closer to the higher altitude Cerro Punta at El Respingo.

BOCAS DEL TORO

Near the border with Costa Rica, the archipelago of **Bocas del Toro** ⑳ is comprised of seven islands and another 200 or so islets renowned for their unspoiled beaches and laid back, Caribbean vibes. The English-speaking islands have become ecotourism hotspots, with isolated rainforest lodges and over-water bungalows where snorkeling and surfing are as easy as rolling out of a hammock. Much of the archipelago is uninhabited, aside from the pastel-painted houses on Isla Colón and a few Ngäbe-Buglé communities farther afield, allowing the trickle of tourists to live out their tropical fantasies.

ISLA COLÓN

The hub of all activity in the archipelago, the 62 sq km (24 sq mile) **Isla Colón** is home to Bocas Town, the regional capital. Much of the town's infrastructure dates from the early 1900s, when United Fruit arrived to install banana plantations on the islands, attracting thousands of immigrants from Jamaica and the Colombian islands of San Andrés and Providencia. The town thrived until the 1930s, when banana blight forced the plantations to move to the mainland; it wasn't until recent decades, when tourism picked up, that any sort of development returned.

Bocas Town sits on a small peninsula with a bustling waterfront where boats to the mainland at Almirante or Changuinola closer to the border can be found, as well as boats to other islands. The airport, just outside of town, offers daily flights to Panama City and David.

While upscale travelers usually head straight for the eco-resorts on more remote islands, backpackers tend to base themselves within the

Overwater villas at Punta Caracol Hotel, Isla Colón.

town's weathered wooden houses, which have been converted into quaint hotels, funky restaurants and yoga studios. The only nightlife in the island's is concentrated here and the less developed **Isla Carenero**, often on bars set on decks over the water. There are several surf schools based in Bocas Town, such as Mono Loco (www.monolocosurfschool.com), as well as PADI certified dive schools, like Bocas Dive Center (www.bocasdivecenter.com), which all run trips to outer islands and can arrange all-inclusive packages with accommodations.

Isla Colón isn't much of a beach destination, although the golden sand of **Bluff Beach**, 8km (5 miles) by bicycle or taxi from Bocas Town, is worth the effort if short on time. A better alternative is to go on a tour to Bocas del Drago beach on the far north side of the island, where there's good snorkeling. The tours also usually stop at **Swan's Cay**, a bird sanctuary, and **Starfish Beach**, with lots of tropical fish and a seabed full of starfish. The other option is to take a boat to nearby **Isla Bastimentos**.

Additionally, there are several large resorts on remote parts of Isla Colón, such as the air-conditioned Playa Tortuga (www.hotelplayatortuga.com) at Playa Big Creek and the rustic bungalows set directly over turquoise waters at Punta Caracol Acqua Lodge (www.puntacaracol.com.pa).

ISLA BASTIMENTOS

The second largest island in the Bocas del Toro archipelago, **Isla Bastimentos** is dominated by the **Isla Bastimentos National Marine Park**, which includes jungle-backed beaches with powdery white sand and the pristine coral formations just off-shore. Bastimentos is much more relaxed than Bocas Town, with just one small creole town of 200 called **Old Bank** on the western corner of the island, a 15-minute boat ride from Isla Colón. There are a few basic hostels in town, though many come to stay at more isolated resorts like the Red Frog Beach Club (www.redfrogbeach.com) or Tranquilo Bay (www.tranquilobay.com). The nearest beach to Old Bank is **Wizard Beach**, a short walk away and

Kuna Yala women.

a beginner surf spot, though **Red Frog Beach** is much better and can easily be reached on a day trip from Bocas Town. The only other communities on Bastimentos are at Bahía Honda and Salt Creek Village, home to Ngäbe people and one nice resort, La Loma Jungle Lodge (www.thejunglelodge.com), which has its own cacao farm.

The national park extends 12,950 hectares (32,000 acres), most of which cover the reefs, which are notable for their wealth of coral species, fish, and marine invertebrates that range from healthy populations of Elkhorn coral to spotted eagle rays. Leatherback turtles and hawksbill turtles, among others, nest on the 5.6km-long (3.5 miles) Playa Larga on the northern shore. The Zapatilla Cays, named for their resemblance to footprints, are uninhabited inlets with turquoise waters and swaying palms, widely regarded as the best beaches in Bocas.

OTHER ISLANDS

Off the southern end of Isla Bastimentos is **Crawl Cay**, about 30 minutes by boat from Bocas Town. The shallow water surrounding the cay is home to soft and hard coral that make it a favorite of divers and snorkelers. Additionally, there are two simple restaurants on the cay, making it a popular day trip.

South of Isla Colón is **Isla Cristóbal**, one of the larger islands in the archipelago. While the island itself is of little interest, an enclosed bay, **Laguna Bocatorito**, is a breeding site for bottlenose dolphins. They are best seen from June to September, when they often swim right up to the boats.

COMARCA KUNA YALA

The semi-autonomous indigenous province of the Kuna Yala, sometimes referred to as the San Blas archipelago, is a paradisiacal place consisting of 350 of the Caribbean's most spectacular small islands and cays. Many of the islands are just a strip of powdery white

sand backed by a few palm trees and ringed with untouched coral reefs. This is the home of the Kuna who have maintained their cultural identity and control all aspects of tourism to the islands.

Despite the spectacular setting, the Kuna have not allowed mass tourism to permeate the islands. There are no five-star lodges here, just rustic bungalows that lack modern amenities. Even getting hold of them is difficult. Still, with the ability to take quick flights from Panama City to several islands or drive in a short amount of time into the Comarca on the El Llano–Cartí road and take a boat, the effort to reach the region is not nearly as difficult as it once was.

ISLA EL PORVENIR AND THE WEST

El Porvenir is the base for the western half of the **Comarca Kuna Yala** ㉑. The most regular flights to the region from Panama City land on the tiny airstrip here. There's a small museum and government offices, although little else other than the experience of immersing

An islet in the Comarca Kuna Yala.

yourself in Kuna life. Hotel El Porvenir (www.hotelporvenir.com) offers rooms just beside the airstrip, though there are better, more expensive accommodations on nearby islands, such as Cabañas Narasgandup (www.sanblaskunayala.com). Many travelers catch a boat elsewhere as soon as they land or simply take day trips.

Tiny Isla Hierba has the closest good beach to El Porvenir, while for snorkeling, **Isla Perro** – with a sunken boat off shore – is better. Not much farther out you come to **Isla Pelicano**, which has a white sandy beach. Many of the lodges near El Porvenir will include transportation to these islands in their rates.

The stunning chain of cays called the **Cayos Holandéses** has the best marine life in the area, although they're 20km (13 miles) away. They have few amenities and the 1.5-hour boat ride each way can be expensive for solo travelers.

THE EASTERN COMARCA

Less visited than the west, the eastern half of the Comarca Kuna Yala is more remote and has been more westernized.

Air Panama flights from Panama City go to Achutupu, Corazón de Jesús, and Playón Chico, but only sporadically, and without a yacht there's little other way of getting there. Some of the better accommodations in the region can be found here, however, such as Yandup Island Lodge (www.yandupisland.com). Still, the marine life in this region is quite good, with some of the highest concentrations of coral in Panama.

THE DARIÉN PROVINCE

On its journey between Alaska and southern Chile, the Pan-American highway makes one break, which is in Panama's Darién Province, bordering Colombia. The Darién Gap, as it is called, is composed of nearly a million hectares (2.4 million acres) of virgin rainforest which teems with diverse flora and fauna, all within the boundaries of the Darién National Park, Panama's largest protected area and a Unesco Biosphere Reserve. While much of the interior is rugged and difficult to reach, the coastlines offer some opportunities to travelers.

⊘ THE KUNA YALA

Spread out across 49 communities in the Comarca, there are an estimated 50,000 Kuna people, also known as Guna, living in much in the same way they have for centuries. During the time of conquest, many were living in what is today known as the Darién, but fighting with the Catio people and Spanish forced them to the islands. Within the Comarca, each community has its own political organization, led by a political and spiritual leader called a *saila*, who sings the legends and laws of the Kuna people. He is accompanied by one or two *voceros*, who help interpret the songs. Kuna families are traditionally matrilineal, as the groom becomes a part of the bride's family and takes her last name.

In Panama City, the Kuna, who speak a Chibchan language, stand out as they wander through Casco Viejo, wearing their brightly colored headscarves, gold septum rings, and arms and legs covered with beaded bracelets. The Kuna are most famous for their colorful *molas*, a textile art form made of appliqué and reverse appliqué techniques, which are worn daily by most Kuna women. Trade of the *molas*, along with that of lobster and coconuts, has allowed the Kuna to function independently while other indigenous groups in Panama have had much difficulty in maintaining their culture.

WESTERN DARIÉN

Before the Pan-American Highway ends near the town of Metetí, the owners of the more established birding lodges (Canopy Tower and Canopy Lodge) operate Canopy Camp Darien (www.canopytower.com/canopy-camp). This upscale, all-inclusive tent camp borders the edge of the 26,000-hectare (65,000-acre) **Serrania Filo del Tallo Hydrological Reserve**, which offers opportunities to see harpy eagles and other rare species of birds and mammals.

DARIÉN NATIONAL PARK

Central America's largest of its kind, **Darién National Park ㉒** is a Unesco World Biosphere Reserve, covers 575,000 hectares (1.4 million acres). Rarely visited, it is rich with biodiversity, ranging from coastal lagoons to untouched rainforest where jaguars and ocelots have been allowed to flourish. It's one of the top ten birdwatching destinations on earth, where rare species like red-throated caracaras and golden-headed quetzals are seen with ease.

Without a guide, the park is inaccessible. Apart from Ancon Expeditions (www.anconexpeditions.com), few guides are equipped to handle trips to either of the access points at Cerro Pirre peak on the north side of the park, or the Cana Field Station toward the southeast. Amenities are non-existent other than simple bunks at the ranger stations. From either entrance point, trails lead deep into the interior of the park and some rivers can be traversed by dugout canoe.

THE SOUTH COAST

Most who come to **Piñas Bay** do so for one reason: sport fishing. Within 20km (12 miles) of the shore, hundreds of fishing records have been broken, a fame that attracts an elite clientele. They stay at the surprisingly simple **Tropic Star Lodge** (www.tropicstar.com), which was founded as a private fishing retreat for a Texas oil tycoon. Billfish like black marlin and sailfish are caught from a fleet of 9.4-meter (31ft) Bertram boats that ply the waters off Zane Grey reef.

Dawn at Cerro Pirre peak in Darién National Park.

Tourists exploring the Mayan temple at Caracol, Belize.

CENTRAL AMERICA

TRAVEL TIPS

OVERVIEW

ACCOMMODATIONS

Central America offers accommodations of all types, from seedy and ramshackle to ultra-luxurious. Very remote destinations tend to have options on the extreme ends of the spectrum, including luxury hotels or eco lodges, along with sketchy sailor hangouts where you won't want to take the kids. In most places you will be expected to drop toilet paper in a waste basket, not the toilet itself, because the plumbing can't cope. Major cities, particularly the capitals, will tend to have the greatest variety of accommodations, from hostels to luxury chain hotels catering to business travelers. Quality in most countries is improving, and nearly all hotels will offer guests wireless internet – although some business hotels will charge a fee.

CLIMATE AND WHEN TO GO

In Central America, temperature depends greatly on altitude above sea level, and temperate climates can be found among mountain landscapes away from the coasts. Hot, tropical temperatures tend to prevail throughout the year in the lowlands and islands. There's usually still plenty of sunshine during the wetter months, although humidity will be at its highest. Most visitors tend to plan their travels around the dry season in the region, which is roughly from November through May. The rainy season lasts from around April to December, while hurricanes typically appear in the region from September to November, or in June and July in the Yucatan.

Take light, breathable summer clothes, plus some additional warm layers if you plan on spending time in the mountains. Note that shorts and very skimpy tops are frowned upon in churches. In the highlands, a sweater should suffice in the evenings. Good hiking boots are an essential investment for trekking. Pack some high-factor sunscreen and lip salve, and bring or buy a hat. A money belt is handy so that you can avoid carrying all your money in one place. Don't forget rechargeable batteries and a recharger for any electrical equipment, perhaps taking along a multi-outlet charging strip for rooms with just one outlet.

CRIME AND SAFETY

The crime rate is generally high in Central America, but risks can be minimized by taking a few basic precautions:

Expensive jewelry should not be worn and large amounts of money and valuable watches should be kept out of sight.

Scam attempts abound, including soiling clothes with all manner of substances. Ignore offers of help by passers-by and clean up in a safe place.

Wear a money belt when traveling.

Keep an eye on your possessions at all times, especially on beaches, and use hotel safes whenever possible (but take a verified list of what you have deposited).

Do not leave valuables in cars.

Avoid walking alone and in deserted areas after dark. Traveling alone after dusk is not advisable.

Never carry packages for other people without checking the contents.

Radio taxis are safer than curbside taxis after dark.

Don't hitchhike. For journeys overland choose well-known and established bus companies when possible.

Carry your passport at all times – and leave a photocopy in your hotel.

For specific inquiries, contact your embassy. The US State Department and the British Foreign Office both publish detailed information on all Central American countries and offer advice to travelers. Their websites are, respectively:
US: http://travel.state.gov
UK: www.fco.gov.uk

EMBASSIES AND CONSULATES

The US, Canada, and the UK have embassies and consulates throughout Central America, while services for residents of Australia, New Zealand, Ireland, and South Africa tend to be limited. For directories of diplomatic services, see the following web pages:
US: www.usembassy.gov
UK: www.fco.gov.uk
Canada: www.international.gc.ca
Australia: www.dfat.gov.au
Ireland: www.dfa.ie
New Zealand: www.mfat.govt.nz

ENTRY REQUIREMENTS AND CUSTOMS REGULATIONS

Visas

Residents from major English-speaking countries rarely need visas to travel in Central America, as long as passports are valid for more than six months. It is essential to check current entry requirements well in advance of departure.

Customs

In many countries, luggage is X-rayed as it passes through customs, and it is illegal to introduce food and plants. In general, if you are taking $10,000 or more in currency it must be declared. Check the individual country regulations for the introduction of pets. As narcotics smuggling is a problem throughout the region, be prepared for frequent checks. If you are coming to live in Central America, the entry of household goods is likely to be a time-consuming affair in most of the region.

ETIQUETTE

Central Americans appreciate courtesy and will be offended by someone who is incapable of saying a simple 'buenos días' (before noon) or 'buenas tardes' (later in the day), when starting a conversation. Locations such as churches and restaurants may refuse entry to improperly dressed people. Visitors should, in any case, show respect for local sensibilities by not wearing skimpy clothing in inappropriate situations. They should also remember that most people they encounter will have had fewer advantages in life and should be treated with the appropriate respect. At the same time, be firm as well as polite when being approached and always ask for prices in advance of any services.

HEALTH AND MEDICAL CARE

Consult your local public health service before leaving home and be sure to get a certificate for any vaccination you have. The most common illnesses are picked up from contaminated food and water, so you should pay particular attention to what you eat and drink. Be particularly wary of street food, ensuring that it is cooked before your eyes. The quality of tap water in much of Central America is unreliable. You are advised to drink only bottled or boiled water, or to take purifying tablets. Hepatitis, picked up from contaminated food and water, is common, and all travelers should get immunized against the disease.

Malaria occurs in jungle areas of Central America, though the risk is relatively low. Consult with your doctor if you have a concern about a particular region.

Yellow fever, transmitted to humans by mosquitoes, is prevalent in the whole of Central America. You are therefore advised to seek immunization. A yellow-fever shot protects you for 10 years, but is effective only after 10 days, so plan ahead.

Your physician or, in the UK, the Medical Advisory Service for Travellers Abroad (MASTA), tel: 0906-822-4100; www.masta-travel-health.com, will advise you about other tropical diseases that may be endemic in the area you are visiting – such as dengue fever and the Zika virus. All travelers should check that they are inoculated against tetanus, typhoid, and polio. You should take with you some form of remedy for stomach upsets and diarrhea, which is likely to be the main complaint of most travelers. Imodium is a useful travel companion, but note that this medication treats the symptoms rather than the cause. Sipping water with a pinch of salt and sugar added can help rehydrate you after a bout of diarrhea.

The other main cause of illness is the heat. Have respect for the power of the tropical sun: wear a hat, use high-factor sunscreen, and be sure to drink plenty of fluids.

LOST PROPERTY

Be careful with your property as theft is a problem in many cities and on domestic bus routes. Do not necessarily expect lost property to be returned, but a quick return or telephone call to your hotel or the restaurant you were eating in may well help you recover that misplaced item.

MONEY

Changing money

You can change money in banks, casas de cambio (exchange bureaus), and larger hotels; casas de cambio usually give the best rate of exchange. US dollars are the most convenient foreign cash and are the official currency of Panama and El Salvador, but avoid denominations greater than $50 bills because they may not be accepted for fear they could be fake or drug money. Also, only bring bills in good condition, because some exchange bureaus can be sniffy about old ones. It is worth using a calculator, as some rates of exchange run into the thousands.

Cash

Unless staying trapped inside a beach resort, you will always need to carry some local cash with you, of course, and should think ahead if you are traveling into a rural area for some time, but try not to exceed the amount covered by your insurance policy. It is also advisable to hoard coins and small bills when you get them, as exact change is often in short supply, especially outside the cities.

Credit and debit cards are also widely accepted, with ATMs (cash machines) located in most cities. Before leaving home, memorize your PIN, and check handling fees and coverage in the event of loss or robbery. Many establishments also add their own supplementary charges.

Traveler's checks in US dollars have lost much of their convenience with the spread of ATMs. While generally safe and acceptable all over Central America, they may not be the best option as there may be high fees and time involved in cashing them. Pounds sterling and euros are not worth bringing. See the separate Money sections for each country for more detailed information.

Finally, it is worth remembering the advice: pack half the clothes you think you'll need, but twice the money.

Tipping

Many hotels and resorts add a service charge to the bill; inquire when you're there, and if not, then tipping between 10 and 15 percent will generally suffice. Visitors will often tip exceptional guides as well; in this case, 10 percent is the norm.

PHOTOGRAPHY

Digital photography has taken over most of Central America, just like the rest of the world. Film is still available in larger centers, although it can be expensive. Note that it is forbidden to photograph military sites (including ports, transportation terminals, and bridges). It is best to ask permission if you are unsure. Many people, particularly from indigenous cultures, are sensitive about having their photo taken, so always ask permission first. Many will ask for a tip (propina).

SHOPPING

Many of Central America's best bargains are still to be found in the local markets, where prices are low and the choice of goods extensive. Jewelry, textiles, sweaters, ponchos, and leather goods are all widely produced. A certain amount of haggling with traders is expected, but be careful not to go too far; think of your income compared to theirs.

TELECOMMUNICATIONS

Central America has gleefully participated in the global boom in mobile telecommunications, particularly as many state-owned telephone companies were woefully slow to extend service. In most countries, it is possible to buy GSM SIM cards for use with unlocked cellphones; nevertheless, check to see if your phone runs on the right bandwidth. Access to the internet is common in most hotels and the occasional internet café, though it can be painfully slow outside of the main towns. Hotel rates for telephone calls are typically very high in international hotel chains, but there are plenty of kiosks offering telephone services – sometimes right on the street. Rollout of 3G and 4G networks allows you to use VOIP for long-distance calls.

TOURIST INFORMATION

While ever-increasing travel information is available on the internet, tourist offices at airports and large bus and ferry terminals will also have information on accommodations and sights to help you when you arrive. Smaller destinations that have a fair number of tourist arrivals – like Copán Ruinas, Bocas del Toro, or Granada – also have tourism offices in town. Better first-hand information will often be available at smaller hotels catering to foreign visitors.

TOUR OPERATORS

You can make reservations for tailor-made trips to the world's most exciting destinations with **Insight Guides** – visit www.insightguides.com to speak to a local expert.

In the US

Exito travel, specializes in airline tickets to Latin America, 108 Rutgers Ave, Fort Collins, CO 80525, tel: 800-655-4053 from the US, 800-670-2605 from Canada, www.exitotravel.com.
Viaventure, offers bespoke tours to every Central American country, tel: 502-7934-6687, www.viaventure.com

In the UK

Latin American Travel Association, produces a useful guide to Latin America and lists all the main travel companies that operate there. Tel: 020-8715 2913, www.lata.org.
Dragoman Overland, adventure group tours. Camp Green, Debenham, Suffolk IP14 6LA, tel: 01728-861133, www.dragoman.com.
Exodus, adventure group tours. Grange Mills, Weir Road, London SW12, tel: 020-8675 5550, www.exodus.co.uk.
Explore Worldwide, adventure group tours. Nelson House, 55 Victoria Road, Farnborough, Hampshire, GU14 7PA, tel: 0845-291 4542, www.explore.co.uk.
Journey Latin America, flights, tailor-made itineraries, escorted tours, and adventure trips. 12–13 Heathfield Terrace, Chiswick, London W4 4JE, tel: 020-3582 8754, www.journeylatin america.co.uk.
STA, specialists in student and under-26 fares, tours, and hotels, with 400 branches worldwide. Tel: 0871-2300040, www.statravel.co.uk.
Trailfinders, long-haul flights and tailor-made vacations. 194 Kensington High Street, W8 7RG, tel: 0845-0546060, www.trailfinders.com.

In Australia/New Zealand

STA, specialists in student and under-26 travel. 841 George Street, Sydney 2000, NSW, tel: 02-9212 1255, call center 134-783, www.statravel.com.au. 130 Cuba Street, Wellington 6001, tel: 0800474 400, www.statravel.co.nz.

In Canada

Canoe.ca, Online travel service that organizes trips to much of Central America, 333 King Street, Toronto, ON, M5A 3X5, http://travel.canoe.ca.

In Ireland

Trailfinders, long-haul flights and tailor-made vacations. 4/5 Dawson Street, Dublin 2, tel: 01-677 7888.

TRANSPORTATION

Getting there

The normal way to arrive in Central America is, of course, by plane. The main departure hubs for flights from Europe are Madrid (where UK passengers join flights booked from London or other UK airports), and Miami, New York, and Houston in the US. There are flights to San José, San Pedro Sula, and other Central American destinations from Toronto, Canada. Numerous cruise ships, however, also call at ports along the Caribbean coast of Central America, sometimes continuing on through the Panama Canal. There is no way to arrive directly by road as none have been built to cross the Darien Gap between Panama and Colombia.

Getting around

Most travel is done by overland bus or plane, with ferries playing a great role in the islands. Safety along the main lines has improved much in recent years, although irresponsible bus and truck drivers are a problem. Car rental is generally quite inexpensive throughout the region, however mandatory insurance in some countries will drive up the cost significantly. Driving is relatively straightforward if one is careful to expect the unexpected and drives defensively.

WHAT TO READ

The Full Montezuma by Peter Moore. The tale of one couple's hilarious travels around Central America, from Mayan sites to tropical beaches. *Enrique's Journey* by Sonia Nazario. A visceral telling of the experience of illegal immigration from Central America to the United States. *The Maya* by Michael D. Coe and Stephen D. Houston. This introduction to Central America's most important civilization is a must read for those interested in the region.

Other Insight Guides titles covering Central America include *Guatemala, Belize and the Yucatan*, *Mexico, Belize*, and *Costa Rica*.

WOMEN TRAVELERS

While Latin American courtesy dictates a certain deference to women, machismo and prejudice about 'liberal' attitudes may easily make some men think that foreign women – particularly those traveling alone – are easily seduced. Advances can be irritating but are rarely aggressive. If politeness fails, it is perfectly fine simply to leave. In the street, refusal to acknowledge 'chat-up' attempts usually works, except with the most persistent. It is normally easy and safe to join other travelers on the backpacking circuit.

SOUTHERN MEXICO

FACT FILE

Area: 1,972,500 sq km (758,000 sq miles) (whole of Mexico)
Capital: Mexico City
Population: 122 million (*Mexico)
Currency: Peso
Language: Spanish
Weights and measures: Metric
Electricity: 110 volts, 60-cycle current.
Dialling code: 52
Internet abbreviation: .mx

GETTING THERE

By air from the US and Canada

Frequent flights, scheduled and charter, run to Cancún from every part of the US and Canada. There are also scheduled flights to Mérida from Miami and Houston, and to Cozumel from Atlanta, Dallas, Charlotte, Houston, Newark, and Toronto. Both airports have additional charter and seasonal services.

By air from Europe

Direct flights to Cancún from Europe are provided by Iberia from Madrid, British Airways from London, and Air Berlin from Düsseldorf, but there are also many charter flights. The most common way to get there by scheduled flight is via a change in the US, usually in Miami or Houston.

GETTING AROUND

The Yucatán is easy to get to and to get around. There are abundant international flights into Cancún, and to some other airports. Unless you have a car, buses provide the main means of getting around, but

Mexico's domestic flight network can be useful for making short hops quickly. Aeroméxico Connect and Interjet are the main domestic airlines.

Cancún Airport (www.cancun-airport.com) is 15km (9 miles) south of the city and has two main terminals. Most US and European airlines use Terminal 3; most Mexican airlines, Air Canada, and some others use Terminal 2. A free shuttle bus runs between them. ADO airport buses run every 30 minutes from Terminal 2 to the bus station in downtown Cancún, and once or twice an hour to Playa del Carmen.

Ferries to the islands

Cozumel

Passenger ferries run from **Playa del Carmen**. The two companies, Mexico and Ultramar, run ferries almost every hour, daily 6am–11pm. A one-way fare is about US$12. Car ferries are operated by Transbordadores del Caribe (www.transcaribe.net) and run from **Puerto Calica**, south of Playa, 2–4 times daily.

Holbox

The ferry port is tiny **Chiquilá**, a 2–3-hour drive from Cancún. Boats make the crossing every 1–2 hours between 6am–7pm; the fare is about US$6. Second-class buses run to Chiquilá and back from Cancún and Mérida. Drivers can leave cars in safe parking lots in Chiquilá for about US$5 a day.

Isla Mujeres

There are passenger ferries from **Puerto Juárez**, north of Cancún, run by the Magaña and Ultramar companies. Both sail every 30 minutes from 6am–midnight with the same fare, around US$6. Buses R-1 and R-13 run to Puerto Juárez from Av Tulum in Cancún. Car ferries run

from **Punta Sam**, five times each way daily.

By bus

The bus is a basic Mexican institution: every village has a bus or *combi* service of some sort, so there really is nowhere that cannot be reached by public transportation. **First-class** buses are air-conditioned, modern, and very comfortable. All luggage is checked in, and buses are usually very punctual. **Second-class** buses provide local services. They are cheaper, less comfortable, and naturally slower than first-class. There are also *intermedio* services, which stop often but have first-class comfort. The most important are the **Riviera** shuttle buses that run every 15 minutes between Cancún and Playa del Carmen, and Mayab buses (one or more each hour) which run the length of the Riviera between Cancún and Tulum.

Car rental

All the main international chains have franchises in Mexico and you can now get very good rates by booking online. If you decide to rent a car once you're in Mexico, you will often get better deals from small local agencies, particularly in Mérida. To rent a car in Mexico you must be over 21 and have your driving licence, passport, and a credit card.

Taxis

Most Mexican taxis do not have meters; instead there are fixed rates for each area, which are posted at taxi stands. In Cancún taxi rates are higher in the Hotel Zone than in the city. The general rules are: get an idea of what the correct rates should be, and always agree a fare before getting into a cab.

A-Z

Accommodations

The Yucatán can cater to pretty much all tastes: options run from glittering beach palaces to small town hotels with whirring roof fans. For extra graciousness, there are elegant hotels in restored colonial *haciendas*, and there's a growing number of charming, individually run small hotels and B&Bs, especially in Mérida and Campeche. As alternatives to big resorts, the coasts and islands offer a seductive variety of romantic palm-roofed cabins by the beach – from basic to luxury standard.

Hotel prices are higher overall – often a lot higher – in Cancún, Isla Mujeres, Cozumel, and the *Riviera Maya* than in the rest of the Yucatán, and have soared recently in Tulum. Hotel rates, especially in resort areas, rise about 10 or 15 percent in the peak season, with additional price hikes for Christmas, New Year, and Easter.

Arts

The relics of ancient Maya civilization naturally provide the core of the Yucatán's museums. The region's most important collections of Maya artifacts are in Mérida's Museo de Antropología e Historia and Campeche's Museo de Cultura Maya, dramatically located in the old Spanish fort of San Miguel south of the town. There are also impressive displays in the museums at the Maya sites of Chichén Itzá, Uxmal, Dzibilchaltún, and Palenque.

Mérida is the only city in the region that has an established contemporary art scene, with an attractive showcase in the form of the MACAY museum (www.macay.org). Temporary art exhibitions are also shown in Museo de la Ciudad and Centro Cultural de Olimpo on the Plaza Mayor.

Budgeting for your trip

The *Riviera Maya* has become increasingly expensive, but Yucatán state is cheaper, and costs fall radically in Campeche and Chiapas. To be comfortable, expect to spend around US$120 a day per person, although not traveling solo will obviously cut costs.

Airport transfer: *Colectivo* minibuses from either terminal direct to the beach hotels in Cancún re about US$15 per person, while taxis cost a rip-off US$60 to the Cancún hotel zone. From the airports in Mérida and Cozumel, taxis charge about US$15 to town.

Car rental: Rates generally start around US$60 per day, including full insurance in high season; cheaper rates are negotiable off-season. Four-wheel-drive vehicles start around US$70 per day.

Gasoline: $2.50 a gallon

Accommodations: Rustic beach bungalows and dorms (usually cold or shared showers and less privacy) for under $40 per night (double occupancy) can still be found in rural villages and isolated beach towns, though expect to pay anywhere from $70 to $120 a night (double occupancy) for moderate lodging (private baths, hot water, some views, parking, extra amenities).

Food: Street food can often be had for less than $1, while local places serve full meals for $5–10. In resorts and tourist areas the prices jump dramatically, ranging from $20–60 per meal, per person.

Museums and attractions: Virtually all archeological sites and major museums in Mexico are administered by the Instituto Nacional de Antropología e Historia (INAH). There are a few variations, but nearly all sites are open daily, 8am–5pm; museums are usually open the same hours, but are closed on Mondays. INAH has a standard set of charges and entry fees: Chichén Itzá costs US$13; Uxmal, Palenque and other large sites are $6–8; smaller sites charge $2–4. Museums cost $3–6.

Children

As a well-developed tourist area, the Riviera Maya naturally has extensive, purpose-built facilities for families that are not found elsewhere in the region, and every hotel over a certain size has a pool. However commercial they may feel to more hardened travelers, centers such as AquaWorld in Cancún and 'eco-parks' like Xcaret and Xel-Há provide a very safe, well-organized introduction to tropical nature, as well as activities such as snorkeling, and are likely to appeal to kids. Note that some luxury

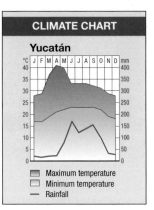

resorts on the Riviera Maya have a no kids policy.

Climate

The Yucatán is very flat and low-lying, so it's nearly always hot but rarely too humid inland around the major ruins. The central lowland forests in the southern Yucatán are hot and pretty humid all year round, but most manageable in the dry season, which starts in December and runs through April.

Severe storms can strike during hurricane season (June to October), but warnings are usually excellent locally, and Mexico has very high-standard hurricane precautions. If you hear of a storm, hotel owners will be able to pass on instructions.

Crime and safety

The Yucatán Peninsula has a much lower level of crime of any kind than other parts of Mexico. There's little or no threat from drug traffickers in this part of Mexico, but there is some petty crime such as bag thefts and pickpocketing in parts of the Riviera Maya, notably Cancún, Playa del Carmen, and Tulum. Elsewhere, be particularly careful not to leave anything valuable on the beach while swimming, and do not leave valuables in budget hotel rooms or basic beach cabañas that are easily broken into.

Customs regulations

Limits on goods that can be carried are similar to those in most countries. There are severe penalties for carrying drugs, weapons, or (when leaving) any item from any archeological site.

Disabled travelers

Disabled travelers will have a hard time in the Maya region, except in Cancún where the sidewalks are smooth and the hotels have elevators. Access for wheelchair users is usually non-existent everywhere else, and mobility is compounded by potholed sidewalks and roads, cobblestones, and an almost complete absence of elevators outside the five-star city-center hotels.

Eating out

In Mexico, the *tortilla* is also used as the basis of a number of delicious dishes that are now familiar all over the world. *Enchiladas* are *tortillas* stuffed with ground beef or cheese; *quesadillas* are *tortillas* covered with melted cheese; *tacos* are fried, filled *tortillas*, and *tostadas* are crispy, deep-fried *tortillas* served with salad. Other variants include *flautas*, *chimichangas*, and *tlacoyos*. Popular Yucatecan dishes include *cochinita pibil* (roasted suckling pig that is marinated with achiote), *papadzules* (tacos filled with hard-boiled eggs), and *sopa de lima* (chicken and tortilla soup with lime).

You will find plentiful seafood served near the coast. Snapper, grouper, barracuda, and shark are all popular, while lobster is on many upscale restaurant menus, as well as shrimp, crab, and conch; ceviche (raw seafood marinated in lime juice) is a favorite in many areas.

Restaurants

The humble *taco* cart and other street stands are ubiquitous in

Salbutes are puffed, deep fried tortillas.

places where locals live; the food is often at rock bottom prices and sometimes better than anything you will find in upscale restaurants. In resort areas along the Riviera Maya you will find many international chain restaurants, as well as most of the big American fast-food outlets and home-grown equivalents like Pollo Campero, which sells fried chicken.

Embassies and consulates

In Cancún

Canadian Consulate: Centro Empresarial, Oficina E7, Blvd Kukulcán Km 12; tel: 998 883 3360
British Vice-Consulate: Hotel Royal Sands, Blvd Kukulcán Km 13.5; tel: 998 881 0184
US Consulate: Blvd Kukulcán Km 13, Torre La Europea; tel: 998 883 0272

Emergencies

In **Mérida** the Tourist Police (tel: 999 925 2555) wear brown-and-white uniforms and patrol on foot or motorcycles. They are there to help, so don't be afraid to ask for assistance if you need it.
Police 999 925 2034

In Cancún

Police 060
Tourist Police 998 885 2277
Red Cross 998 884 1616

Etiquette

Politeness, a smile, and an effort to speak a little Spanish will help you get more out of Mexico. Public nudity is offensive in most of the region, but topless and nude bathing are now accepted in trendier parts of the Riviera Maya (Playa del Carmen, away from the main town beach, and Tulum).

Festivals

January–February

Carnival, a week-long pre-Lenten celebration with parades, floats, and dances, celebated in Cozumel, Campeche, Cancún, and several other towns.
La Candelaria, on Feb 2nd and around, in Valladolid and Chicxulub, is a Christian festival celebrating the presentation of Jesus at the Temple.

March–April

Equinox and Descent of Kukulcán, in Chichén Itzá on March 21.
Easter, when Ticul, Acanceh, and many other towns hold celebrations.

June

Marine Day fishing tournament in Cozumel. Some towns hold a fiesta in honor of San Pedro and San Pablo.

September

San Román, a week-long fiesta, is held in Campeche.
Cristo de las Ampollas (Christ of the Blisters), in Mérida until October.

October

Day of the Dead (*Hanal Pixan*), marked across the region.

November–December

Yucatán State Fair, in Xmatkuil, south of Mérida.
Virgin of Guadalupe, on December 12 and preceding days; processions all over Mexico.

Gay and lesbian travelers

Homosexuality is legal in Mexico, since there are no federal laws forbidding it, but cruising zones are occasionally targeted by police in campaigns to protect 'public morality,' making discretion wise. Cancún, Playa and Tulum are the exceptions, as they're much more in tune with US resorts than rural Mexico.

Health and medical care

It is essential to have a comprehensive travel insurance policy, with full medical cover including the option of repatriation by air in an emergency, when traveling in Mexico. There are no special precautions required, but it is advisable to be inoculated against tetanus, typhoid, and hepatitis A.

In the main cities and tourist areas there are well-equipped private hospitals with English-speaking staff that are the best places to head for to if you need any kind of treatment. In rural areas, there are public health centers (Centros de Salud), which are more basic but can still deal with emergencies. In most of Mexico there is a common phone number to call for all emergency services: 066 or 060.

Private clinics

Cancún: Amerimed Hospital, Av Tulum Sur Mza, 260; tel: 998 881 3400; www.amerimed.com.mx
Mérida: Centro Médico de las Américas, Calle 54, 365, off Av Pérez Ponce; tel: 999 927 3199; www.centromedicodelasamericas.com.mx

Media

Yucatán Today, a free monthly, is widely available and is very informative about activities and tourist amenities in Yucatán state. *The News*, an English-language daily produced in Mexico City, is available at some newsstands, and a special local Cancún edition of the *Miami Herald* is widely distributed, and often free in hotels. There are also innumerable free booklets and brochures including maps and information about the region: *Cancún Tips* is the best known, and distributed free to passengers arriving at Cancún Airport.

Money

The Mexican peso stands around 20 or 22 pesos to the dollar. Casas de Cambio change money, although the exchange rate is often better at a bank. ATMs (cash machines) are easy to find, but not in the more remote beach and rural areas. Along the Riviera Maya, dollars are widely accepted.

Opening hours

Banking hours are usually from 9am to any time between 3 and 7pm. Many stores close at lunchtime for a lengthy break, reopening around 4 or 5pm and remaining open until late evening. Larger stores and malls stay open all day.

Postal services

Post offices usually stay open all day (mornings only on Saturdays) but mail deliveries are very slow. The Mexican post office has a reliable courier service, Mexpost, and you should use this rather than standard mail when sending anything home.

Public holidays

January 1 New Year's Day
February 5 Constitution Day
February 24 Day of the Flag
March 21 Benito Juárez's birthday
March/April Good Friday and Easter Sunday
May 1 Labor Day
May 5 Victory Day
September 16 Independence Day
October 12 Día de la Raza
November 2 Day of the Dead
November 20 Revolution Day
December 12 Day of Our Lady of Guadalupe
December 25 Christmas Day

Shopping

Mérida is a good destination for traditional Yucatecan products like hammocks, baskets, belts, *huipiles* (embroidered smocks), Panama hats, *guayaberas* (loose shirts with large pockets), and many other kinds of craftwork, though small markets and stores can be found across the region. In Cancún, the Hotel Zone is packed with ritzy shopping malls, or plazas, lined with international designer stores.

Telecommunications

Telephones

In most towns there are private phone offices known as Casetas de Larga Distancia, though Skype or other internet call systems can cut costs considerably. For calls within Mexico, you must first dial an access code (01) before dialing the area code and number; for calls to the US and Canada use the prefix 00-1; for the rest of the world 00 followed by the country code.

Cellphone coverage is now good in most of the Yucatán Peninsula, but charges are high if you use a foreign cellphone. Mexican cellphone numbers have the same three-digit area codes, but the number after that often begins 11 or 01, and when calling from a local phone you may need to use a different access code

(044 or 045) rather than 01.
Operator assistance with making an international call **090**
Operator assistance with making a domestic call **020**

Internet

Even the smallest town seems to have at least one internet café, though nearly all hotels and many restaurants and cafés offer free Wi-Fi connections now.

Time zone

US Central standard time; GMT minus 6 hours.

Tourist information

The **State of Yucatán** has a useful tourism website (http://yucatan.travel/en/). You will find offices in downtown **Mérida** (Teatro Peón Contreras, Calle 60; tel: 999 930 3760) and in Campeche (Casa Seis, Plaza Principal; tel: 981 811 9229). In other towns there are local offices that do not give information by phone but can be useful for getting maps and leaflets on local tours.

Visas and passports

All visitors, including Canadian and US citizens, require a valid passport to enter Mexico. Visitors will be issued with a tourist card upon arrival, which will be marked with the permitted length of stay (usually 180 days). The card must be retained during a stay and surrendered on leaving the country.

What to read

Yucatán Before and After the Conquest by Diego de Landa, translated by William Gates. On-the-spot reporting of Maya culture from a friar who witnessed the advance of the conquistadors.
Incidents of Travel in Central America, Chiapas and Yucatán by John L. Stephens. One of the finest travel books ever written. Stephens and artist Catherwood traveled through the region during the Central American War but still managed to rediscover many ruins (including Copán) that were unknown in the West.
A Guide to the Birds of Mexico and Northern Central America by Steve N.G. Howell. The definitive reference book of the region's birds.

GUATEMALA

FACT FILE

Area: 108,888 sq km (42,042 sq miles)
Capital: Guatemala City
Population: 15.47 million
Currency: Guatemalan quetzal
Weights and measures: Generally metric
Electricity: 110 volts
Dialling code: 502
Internet abbreviation: GT

GETTING THERE

By air from the US, Canada, Europe, Australia, and New Zealand

Most flights to Guatemala are routed through US hub cities, including Atlanta, Chicago, Dallas, Houston, Los Angeles, Miami, and Newark. You'll also find flights via other Mexican and Central American hubs, including El Salvador (with Avianca; www.avianca.com), Mexico City (Aeroméxico; www.aeromexico.com and Interjet; www.interjet.com), and Panama (Copa; www.copair.com). Flying from Canada, you'll have to travel via one of the US gateway cities.

The main direct air itinerary linking Europe to Guatemala is from Madrid, flying with Spanish airline Iberia (www.copair.com). Travelers from the UK and Ireland can also choose to fly via one of the US gateway cities, or via Mexican or Central American hubs. All international flights land at La Aurora International Airport (tel: 502 2332 6084), 4 miles (6km) south of Guatemala City, except for a few regional flights from Belize and Cancún which land at Mundo Maya Airport in Flores (near Tikal).

By road

Buses are a popular way to enter Guatemala. Several bus services run from Mexico, Honduras, Belize, and El Salvador into Guatemala with the San Salvador–Guatemala City connection among the most frequent.

GETTING AROUND

Guatemala is a relatively small country, but the mountainous terrain and ancient buses mean that travel can be time-consuming. Stick to the main highways and things move reasonably well, but many of the minor routes are unpaved, and the going can be slow.

A public bus service departs from outside Aurora International Airport heading for Guatemala City's historic center, Zona 1, but it's easiest and safer to travel by taxi; expect to pay around US$12–14 to travel into Zona 1. Travelers to Antigua can catch one of the shuttle buses (around US$12) leaving at fairly regular intervals.

By air

The only scheduled domestic flight currently in operation is the 50-minute Guatemala City–Flores flight (to visit Tikal), which saves an 8–10-hour trip by road – although you can expect to pay a fairly steep US$210–240 for a round-trip ticket. Avianca (www.avianca.com) and TAG (www.tag.com.gt) both offer flights.

By bus

The regular Guatemalan bus, called a camioneta, is an old North American school bus. It's three to a seat, and as many as possible standing in the aisle. Progress is always pretty slow, but never dull. Expect to pay about Q8 an hour. There are also first-class buses (pullmanes) that connect the major towns along the main highways and into Mexico and the other Central American countries. They are a little quicker, don't stop so frequently, and you'll have a seat reservation. Expect to pay Q10–12 an hour.

Shuttle buses, usually modern minibuses, provide a useful, fast, and comfortable alternative. They mainly cover the prime tourist destinations, but are increasingly common throughout the country. Expect to pay about US$5 per hour.

Another method of transportation now common in Guatemala is non-tourist minibuses (microbuses) which have replaced the old chicken buses on many paved-road routes.

By boat

Boats connect the villages around Lago de Atitlán, Puerto Barrios, and Livingston, and Livingston and Río Dulce town. These routes all have daily services, and it's usually not necessary to make advance reservations.

By car

Driving in Guatemala can be a hairraising experience due to a combination of local practices – such as overtaking on blind corners – and the rough, unpaved condition of many roads bar the main ones. Traffic congestion is high in the capital, and the Interamericana and the highway to Puerto Barrios tend to be busy. Renting a car here costs US$35–70 a day.

A–Z

Accommodations

Accommodations in Guatemala range from luxury colonial hotels to backpackers' hostels. There are plenty of budget hotels to choose from and an increasing number of boutique places. Pensiones or *hospedajes* have very basic rooms, and these guesthouses are usually run by local families. Room rates are at their highest during Semana Santa (the week leading up to Easter Sunday), Christmas to New Year, and July and August. Keep in mind that hotels sell out quickly during Semana Santa, particularly in hotspots like Antigua, so book far in advance.

Budgeting for your trip

Guatemala is an inexpensive country in which to travel. Both accommodations and food are very affordable, so you can easily save in those areas, and then have extra for organized tours (where costs can add up) as well as souvenir-shopping – it's hard to leave Guatemala without at least a few pieces of its lovely colorful weavings. Backpackers can budget US$25 per day or less (for a hotel stay, food from a comedor/market stand and travel); 'mid-range' travelers perhaps US$40–50 per person a day; and for those looking to travel in real comfort, US$80–120 per person a day. The Guatemalan currency is the quetzal, and has been fairly stable over the last decade.

Children

Guatemala is an inviting county for kids. For starters, kids are often enthusiastically embraced – at restaurants, stores, hotels, and even museums. In fact, the staffers will

usually go out of their way to provide an extra bed or a child's portion. Guatemala's colorful, fascinating culture is also very accessible to the younger set, from weaving co-ops where they can observe Maya craftspeople to Maya temples that look right out of ancient picturebooks. And kid-friendly outdoor activities abound, including ziplining.

Climate

The Maya region is subtropical, and temperatures are governed far less by the seasons than by altitude. The rainy season is from May to October, but it very rarely rains all day. Often mornings are clear, followed by an afternoon downpour. In most of the region, maximum temperatures are kept to a moderate level (25–30°C/75–85°F), because of cloud cover, and nights are warm. November to April is the dry season, when the skies are usually clear. At this time of year it can get quite chilly at night anywhere in the region, but especially in the Guatemalan and Chiapas highlands, where frosts are not unknown in high-altitude towns. On the coast, severe storms can strike during hurricane season (June to October), but warnings are usually excellent locally. It is worth bearing in mind that at the height of the rainy season, visiting Petén's more remote ruins can land you in thigh-deep mud.

What to wear

Pack lightweight, breathable clothing, and sturdy walking shoes. For

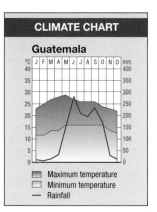

CLIMATE CHART
Guatemala

Maximum temperature
Minimum temperature
Rainfall

hiking, consider wearing long sleeves and lights pants to guard against bugs. Also, remember to bring appropriate items to guard against the sun, particularly if you have sensitive skin – wide-brimmed hats, sunscreen, long sleeves. In the big cities, dining and nightlife can require more formal wear – dress shirts for men, and a skirt or dress for women. The highlands gets chilly, so bring a light jacket or fleece.

Crime and safety

It's important to take some basic precautions when visiting Guatemala – but keep in mind that crime against tourists is still relatively rare, and the majority of visitors will not experience trouble of any kind. Having said that, general crime levels are high in Guatemala, and tourists have been targeted by (occasionally armed) criminals on the roads and on buses. It's a good idea to register with your embassy on arrival and to keep abreast of what's going on – Inguat, the Guatemalan tourist board, provides up-to-date security information via their Asistur line which can be reached on tel: 1500. The US State Department (http://travel.state.gov/travel) and the UK Foreign and Commonwealth Office's travel advice pages for Guatemala also give a solid overview of the current security situation (www.fco.gov.uk).

Customs regulations

Duty free: 80 cigarettes or 100g of tobacco; 1.5l of alcohol; cameras for personal use; no restriction on perfume. Restricted items: fresh food.

Papayas and mangoes at the market in Santiago de Atitlán.

Disabled travelers

Travelers with disabilities will find it challenging to travel in Guatemala. Access for wheelchair users is generally minimal, and mobility is hampered by potholed sidewalks and roads, cobblestones, and a lack of elevators outside of five-star city-center hotels. Travel by public transportation is also difficult, but note that a number of privately run shuttles that ply the main tourism towns can assist passengers with disabilities. Thankfully, many Guatemalan hotels are low-rise, so even outside the more upscale hotels with their elevators and ramps, you shouldn't have too much of a problem finding accessible sleeping quarters. There are organizations that will direct you to tour operators that are well set up for disabled travelers. Try Twin Peaks (Press Box 129, Vancouver, WA 98666; tel: 360-694 2462; www.twinpeakstravel.com) or consult the website Global Access (www.global accessnews.com) for excellent travel advice for the disabled.

Eating out

Guatemala has a range of eateries, from upscale restaurants in the big cities to comedores, which are the local equivalent of an American diner. Guatemala also abounds with tasty street snacks – like pupusas, thick corn tortillas packed with fillings like cheese and pork – but note that hygiene standards on the street can vary, so take care.

Maize stars in some from on most Guatemalan menus, including tortillas, which are best served while still warm – often wrapped inside a cotton cloth. After maize, beans (frijoles) are the second fundamental ingredient in the regional diet. Black beans are the most popular variety, but red pinto (literally 'painted') beans are also eaten. Chilies are native to the region, with over 100 varieties. Chili is commonly served in a salsa sauce that you will find at every dinner table. In Guatemala this salsa is often just called picante (spice) and can be from a bottle or freshly made. As for fresh fruits: bananas are everywhere, while avocados, tomatoes, blueberries, raspberries, apples, oranges, limes, papayas, and mangoes also feature. The creamy pink flesh of the zapote fruit, for example, is amazing. Also

wonderfully fresh are fruit juices and licuados, a type of fruit milkshake. Historically, turkey, wild pig, and iguana were all eaten, but, except in jungle areas, you will find that these days chicken, pork, and beef are the meats specified on most menus, either grilled, fried, or in a stew. You will find plentiful seafood served near the coast. Snapper, grouper, barracuda, and shark are all popular, while lobster is on many upscale restaurant menus, as well as shrimp, crab, and conch; ceviche (raw seafood marinated in lime juice) is a favorite in many areas.

Embassies and consulates

Canada: 8th floor, Edificio Edyma Plaza, 13a Calle 8-44, Zona 10, Guatemala City; tel: 2333 6102; www.canadainternational.gc.ca
UK: 11th floor, Torre Internacional, 16a Calle 00-55, Zona 10, Guatemala City; tel: 2367 5425; http://ukin guatemala.fco.gov.uk
US: Av La Reforma 7-01, Zona 10, Guatemala City; tel: 2326 4000; http://guatemala.usembassy.gov

Emergencies

In case of any emergency, dial 1500 from anywhere in Guatemala, which connects you to a bilingual operator who will put you in contact with the police, fire department, or ambulance. For National Police, you can also call 110.

Etiquette

Politeness, a smile, and an effort to speak a little Spanish will help you get more out of Guatemala. Avoid being openly critical of the country's problems, including corruption, inefficiency, and poverty – Guatemalans recognize their country's difficulties, but some are sensitive to criticism.

Try not to talk too loudly, as the Maya in particular find Westerners overbearingly loud. If you visit one of the smaller highland markets in Guatemala (not Chichicastenango or San Francisco El Alto), one of the most interesting aspects is how quiet the whole affair is, with business being conducted sotto voce.

Public nudity is offensive in most of the region. It's also advisable to cover your legs and shoulders when you visit churches – short shorts are usually frowned upon.

Festivals

January
El Cristo Negro, Esquipulas, January 15. Pilgrims from around the country – and the world – descend on the Basilica to pay tribute to the Black Christ.

April
Holy Week. Religious ceremonies and processions across the country, from Antigua to Quetzaltenango.

July
La Fiesta Nacional Indígena de Guatemala, Cobán, late July to early August. One of the region's great celebrations of Maya culture, with rollicking street fairs, parades, and parties.

August
Fiesta de la Virgen de la Asunción, countrywide, August 15. The patron saint of Guatemala City is celebrated around the country, with parades, fairs, and concerts.

September
Guatemala's Independence Day, countrywide, September 15. A national holiday, with parades and concerts, around the nation.

November
Día de los Muertos (All Saints' Day), countrywide, November 1. Guatemalans remember the dead, with flowers, visits to the cemetery, and other colorful celebrations, including flying massive kites in Todos Santos.
National Garifuna Day, Livingston, November 26. The Garifuna of Livingston party during the days leading up to and after November 26, with Garifuna food, music, and dance.

December
Quema del Diablo, countrywide, December 7. Bonfires light up the streets in towns around the country as effigies of Satan, old furniture, and are burned.
Fiesta de Santo Tomás, Chichicastenango, December 21. The patron saint of Chichicastenango is celebrated with parades, fireworks, fairs, and the famous Palo Volador ('flying pole').

Gay and lesbian travelers

Guatemala has a small gay scene, centered in the capital where there are a few gay clubs and bars. While it's best to be discreet (holding hands in public is unwise), most gays and lesbians find little local hostility. Exercise common sense and avoid the more macho men-only cantinas.

Health and medical care

Hygiene standards are much better than in many other parts of the developing world, but diarrhea may still strike no matter how careful you are. Stomach upsets are likely to be your main concern, but you should also be inoculated against polio, cholera, tetanus, typhoid, and hepatitis A. None of these diseases is at all common in the Maya countries, immunization is not a mandatory requirement, and the risk is very low, but every year there are cases.

Mosquitoes are likely to be much more of a concern, and it's imperative to minimize the chances of being bitten, especially in remote, lowland areas. Diligently apply repellent (*repelente*) to all exposed areas of skin, especially around your ankles.

Malaria is present in rainforest (and some lowland) areas but is not at all common across the region. There have been no reports of chloroquine-resistant strains of mosquito in the region, but for the latest information check with a specialized travel health clinic before you go.

Dengue fever, carried by a daytime mosquito, is on the increase worldwide, and there have been a few outbreaks in the Maya region. It's normally caught by being bitten near pools or puddles of dirty, stagnant water. The symptoms are fever, severe headache, complete loss of energy, and usually a skin rash. There is one rare strain, **dengue hemorrhagic**, that can be very serious but is rarely fatal in adults: in most cases the body heals itself within a few days. There's no vaccine for any strain of dengue, so you should take great precaution against being bitten; the only remedy is to take complete rest until the dengue clears, which seriously interrupts your holiday. Take high-factor sunscreen, a hat for protection against the sun, and drink plenty of (bottled) water to avoid dehydration, especially at high altitudes.

Don't drink tap water and don't brush your teeth with it – contaminated water can transmit the hepatitis A virus and is a major cause of

sickness in Guatemala. In the cities, drinking water is heavily chlorinated but should still be avoided.

Insurance

You must have medical insurance before coming to Guatemala. Public hospitals should generally be avoided if possible; the private sector is more efficient and better equipped. Your embassy will have a list of English-speaking doctors and dentists. In remote areas, it may be best to get to a city as soon as possible if you can travel. Keep all receipts and contact your insurance company immediately if you do need medical treatment.

Alerta Médica is a private medical emergency assistance service. Contact them by phoning **1711**.

Hospitals

Centro Médico, 6 Av 3-47, Zona 10, Guatemala City; tel: 2332 3555
Santa Lucía Hospital, Calzada Santa Lucía Sur 7, Antigua; tel: 7832 3122
Centro Médico Galeno, 2 Calle 3-08, Zona 3, Cobán; tel: 7952 3175

Media

The main daily newspapers are *Prensa Libre*, *Siglo XXI*, *El Periódico*, and *La Hora*. All are published in Spanish. The *Guatemala Times* (www.guatemala-times.com) is a good online source of news. There is also the free, monthly English-language magazine *The Revue* (www.revuemag.com), produced in Antigua. There are hundreds of radio stations, devoted to everything from merengue to Evangelical worship. La Marca (94.1 FM) is a popular reggaetón station, while Atmosfera (96.5 FM) plays rock and indie. You'll also find dozens of television stations in Guatemala, and several foreign channels (including CNN) are broadcast on cable, which is available in most of the main towns.

Money

Debit cards are the most popular way to access money, and credit cards are useful in hotels, restaurants, and stores. Visa and MasterCard are widely recognized. Most towns will have an ATM or two for 24-hour withdrawals. **Travelers' checks** can be cashed in many banks. Make sure you get your travelers' checks issued in US dollars (other currencies are rarely

accepted) and from an established name such as Thomas Cook or American Express. **The Guatemalan** quetzal comes in Q0.50, Q1, Q5, Q10, Q20, Q50, Q100, and Q200 bills. It is divided into 100 centavos.

Opening hours

Businesses and offices are generally open between 9am and 5pm, but they often close for an hour or two between noon and 2pm. Many banks stay open until 7pm (and even 8pm), especially in tourism-orientated towns. Archeological sites are usually open daily from 8am to 5pm (Tikal from 4am to 8pm), and nature reserves are also usually open daily, such as the Quetzal Reserve (6am–4pm) and Cerro Cahuí (6.30am to dusk).

Postal services

There are post offices (*correos*) in every town. Air mail takes between three days and a week to reach North America, but between one and two weeks to get to Europe. The postal service is quite reliable, but many people choose to use a courier company to send anything important overseas.

Public holidays

January 1 New Year's Day
Semana Santa Holy Week, the four days preceding Easter
May 1 Labor Day
June 30 Army Day, anniversary of the 1871 revolution
August 15 Guatemala City fiesta
September 15 Independence Day
October 12 Discovery of America
October 20 Revolution Day
November 1 All Saints' Day
December 24 Christmas Eve
December 25 Christmas Day
December 31 New Year's Eve

Shopping

Few visitors leave Guatemala without at least a few Guatemalan crafts (*artesanías*), which reveal the country's rich Maya cultural traditions. Don't miss a trip to the highlands, where every village has its own craft specialty or designs – and its own market day. Undoubtedly, Guatemala's grandest craft is textiles, which are woven into a rainbow of brilliant colors. Markets in Guatemala City and Antigua

Procession for Semana Santa, Antigua.

feature an excellent assortment of highland crafts, from textiles to basketry to silver to ceramics, while the large highland markets of Chichicastenango and San Francisco el Alto are also splendid.

Telecommunications

Telephones

Cellular coverage is extensive across most of the country, and compatible with many North American cellphones. Pay-as-you-go cellphones come cheap, and inserting a local SIM card into your own handset is also a possibility if your phone is unlocked. To make a collect-call (reverse charge call) to the US, Canada, and Mexico from Guatemala, tel: 147120 from a Telgua phone. Local calls in Guatemala are very cheap, at around US$0.10 per minute; national calls work out at around US$0.35 per minute.

You can buy a local prepaid phone card, such as a Telgua one, which you insert in street telephones to make calls. Using an international phone charge card is another option. All the main North American telecoms companies issue these, including AT&T, Canada Direct, MCI, and Sprint; get in touch with your phone company before you leave. Directory Assistance is 124 and the International Call Operator is 171.

Internet

Increasingly, hotels in Guatemala have free or inexpensive Wi-Fi. Otherwise, there is an abundant number of internet cafés throughout the country. Rates are around US$0.80–3 an hour. Connection speeds are usually rapid in the main centers, much less so once you get off the beaten track. Wi-Fi is widespread in towns popular with tourists, though connections are usually slow.

Time zone

US Central standard time; GMT minus 6 hours.

Tourist information

Inguat (www.visitguatemala.com), the Guatemalan tourist board, has offices throughout the country.
Guatemala City: 7 Av 1-17, Zona 4, Centro Cívico; tel: (502) 2421 2800; email: info@inguat.gob.gt. Also has a kiosk at the airport (email: info-aeropuertoaurora@inguat.gob.gt.
Antigua: 2 Calle Oriente No. 11 Casa del Turista; tel: (502) 7832 3782; email: info-antigua@inguat.gob.gt
Quetzaltenango: 7 Calle 11-35, Zona 1, Edificio Casa de la Cultura; tel: (502) 7761 4931; email: info-xela@inguat.gob.gt
Panajachel: Calle Principal 0-87, Zona 2 Panajachel, Solola; tel: (502) 2421 2953; email: info-panajachel@inguat.gob.gt
Isla de Flores: Playa Sur, Flores, Petén; tel: (502) 4210 9992; email: info-ciudadflores@inguat.gob.gt. Also has a kiosk at Petén's airport (email: info-mundomaya@inguat.gob.gt).

Antigua has tourist police (corner of 4 Av Norte and the plaza), who can help with security problems.

Other helpful websites:
www.aroundantigua.com
www.atitlan.com
www.lanic.utexas.edu
www.mayaparadise.com
www.quetzalnet.com
www.visitguatemala.com

Visas and passports

All visitors require a valid passport to enter Guatemala for stays of up to 90 days; citizens other than those of the USA, UK, most EU states, Canada, Australia, and New Zealand will also need a Guatemalan visa, which they can obtain from a Guatemalan embassy or consulate. The initial 90-day period can be extended by a further 90 days by visiting Migración in Guatemala City (6 Avenida 3-11, Zona 4; tel: 2411 2411). The extension will cost you US$17. There is no charge if you enter or leave overland at one of the more remote border crossings, though officials often demand a small fee.

There's a $30 departure tax on all international flights, but it's usually included in your ticket price; confirm with your airline. Separately, you often have to pay an airport security fee of around Q20 in cash at the airport.

What to read

The Ancient Maya by Robert Sharer. Authoritative, formidable study of the Maya.
Popol Vuh translated by Dennis Tedlock. The K'iche' 'bible,' the masterful book of creation that is both one of the most important pre-Columbian texts in the Americas and also an incredibly rich and imaginative read.
Sweet Waist of America by Anthony Daniels. Mainly concerned with Guatemala, the book was written toward the end of the civil war. Daniels interviews a cross-section of Central American society including Guatemalan soldiers, priests, schoolchildren, and two military dictators.
I, Rigoberta Menchú – an Indian Woman in Guatemala by Rigoberta Menchú. Extremely harrowing autobiography of the K'iche' Maya Nobel Prize winner, who lost her mother, father, and brothers in the civil war. The second volume, *Crossing Borders*, is a much lighter, more optimistic read, dealing with her life in exile and her return to Guatemala.

BELIZE

FACT FILE

Area: 22,965 sq km (8,867 sq miles)
Capital: Belmopan
Population: 331,900
Currency: Belize dollar
Weights and measures: The British Imperial system is generally used, with speed and road signs in miles.
Electricity: 110 volts
Dialling code: 501
Internet abbreviation: BZ

GETTING THERE

By air from the US, Canada, Europe, Australia, and New Zealand

Numerous airlines fly nonstop or direct from the US and Canada to Belize (Aeromexico: www.aeromexico.com; Air Canada: www.aircanada.com; American Airlines: www.aa.com; British Airways: www.britishairways.com; Delta: www.delta.com; United Airlines: www.united.com; WestJet: www.westjet.com). From Europe, Australia, and New Zealand, flights travel via hubs in the US, including Miami and Houston. All international flights into Belize land at the Philip S.W. Goldson International Airport, which is 10 miles (16km) northwest of Belize City on the George Price (Northern) Highway. Belizean carrier Tropic Air (www.tropicair.com) offers flights between Cancún and Belize City.

GETTING AROUND

There is a taxi rank outside the airport. Rates into Belize City are fixed and are fairly hefty for the 20-minute ride (B$50/US$25). One way to save is to share the taxi with other travelers. Rates to other parts of Belize can be negotiated (confirm the price before you get in).

By air

Small plane services cover most of Belize. This is by far the most convenient way to get around. Most of the flights run on time and few take longer than a half hour. The most popular destinations are from the International Airport to San Pedro on Ambergris Caye (which takes 20 minutes, and gives you spectacular views of the coral reef), and to Placencia and Dangriga, both in the south.

National operators
Maya Island Air
Tel: 223-1140
www.mayaairways.com
Tropic Air
Tel: 226 2012
www.tropicair.com

By boat

The alternative to flying to Caye Caulker or Ambergris Caye is to take a boat service from Belize City. The two main companies are San Pedro Belize Express Water Taxi (tel: 223 2225, www.belizewatertaxi.com), which departs from North Front Street, near Tourist Village, and the Ocean Ferry Belize (tel: 223 0033, www.oceanferrybelize.com), leaving from North Front Street, near Swing Bridge.

By bus

Buses run at least hourly between Belize City and the major towns to the north, west, and south. Most are the non-air-conditioned US school bus variety. The main bus station in Belize City is just west of the center, and is used by all companies serving all the towns and main roads in Belize; smaller bus lines serving some villages depart from nearby streets. Most buses will stop whenever requested, but Express buses,

which cost a little more, only stop in the main towns.

By car

Having your own wheels can come in very handy in the interior of Belize, but note that renting a car is expensive and a large damage deposit, taken by credit card, is required; insurance is about US$15–20 a day. The other drawback is the bad condition of some roads; in particular, take great care with the deep potholes, which can cause damage to the car (and, potentially, the people inside it) unless negotiated cautiously. Both the companies below have offices at the International Airport and in Belize City.
Budget
Km4, George Price (Northern) Highway, Belize City
Tel: 223 2435
www.budget-belize.com
Crystal Auto Rental
Km8, George Price (Northern) Highway, Belize City
Tel: 223 1600, toll-free in Belize: 0800-777-7777
www.crystal-belize.com
This is the largest rental fleet in Belize, excellent value, and the only company that allows you to take its vehicles to Tikal.

A–Z

Accommodations

Belize has a wonderfully diverse array of accommodations, from comfortable budget hotels to luxurious beach resorts to eco-friendly jungle lodges. Also a bonus: many resorts, both in the cayes and inland, offer a wide variety of tours, including diving and fishing, exploring Maya ruins, birdwatching, kayaking, and caving. Looking for serious pampering? You'll find that too, from lavish resorts on the cayes where you can enjoy sunrise yoga and candlelit massages to jungle hideaways with Maya-inspired treatments. Note that there is a compulsory government hotel tax of 9 percent added to prices, and many hotels add a service charge of 5–10 percent. Hotel prices vary greatly depending on the season. High-season rates are usually charged between mid-November to mid-May, but can vary between hotels. Prices may drop dramatically in the low season.

Budgeting for your trip

Overall, Belize is up to 40 to 50 percent more expensive than its Central American counterparts. That said, you can still find plenty of budget options, including for food, transportation, and accommodations, across the country. A main course at an upscale restaurant starts at Bz$50; at a moderate restaurant, Bz$35; and at a budget restaurant, you can dine on a hearty meal, particularly at lunchtime, for as little as Bz$12.

Accommodations prices also cover the spectrum: Average prices range from $Bz50 at a simple budget guesthouse to $Bz150–250 for a decent mid-range hotel to $Bz400–500 and up for luxe resorts. Buses are perhaps the best transportation deal in the country (see page 344), while getting around by plane is more expensive but much faster (see page 344).

Exchange rates are stable, with the national currency, the **Belize dollar**, conveniently fixed at the rate of two to the US dollar (Bz$2=US$1). US dollars (cash and travelers' checks) are also accepted everywhere – and in some places even preferred – as currency. A cautionary note: This simple dual currency system can present challenges, as you'll constantly need to ask which dollar is being referred to; it's easy to assume the price of your hotel room or trip is in Belize dollars, only to discover on payment that the price is in US dollars – a common misunderstanding.

Children

Belize is a very child-friendly destination, and there is plenty to delight children. In particular, Belize is an excellent place to introduce children to the natural world – and the importance of protecting and sustaining it – with numerous opportunities for jungle treks, wildlife spotting, and snorkeling. Top sights and activities that are often popular include the Belize Zoo, the Community Baboon Sanctuary, cave-tubing in Cayo, and swimming in the Caribbean waters on the cayes. The more upscale resorts and hotels have a number of amenities for children, including cribs, high chairs, childcare amenities, and children's menus. Also, the hotel staff can often help you find recommended local babysitters.

Climate

Belize enjoys a subtropical climate, tempered by brisk prevailing tradewinds from the Caribbean Sea. There are two seasons: the rainy season is from June to January, with a brief dry period in August; the dry season is from February to May. It should be stressed that this is a flexible division, and torrential tropical downpours can occur at any time of the year. Most visitors come to Belize during the winter months of the northern hemisphere – note, though, that this is generally when airfare prices are highest and hotels fill up. December and January are the coolest months, but even so, the temperature rarely falls below 55°F (13°C) at night. In the steamier months, the coastal temperatures usually reach 96°F (36°C); inland can be hotter.

What to wear

Belize is all about the great outdoors – no matter what time of year, you'll spend the bulk of your time outside, whether on the beach, or in the jungle or the cool mountains. The heat and year-round humidity dictate lightweight clothing of natural fibers. On the cayes, you can get by in shorts, a T-shirt, and sandals most of the time, or just bare feet and a swimsuit. However, most of the larger resorts maintain a trendy profile after dark, so pack a more formal tropical outfit to wear under the thatched roof at dinner. Most of the time, you'll need to dress for the weather rather than for style. Don't underestimate the power of the tropical sun: it can burn you in a half hour or less. The two absolute essentials that you will use are sunscreen and insect repellent. Bring them with you: sunscreen is surprisingly expensive here.

Crime and safety

It's important to take some basic precautions when visiting Belize, but overall it's a fairly safe country – crime against tourists is relatively rare. The city where you'll need to be most careful is Belize City, which has long had a sketchy reputation. While it's generally safe during the day, after dark it's best to take taxis to get around. Elsewhere, be particularly careful not to leave anything valuable on the beach while swimming, and do not leave valuables in budget hotel rooms or basic beach *cabañas* that are easily broken into. If in doubt, ask hotels to lock up your bag when you go out. Also, make sure that any guide you hire has official credentials – all legal tour guides in Belize are licensed and will have a photo ID. Marijuana (called *ganja* in Belize) is illegal throughout the region, as are other drugs. If you get into any trouble with the police, the first thing to do is to contact your embassy (see page 346).

It's always a good idea to stay abreast of the current safety situation in your destination by checking the travel advice pages from the US State Department (travel.state.gov/travel) and the UK Foreign and Commonwealth Office (www.fco.gov.uk). In addition to its regular police force, Belize has special tourism police, operating from local police stations.

Customs regulations

Removal, sale, and exportation of the following are prohibited by law in Belize: any kind of coral without a license, archeological artifacts, orchids; shells, fish, crustaceans, turtles, and materials from turtles.

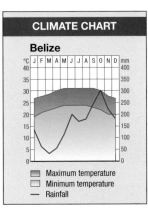

CLIMATE CHART

Belize

Maximum temperature
Minimum temperature
Rainfall

Disabled travelers

Mobility-challenged visitors will find it challenging to travel in Belize, though the infrastructure is slowly improving and a number of tour companies now offer services and contingency plans for those with disabilities. Public transportation is not equipped for wheelchairs, but minibus taxis are plentiful and drivers will assist you when asked. Streets in many areas can be difficult to negotiate, as they are mostly unpaved and sidewalks are few and far between. Not many hotels are equipped for travelers with disabilities, so it's imperative to ask about a hotel's accessibility when you call to make a reservation; note that the newer and higher-end resorts, particularly in well-touristed areas like Ambergris Caye, are more likely to have amenities for travelers with disabilities.

Eating out

Belizean cuisine is best described in the plural – cuisines. Wander through most any town or village, and you'll encounter a delightful and distinctive mix of Latin American, Caribbean, Creole, and Garífuna options, not to mention delicacies from farther afield – Taiwan, Thailand, and Lebanon to name but a few. And then there's the seafood: fresh and plentiful, the fresh fish and shellfish – particular the succulent and mildly sweet lobster – is, not surprisingly, the highlight for most visitors. Happily, you'll find it everywhere from the cayes to the coast to the inland communities. Just make sure to time your visit with lobster season (June 15–February 15). But at the heart of Belizean cuisine is the ultimate comfort food: rice and beans. This ubiquitous dish, with stewed chicken or beef, is the local daily fuel. The most successful Belizean beer, Belikin, with a Maya temple on the label, is consumed and sold everywhere, from local beach bars to convenience stores. It comes in a variety of styles, from dark and rich to light and sparkling. But the finest alcohol in Belize is undoubtedly rum. There are several local brands of rum, including Caribbean and Durleys (which is also called 'parrot rum' because of its company logo). One of the best, though, is Travellers One Barrel Rum. Travellers is Belize's oldest rum distillery, which

was launched originally as a bar in 1953 by Jaime Omario Perdomo Sr.

Dining out in Belize is decidedly casual, from laidback beach eateries to jungle lodge restaurants, and often include outdoor seating – with gorgeous views, whether the sparkling Caribbean or the tangled rainforest. Lunch is usually the main meal of the day. Though most places also serve dinner, eating out late is not a Belizean custom. Plan to arrive by 8pm for the best range of options.

Embassies and consulates

Canada: Consulate of Canada, 80 Princess Margaret Drive, Belize City; tel: 223 1060; www.embassy-canada.com/belize.html
UK: Embassy Square, PO Box 91, Belmopan; tel: 822 2146; http://ukinbelize.fco.gov.uk
US: Floral Park Road, Belmopan; tel: 822 4011; http://belize.usembassy.gov
Australia: Belize doesn't have an Australian consulate or embassy; instead, the Australian Embassy in Mexico City (Rubén Dario 55, tel: 55-1101-2200; www.mexico.embassy.gov.au) can assist.

Emergencies

Police 90 or 911
To report a crime 227 2222 (Belize City)
Ambulance/Fire 90 (Belize City only)

Etiquette

Politeness and a smile goes a long way while traveling in Belize. And, although Belize is a very casual country – shorts and sandals are the unofficial uniform throughout the cayes and the coast – there are plenty of occasions that call for dressier outfits, such as dining out at an upscale restaurant, attending church, or visiting a local's home for a party. In general, it's best to avoid being openly critical of the region's problems, including crime and dilapidated houses – Belizeans recognize their country's difficulties, but some are sensitive to criticism. If you have an appointment, get there on time, but don't be too surprised if you have to wait around a while – the definition of punctuality is loose here. If you add some flexibility to your travel plans, and expect the odd delay, you will have a far less frustrating time if you get held up.

Festivals

Party time in Belize peaks during the annual September festivities, when the two most significant events in the country's history are celebrated: the Battle of St George's Caye Day on September 10 commemorates the 1798 sea battle which finally removed Spanish claims to Belize, while Independence Day on September 21 marks the day that British rule came to an end in 1981. Keeping the party going, Garífuna Settlement Day, on November 19, commemorates the 1832 arrival of the largest group of Garífuna to Belize's southern shores, and is a non-stop fiesta. The best place to enjoy this is in Dangriga, where the celebratory music and dancing starts on the evening before Settlement Day. The mestizo and Maya communities have their own religious and other events, particularly at Easter time – costume parades begin the weekend before Lent. Other top festivals during the year include the lobster festivals in San Pedro, Caye Caulker, and Placencia, marking the official start of lobster season, where you can feast on the famous crustacean in all its permutations, including grilled and in tangy ceviche.

Gay and lesbian travelers

Belize overall is not a gay-friendly country, and local LBGT people often keep their sexuality a secret. Few people will make their disapproval obvious to foreigners, however, and many openly welcome the gay cruises that visit the country. San Pedro is probably your best bet for a hassle-free time. However, Belize's Supreme Court overturned the country's anti-gay law in August 2016, in a landmark ruling. Belize is the first country in the Caribbean to do so, and the hope is that other countries in the region will follow suit.

Health and medical care

Hygiene standards are much better than in many other parts of the developing world, but diarrhea may still strike no matter how careful you are. Stomach upsets are likely to be your main concern, but you should also be inoculated against polio, cholera, tetanus, typhoid, and hepatitis. None of these diseases are at all common in Belize – immunization is not a mandatory requirement and the risk is very low – but every year there are cases.

Mosquitoes are likely to be much more of a concern, and it's imperative to minimize the chances of being bitten, especially in remote, lowland areas. Diligently apply insect repellent with a high DEET content to all exposed areas of skin, especially around your ankles. There is malaria in some parts of Belize. Most travelers visiting the cayes or San Ignacio don't need to worry too much, but if you are heading for extended stays in jungle areas, it is advisable to begin a course of anti-malaria tablets.

Dengue fever, carried by a daytime mosquito, is on the increase worldwide, and there have been a few outbreaks in and around Belize. It's normally caught as a result of being bitten near pools or puddles of dirty, stagnant water. There is one rare strain, dengue hemorrhagic, that can be very serious, but it is rarely fatal in adults: in most cases the body heals itself within a few days. There's no vaccine for any strain of dengue, so you should take great precaution against being bitten.

Belize has a fairly high number of reported cases of AIDS. The problem is being traced partly to foreign visitors – particularly those from elsewhere in Central America and from the United States. Visitors are advised to practice safe sex; condoms are inexpensive and widely available at pharmacies.

Take high-factor sunscreen, a hat for protection against the sun, and drink plenty of (bottled) water to avoid dehydration, especially at high altitudes. The quality of food and its preparation in Belize is good so there is not as great a risk of stomach problems as in neighboring countries. Tap water is potable in most of Belize, but in some parts of the cayes or in the south of Belize, it's not recommended for drinking. Instead, drink bottled water, sold at all gas stations and stores.

If you require the services of a physician, your hotel should be able to recommend one nearby. If you need daily medication, bring an ample supply since your brand may be unavailable or extremely expensive in Belize.

Few pharmacies are open late at night or on weekends and, should you need urgent medical attention, be warned: district hospitals are supposed to have doctors on call at night and on weekends, but serious illnesses or injuries are usually referred to the Karl Heusner Memorial Hospital in Belize City. So, if the worst happens and you have the option, your best bet is to go directly there. Belize Medical Associates (tel: 223 0303), next to the hospital in Belize City provides a more rapid service, although it is more expensive.

Public hospitals

Karl Heusner Memorial Hospital, Belize City
Tel: 223 1548
www.khmh.bz
Corozal Hospital
Tel: 422 2076
Dangriga Hospital
Tel: 522 2078
Orange Walk Hospital
Tel: 322 2072
Punta Gorda Hospital
Tel: 722 2026
San Ignacio Hospital
Tel: 824 2066

Media

For English speakers traveling around Central America, Belize's English-language media is a pleasant bonus. You can keep up with both local and international news here, with daily national newspapers and many spirited TV and radio shows. Major newspapers include The Amandala, The Belize Times, The Guardian and The Reporter. In radio, Love FM offers music and news, and has one of the most extensive networks in the country. Another major station is KREM FM, with local talk and music. The two main TV stations are **Channel 5**, the country's best broadcaster, with top-notch news programs, and **Channel 7**, which features a mix of American and Belizean programming.

Money

Debit cards are the most popular way to access money, and credit cards are useful in upscale hotels, restaurants, and stores. Visa and MasterCard are widely recognized. Most towns have an ATM or two for 24-hour withdrawals. In many places it is possible to arrange a cash advance on your credit card, though this is often time-consuming and you'll usually need to pay a fee.

Travelers' checks can be cashed in many banks, but smaller branches may take a long time over it, so try to use city branches instead. Make sure you get your travelers' checks issued in US dollars (other currencies are rarely accepted) and from an established name such as Thomas Cook or American Express. In Belize, US-dollar travelers' checks can be used as currency in some stores.

US dollar bills are accepted almost everywhere, because the Belize dollar is pegged to the US dollar at a rate of Bz$2 to US$1. Some prices are quoted in US dollars, so it is important to check which currency a price is in before agreeing to it. Belizean dollars, with bills from Bz$2 to Bz$100, are divided into 100 cents.

Opening hours

Most stores and offices are open Mon–Fri 8am–noon, with afternoon hours from 1 to 5 or 6pm. Most banks open Mon–Fri 8am–3 or 4pm; some are also open until noon on Saturdays. Almost everything is closed on public holidays.

Postal services

Belize City Post Office is on the north side of the Swing Bridge (near the intersection of Queen and North Front streets). Belizean stamps are beautiful, with depictions of native flora and fauna, and are prized by collectors. The country provides one of the most economical and reliable postal systems in Central America. Allow around 4–7 days for mail to arrive in the US and around two weeks (often less) to Europe, Asia, or Australia. The post office is open 8am–noon and 1–4.30pm.

Public holidays

January 1 New Year's Day
March 9 Baron Bliss Day
March/April Easter weekend
May 1 Labor Day
May 24 Commonwealth Day
September 10 St George's Caye Day
September 21 Independence Day
October 12 Pan-American Day
November 19 Garífuna Settlement Day
December 25 Christmas Day
December 26 Boxing Day

Shopping

Belize produces a wide variety of artisan crafts that make for great souvenirs. Look for carvings made of *zericote*, a two-toned wood that grows only in Belize and surrounding areas. Slate carvers, who often sell their wares at Maya sites, create detailed reproductions of Maya gods and stelae. In the Maya villages in southern Belize, keep an eye out for colourful embroidery, though note that quality is generally better in Guatemala. Maya, Garífuna and Creole villages create great basketware, including small, tightly woven 'jippy jappa' baskets. One delicious souvenir is a bottle of Marie Sharp's Pepper Sauce, made from Belizean *habañero* peppers. This spicy accompaniment to rice and beans tops every restaurant table in the country, and you'll find bottles of the spicy stuff and souvenir shops across the country.

Telecommunications

Telephones

The country's main telephone and cell phone provider is Belize Telemedia Ltd (www.belizetelemedia.net). Cellphone coverage is best in towns and cities. Most North American cellphones should work in Belize, but only tri-band or multi-band European phones will pick up a signal. Public telephones are available throughout Belize, except in the more remote areas where you will often only find a community phone in someone's house. International phone cards are the cheapest way to make international calls when using a public telephone. Your hotel will also have fixed rates for national and international calls.

Directory Assistance 113
International Call Operator 114

Internet

Throughout the country, you can find access to the internet. Most hotels, resorts, and other accommodation offer Wi-Fi, usually for free, but occasionally for a fee. Restaurants and cafés, particularly in the tourist hubs, also have Wi-Fi and will allow you to use it for free. This means, of course, that internet cafés are now few and far between, though you'll still find a couple in major towns, with prices starting are around Bz\$10 for an hour.

Time zone

US Central standard time; GMT minus 6 hours.

Tourist information

The official Belize Tourism Board website, www.travelbelize.org, has a broad range of information, from sights and attractions to outdoor adventures to accommodations. There are Belize Tourism offices in Belize City and in main towns around the country, including in Placencia and San Pedro. The Belize Tourism Industry Association (BTIA; www.btia.org) represents many of the tourism-related businesses in the country and produces the annual *Destination Belize* magazine (www.destinationbelize.com), which is filled with helpful information and available free from tourist offices and many hotels. Note also that a number of towns and regions in Belize have developed their own tourism-friendly websites, often focusing on current news and local information – two of these are www.ambergriscaye.com and www.corozal.com. Other helpful websites include www.gov.uk/foreign-travel-advice/belize, the government's own website, which has an overview of current politics and tourism trends; and www.channel5belize.com, the local news station, which covers Belize news and headlines.

Belize Tourism Board
64 Regent Street, Belize City; tel: 227 2420 (toll-free: 1-800-624-0686); www.travelbelize.org; 8am–noon and 1–5pm.

For further information on Belize's ecology and protected areas, contact: **Belize Audubon Society**, 12 Fort Street, Belize City; tel: 223 5004; www.belizeaudubon.org; Mon–Fri 8am–5pm. Belize's oldest conservation organization.

The Belize Zoo and Tropical Education Center, Ladyville GPO, Belize City; tel: 822 8000; www.belizezoo.org.

For more detailed information about Maya archeological sites, or for permission to visit certain sites in the region, contact the **Belize Institute of Archaeology**, Museum Building, Culvert Road, Belmopan; tel: 822 2106; http://nichbelize.org.

Visas and passports

Visas are not required by most nationalities, including citizens of the United States, United Kingdom, Canada, Australia, New Zealand, South Africa, and CARICOM (Caribbean Community) countries, as well as most members of the

European Union. It is advisable to check with your nearest consulate or embassy before travel as requirements do change. All people from the above countries still need an international passport that is valid for at least six months, and an onward or round-trip air ticket. All visitors are permitted to stay up to 30 days. To apply for an extension visit any Immigration Office. A moderate fee is charged, and applicants must demonstrate sufficient funds for the remainder of their stay, as well as an onward ticket. Note that there's a departure tax of US\$30 to leave the country, by land or sea (payable even if you're on a day trip to Tikal).

What to read

Many of the best books written about Belize or by Belizean authors are published in the country and may not be available elsewhere. Cubola Productions (www.cubola.com) is Belize's foremost publisher. Angelus Press (www.angeluspress.com) in Belize City also offers a mail-order service for a variety of titles.

A Belize Rainforest: The Community Baboon Sanctuary by Horwich and Lyon. Everything you wanted to know about howler monkeys and much more.

Jaguar: One Man's Struggle to Establish the World's First Jaguar Preserve by Alan Rabinowitz. The personal story of how wildlife biologist Rabinowitz's 1983 study of jaguars in the Cockscomb Basin of south-central Belize led to the creation of the Jaguar Reserve.

The Maya by Michael D. Coe. An excellent general introduction to the subject.

Maya Cities and Sacred Caves by Jaime Awe. A short guide to Belize's publicly accessible Maya sites and an excellent summary of ancient Maya history.

Time Among the Maya by Ronald Wright. An entertaining and informative account of the author's journeys around Central America, with insights into Maya culture.

Birds of Belize by H. Lee Jones. By far the best and most comprehensive fully illustrated guide to all species recorded in Belize.

Rainforest Remedies – 100 Healing Herbs of Belize by Rosita Arvigo and Michael Balick. Fascinating guide to the endemic plantlife of Belize, illustrated with line drawings.

EL SALVADOR

FACT FILE

Area: 21,041 sq km (8,124 sq miles)
Capital: San Salvador
Population: 6.34 million
Currency: US Dollar
Language: Spanish
Weights and measures: Metric
Electricity: 110-120 volts, 60-cycle current.
Dialling code: 503
Internet abbreviation: .sv

GETTING THERE

By air

From Europe: Iberia offers scheduled, direct flights, from Madrid, though many will connect through the US.
From/via US: Collectively, American Airlines, Avianca, Delta, Spirit Airlines, and United fly direct to San Salvador from many points in the US (see page 339 for airline websites).
From Canada: Air Canada offer direct flights from Toronto, while Air Transat offers seasonal service from Montreal-Trudeau.

GETTING AROUND

To and from the airport

Monseñor Óscar Arnulfo Romero International Airport, located about 45km (31 miles) southeast of San Salvador, is the country's only international airport. Official airport taxis wait outside and run trips to the capital, as well as points along the coast. Public bus 138 also runs to the capital.

By bus

San Salvador has several bus terminals, including Fenadesal for points east and Occidental for points west. International bus companies such as Tica Bus (www.ticabus.com), Pullmantur (www.pullmantur.com), and Transporte del Sol (http://transportedel-sol.com) service routes between San Salvador and neighboring countries.

By sea

Cruise lines such as Crystal, Princess, and Oceania make port at Acajutla west of San Salvador, often continuing to or coming from the Panama Canal.

By road

El Salvador's best road is the Pan-American Highway, which passes through El Salvador between San Miguel in the East and San Salvador in the West. Outside of this main route, roads vary from paved to semi-paved to pothole-ridden dirt. Most car rental agencies insist that the driver is over 21 years of age, holds a valid passport and driver's license, and has a valid credit card for a deposit (not cash).

In San Salvador:

By bus

SITRAMSS is San Salvador's integrated bus system with its own lanes and stations. It runs on set schedules and is the most economical way to get around the city and surrounding suburbs.

By taxi

Taxis are safe, cheap, and plentiful.

Accommodations

In San Salvador, the best and largest hotels, mostly multinational chains, are found in the south and west of the city in Colonia San Benito and Colonia Escalón, as well as to the north of the city near the Metrocentro Mall. Outside of the capital and a few beach areas, most hotels are independently owned cinderblock structures with basic amenities. There is no high season in El Salvador, so prices rarely change. However, during holidays hotels do tend to fill up faster, so it is best to make reservations at least a month in advance.

Budgeting for your trip

Aside from a few luxury hotels and resorts, there is little in El Salvador that will drive up your budget. The country is more or less on par with Honduras and Guatemala even though the currency is the US dollar.
Airport transfer: From SAL it is a 40-minute ride (about US$30–40 by taxi) between downtown San Salvador and the airport.
Car rental: Rates generally start around US$55 per day, including full insurance in high season; cheaper rates are negotiable off-season. Four-wheel-drive vehicles start around US$75 per day.
Gasoline: $2.77 per gallon
Accommodations: Basic hotels (usually cold or shared showers and no Wi-Fi) for under $30 per night (double occupancy) dominate small mountain and remote beach areas. In the city and main beach resorts, especially at the beach, they fill up fast in the high season and on weekends. To upgrade the comfort level, expect to pay at least $70 to $90 a night (double occupancy) for moderate lodging (private baths, hot water, some views, parking, and extra amenities).
Food: A meal of streetside *pupusas* will cost no more than $1–2, while the majority of local restaurants average around $10. Steakhouses, hotel restaurants and other more formal establishments rarely go beyond $30 per per meal per person.

Museums and attractions: Entrance to Salvadoran museums and national parks tends to be inexpensive, often costing under $3.

Children

El Salvador is an easy place to travel with children as they are welcome everywhere. In San Salvador, there's a children's museum, the Tin-Marin (www.tinmarin.org) with its own butterfly garden. The Pacific coast is always reliable with kids, especially if you can line up a visit to coincide with turtle nesting season (August to December) on beaches like Los Cóbanos and Barra de Santiago. Indigo-dyeing demonstrations in Chalcuapa are always a big hit, as is a visit to the Mayan site of Joya de Cerén, the Pompeii of the Americas.

Climate

El Salvador's tropical climate has distinct wet and dry seasons. The summer, or dry season, runs from about December to April, while winter, or the rainy season, is the rest of the year. Even during the rainy season many of the days are clear, with a bright sun in the mornings and rain coming only later in the day.

Temperatures are consistent throughout the year with the lowlands being hot and humid, while the central plateau and mountain areas are more moderate. The average temperature in San Salvador is 23°C (73°F), while on the coast the average high is 27°C (80°F).

Crime and safety

In San Salvador, precautions should be taken against petty crime such as pickpocketing and theft, especially in the center. Leave valuables in a locked safe at the hotel or don't bring them to El Salvador at all. Stick to well trafficked streets at night and hotel taxis. There has been an uptick in gang activity in the capital in recent years, although overall violent crime is down. On beaches, keep a close eye on your belongings.

Customs regulations

Visitors to El Salvador can bring in no more than 200 cigarettes or 50 cigars, 2L of alcohol, and gifts worth up to $500. Like elsewhere in the region, there are heavy restrictions on the import and export of plants, animals, vegetables, and fruit.

Disabled travelers

With many large shopping malls and multinational chain hotels and restaurants that are equipped with ramps and elevators, El Salvador does have some limited amenities for mobility-impaired travelers. Outside of San Salvador and major resorts, however, such amenities are nonexistent. Still, the lingering effects of civil wars and landmines have left a significant segment of the population disabled, so the public tends to be particularly understanding and helpful to travelers with disabilities.

Eating out

What to eat

Much of Salvadoran cuisine is a blend of Spanish and indigenous recipes and ingredients. El Salvador's most famous recipe is the *pupusa*, a thick, hand-pressed corn tortilla that can be stuffed with fillings such as cheese, *chicharrón* (fried pork crackling), beans, *loroco* (a native flower) or *ayote* (squash). *Pupusas* are inexpensive and are usually grilled on street stands. They are usually served with *curtido*: pickled onions, cabbage and carrots. Salvadoran *tamales*, of which there are many varieties, are steamed in plantain leaves and stuffed with ingredients like corn, black beans, or chicken. Other popular dishes include *yuca frita* (fried yuca), *panes rellenos* (turkey or chicken sandwiches), and *carne asada* (grilled steak).

Restaurants

Most of the restaurants in El Salvador are informal affairs. Some of the best food in the country comes from rural, country-style restaurants, or beachfront eateries sourcing their food from local fishermen. In San Salvador, there are more cosmopolitan restaurants serving sushi, Peruvian, or contemporary Salvadoran food, although even there the atmosphere isn't particularly stuffy. From Monday to Saturday, most restaurants in the capital will open from noon–3pm and 7–10 pm. In the countryside, many restaurants open just during the day.

Embassies and consulates

The following are in San Salvador:
Canada: 63 Av. Sur y Alameda Roosevelt, Local 6, Nivel Lobby II, tel: 7045 6601; www.canadainternational.gc.ca/el_salvador-salvador/
South Africa: (Consulate) Boulevard Merliot y Av. Las Carretas, Edif. Bolsa de Valores, Nivel 2, Ciudad Merliot, Ant. C., tel: 2133 3700.
UK: Torre Futura, 14th Floor, Colonia Escalón, tel: 2511 5757, www.gov.uk/government/world/organisations/british-embassy-san-salvador.
US: Final Boulevard Santa Elena, Antiguo Cuscatlán, tel: 2501 2999; https://sansalvador.usembassy.gov.

Emergencies

Dial **911** anywhere in El Salvador for emergency assistance.
Reporting a crime: tel: 911 (24 hours).

Etiquette

Salvadorans tend to be conservative and friendly, saying hello when sitting next to someone and preempting any conversation with *buenos días* (good morning) or *buenas tardes* (good afternoon/evening). In business and more formal settings, appearance and grooming is expected to be tidy. Even in beach areas away from the beach, wearing bikinis or going shirtless will attract unwanted stares.

Festivals

February
International Permanent Festival of Art and Culture, Suchitoto, an annual art and culture festival.

March
Semana Santa, Holy Week celebrations occur around the country, with masses and feasts, all culminating on mass on Easter Sunday.

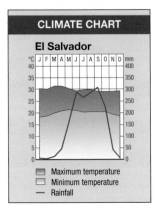

CLIMATE CHART

El Salvador

- Maximum temperature
- Minimum temperature
— Rainfall

May

Fiesta de las Flores y Palmas, Panchimalco, a flower festival with costumes and plant filled street that dates to Mayan times to celebrate the arrival of the rainy season.

July

Copa Quicksilver, Punta Rocas, the country's top surf competition, which attracts big name national and international surfers.

August

Las Bolas de Fuego, Nejapa, a century old tradition in a small community north of San Salvador where kerosene-soaked, flaming rag balls are thrown at one another.
Fiestas Agostinas, San Salvador, to celebrate the capital's patron saint, the Divine Savior of the World (aka Jesus Christ). While mass and religious activities are common, many families use the opportunity to vacation.

September

Día de Independencia, there are celebrations around the country to commemorate independence from Spain on September 15, with parades, fireworks and traditional foods.

November

Carnaval, San Miguel, a week-long party, the country's biggest, with dancing, parades and heavy drinking.

Gay and lesbian travelers

While there are laws to prevent discrimination against the LGBT community in El Salvador, there is still widespread anti-gay harassment and violence in the conservative country. A law in 2015 increased penalties for hate crimes based on sexual orientation, but public attitudes have yet to adjust and caution is advised wherever possible.

Health and medical care

El Salvador is known for having a poor health care network, especially in rural areas. However, there are private clinics, most of them concentrated in the capital. For medical emergencies in the San Salvador area, you can contact:
Consejo Superior de Salud Publica, tel: 2561 2525, www.cssp.gob.sv.
Gastroclínica Escalón, tel: 2263 5572.
Hospital de Diagnóstico y Emergencias, tel: 2506 2000

Media

Daily Spanish-language newspapers include: *El Diario de Hoy*, *Diario Co Latino* and *La Prensa Gráfica*. Additionally, there is El Faro (www.elfaro.net), the country's first digital newspaper, which was founded in 1998 and also has event listings.

Money

As the US dollar is the official currency, changing money tends to be quite easy. ATMs are widespread, especially in San Salvador. Currency exchange offices are at the airport, though most banks can exchange euros and regional currencies as well.

Opening hours

Business opening hours, including banks, are generally Monday through Friday 8.30am–5pm and Saturdays until noon. In rural towns, many businesses will close for 1–2 hours over the midday period. Many tourist attractions are open on Sundays, but close on Mondays.

Postal services

Nearly every small town in El Salvador has a post office, listed as Correos (www.correos.gob.sv). International courier services like FedEx and DHL can be found in San Salvador.

Public holidays

January 1 New Year's Day
March/April Semana Santa (Thursday–Sunday)
April 11 Juan Santamaría Day
May 1 Labor Day
August 1–6 Festival of El Salvador
September 15 Independence Day
October 12 Día de la Raza
November 2 All Souls' Day
December 24, 25 and 31 Christmas and New Year's

Shopping

While San Salvador is better known for its flashy malls with international designer stores, there are local handicrafts all over the country with more cultural value. Salvadoran coffee is of renowned quality, while woven hammocks, Mayan handicrafts and fabrics dyed with indigo can be found at craft markets around the capital and elsewhere in the country.

Telecommunications

Telephones

The international code for El Salvador is 503. Most operators offer cell phone service using GSM technology (1800 MHz and 850 MHz).

Internet

Internet cafés are becoming scarce, but public internet access and Wi-Fi spots can be found everywhere. Most hotels offer a computer for internet service, Wi-Fi, or both.

Time zone

El Salvador is on North America's Central Standard Time which means it is six hours behind GMT. It does not observe Daylight Savings, so this time difference increases one hour during the northern summer months.

Tourist information

The following offices are particularly good:
CORSATUR, http://elsalvador.travel/en, has offices in central San Salvador, Suchitoto, Nahuizalco, and Puerto la Libertad. Each office is equipped with an English-speaking employee who can help with any questions.
Casas de Cultura, community centers found in nearly every town in El Salvador, generally have local information, maps and brochures available.

Visas and passports

Citizens of the US, Canada, UK, Ireland, Australia, New Zealand, and South Africa need a passport valid for at least six months beyond the date of entry to El Salvador, as well as a tourist card, which can be purchased for $10 on arrival. Travelers may remain in the country for 90 days.

What to read

La Diáspora, Horacio Castellanos Moya, recounts the struggles of exiles from El Salvador's civil war.
The Massacre at El Mozote, Mark Danner, detailing the 1981 murder of hundreds at the hands of a US trained Salvadoran army battalion that was nearly forgotten.
Land of Childhood, Claudia Lars, a rich memoir that explores the folklore and cultural traditions of El Salvador at the turn of the century.

HONDURAS

FACT FILE

Area: 112,500 sq km (43,400 sq miles)
Capital: Tegucigalpa
Population: 8 million
Currency: Lempira
Language: Spanish
Weights and measures: Metric
Electricity: 110-120 volts, 60-cycle current.
Dialling code: 504
Internet abbreviation: .hn

GETTING THERE

By air

From Europe: Air Europa offers scheduled, direct flights, from Madrid to San Pedro Sula, while the alternative is to connect in the US.
From/via US: AeroMexico, American Airlines, Avianca, Choice Air, Copa Airlines, Delta, Spirit Airlines, United.
From Canada: Avianca offers flights from Toronto with a stop in San Salvador, while Sun Wing has seasonal flights from Toronto and Montreal to La Ceiba and Roatán.

GETTING AROUND

To and from the airport

There are four international airports in Honduras, with flights split between the four. San Pedro Sula handles the most traffic, closely followed by Tegucigalpa. Roatán and La Ceiba handle mostly regional flights. San Pedro Sula's Ramón Villeda Morales International Airport (SAP) sits 15km (9 miles) east of the city on the road to La Ceiba. Official airport taxis

wait outside, while bus company Hedman Alas (www.hedmanalas.com) has a terminal at the airport with frequent buses to La Ceiba and to their main hub in downtown San Pedro Sula. Tegucigalpa's Tocontín International Airport (TGU) is 6km (4 miles) south of the center on the highway to Choluteca. Official airport taxis and less expensive unofficial ones wait outside.

By air

Domestic airlines are reasonably priced and quick, making them a great alternative to traveling across the country or a quick trip to the Bay Islands. Aerolineas Sosa (www.aerolineasosahn.com) and CM Airlines (www.cmairlines.com) are the two domestic airlines in Honduras and fly to all of the Bay Islands, Copán, La Ceiba, Tegucigalpa, San Pedro Sula, and Puerto Lempira.

Keep in mind that local airlines allow one checked bag, up to 16kg (35lbs), per passenger, depending on the fare class purchased; fees for excess baggage start at $35.

By bus

San Pedro Sula's Gran Central Metropolitana de Autobuses is located a few kilometres south of the city center, and is the transportation hub of the country. Dozens of bus companies operate here, with frequent service to major destinations such as Tegucigalpa, Tela, La Ceiba and Copán, as well as more offbeat destinations. Hedman Alas (www.hedmanalas.com), which runs to Guatemala as well, and Viana Clase de Oro (www.vianatransportes.com). For long distances buses, Tica Bus (www.ticabus.com) stops in Tegucigalpa, San Pedro Sula and La Ceiba, connecting to capitals throughout Central America.

By sea

Cruise ships dock at two ports on the Bay Island of Roatán throughout the year. Most major Caribbean cruise lines stop here on various itineraries round the Gulf of Mexico or en route to the Panama Canal. Princess, Norwegian, Carnival, Royal Caribbean and MSC all make port at Roatán. Private yachts are also a popular way to travel to and from the Bay Islands or along the mainland coast, while ferries travel between La Ceiba and the Roatán and Utila several times per day.

By road

Honduras has three good highways: between San Pedro Sula and Tegucigalpa; along the North Coast; and between San Pedro Sula and Copán. Outside of these routes the roads are rarely paved and often filled with potholes. The majority of rental cars are manual transmission; automatics cost considerably more. Most agencies insist that the driver is over 21 years of age, holds a valid passport and driver's license, and has a valid credit card for a deposit (not cash). If traveling outside the main cities, renting a 4x4 is a must.

In San Pedro Sula

By bus

San Pedro Sula's bus system is confusing and of little use to most travelers. Almost every site of interest to the traveler is within the Circunvalación, which can be explored on foot during the day.

By taxi

Taxis are by far the best way of getting around San Pedro Sula. They are everywhere and very cheap. If they don't have a meter negotiate a price before getting in.

A-Z

Accommodations

With a few exceptions, many of the best hotels in San Pedro Sula are along the Circunvalación, a beltway that circles the city. Most hotels are business oriented, as few tourists end up staying in the city. Some good boutique hotels have opened in residential areas outside the center.

The high tourist season in Honduras is during the dry season, running roughly from January to June, as well as national holidays. Aside from the Bay Islands and some resorts along the North Coast, most hotels do not have high-season rates.

Budgeting for your trip

Honduras is one of, if not the most, inexpensive places in all of Latin America, especially away from cities and resort areas (which can sometimes feel like a separate universe). The currency, the Lempira, has been losing value against the dollar and euro in recent years, making Honduras as cheap as it has ever been.

Airport transfer: From SAP it is a 20-minute ride (about US$10–15 by taxi) between downtown San José and the airport.

Car rental: Rates generally start around US$50 per day, including full insurance in high season; cheaper rates negotiable off-season. Four-wheel-drive vehicles start around US$70 per day and are recommend if traveling outside of the main routes.

Gasoline: $3.25 per gallon

Accommodations: Rustic cabins (usually cold or shared showers and less privacy) for under $20 per night (double occupancy) can be found in rural villages all over the country, even in national parks. For a middle of the road hotel with hot water and Wi-Fi, expect to pay at least $50 to $70 a night (double occupancy). Upscale beach resorts or jungle lodges start at around $150 a night.

Food: The most expensive restaurants are at luxury hotels, otherwise, you'll rarely spend more than $20–30 on a good meal in Honduras. Street eats and traditional restaurants are extremely cheap, rarely more than $5 or $10 a meal.

Museums and attractions: Most museums and attractions cost just a few dollars to visit, although some of the most popular ones, like the Copán ruins, are more expensive ($10–$15). Most museums offer lower rates for students and children.

Children

Honduras is a very family friendly destination. Most major tourists areas welcome kids and there are child-focused activities in the country. In Tegucigalpa, there's Chiminike (www.chiminike.org), an interactive children's museum on the southern edge of town. Aside from beaches, Roatán has an all-in-one island theme park called Gumbalimba (www.gumbalimbapark.com), with a nature preserve, canopy tour, monkey island and various water sports. In and around the ruins of Copán, there's Macaw Mountain (www.macawmountain.org), a bird park, and Alas Encantadas, a butterfly house. In the buffer zone along Pico Bonito National Park, there are trails to waterfalls and kid-appropriate whitewater rafting on the Cangrejal River.

Climate

In most cases, Honduras is always hot, unless you are in the mountains. The temperature doesn't fluctuate much throughout the year. There are two main seasons in Honduras: wet and dry. The rainy season runs from about May to November in the interior, while on the North Coast and on the Bay Islands rains are more likely from September to January. Rainy season discounts can be had along the coast, though rarely do they occur elsewhere in the country. Hurricane season runs from August to November.

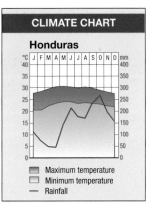

CLIMATE CHART

Honduras

Maximum temperature
Minimum temperature
Rainfall

Temperatures

Temperatures tend be hotter and more humid along the Caribbean coast, with highs averaging 34°C (93°F), while highland areas are cooler, averaging 20°C (68°F).

Crime and safety

In recent years crime has become a major cause for concern in Honduras. San Pedro Sula was even named the murder capital of the world for a while. Drug trafficking and gang activity have made parts of urban areas of San Pedro Sula, La Ceiba, and Tegucigalpa off limits. Use common sense when walking around, traveling only by taxi at night, and only carrying as much cash as you need. Still, most crime is limited to pickpocketing and minor theft, and in tourist destinations Honduras is as safe as anywhere else in the region.

Customs regulations

Visitors entering Honduras may also bring in no more than 400 cigarettes, 500 grams of pipe tobacco, or 50 cigars, and 2.5 liters of alcoholic beverages per adult.

Disabled travelers

Outside of major resorts and chain hotels in main cities, few areas of Honduras are accessible to travelers with disabilities. Few national parks are set up for wheelchairs, while sidewalks and streets are often bumpy or filled with cobblestones. Bay Island ferries are accessible, however.

Eating out

What to eat

While Honduran cuisine isn't catching on worldwide like Mexican, there are some reliable recipes worth seeking out. The *plato típico*, the hearty national dish, is a pile of beef, plantains, beans, pickled cabbage, cream, and tortillas. The most common street snack and fast food in the country is the *baleada*, the Honduran version of a taco. It's a thick, folded tortilla stuffed with refried beans, fresh cheese and cream, plus chicken, pork, or beef on special occasions. The food gets even heavier in the highlands, where *chuletas de cerdo*, or pork chops, and thick cuts of steak dominate most restaurant menus. Fish can be prepared a number of ways. In the interior, find it

A typical meal of fish, shrimp, rice, beans, and fried plantain.

estilo de Yojoa, or fried whole. On the north coast, fish might be sautéed with garlic, grilled, or marinated with citrus in ceviche. *Pollo frito*, or fried chicken, is found everywhere.

Restaurants

There's not much a fine dining scene anywhere in Honduras. When going out, many Hondurans dine at rustic country eateries or American chain restaurants, but in some major cities and tourists areas you'll find good Peruvian, French, and BBQ restaurants. In rural areas many restaurants open for around lunchtime and close by dark, while in large cities and tourists areas they might be open from noon–3pm and 5–10pm.

Embassies and consulates

The following are in Tegucigalpa
Canada: Plaza Ficohsa (3rd floor), Boulevard San Juan Bosco, Colonia Payaquí, tel: 2232 4551; www.canada international.gc.ca/costa_rica/contact-honduras-contactez.aspx?lang=eng
US: Avenida La Paz, tel: 2236 9320; http://hn.usembassy.gov.
  The following is in San Pedro Sula
South Africa: Avenida 2 at Calle 12, Barrio Las Acacias, Casa 104, tel: 552 2093.
  UK visitors are referred to the embassy In Guatemala City
UK: Edificio Torre Internacional, Nivel 11, 16 Calle 0-55, Zona 10, tel: (502) 2380 7300, www.gov.uk/government/world/honduras.

Emergencies

Dial 198 anywhere in Honduras for emergency assistance.
Reporting a crime: tel: 2237 6571.

Etiquette

In general Hondurans are laid back and easy going. It's considered polite to greet anyone you speak with a general *buenas días* (in the morning), *buenas tardes* (after midday), or *buenas noches* (after dark). Men shake hands while women embrace. Kissing on the cheek is not customary in the country. When meeting with an elderly person, address them as Don or Doña, followed by their first name.

Festivals

February
The Feria de la Virgen de Suyapa, outside of Tegucigalpa, is revered by Catholics around the country, who honor the Saint's Feast Day, with processions and Mass at the Basílica de Suyapa and other churches around the country.

March
Semana Santa in Comayagua is the biggest Holy Week festival in the country, featuring an entire week of elaborate processions with bright costumes and brightly colored sawdust carpets, called *alfombras*.

April
Garífuna Day, on the Bay Islands and in Garífuna towns on the North Coast, involves dancing, drumming, and lots of Guifiti, the local hooch. The festival, from April 12 to 16, celebrates the arrival of the Garífuna on Roatán in 1797.

May
Feria de San Isidro. Hundreds of thousands descend on the north coast town of La Ceiba for their

version of Carnaval, which includes parades through downtown and all-night partyng on the beaches.

June
Feria Juniana, San Pedro Sula's biggest Party includes concerts and cultural performances around the city, as well as a parade around Avenida Circunvalación on June 29.

July
Garífuna Festival, Bajamar. The tiny Garífuna community near Puerto Cortés attracts Garífuna from around the country to partake in this vibrant, weeks long festival.

August
Sun Jam Festival, Utila. On tiny Water Cay, a limited crowd of 1,500 comes to this all-night rave and electronic music party that has taken place each year since 1996.

Gay and lesbian travelers

While the Bay Islands are an exception, most of Honduras is not particularly gay friendly. The few gay and lesbian bars in major cities are underground and rarely last very long. Murders of LGBT people are not unheard of, so discretion is advised.

Health and medical care

Many doctors in Honduras, especially in San Pedro Sula and Tegucigalpa, speak basic English. Contact your embassy for an updated list. For medical emergencies in San Pedro Sula there's Hospital Centro Médico Betesda at 11a Av. NO and 11a Calle NO (tel 516 0900); in Tegucigalpa there's the Honduras Medical Center (http://hmc.com.hn), on Av. Juan Lindo.

Media

There are five main daily Spanish newspapers in Honduras, all of which are owned by politicians: *El Heraldo*, *La Prensa*, *La Tribuna*, *El Tiempo*, and *El Nuevo Día*. The Bay Islands have a monthly English-language magazine, the *Bay Islands Voice* (www.bayislandsvoice.com).

Money

Private banks are the best places to exchange money, though hotels may also do it at a higher rate. If you have any leftover lempiras, it's best to change them to euros or dollars before you get on the plane. ATMs are fairly widespread and major credit cards are widely accepted. US dollars are an unofficial second currency.

Opening hours

General business hours are generally 9am–5pm, while banks are Mon–Fri 8.30am–4.30pm, and on Saturday from 9am–noon.

Postal services

While the Honduran postal system, the Correo Nacional, is generally reliable, when sending things of value it's best use international courier services like FedEx, EMS, or DHL, which have offices in San Pedro Sula, Tegucigalpa, and several other larger cities.

Public holidays

January 1 New Year's Day
March/April Maundy Thursday
March/April Good Friday
April 14 Day of the Americas
May 1 Labor Day
August 15 Mother's Day
September 15 Independence Day
October 3 Morazán Day
October 12 Columbus Day
October 21 Armed Forces Day
December 25 Christmas Day

Shopping

Some of the best souvenirs in Honduras are handicrafts created by

Honduran currency.

indigenous groups, such as the black and white ceramics made by the Lenca culture in the Western highlands near Gracias. Along the coast, the Garifuna carve wood and coconuts into figurines, while tribes in La Mosquitia paint on tree bark canvases. Handicrafts from many parts of the country can be found in San Pedro Sula's Guamilito Market, in the many stores in the town of Copán Ruínas and near Tegucigalpa in Valle de Ángeles. Santa Rosa de Copán and Choluteca are good places to pick up cigars, many of which are produced by Cuban exiles and of top quality. For fine leather products, such as hats, purses, and wallets, local brand Danilo's (www.danilos.com) has outlets in San Pedro Sula.

Telecommunications

Telephones
The international code for Costa Rica is 504. To make a call from a public phone, which are increasingly rare, you will need a phone card (*tarjeta telefónica*), available at most stores and pharmacies. Most operators offer cellphone service using GSM technology, which most major providers use. To make local calls you can buy a local SIM card, though your provider may have to unlock your phone.

Internet
Internet cafés, once widespread, are now quite rare in Honduras, as free Wi-Fi is in nearly every hotel, restaurant, mall, and café. Most also hotels offer a computer with internet service for guest use.

Time zone

Honduras is on North America's Central Standard Time, which means it is six hours behind GMT, although it does not follow daylight savings; therefore, there is a one-hour time difference during the summer.

Tourist information

Honduras lacks a budget for tourist information offices, so they are few and far between. They generally lack resources, though tour desks and even hotel concierges can help fill in some of the blanks. The main tourist office is the **Instituto Hondureño de Turismo**, Colonia San Carlos (tel: 2222 2124, Mon–Fri 9am–5pm) in Tegucigalpa. They have good information and maps, although they're not entirely user-friendly. More useful are their stands in airports around the country.

Visas and passports

Citizens of the United States, Canada, and the UK require valid passports to enter Honduras. Tourist cards, distributed on arriving international flights or at border crossings, are good for stays of up to 90 days. Keep a copy of your tourist card for presentation upon departure from Honduras. (If you lose it, you'll have to pay a small fine.)

What to Read

Don't Be Afraid, Gringo: A Honduran Woman Speaks From The Heart: The Story of Elvia Alvarado, an autobiographical account of one campesino woman's life of struggle.
Prisión Verde, Ramón Amaya Amador, a worker on a banana plantation details their daily life.
Bananas! How The United Fruit Company Shaped the World, Peter Chapman, a non-fiction book about United Fruit and their influence in shaping Honduras and neighboring countries.
The Mosquito Coast, Paul Theroux, a fictional account of an egotistical inventor, frustrated with the US, who moves his family to the jungles of La Mosquitia.
Far Tortuga, Peter Matthiessen, a poetic account of a group of turtles from Roatán traveling to the Mosquito Coast.

NICARAGUA

FACT FILE

Area: 130,375 sq km (50,300 sq miles)
Capital: Managua
Population: 6.3 million
Currency: Córdoba
Language: Spanish
Weights and measures: Metric
Electricity: 110 volts, 60-cycle current.
Dialling code: 505
Internet abbreviation: .ni

GETTING THERE

By air

From Europe: There are no direct flights from Europe to Nicaragua, so flights will have a layover in the US, Panama, or Costa Rica.
From/via US: American Airlines, Avianca, Delta, Spirit Airlines, and United (see page 339) offer direct flights from several US cities such as Miami, Houston, and Los Angeles.
From Canada: Canada flights to Nicaragua will connect in the US or elsewhere in Central America.

GETTING AROUND

To and from the airport

Augusto C. Sandino International Airport (MGA) 10km (6 miles) east of downtown Managua is Nicaragua's main international airport; however, some flights also go direct to the Corn Islands or the Costa Esmeralda airport on the Pacific coast. Outside, official airport taxis offer transfers to Managua, while numerous shuttle companies like Adelante Express (www.adelanteexpress.com) and Nicaroads (www.nicaroads.com) connect to Granada and the Pacific Coast.

By air

As the largest country by area in Central America, getting around by land can be time-consuming, particularly to remote destinations far from highways. A domestic terminal at Augusto C. Sandino International Airport in Managua is the home of local carrier La Costeña (tel: 505 2263 2142; www.lacostena.com.ni), which has a small fleet of propeller planes that connect to little used airstrips around the country, including at the Costa Esmeralda, Ometepe, Puerto Cabezas, San Carlos, Bluefields, and the Corn Islands. Checked baggage is limited to 18kg (35lbs), per passenger. Surfboards are an additional $10 per board (limit two per passenger).

By bus

Few cities in Nicaragua have anything even remotely resembling a bus terminal, though Managua is an exception. While chicken buses – the recycled American school buses – leave for cities around the country from the Mercado Roberto Huembes (serving the south) or the Mercado Mayoreo (serving the north and east), more comfortable minibuses depart from the UCA (pronounced 'ooka') Terminal, 1 block from the Rotonda Metro Centro from 6am–9pm.

For reaching other Central American capitals, both Tica Bus (www.ticabus.com) and Trans Nica (www.transnica.com) have daily departures on comfortable, air-conditioned buses.

By sea

While Princess, NCL, and other international cruise lines are increasingly docking at San Juan del Sur on the Pacific Coast, most water routes are regional. Ferries ply the waters between Bluefields and the Corn Islands, as well as across Lake Nicaragua and Lake Managua.

By road

Traveling by rental car is one of the easiest ways to get around Nicaragua, though it can be time-consuming as truck traffic and single-lane roads can suddenly turn a regional drive into an all-day affair. Aside from the Pan-American Highway and CA-4 between Managua and Granada, the roads can be quite rough and may require a 4x4. For getting off the beaten track, driving is often your only option. Rental agencies, most based in Managua, insist that the driver is over 21 years of age, holds a valid passport and driver's license, and has a valid credit card for a deposit (not cash).

In Managua

By bus

Public buses are geared for the local population and tend to be crowded, dangerous and not particularly convenient for tourists anyway.

By taxi

Taxis are cheap and everywhere in Managua and are by far the best way to get around. There are no meters, so fares will need to be negotiated on getting in the cab. Bear in mind that fares tend to be double at night. Overcharging foreigners is normal as well, so be prepared to haggle.

A–Z

Accommodations

Travelers in Managua tend to gravitate toward a few districts. Backpackers stick close to the offices of bus companies in Barrio Martha

Quezada, where most hotels are found. In the Microcentro, south of downtown, most of the more upscale and mid-range accommodations can be found. Unless there's a specific reason to stay in Managua, such as an early flight, most will soon flee the city for more attractive destinations around the country. Note that high season in Nicaragua is from November to April, and low season is from May to October, when there is the most rain. During the low season, room prices in some regions may be discounted, though the Pacific coast tends to stay dry throughout the year and prices don't fluctuate much. Note that rates for many beach resorts and ecolodges often include meals, transportation, and tours.

Budgeting for your trip

Nicaragua can be both an expensive and cheap destination. While there are several ultra-luxury resorts with service that rivals anywhere in the world, much of the country tends to be inexpensive. DIY tours of the country allow you to enjoy the landscape independently and are not much more than a package tour of the country. The currency, the Córdoba, has been losing value in recent years, making the country more affordable than ever.

Airport transfer: From MGA it is a 15-minute ride (about US$20–25 by taxi) to the Microcentro.

Car rental: Rates generally start around US$50 per day, including full insurance in high season; cheaper rates negotiable off-season. Four-wheel-drive vehicles start around US$70 per day.

A local bus in Granada.

Gasoline: $3.39 per gallon

Accommodations: No-frills hotels with cold showers can be found for less than $25 per night (double occupancy) in rural areas, while dorm beds at hostels can be had for even less in most cases. For nicer accommodations with private hot water showers and modern amenities, expect to pay around $50–80 a night (double occupancy), going up to $400 for the nicest resorts.

Food: Eating in Nicaragua tends to be inexpensive, even in tourist towns. Market meals and street food can fill your belly for less than a dollar, while local restaurants rarely cost more than $10 for a meal. Restaurants in resorts can cost as much as $30–50 per meal, per person.

Museums and attractions: Museum admission tends to be very inexpensive in Nicaragua, with prices for foreigners, which are considerably higher than nationals, maxing out at about $5. National park fees are usually around $10.

Children

Nicaragua is a family-friendly country and locals bring their kids with them wherever they go. In Managua, kids will appreciate the atmosphere of the breezy waterfront at Puerto Salvador Allende, although for the best attractions families should get out of the city. There are family-friendly chocolate-making classes at Granada's Choco Museo, while not far away, kayaking and fishing trips on Lake Nicaragua from the Lord of the Flies-like Jicaro Island Ecolodge make for one-of-a-kind adventures. Volcanoes like Cerro Negor offer

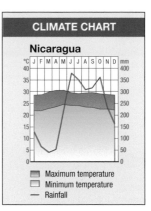

CLIMATE CHART

Nicaragua

sandboarding, while lakes like Apoyo Lagoon are submerged in thick rainforest where there are opportunities to spot howler and capuchin monkeys. The beaches and snorkeling on the Corn Islands and along the Costa Esmeralda north of San Juan del Sur are definite crowd-pleasers.

Climate

Nicaragua has two seasons: rainy and dry. The rainy season lasts from July to December and for much of the period the rain comes in short but intense tropical downpours once a day. During the dry season, from January to June, the landscape tends to dry out, especially in the Pacific lowlands. Temperatures are hot year-round, varying primarily by location. Along the coasts, temperatures range between 22°C–30°C (72°–86°F), though can easily hover above 38°C (100°F) in May, the hottest month. The interior of the country tends to be about 5°C (9°F) cooler, while in the mountains it's about 10°C (18°F) cooler.

Crime and safety

Compared with neighboring Honduras and El Salvador, crime in Nicaragua is significantly lower, which many believe is the result of one of the region's most modern police forces. Still, common sense measures should be taken while traveling, particularly in Managua. Most crimes are petty, limited to pickpocketing and cellphone grabbing. Preventative measures include carrying only as much cash as you need and leaving valuables at home or locked in a hotel safe. Take taxis whenever possible in the city, especially at night.

Customs regulations

Personal effects may be taken into the country, including up to 500g (18oz) of tobacco and 3 liters (102 fl oz) of wine or liquor (if over 21). Carry prescription drugs in original containers.

Disabled travelers

Outside of ramps and elevators in malls and international chain hotels in Managua, as well as a few resorts, very few provisions have been made for disabled travelers in Nicaragua. However, the country has a significant disabled population because of landmines and violence in the 1970s, so people in general tend to be understanding of the needs of less able-bodied travelers.

Eating out

What to eat

The origins of Nicaragua's most famous dish, *gallo pinto* (literally, painted rooster), trace back to a former province called Guanacaste, that is now a part of Costa Rica. Still, Nicaraguans claim the dish, which is comprised of seasoned rice and black or red beans mixed with onion, cilantro, garlic, and peppers. Bananas and plantains find their way into almost in dish as *tajadas* (plantain chips), *tostones* (pressed and fried in oil), and *maduros* (slow roasted with sugar). In Granada, the most famous dish is *vigorón*, a plate of boiled yuca topped with fried pork skin and cabbage slaw that's served on a banana leaf. *Nacatamales*, Nicaragua's version of the *tamale*, is served in markets and restaurants around the country, often with distinct regional preparations.

Restaurants

Outside of a few restaurants in Managua and a handful of coastal resorts, most dining in Nicaragua is a very casual affair. Throughout the country, most restaurants open for lunch from about noon–3pm and for dinner from about 6–10pm.

Embassies and consulates

The following are in Managua:
Canada: De Los Pepitos, Building 5, tel: 2268 0433; http://nicaragua.gc.ca.
South Africa: (Consulate), Lomas de Guadalupe 31, tel: 2270 5634.
US: Kilómetro 5 ½ Carretera Sur, tel: 2252 7100; https://ni.usembassy.gov.

The following is in San José, Costa Rica
UK: Edificio Centro Colón, 11th Floor, in tel: 2258 2025, www.gov.uk/govern ment/world/nicaragua

Emergencies

Dial 118 anywhere in Nicaragua for emergency assistance.

Etiquette

Nicaraguans are generally open and friendly, eager to hold conversations with foreigners. Like elsewhere in the region, beginning a conversation with *hola* or *buenos dias*, as well as addressing strangers with '*usted*' rather than '*tú*' is considered polite. The terms Don (men) and Doña (women) followed by first names is often used to address older Nicaraguans. Even poor *campesinos* tend to take care of how they dress, making sure to tuck in their shirts, so grungy backpacker gear and skimpy swimsuits may attract stares in some places.

Festivals

February

Festival Poesia Nicaragua, the country's international poetry festival runs for one week at the end of February, each year celebrating the work of one Nicaraguan poet and attracting visitors from more than 50 countries who give readings around town.

March

Semana Santa, Holy Week celebrations take place around Nicaragua, and are most festive in colonial towns like Granada and León. Many Nicaraguans use the break to travel and beach resorts tend to fill up months in advance.

May

Tulululu, in Bluefields, is devoted to the Maypole celebrations in honor of the rain and on the last day of the month, a chain dance begins in the Old Bank neighborhood and eventually marches across town to Cotton Tree neighborhood.

July

Sandinista Day, on July 19, celebrations make the end of the Sandinista revolution when the Somoza regime gave up power in 1979. The largest celebrations take place in Managua.

August

Crab Soup Festival, the Corn Islands. Each year on the 27th (Big Corn) and the 29th (Little Corn), in commemoration of the end of slavery, residents dance, march, and eat crab soup.
International Fishing Tournament, Rio San Juan, a competition among top regional fishermen.

September

San Jeronimo, on the last day of September in Masaya, with religious processions celebrating the saint and a Torovenado parade with folkloric characters.

October

Los Aguizotes, on the last Friday of the month in Masaya, the gates of hell open (allegedly), and devils and demons parade around town in the regional version of Halloween.

November

Garífuna Day, in Orinoco and elsewhere along the Caribbean coast on the 19th, with lots of drumming, music and the sampling of traditional foods.

Gay and lesbian travelers

While Managua and coastal communities filled with expats are generally LGBT-friendly and have gay clubs and a gay parade, rural areas tend to be more conservative and are not always as open-minded. While violence against gay and lesbian travelers is rare, keeping public displays of affection to a minimum is recommended to mitigate safety concerns.

Health and medical care

Nicaragua has a spotty record on health care, with many rural communities lacking access to basic supplies. Still, there are modern hospitals and foreign-trained English speaking doctors available in many parts of the country.

For medical emergencies in the Managua area, you can contact:
Hospital Bautista, tel: 2249 7070, www.hospitalbautistanicaragua.com
Metropolitano Hospital Vivian Pellas, tel: 2255 6900, www.metropolitano.com.ni

Media

Daily Spanish-language newspapers include: La Tribuna, *El Nueno*

Diario, La Prensa, El Mercurio, and *La Jornada*. There are no English-language papers in print.

Money

Money can be exchanged with street money changers and gas stations, though banks and airports tend to be the most secure. Hotels will often change money for a fee and some resort areas use the US dollar as a second currency. ATMs are widespread and generally offer the best rates. It's important to carry small bills, as taxi drivers and store clerks are notorious for not having enough change.

Opening hours

Bank hours are generally 8.30am–4pm during the week, with some opening for a half-day on Saturday. Malls and store tend to open from 10am–8pm, although in rural areas that's not always the case.

Postal services

Correos de Nicaragua post offices has branches all over the country, with the main branch in Managua, the Palacio de Correos, at 2a Ave NO y 5a Calle NO. International courier services like FedEx and DHL are more secure for anything of value.

Carnival time.

Public holidays

January 1 New Year's Day
March/April Holy Week (Thurs, Fri, and Sat before Easter Sunday)
April 11 Juan Santamaría Day
May 1 Labor Day
July 19 Liberation Day
September 14 Battle of San Jacinto
September 15 Independence Day
November 2 Day of the Dead
December 8 La Purisma
December 25 Christmas Day

Shopping

Managua is home to a handful of posh, air-conditioned shopping malls like the Galerias de Santo Domingo and Multi Centro Las Americas, though you'll find more interesting souvenirs out in the provinces. Fair trade stores in different parts of the country sell items like woven pine needle baskets from Jalapa, furniture from Masatepe, leather from Estelí, and hammocks from Masaya. In Estelí, cigars are an excellent purchase and the quality rivals that of Cuba, while Flor de Caña rum can be picked up all over the country.

Telecommunications

Telephones

The international code for Nicaragua is 505. Most operators offer cellphone service using GSM technology (1800 MHz and 850 MHz).

Internet

Free Wi-Fi hotspots can be found in malls, cafés, and some public parks, replacing the inexpensive cyber cafés that used to be the primary method of online access in Nicaragua. Most hotels offer free connections, though multinational chains sometimes charge a fee.

Time zone

Nicaragua is on North America's Central Standard Time, which means it is six hours behind GMT. It does not observe Daylight Savings, so this time difference increases one hour during the northern summer months. The sun sets year-round around 6pm.

Tourist information

Intur – The Nicaragua Tourism Board, inside Managua's Crowne Plaza Hotel, offers general information and maps, plus has smaller offices around the country. http://visitnicaragua.us

Visas and passports

Citizens of the US, Canada, UK, Ireland, Australia, New Zealand, and South Africa need only a passport valid for at least six months beyond the date of entry to Nicaragua for a stay of 90 days. A tourist card must be purchased on arrival for $10. There is a $35 exit fee upon leaving Nicaragua by air, though it is usually included in the price of a ticket.

What to read

Azul, by Rubén Darío, the first book of poems from the native poet helped launch the Modernista form of literature.
The Jaguar Smile, A Nicaraguan Journey, by Salman Rushdie, puts a human face on Nicaragua through its politics, poetry and land amidst the horrors of the revolution.
Nicaragua: Living in the Shadow of the Eagle, by Thomas Walker and Christine Wade, provides in-depth coverage of the breadth of US influence on Nicaragua.
The Nationalist in Nicaragua, by Thomas Belt, is an early travelogue, first published in 1874, that explores the country's tropical forests, rivers and lakes.

COSTA RICA

FACT FILE

Area: 51,000 sq km (19,700 sq miles)
Capital: San José
Population: 5 million
Currency: Colón
Language: Spanish
Weights and measures: Metric
Electricity: 110 volts, 60-cycle current.
Dialling code: 506
Internet abbreviation: .cr

GETTING THERE

By air

From Europe: Iberia flies direct from Madrid and British Airways flies direct from London. The alternative is to connect in the US.
From via/US: Alaska Airlines, American Airlines, Air Berlin, Avianca, Copa Airlines, Delta, Frontier Airlines, JetBlue, Sansa, Spirit Airlines, United, US Airways, West Jet.
From Canada: Air Canada offer direct flights from Toronto; Vancouver trips go through Houston or Dallas; flights from Montreal stop in the eastern US.

For airline information, see page 339.

GETTING AROUND

To and from the airport

Most international flights arrive in Costa Rica at Juan Santamaría Airport (SJO) about 16km (10 miles) from San José, although Daniel Oduber International Airport (LIR) in Liberia also handles international flights. Taxi Unidos (www.taxiaeropuerto.com) is the official airport taxi company and has a fleet of orange vehicles, but Uber is also a good option. There are also unlicensed

taxis at the airports but fares can be significantly higher. Buses into town, operated by TUASA, leave from a stop close to the terminal exit between 4.30am and 11pm and cost less than US$1. Most buses from Guanacaste and Puntarenas beaches to the capital also stop at the airport.

By air

Domestic flights (vuelos locales) are reasonably priced and are a comfortable alternative to many hours on bad roads. Nature Air (www.natureair. com) and **SANSA** (www.flysansa.com) fly to Arenal, Liberia, Tamarindo, Nosara, Tambor, Quepos, Palmar Sur, Puerto Jiménez, Drake Bay, Punta Islita, Tortuguero, Bocas del Toro, Panamá, and Granada and Managua, Nicaragua, with additional destinations available for chartered flights. Surfboards are accepted if there is space available, for an extra charge.

Keep in mind that local airlines allow one checked bag, up to 18kg (40lbs), per passenger, depending on the fare class purchased; fees for excess baggage vary from $7 to $60. On SANSA, any bag weighing more than 14kg (30lbs) is charged $1 for each additional 450 grams (1lb).

By bus

San José has no central terminal for long-distance buses, each bus hub handles travel to a certain region. Major ones include the 'Coca-Cola,' near a former bottling plant at Calle 16, Avenida 1–3, the departure point for the Central Pacific; the Caribbean bus terminal, Calle Central, Avenida 11 (just east of the Children's Museum); and MUSOC, Calle Central, Avenida 30, to San Isidro (the hub for buses to the Southern Zone). Tica Bus (tel: 2296 9788; www.ticabus.com) and Trans Nica (tel: 2223 4242; www.transnica.

com) have daily buses to neighboring Central American countries.

By sea

Cruise ships come into Puerto Limón on the Caribbean coast and Puerto Caldera and Puntarenas on the Pacific. Princess, Norwegian, Carnival, Windstar, Holland America, and many other major cruise lines stop in Costa Rica, often coming from or going to the Panama Canal.

By road

Pothole-filled, unlit roads, careless (to put it mildly) drivers, and poor signage and road markings conspire to make driving in Costa Rica a definite challenge, but it makes sense for off-the-beaten-path trips outside San José. The majority of rental cars are manual transmission; automatics cost considerably more. Most agencies insist that the driver is over 21 years of age, holds a valid passport and driver's license, and has a valid credit card for a deposit (not cash).

In San José

By bus

The Sabana Cementerio bus cuts across town in both directions, just north and south of the center; ask for the stop closest to you (¿Dónde está la parada para el Sabana Cementerio?). All other buses leave for the suburbs from their respective quadrants; for example, those heading west (Rohrmoser, Escazú, Santa Ana) leave from the Coca-Cola area; ones heading east (Los Yoses, San Pedro, Curridabat) leave from near the east end of the pedestrian walkway. Check out www.busmapscr.com for route maps.

By rail

Commuter rail service, the Tren Urbano, runs every half hour between

San José and Heredia or Cartago, departing from San José's Atlantic Station. For a detailed schedule see www.incofer.go.cr.

By taxi

Taxis are by far the easiest way of getting around San José; they are widely used and relatively inexpensive. You'll rarely have to wait long, although it is sometimes difficult to catch a cab in a rainy rush hour. All taxis should have operational meters *(marías)*; be sure the drivers use them. If not, negotiate before getting in. In San José, Uber (www.uber.com) is secure and often less expensive than traditional taxis.

A–Z

Acccommodations

The most popular places to stay in San José are in *el puro centro*, right downtown near the Plaza de la Cultura and in historic Barrio Amón, which has some boutique hotels with character. More relaxed hotels can be found outside the center in Escazú, Santa Ana, Alajuela, or Heredia. Note that high season in Costa Rica is from November 1 to April 30, and low season is from May 1 to October 31, excluding July and August, when greater demand means higher prices. During the low season, room prices may be discounted by as much as 40 percent. Reservations made, but not paid for, may not be held, especially during high season. Note that rates for remote lodges in areas such as Tortuguero or the Osa Peninsula may appear high but they usually include meals, transportation, and tours.

Budgeting for your trip

Many visitors find Costa Rica more expensive than they expected. It still can be an economical destination, and much of Costa Rica can be enjoyed independently, allowing you to keep costs down – although an itinerary organized by a tour operator may be worth the extra cost in time savings. The currency, the Colon, is one of the most stable in the region. **Airport transfer:** From SJO it is a 20-minute ride (about US$20–30 by taxi or Uber) between downtown San José and the airport.

Car rental: Rates generally start around US$70 per day, including full insurance in high season; cheaper rates are negotiable off-season. Four-wheel-drive vehicles start at around US$80 per day.

Gasoline: $3.57 per gallon

Accommodations: Cheap cabins (usually cold or shared showers) for under $25 per night (double occupancy) abound, especially at the beach – but they fill up fast in high season and on weekends. To upgrade the comfort level, expect to pay at least $70 to $90 a night (double occupancy) for moderate lodging (private baths, hot water, some views, parking, and extra amenities).

Food: Most local restaurants are very reasonably priced, ranging from a few dollars for a simple meal to $50 for two people at an above average restaurant. Luxury hotel restaurants are sometimes excessively priced, often costing as much as $30–50 per meal, per person.

Museums and attractions: Attractions sometimes charge one price for tourists, and a lower one for Costa Ricans. Many of the smaller museums are free; the rest range from less than $1 to $15, usually with student and child rates. National park admission fees vary, but are usually around $10.

Children

Costa Ricans adore children and they are welcome everywhere. The San José area has any number of child-focused activities, but one of the best is the interactive exhibits at the Museo de los Niños, housed in a castle-like former prison. Children usually enjoy La Paz Waterfall Gardens in Varablanca. For seaside fun, Tamarindo on the North Pacific is a good beginner's beach for fledgling surfers. Punta Uva on the southern Caribbean coast and sheltered Playa Manuel Antonio on the central Pacific coast provide child-friendly snorkeling and swimming. Older children may want to stay up for the mystical, nocturnal spectacle of giant sea turtles laying eggs at Tamarindo, Tortuguero, or Ostional.

Climate

Costa Rica has two seasons; the rainy or green season, which Costa Ricans call winter *(invierno)*, and the dry season or summer *(verano)*. In the Central Valley, the rainy season

lasts from May through November and the dry season from December through April. Even during the rainy season, most mornings are bright and sunny. During the rainy season there are fewer tourists and you can take advantage of green-season discounts in hotels. Rain can fall at any time on the Caribbean coast but October is usually the driest month. Be prepared for higher humidity on the Caribbean coast.

The average temperature in San José is 24°C (75°F). In the highlands, temperatures drop approximately 0.6°C for each 100 meters (500ft) of elevation. The temperature on the coasts varies from the mid-20s°C (70s°F) to the 30s°C (low 90s°F).

Crime and safety

Theft can be a problem in Costa Rica. Pickpocketing, chain and watch snatching, backpack grabbing, and other thefts are becoming more common, especially in downtown San José and popular beach towns. It is, for the most part, non-violent, snatch-and-run thievery. Do not be paranoid and frightened, but do be vigilant. Carry only as much cash as you will need. Leave your backpack, passport, and jewelry in the hotel, preferably in a locked office. Keep an eye on wallets and shoulder bags. If you buy valuable items, make your return trip by taxi. Avoid deserted streets at night and walking in isolated areas.

Customs regulations

Personal effects may be taken into the country and up to six rolls of film, 500g (18oz) of tobacco, 2kg (4lbs) of candy, and 5 liters (170 fl oz) of wine or liquor (if over 21). Carry

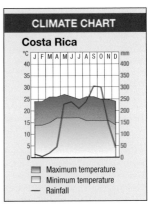

prescription drugs in original containers. Anyone caught with illegal drugs can face 8 to 20 years in jail with no bail.

Disabled travelers

Much of Costa Rica's claim to fame is based around rugged nature, and the country's buckled and potholed roads and sidewalks (where they exist) can be difficult to navigate at the best of times. Definitions of 'accessible' vary widely – call ahead with specific questions to avoid disappointment. A variety of attractions, including the Poás and Irazú volcanoes, and Carara National Park, are set up to facilitate travelers in wheelchairs, and a handful of local companies organize excursions or arrange transportation.

Eating out

What to eat

The classic Costa Rican dish of *gallo pinto* (literally, painted rooster) is rice and black or red beans mixed with seasonings including onion, cilantro (coriander), garlic, and finely chopped bell peppers. Guanacaste, the northwestern province that once was part of Nicaragua, claims to have originated this dish. While predominantly a breakfast dish in the city, rural Costa Ricans eat *gallo pinto* three times daily, accompanied by homemade corn tortillas. For breakfast they order it with scrambled or fried eggs and sour cream, or natilla.

For lunch, many have a *casado* – a hearty combination including rice, beans, cabbage salad, fried sweet plantains, and sauced chicken, fish, or beef. *Picadillos* are served in every Tico home: diced potatoes, chayotes (water squash or vegetable pears) or string beans mixed with finely chopped meat, tomatoes, onions, culantro, bell peppers, and whatever the cook feels may add flavor to the pot. Leftover *picadillos*, fried with rice, are served for breakfast, usually with hot tortillas; this combination is called *amanecido*.

Restaurants

Costa Rica's culinary offerings are very cosmopolitan, along with traditional local fare (*comida típica*). Monday to Saturday, most bars/restaurants open any time from 8.30am to 11am, and stay open until around midnight or 2am in cities. On Sunday, some may close earlier,

others do not bother to open at all. Out in the campo, you will have to eat early or go hungry. Even in many tourist areas, restaurants close early. Friday and Saturday nights are busy, but earlier in the week you may find happy hours and other offers.

Embassies and consulates

The following are in San José:
Canada: Oficentro La Sábana, Bldg 5, tel: 2242 4400; http://costarica.gc.ca.
South Africa: (Consulate), 150 meters/yds west of entrance to Pacific Rail Terminal, Downtown, tel: 222 1470 or 223 8223.
UK: Edificio Centro Colón, 11th Floor, tel: 2258 2025, www.gov.uk/government/world/costa-rica.
US: Vía 104, Calle 98, Provincia de San José, tel: 2519 2000; http://costarica.usembassy.gov.

Emergencies

Dial 911 anywhere in Costa Rica for emergency assistance.
Car Accidents: tel: 800-8726 7486 (Transit Police in San José) and 800-800 8001 (National Insurance Institute in San José).
Reporting a crime: tel: 2295 3272 or 911 (OIJ in San José, 24 hours).

Etiquette

Preceding any request with *Me puede hacer el favor de...* (Could you do me the favor of...) will go a long way to ensuring the best service. While you'll see Costa Ricans snapping their fingers at wait staff and calling out *muchacha* or *muchacho* (girl or boy), foreigners should stick to the more respectful *Disculpe, señor/a* (Excuse me sir/ma'am). People shake hands when first introduced. Women usually greet each other with a kiss on the cheek and say goodbye in the same fashion; this also applies when a friendly relationship exists, and men and women often greet each other in the same way. Elderly Costa Ricans are commonly addressed as Don (men) or Doña (women) followed by their first name.

Festivals

January

Fiestas Palmares, in Palmares near Alajuela, a two week cowboy party with horse parades, rodeos, musical performances, rides, and beer.

February

Fiestas de los Diablitos, Festival of the Little Devils, Rey Curre, with masks, costumes, and dancing reenactments of the victory over the Spanish.
Liberia Fiestas, where folkloric traditions are celebrated with concerts and parties around Liberia.

March

National Orchid Show, San José, with 300-plus species of orchids displayed.

April

Día de Juan Santamaría, celebrated around the country to honor national hero, Juan Santamaria, who helped Costa Rica defeat William Walker.

July

Virgin of the Sea Fiestas, Puntarenas, with food, music, and religious activities to honor the town's patron saint.
Annexation of Guanacaste Day, Liberia, celebrating the day the province chose Costa Rica over Nicaragua.

August

Día de la Virgen de los Ángeles, Cartago, Costa Rica's largest religious holiday, where pilgrims march on foot or on their knees to the Basilica de Los Ángeles to pay honor to La Negrita, the black Virgin

October

Carnaval, in Puerto Límon and Puerto Viejo, with costumes, parades through town, live music, and feasts.
Día de la Raza, commemorating Columbus' discovery of the New World.

November

Día de los Inocentes, countrywide, paying respect to the dead.

December

El Tope Nacional, San José, the national horse parade.
San Jose Carnival, with parades and live music.

Gay and lesbian travelers

Relatively free of active oppression and intolerance, Costa Rica has become a favorite spot for LGBT travelers from around the region. It now even has its own Gay Pride Parade (June). San José and Manuel Antonio have clusters of gay-only and gay-friendly hotels, restaurants, and bars. The general public tends to be uncomfortable with same-sex displays of affection, however.

Health and medical care

Costa Rica has an excellent health-care system, much less expensive than in the US. Many doctors are trained in the US or Europe and speak English, especially those at private clinics. In some remote communities, you can get help through the public clinic system, called **EBAIS**. For medical emergencies in the San José area: **Hospital de los Niños**, tel: 2523 3600 (for children). **Hospital San Juan de Díos**, tel: 2547 8000 **Clínica Católica**, Guadalupe, tel: 2246 3000 **Hospital San José CIMA**, Escazú, tel: 2208 1000, www.hospitalsanjose.net

Media

Daily Spanish-language newspapers include: *La Nación*, *La Prensa Libre*, *La República*, and *Al Día*. The *Tico Times* (www.ticotimes.net), published weekly on Friday, is widely available at most newsstands in central San José, Cartago, Heredia, and Alajuela. It gives the week's news in Costa Rica and up-to-date listings of what's happening, and where.

Money

Private banks are the best places to exchange money if you want to avoid long lines. Your hotel may also change money for you. Some banks now handle euros as well as dollars. Money can be exchanged at the airport (BAC San José) from 5am to 10pm – if you have colones, it's best to change them to euros or dollars before you get on the plane. ATMs are fairly widespread and major credit cards are widely accepted. US dollars are an unofficial second currency.

Opening hours

Business opening hours are generally 8am–5pm, often with a lunch break from noon–1pm. Retail stores are usually open Mon–Sat from 9am until 6 or 7pm. State banks usually open Mon–Fri from 8.30am–3.30pm and some are also open on Saturday morning.

Postal services

The central post office is at Ca. 2, Avenida 1–3, tel: 2223 9766. Mail can be received there in the general delivery section *(Lista de Correos)*. Outgoing items should be mailed at either a hotel desk or a post office. It is usually difficult, time-consuming, and expensive to receive packages in the mail. The most popular international courier services are FedEx and DHL. Consult the *Yellow Pages* for numbers.

Public holidays

January 1 New Year's Day
March/April Good Thursday
March/April Good Friday
April 11 Juan Santamaría Day
May 1 Labor Day
July 25 Annexation Day
August 2 Virgin of Los Angeles Day
August 15 Mother's Day
September 15 Independence Day
October 12 Meeting of the Cultures Day
December 25 Christmas Day

Shopping

Costa Rica's selection of souvenirs has been increasing slowly but steadily over the past few years. The traditional classics – miniature ox-carts, wood products, indigenous masks, and coffee – are now sold alongside locally produced CDs that rival any world-music offering. Bartering is low-key, but you can usually get a discount off the price by paying cash. Costa Rican coffee is excellent and relatively inexpensive, with top-quality Coopedota coffee from the Tarrazú region available in some supermarkets. The mountain town of Sarchí is known for its intricately painted woodwork. Papaya Music releases are available at Universal, Lehman's, and many other stores, featuring local legends and traditional tunes.

Telecommunications

Telephones
The international code for Costa Rica is 506. To make a call from a public phone, you will need a phone card *(tarjeta telefónica)*, available at most stores and pharmacies. Most operators offer cellphone service using GSM technology (1800 MHz and 850 MHz).

Internet
Inexpensive internet cafés are slowly disappearing as there is now public internet access and Wi-Fi spots in just about any town of any size. Most hotels offer a computer with internet service, Wi-Fi, or both. Eateries such as Bagelmen's outlets in San José and Denny's at the Hotel Irazú are popular wireless hotspots.

Time zone

Costa Rica is on North America's Central Standard Time which means it is six hours behind GMT. It does not observe Daylight Savings, so this time difference increases one hour during the northern summer months. Since Costa Rica is close to the equator, the number of daylight hours does not vary much from season to season; the sun sets year-round more or less around 6pm.

Tourist information

The following offices are particularly good:
ICT Avenida Central, pedestrian walkway office, tel: 2222 1090, Mon–Fri 9am–5pm, closed noon to 1pm. Good information and maps.
ICT Central Office, East Side of Juan Pablo II Bridge, over the highway General Cañas, tel: 2299 5800, 866 267 8274 (from the US), 8am–4pm. Staffed by bilingual operators.
National Parks Information, tel: 2283 8004 or 192, www.costarica-national parks.com. Official government site for extensive information on all national parks.

Visas and passports

Citizens of the US, Canada, UK, Ireland, Australia, New Zealand, and South Africa need only a passport valid for at least six months beyond the date of entry to Costa Rica. Travelers may remain for 90 days. If you leave the country for 72 hours, when you return you will be allowed another 90 days.

What to read

Green Phoenix: Restoring the Tropical Forests of Guanacaste, William Allen, a fresh look at saving the world's tropical forests.
Costa Rica: A Traveler's Literary Companion, edited by Barbara Ras, includes short stories set around Costa Rica.
The Birds of Costa Rica, Richard Garrigues and Robert Dean, a field guide to the country's bird life.
Happier Than a Billionaire, Nadine Hays Pisani, how an American woman quit her job and relocated to the beach in Central America.

PANAMA

FACT FILE

Area: 77,000 sq km (30,000 sq miles)
Capital: Panama City
Population: 4 million
Currency: Balboa
Language: Spanish
Weights and measures: Metric
Electricity: 110-120 volts, 60-cycle current.
Dialling code: 507
Internet abbreviation: .pa

GETTING THERE

By air

From Europe: Luftansa offers scheduled, direct flights from Frankfurt, while KLM has direct flights from Amsterdam. The alternative is to connect in the US.
From via/US: American Airlines, Avianca, Copa Airlines, Delta, Spirit, and United.
From Canada: Avianca offers several weekly direct flights from Toronto, while other airlines connect in the US.

For airline contact details, see page 339.

GETTING AROUND

To and from the airport

Panama's Tocumen International Airport is 30km (19mi) east of Panama City. Official airport taxis can be hired inside the airport. Uber is also a good option. Some business hotels offer transfers, though you should make arrangements in advance for a pick up.

By air

From Albrook Marcus A. Gelabert airport, 1.5km (1 mile) west of the center, Air Panama (www.airpanama.com) offers domestic flights to more than a dozen destinations within Panama, including Kuna Yala (the San Blas Islands), David, Chitré, the Pearl Islands and Bocas del Toro. As drives can be long and roads rough, not to mention some island destinations are otherwise inaccessible without a private yacht, internal flights can save a considerable amount of travel time.

Air Panama flights allow one checked bag, up to 14kg (30lbs), per passenger, with the exception of flights to David, which allow 30kg (66lbs).

By bus

Beside Albrook airport and the Albrook metro station is the Albrook bus terminal, the city's modern bus station. Here there are bus lines to all parts of the country, with many buses per day making the trip to David. For long distances buses, Tica Bus (www.ticabus.com) goes direct to San José, continuing on to capitals throughout Central America. Expreso Panama (www.expresopanama.com) also goes to San José.

By sea

Many major cruise lines have a trip through the Panama Canal on their itineraries, plus stops in Panama City and Colón where shore excursions can be arranged. Private yachts are also a popular way to travel to the Kuna Yala (San Blas Islands) and sometimes continuing to Cartagena, Colombia. Most trips begin in Portobelo outside of Colón. Ferries also make the trip from Panama City to Taboga Island and the Pearl Islands.

By road

The Pan-American Highway is paved for almost the entire length of Panama, stopping for the Darién Gap, the roadless jungle region that borders Colombia. Roads that branch off the highway to main towns are usually good, though others can be rough and filled with potholes. Most rental car agencies require that the driver is over 21 years of age, holds a valid passport and driver's license, and has a valid credit card for a deposit (not cash). If traveling outside the main cities, particularly on mountain roads, renting a 4x4 is a must.

In Panama City:

By metro

A new metro system opened in 2014, running for about 5km (8 miles) from the Albrook bus terminal and mall through the city to the town of Los Andes. Many of the stops are away from tourist areas, though some are useful, such as the Cinco de Mayo stop that is near Casco Viejo.

By taxi

Taxis are by far the best way of getting around Panama City. They are everywhere and very cheap. If they don't have a meter negotiate a price before getting in. Smartphone apps like Uber and Easy Taxi are very useful here.

A-Z

Accommodations

Most hotels in Panama City are found within a few neighborhoods. For hip boutique hotels that are often as much of the nightlife scene as near it, Casco Viejo, with hotels like the American Trade (www.acehotel.com/panama) and Tantalo (www.tantalohotel.com, is the place to be. More corporate hotels like the Bristol (www.thebristol.com) and budget accommodations are scattered around a few adjoining neighborhoods like Obarrio, Bellavista, Marbella, and El Cangrejo.

The high tourist season in Panama is during the dry season, running roughly from December to mid-March, as well as national holidays. During the rainy season some resort hotels in Bocas del Toro and along Pacific beaches will offer low season rates.

Budgeting for your trip

As it is one of the most developed nations in the region, Panama can be much more expensive than countries farther north. The currency, the Balboa, is the dollar, though Panama does have its own set of coins that correspond to those in the US.

Airport transfer: From PTY it is a 30–60 minute ride (about US$20–25 by taxi) between the city center and the airport, depending heavily on traffic.

Car rental: Rates generally start around US$40 per day, including full insurance in high season; cheaper rates are negotiable off-season. Four-wheel-drive vehicles start around US$60 per day and are recommended if traveling on mountain roads.

Gasoline: $2.19 per gallon

Accommodations: In rural areas and remote beaches, some rustic hotels can be found for around $50–60 per night (double occupancy). For a middle-of-the-road hotel with hot water, air-conditioning, and Wi-Fi, expect to pay about at least $70 to $100 a night (double occupancy), while luxury hotels and resorts range from about $150 to $500 a night.

Food: Panama City has Central America's best restaurant scene, though the best restaurants average $60 per person. Meals at simple restaurants average about $20 per person, while those in rural areas are half of that.

Museums and attractions: Museums in Panama usually have two prices: one for Panamanians and one for foreigners. Most of the big museums and attractions have admission prices ranging from $10–22, while smaller museums outside of Panama City might cost just a few dollars. Most museums and attractions also offer lower rates for students and children.

Children

Panama is one of the most family friendly places in Central America. Kids are welcome everywhere and most major tourist destinations have numerous activities for kids. Everywhere in the country is a learning opportunity. Watching the ships pass through the Panama Canal, visiting an Emberá village in Gamboa, and seeking out diverse flora and fauna in national parks are just some of the exceptional experiences that kids can take advantage of. Of course, wherever you are in Panama, you are never far from a beach and very few resorts are adults-only.

Climate

In Panama, there are two seasons, wet and dry. The dry season runs from December to mid-March, while the rainy season is the rest of the year (though this doesn't mean rain all day long by any means). Temperatures don't change much throughout the year, though they can vary by location. Temperatures tend to be hotter, more humid, and rainier along the Caribbean coast than the Pacific. In Panama City highs average 32°C (90°F), while highland areas are cooler, averaging 26°C (75°F).

Crime and safety

Panama is relatively safe, especially compared to other countries in the region, However, it is important to take some precautions when walking around – especially at night, when you should stick to well-lit areas and leave valuables at home. Most crime, primarily petty theft, is confined to the three largest cities: Panama City, Colón, and David.

Customs regulations

Visitors entering Panama may bring in no more than 200 cigarettes and 3 liters of alcoholic beverages per adult tax free. Cameras, jewelry, and fishing and diving gear for personal use are permitted duty-free.

Disabled travelers

Panama is more accessible to people with disabilities than other Central American countries, with most large hotels and resorts having

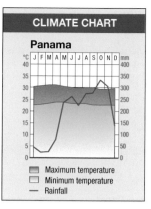

CLIMATE CHART

Panama

amenities. Still, in rugged, rural areas and national parks, getting around will be difficult.

Eating out

What to eat

Traditional Panamanian cuisine tends to be heavy and incorporate a lot of protein, whether it is fish, pork or beef.

Some staple dishes include *hojaldre*, a type of fried bread, and *guacho*, a succulent, seasoned risotto-like rice dish. *Pargo frito*, whole fried red snapper, is popular in Afro-Panamanian communities, as are recipes like *sous*, which are pickled pig's feet. Seafood is popular everywhere, and includes ceviches and *cocteles*, plus grilled or fried filets.

Restaurants

Panama has the best restaurant scene in Central America. It's not just in Panama City either. You find classically trained chefs on remote beaches in the Azuero peninsula or cooking out of a hostel in Bocas del Toro. In Panama City there are modern Panamanian restaurants, Greek restaurants, American chains, hip coffee roasters, and even Vietnamese restaurants.

In rural areas many restaurants open around lunchtime and close by dark, while in urban areas they might be open from noon–3pm and from 5–10pm.

Embassies and consulates

The following are in Panama City
Canada: Torres de las Americas Tower A, 11th floor, Punta Pacifica, tel: 294-2500; www.canadainternational. gc.ca/panama

US: Demetrio Basilio Lakas Avenue, Clayton, tel: 207 7000; http://pa.usembassy.gov.
UK: Calle 53 Este at Nicanor de Obarrio, which can also provide service to Australian and New Zealand citizens.

Emergencies

Dial **103** anywhere in Panama for emergency assistance. For reporting a crime, dial **104**.

Etiquette

Panama is quite relaxed, even in Panama City. While flip-flops, shorts, and tank tops will probably be looked down upon in Panama City, in the rest of the country, few will take issue. Tardiness is very common, so don't be surprised if someone shows up to dinner 30 minutes late. It's considered polite to greet anyone you speak with a general *buenas días* before launching into a conversation. Most Panamanians greet each other with a light kiss on the right cheek, though shaking hands is accepted too. In indigenous areas, particularly Kuna Yala (San Blas), many request money to have their photo taken.

Festivals

January
Feria de las Flores y del Café, in Boquete, is one of the world's most important flower festivals, drawing thousands of people to Boquete for 10 days for exotic flower displays, games and parades.
Jazz Festival, Panama City, runs for three days in late January, attracting both national and international musicians who play in a variety of venus around town.

February
The Feria de la Virgen de Suyapa, outside of Tegucigalpa, is revered by Catholics around the country, who honor the Saint's Feast Day with processions and Mass at the Basílica de Suyapa and other churches around the country.
Carnaval is big in Panama. The four days preceding Ash Wednesday are a chance for Panamanians to really party. Panama City and the Azuero Peninsula are the biggest celebrations and include parades, music and lots of alcohol and feasting.

March
Semana Santa, during this week (Holy Week), parades, religious processions, and other special events take place across the country. Palm Sunday through Holy Saturday.
Feria de David, in Chiriquí capital, thousands gather over 10 days to see hundreds of exhibitors displaying technological advancements, as well as attend various cultural activities.

April
Feria Internacional del Azuero, in La Villa de Los Santos, is a multi-day country fair with livestock competitions, plus traditional foods and heavy drinking.

June
Festival Patronales de La Virgen de Santa Librada, in Las Tablas, from July 20–22, is best known for its Pollera competition, where the most beautiful pollera costumes are displayed and a Queen is crowned.

September
Feria Internacional del Mar, Bocas del Toro, runs for five days and features stands celebrating local cuisine, handicraft booths and various folkloric presentations.

October
Festival del Cristo Negro, Portobelo, thousands of pilgrims pay homage to the city's wooden black Christ effigy, which is paraded around town every October 21.

November
Panama's two main independence days, November 3 and 4, feature parades and fireworks throughout the country. Smaller celebrations occur on November 10 and for the 'First Call for Independence' and November 28, which honors Independence Day from Spain.

Gay and lesbian travelers

Panama tends to have more progressive attitudes towards the LGBT community than most other countries in the region, particularly in Panama City where there is a vibrant gay scene. Rural areas, however, are less progressive and discretion is advised.

Health and medical care

Panama has a greater range of English-speaking doctors than anywhere else in the region. In Panama City, Punta Pacifica (www.hospitalpuntapacifica.com), on Boulevard Pacifica in Punta Pacifica, is the only John Hopkins-associated hospital in Central America and employs more than 350 specialists, as well as the Centro Médico Paitilla (http://centromedicopaitilla.com), at Avenida Balboa and Calle 53, one of the oldest private hospitals in the region.

Kuna Yala women and girl, San Blas islands.

Boquete's flower festival.

Media

There are a half dozen daily Spanish newspapers in Panama, the biggest being *La Prensa*, which also maintains updated events listings. The English-language *Panama News* (www.thepanamanews.com) is available in many tourist shops and airports. Smaller, regional English publications like the *Bocas Breeze* and *The Pearl Island Times* can be found at Albrook Airport, among other places.

Money

ATMs are widespread and major credit cards are widely accepted. For changing euros or other currencies, go to Banco Nacional locations, including at Tocumen airport.

Opening hours

General business hours are generally 9am–5pm, while banks are open Mon–Fri from 8.30am–4.30pm, and on Saturday from 9am–noon. Shopping malls usually close around 8pm.

Postal services

The central post office, Correos y Telégrafos, is located beside the Mercado de Mariscos in Panama City, though many hotels will also mail postcards and letters for you. International courier services like FedEx, Mail Boxes Etc and DHL have offices all over Panama City.

Public holidays

January 1 New Year's Day
January 9 Martyr's Day
March/April Good Friday
March/April Eater Sunday
May 1 Labor Day
August 15 Founding of Old Panama (Panama City only)
October 12 Hispanic Day
November 2 All Souls' Day
November 3 Independence Day
November 4 Flag Day
November 5 Colón Day (Colón only)
November 10 First Call for Independence
November 28 Independence from Spain
December 8 Mother's Day
December 25 Christmas Day

Shopping

Duty free is touted all over Panama, though it's a mostly overblown claim, outside of the stores at Tocumen airport that sell international brands at the same prices as in the US. For a more authentic shopping experience, Galeria Latina (tel: 314-1985), at Calle 5ta and Avenida A, in Casco Viejo, sells Emberá ceremonial masks and Kuna molas, as well as other indigenous handicrafts. For coffee, you can find locally roasted beans from the best farms around Panama, including Gesha, the most expensive coffee in the world, at Café Unido (www.cafeunido.com) locations. Panama hats, which are actually made in Ecuador, are sold throughout the country at souvenir shops, malls and airports.

Telecommunications

Telephones

The international code for Costa Rica is 507. Public phones have all but disappeared from Panama. Most local operators offer cellphone service using GSM technology, which most major providers use.

Internet

There is free Wi-Fi all over Panama: public parks, major attractions, in malls, plus almost every hotel, restaurant, and café.

Time zone

Panama is five hours behind GMT, though it does not follow daylight savings, therefore it is one hour ahead of Costa Rica.

Tourist information

The Autoridad de Turismo de Panama (www.visitpanama.com) has kiosks in both Tocumen and Albrook airports that supply maps and brochures.

Visas and passports

US, Canadian, British, Australian, and New Zealand passport holders may stay for up to 180 days without a visa. If transiting the Panama Canal as vessel passengers, there is no need to show a passport if not disembarking. Your passport must be valid for at least 3 months from the date of your arrival in the country.

What to read

The Path Between the Seas: The Creation of the Panama Canal 1870-1914 by David McCullough and Panama Fever: The Epic Story of Building the Panama Canal by Matthew Parker, are two of the best reads about the construction of the canal.
Emperors in the Jungle, by John Lindsay-Poland, recounts the history of U.S. military involvement in Panama over the past century.
A Guide to the Birds of Panama, by Robert S. Ridgley and John A. Gwynne, is the essential book for avian enthusiasts.
The Darien Gap: Travels in the Rainforest of Panama, by Martin Mitchinson, explores the wild, roadless region that borders Colombia.

While many in Central America speak some English, particularly in tourist areas, it is good to have basic Spanish phrases at your disposal. In remote areas, it is essential. In general, locals are delighted with foreigners who try to speak the language, and they'll be patient – if sometimes amused. Pronunciation is not difficult. The following is a simplified mini-lesson

VOWELS

a as in *father*
e as in *bed*
i as in *police*
o as in *hole*
u as in *rude*
Consonants are approximately like those in English, the main exceptions being:

c is hard before **a**, **o**, or **u** (as in English), and is soft before **e** or **i**, when it sounds like **s**. Thus, *censo* (census) sounds like *senso*.

g is hard before **a**, **o**, or **u** (as in English), but before **e** or **i** a Spanish **g** sounds like a guttural **h**. G before **ua** is often soft or silent, so that *agua* sounds more like *awa*, and Guadalajara like *Wadalajara*.

h is silent.

j sounds like the English h.

ll sounds like y.

ñ sounds like ny, as in *señor*.

q is followed by **u** as in English, but the combination sounds like **k** instead of like **kw**. *¿Qué quiere usted?* is pronounced: Keh kee-er-eh oosted?

r is often rolled.

x between vowels sounds like a guttural **h**, eg in México or Oaxaca.

y alone, as the word meaning 'and,' is pronounced **ee**.

Note that **ch** and **ll** are separate letters of the Spanish alphabet; if looking in a phone book or dictionary for a word beginning with **ch**, you will find it after the final **c** entry. A name or word beginning with **ll** will be listed after the **l** entry (**ñ** and **rr** are also counted as separate letters.)

SPANISH WORDS/PHRASES

please *por favor*
thank you *gracias*
you're welcome *de nada* (literally, for nothing)
I'm sorry *lo siento*
excuse me *con permiso* (if, for example, you would like to pass) *perdón* (if, for example, you have stepped on someone's foot)
yes *sí*
no *no*
can you speak English? *¿habla (usted) inglés?*
do you understand me? *¿me comprende?/¿me entiende?*
this is good *(esto) está bueno*
this is bad *(esto) está malo*
good morning *buenos días*
good night/evening *buenas noches*
goodbye *adiós*
where is...? *¿dónde está...?*
exit *la salida*
entrance *la entrada*
money *dinero*
credit card *la tarjeta de crédito*
tax *impuesto*

Getting around

airplane *el avión*
airport *el aeropuerto*
ferry boat *el barco*
train station *la estación del ferrocarril*
train *el tren*
first class *primera clase*
second class *segunda clase*

Useful phrases when traveling

how much is a ticket to...? *¿cuánto cuesta un boleto a...?*
I want a ticket to... *quiero un boleto a...*
please stop here *pare aquí, por favor*
please go straight *recto, por favor*
how many kilometers is it from here to...? *¿cuántos kilómetros hay de aquí a...?*
how long does it take to go there? *¿cuánto se tarda en llegar?*
left *a la izquierda*
right *a la derecha*
what is this place called? *¿cómo se llama este lugar?*
I'm going to... *Voy a...*

On the road

car *el carro/el automóvil*
where is a gas station? *¿dónde hay una gasolinera?*
a repair garage *un taller mecánico*
auto parts store *almacén de repuestos*
fill it up, please *lleno, por favor*
please check the oil *cheque el aceite, por favor*
radiator *el radiador*
battery *el acumulador*
I need... *necesito...*
tire *una llanta*
spare wheel *la llanta de repuesto*
towtruck *una grúa*
mechanic *un mecánico*
tune-up *una afinación*
it's broken *está roto/a*
they're broken *están rotos/as*

Taxis

taxi *el taxi*
taxi stand *el sitio de taxis*
please call me a taxi *pídame un taxi, por favor*
what will you charge to take me to...? *¿cuánto me cobra para llevarme a...?*

At the bar/restaurant

In Spanish, *el menú* is not the main menu, but a fixed menu offered each day (usually for lunch) at a lower price. The main menu is *la carta.*
restaurant *un restaurante*
cafe or coffee shop *un café*

please bring me some coffee *un café, por favor*
please bring me... *tráigame por favor...*
beer *una cerveza*
cold water *agua fría*
hot water *agua caliente*
soft drink *un refresco*
daily special *el plato del día/el especial del día*
breakfast *desayuno*
lunch *almuerzo/comida*
dinner *cena*
first course *primer plato*
second course *plato principal*
may I have more beer please? *¿más cerveza, por favor?*
may I have the bill please? *¿me da la cuenta, por favor?*
Waiter! (waitress!) *¡Señor! (¡Señorita! ¡Señora!)*

At the hotel

where is there an inexpensive hotel? *¿dónde hay un hotel económico?*
do you have an air-conditioned room? *¿tiene un cuarto con aire acondicionado?*
do you have a room with bathtub? *¿tiene un cuarto con baño?*
where is... *¿dónde está...*
the dining room? *el comedor?*
key *la llave*
manager *el gerente*
owner (male) *el dueño*
owner (female) *la dueña*
can you cash a traveler's check? *¿puede cambiar un cheque de viajero?*

Shopping

Department store *el departamento*
market, marketplace *el mercado*
souvenir shop *la tienda de recuerditos*
what is the price? *¿cuánto cuesta?*
it's too expensive *es muy caro*
can you give me a discount? *¿me puede dar un descuento?*
do you have...? *¿tiene usted...?*
I will buy this *voy a comprar esto*
please show me another *muéstreme otro (otra) por favor*
just a moment, please *un momento, por favor*

Months of the year

January *enero*
February *febrero*
March *marzo*
April *abril*
May *mayo*
June *junio*
July *julio*
August *agosto*
September *septiembre*

October *octubre*
November *noviembre*
December *diciembre*

Days of the week

Monday *lunes*
Tuesday *martes*
Wednesday *miércoles*
Thursday *jueves*
Friday *viernes*
Saturday *sábado*
Sunday *domingo*

Numbers

1 *uno*
2 *dos*
3 *tres*
4 *cuatro*
5 *cinco*
6 *seis*
7 *siete*
8 *ocho*
9 *nueve*
10 *diez*
11 *once*
12 *doce*
13 *trece*
14 *catorce*
15 *quince*
16 *dieciséis*
17 *diecisiete*
18 *dieciocho*
19 *diecinueve*
20 *veinte*
21 *veintiuno*
25 *veinticinco*
30 *treinta*
40 *cuarenta*
50 *cincuenta*
60 *sesenta*
70 *setenta*
80 *ochenta*
90 *noventa*
100 *cien*

UNDERSTANDING CREOLE

English is the official language of Belize and elsewhere along the Caribbean coast of Central America, but the reality on the streets is somewhat different. There are dozens of Creole languages in the Caribbean; Belize Creole (spoken by about 180,000 people) is a hybrid of English and the diverse language groups of West Africa with a smattering of words derived from Spanish and Nicaraguan Miskito. Essentially vernacular (see examples below), Creole isn't taught, written, or read, so there are no definitive spellings. As is the case with many folk languages, Creole is particularly rich in proverbs. (See the book *Creole Proverbs of Belize* for further information.)

Fowl caca white an tink e lay egg A chicken defecates white and thinks she's laid an egg. (Used in relation to a self-important person)

Dis-ya time no tan like befo time It was different in the old days.

Da weh da lee bwai mi di nyam? What was the little boy eating?

GUATEMALAN AND YUCATECAN GLOSSARY

Aguadas – seasonal water holes in lowland Maya region
Atol – drink made from maize dough or sometimes rice
Ayuntamiento – town hall
Brujo – Maya priest
Cacique – political leader (originally 'native chief' in Carib)
Ceiba – sacred kapok (silk-cotton) tree
Cenote – natural well in the Yucatán
Chapín – colloquial term for a Guatemalan
Chicle – tree sap (from which chewing gum is derived)
Cofrade – *cofradía* member
Cofradía – religious group common among Maya in the Guatemalan highlands
Creole – the people and language of Afro-Caribbean Belize
Criollo – native of Spanish descent
Finca – large farm estate (Guatemalan)
Huipil – Maya women's blouse
Indio – pejorative term for indigenous people
Ladino – Meaning 'Latin,' used for any non-indigenous person, or for those who have adopted Hispanic culture
Long Count – Maya calendar from late Preclassic and early Classic period
Marimba – Guatemalan musical instrument similar to a xylophone
Mestizo – person of mixed indigenous and Spanish heritage, who is generally part of Hispanic or *ladino* society; common term in Mexico
Milpa – traditional maize field
Sacbe – 'white road' between ancient cities or leading to a temple, especially in the Yucatán
Típica – traditional handmade Guatemalan clothes and weavings produced for tourists
Traje – traditional Guatemalan clothing
Yaxche – Yucatec Maya word for the sacred *ceiba* tree

CREDITS

PHOTO CREDITS

Alamy 10T, 44, 69, 83, 84BR, 84BL, 186, 212, 213, 239, 321, 328/329
Alex Havret/Apa Publications 73, 107, 110, 112, 113, 114, 115, 116, 119, 120, 121B, 121T, 122B, 122T, 124, 125, 126, 127, 128, 334/335, 337
AWL Images 100, 106, 134, 184, 197TR, 218/219, 220, 224
Ben Pipe/robertharding/REX/ Shutterstock 16/17
Chan Chich Lodge 185
Coco Bongo 117
Corrie Wingate/Apa Publications 9TL, 19T, 24, 28, 38BL, 38/39T, 39ML, 39BR, 39BL, 39TR, 67, 70, 71, 72, 74, 79, 87, 101T, 105B, 132/133, 135, 138, 139, 140, 142, 143, 147, 148, 149, 150, 151, 152, 153, 154, 155, 157, 158, 160, 161, 162, 163, 171, 172, 173, 174, 175, 176, 177, 178, 179, 182, 183, 188, 189, 190, 191, 192/193, 194, 196B, 197BL, 229, 241BL, 268/269, 271T, 272/273, 276, 277, 279, 280, 281, 282, 283, 284, 285, 286, 288, 289, 290, 292, 293, 295, 296, 298, 299, 300, 301, 303, 304/305T,

305TR, 332, 338/339, 340, 343, 344, 348/349, 360, 368
Dagli Orti/REX/Shutterstock 43, 48, 78
Design Pics Inc/REX/Shutterstock 305BR
Diego Lezama/imageBROKER/REX/ Shutterstock 137
Frans Lanting/FLPA 241TR
Getty Images 1, 4, 7TR, 7ML, 10B, 12/13, 14/15, 18, 20, 22/23, 25, 26/27, 31T, 32, 33, 34, 35, 36, 38BR, 40, 42, 45, 46, 47, 50, 51, 52, 53, 54, 55, 56, 57, 58, 59, 60, 61, 62, 63, 64/65, 66, 68, 75, 76, 77, 80, 81, 82, 84/85T, 85BL, 85TR, 86, 88, 94/95, 96/97, 104, 118, 129, 164/165, 168, 195, 196/197T, 197BR, 198/199, 200, 203, 205, 209, 214B, 216, 223, 234, 238, 240/241T, 240BR, 240BL, 241BR, 242/243, 244, 250, 258, 259, 260, 261, 270, 304BR, 306, 307, 315, 317, 322, 325, 330
Glyn Genin/Apa Publications 305BR
iStock 6ML, 6MR, 6BL, 6MR, 7ML, 7TL, 8T, 9TR, 9BR, 11B, 11T, 19B, 21, 85ML, 85BR, 91, 93, 101B, 105T, 130, 131,

156, 187, 201T, 201B, 204, 206, 211, 221, 236T, 237, 245, 249, 251, 253, 254, 255, 256, 257, 265, 266, 267, 287, 304BL, 309, 310, 312, 316, 323, 354, 355, 357, 364
John Bustos/REX/Shutterstock 252
Leonardo 263
National Numismatic Collection, National Museum of American History 49
Pete Oxford/Minden Pictures/FLPA 241ML
Photoshot 264
Public domain 29, 41
Robert Harding 90, 226, 228, 230, 233, 326
Shutterstock 7MR, 8B, 37, 89, 92, 123, 169, 180, 181, 197ML, 202, 207, 210, 214T, 217, 227, 231, 235, 236B, 262, 271B, 305ML, 313, 314, 318, 319, 320, 324, 327, 352, 356, 359, 366, 367
Sipa Press/REX/Shutterstock 30
SuperStock 7BR, 98/99, 232
This content is subject to copyright.
Xinhua/REX/Shutterstock 31B

COVER CREDITS

Front cover: Xunantunich ruins, Belize *Shutterstock*
Back cover: Arenal Volcano, Costa Rica *iStock*

Front flap: (from top) Palenque, Mexico *iStock*; Snorkeling, San Blas Islands, Panama *iStock*; Cenote, Mexico *Shutterstock*; Antigua,

Guatemala *iStock*
Back flap: Boquete, Panama *iStock*

INSIGHT GUIDE CREDITS

Distribution
UK, Ireland and Europe
Apa Publications (UK) Ltd;
sales@insightguides.com
United States and Canada
Ingram Publisher Services;
ips@ingramcontent.com
Australia and New Zealand
Woodslane; info@woodslane.com.au
Southeast Asia
Apa Publications (SN) Pte;
singaporeoffice@insightguides.com
Hong Kong, Taiwan and China
Apa Publications (HK) Ltd;
hongkongoffice@insightguides.com
Worldwide
Apa Publications (UK) Ltd;
sales@insightguides.com
Special Sales, Content Licensing and CoPublishing
Insight Guides can be purchased in bulk quantities at discounted prices. We can create special editions, personalised jackets and corporate imprints tailored to your needs. sales@insightguides.com
www.insightguides.biz

Printed in China by CTPS

All Rights Reserved
© 2017 Apa Digital (CH) AG and
Apa Publications (UK) Ltd

First Edition 2017

No part of this book may be reproduced, stored in a retrieval system or transmitted in any form or means electronic, mechanical, photocopying, recording or otherwise, without prior written permission from Apa Publications.

Every effort has been made to provide accurate information in this publication, but changes are inevitable. The publisher cannot be responsible for any resulting loss, inconvenience or injury. We would appreciate it if readers would call our attention to any errors or outdated information. We also welcome your suggestions; please contact us at: hello@insightguides.com

www.insightguides.com

Editor: Sarah Clark
Author: Nicholas Gill and AnneLise Sorensen
Head of Production: Rebeka Davies
Picture Editor: Tom Smyth
Cartography: Carte

CONTRIBUTORS

This brand-new *Insight Guide Central America* was commissioned and copyedited by Managing Editor **Sarah Clark**. It was primarily written by **Nicholas Gill**, while **AnneLise Sorensen** provided the Guatemala and Belize chapters.

Writer and photographer Nicholas travels regularly through the Americas for publications such as the *New York Times*, *Wall Street Journal*, and *The Guardian*. He is the co-founder of http://

newworlder.com, exploring regional food. Writer, editor, and photographer AnneLise has written and wine-tasted her way across four continents for outlets including *New York Magazine*, *Time Out*, and *Gourmet*, plus other travel guides inclduing *Insight Guide Belize*. See http://annelisesorensen.com.

Thanks go to **Penny Phenix**, who proofread and indexed the book, and to **Rachel Lawrence**, for her original work on the book's concept.

ABOUT INSIGHT GUIDES

Insight Guides have more than 45 years' experience of publishing high-quality, visual travel guides. We produce 400 full-colour titles, in both print and digital form, covering more than 200 destinations across the globe, in a variety of formats to meet your different needs.

Insight Guides are written by local authors, whose expertise is evident in the extensive historical and cultural

background features. Each destination is carefully researched by regional experts to ensure our guides provide the very latest information. All the reviews in **Insight Guides** are independent; we strive to maintain an impartial view. Our reviews are carefully selected to guide you to the best places to eat, go out and shop, so you can be confident that when we say a place is special, we really mean it.

Legend

City maps

Freeway/Highway/Motorway
Divided Highway
Main Roads
Minor Roads
Pedestrian Roads
Steps
Footpath
Railway
Funicular Railway
Cable Car
Tunnel
City Wall
Important Building
Built Up Area
Other Land
Transport Hub
Park
Pedestrian Area
Bus Station
Tourist Information
Main Post Office
Cathedral/Church
Mosque
Synagogue
Statue/Monument
Beach
Airport

Regional maps

Freeway/Highway/Motorway
(with junction)
Freeway/Highway/Motorway
(under construction)
Divided Highway
Main Road
Secondary Road
Minor Road
Track
Footpath
International Boundary
State/Province Boundary
National Park/Reserve
Marine Park
Ferry Route
Marshland/Swamp
Glacier   Salt Lake
Airport/Airfield
Ancient Site
Border Control
Cable Car
Castle/Castle Ruins
Cave
Chateau/Stately Home
Church/Church Ruins
Crater
Lighthouse
Mountain Peak
Place of Interest
Viewpoint

INDEX

MAIN REFERENCES ARE IN BOLD TYPE